D0903051

What Are the Animals to Us?

What Are the Animals to Us?

Approaches from Science, Religion, Folklore, Literature, and Art

Edited by Dave Aftandilian

Assistant Editors
Marion W. Copeland and David Scofield Wilson

The University of Tennessee Press / Knoxville

Library of Congress Cataloging-in-Publication Data

What are the animals to us? : approaches from science, religion, folklore, literature,
and art / edited by Dave Aftandilian; assistant editors Marion W. Copeland and David
Scofield Wilson.– 1st ed.
    p. cm.
Includes bibliographical references and index.
ISBN-13: 978-1-57233-472-4 (hardcover)
ISBN-10: 1-57233-472-X (hardcover)
  1. Human-animal relationships.
  2. Animals and civilization.
  I. Aftandilian, Dave.
QL85.W43 2006
590–dc22
                    2006007741

Contents

Part 3
Holy Dogs and Scared Bunnies: Animals in Art and Religion

Part 4
Come into Animal Presence: Ethics, Ethology, and Konrad Lorenz

Illustrations

Figures

Plates

Tables

Introduction

Of Bats, Animal Studies, and Real Animals

Dave Aftandilian

Many years ago, the birds and the beasts were preparing for war with each other. The birds came to the bat and asked him to fight for them, but he replied, "I am a beast." Then the beasts asked the bat to fight on their side, but he said, "I am a bird." At the last minute, peace was made, but ever since, both the birds and the beasts have shunned the bat.

So goes the Aesop's fable of "The War Between the Beasts and the Birds" (also known as "The Bat, the Birds, and the Beasts"), first written down by the Roman freedman Phaedrus in the first century c.e.[1] The folklorist Joseph Jacobs later appended the moral "He that is neither one thing nor the other has no friends."[2]

Boria Sax retold this fable and its moral during the opening session of the August 2001 Nature in Legend and Story (NILAS) conference in Davis, California.[3] He likened all of the attendees (himself included) to bats, since our humanistic and social scientific research interests in animals made us unlike most of our disciplinary colleagues, and conversely, our diverse disciplinary specializations made each of us unlike most of our fellow conference-goers.

Boria's point was extremely well taken by everyone at the session. All the members of this decidedly interdisciplinary group had experienced colleagues saying "Huh?" when we explained our research interests in animal studies or had felt the more consequential shunning of our "batty" selves and studies by job search committees and granting agencies. Although interest in animal studies has been growing since the 1980s, whether measured in terms of the number of doctoral dissertations in human-animal studies,[4] number of postsecondary courses taught on "Animals and Society,"[5] number of academic conferences that focus on the role of nonhuman animals in human culture and society,[6] or the seemingly ever-increasing number of monographs and edited collections in the humanities and social sciences that focus on animals,[7] animal studies remains marginalized. Few departments or institutions consistently support animal studies research, despite its growing popularity with students and individual scholars (and, many contributors to this book would argue, its critical importance in reconnecting people to the other species with whom we share the planet). Yet there we were, biologists and anthropologists, folklorists and art historians, literary critics and librarians, all gathered together to investigate the roles that animals have played in various aspects of human cultures past and present.

Diverse as all of our interests, topics, and approaches were, we shared a common goal: answering the question, What are the animals to us? What do certain kinds of animals mean to a given culture or person? To what extent are those meanings idiosyncratic, and to what extent are they shared widely within a given culture or cultures? Consider the bat again, for instance. Why do so many human cultures find the bat anomalous? In addition to the Greeks and Romans, native peoples of southern Nigeria, Australia, and southeastern North America all have similar stories of a contest between the birds and the beasts in which the bat plays a key role because of its anomalous taxonomic position between the two types of creatures.[8] Usually seen only at night, bats have wings and fly like birds but also have teeth and nurse their young like four-footed animals. Contemporary scientific researchers add that bats also share the trait of echolocation, navigating via sonar, with another group of anomalous creatures: dolphins, air-breathing mammals who spend most of their time in the oceans.[9]

Although Claude Lévi-Strauss has famously argued that we can never predict exactly which animals any given culture will find "good to think," exploring cross-cultural folklore and literature about category crossing, "liminal" animals like the bat or the cat (see Lynne S. McNeill's chapter, this volume) or the snake (see chapters by Ria Koopmans–de Bruijn, Dave Aftandilian, and Muffet Jones, this volume) or the dog (see chapters by Laura Hobgood-Oster, Susan Carole Roy, and Anne Alden, this volume) can help direct our attention to certain species that are more likely to be thought than others.[10] For instance, the bear plays a key role in the folklore of many cultures (especially among circumpolar groups in Asia, Europe, and North America) because it walks on two legs and eats many of the same foods that people do; it also symbolically "dies"—goes into hibernation—and is reborn each spring.[11] Animals that undergo transformation as part of their life cycles also often earn starring roles in the human imagination. The butterfly's wonderful metamorphosis from crawling caterpillar to immobile pupa to winged adult, for instance, has come to symbolize the journey of the human soul from birth through life to whatever existence comes after in traditional cultures of every continent.[12]

Of course, the chapters in this volume do far more than merely note that certain animals tend to fire the human imagination more than others. To highlight these contributions, an editor would normally be expected at this point to provide a detailed "road map" to the collection for the reader. Readers seeking such a summary should skip ahead to the introductions to each section; there, Boria Sax, Marion W. Copeland, Laura Hobgood-Oster, and David Scofield Wilson give brief descriptions of each chapter in their respective section and place it in its literary and/or historical context. Chapters were assigned to sections based mainly on their subjects, as is evident in the titles of the sections: "From Totems to Tales: Folklore, Myth, and Animals," "Real Toads in Imaginary Gardens: Animals in Literature and History," "Holy Dogs and Scared Bunnies: Animals in Art and Religion," and "Come into Animal Presence: Ethics, Ethology, and Konrad Lorenz."

But I do want to say a few words here both about the content of this book and about its significance for animal studies. The primary focus of *What Are the*

Animals to Us? is on analyzing cultural products about animals. The contributors to part 1, "From Totems to Tales," for instance, interpret folkloric representations of animals in various cultures. The chapters in part 2, "Real Toads in Imaginary Gardens," concern themselves with literary and historical representations of animals, and part 3, "Holy Dogs and Scared Bunnies," considers the role of animals in art and religion. In the final section of the book, "Come into Animal Presence," the contributors read Lorenz's ethological writings about animals in various cultural contexts—as documents written during the reign of and in part inspired by the concerns of the Third Reich, as constituting one of the founding myths of the field of animal behavior, as still-cited scientific data, as part of a continuing debate over the ethical conduct of science, and as ammunition in the continuing struggle to move away from positivist, reductionist scientific approaches to knowing animals and ourselves. Throughout the book, the contributors avoid specialized or overly theoretical language to make their writings as accessible as possible to scholars from a wide variety of disciplines and to general readers.

The diversity of subject areas represented in the section titles signals one of the primary contributions of this book as a whole: it brings together a wide variety of disciplinary and interdisciplinary approaches to animal studies in one place so that they may be compared and contrasted, and, it is hoped, so that they may cross-fertilize one another in the minds and works of those who read them. Very few (if any) other edited collections include approaches from animal behavior and folklore, literary and religious studies, and the history of science and of art all in one place, making this a truly unique book in that sense. *What Are the Animals to Us?* also shows the reader how using the lens of animal studies can provide us with new insights into familiar topics, from ethology to environmental history, postmodern art to Christian theology.

For instance, in part 1, reading Xiaofei Kang's chapter on fox lore and worship in late imperial China in conjunction with Ria Koopmans–de Bruijn's chapter on serpent mates in Japanese folklore suggests similarities in the use of stories about shapeshifting animals to address changing gender roles in these two cultures that might be productively explored by future comparative studies. Similarly, the connections among serpents and agricultural fertility revealed in both Koopmans–de Bruijn's chapter on Japanese folklore and Dave Aftandilian's chapter on Native American sacred stories, artworks, and rituals suggest a shared cross-cultural understanding of snakes in relation to human culture that would also likely reward further examination. And by including a section on Lorenz's ethological writings as worthy of analysis not just as scientific documents but also as mythological, historical, and sociological texts, *What Are the Animals to Us?* both helps expand the potential source base for animal studies research and contributes to wider discussions of the importance of the language used in scientific writings for affecting how the general public perceives animals.[13]

A second major contribution of *What Are the Animals to Us?* is its breadth of coverage, both in terms of space and time. The chapters examine the roles that animals have played in cultures around the world, from Asia to Europe to North and

South America. The contributors themselves come from not just the more familiar American contexts but also from Norway (Elisabet Sveingar Amundsen) and Portugal (Ana Isabel Queiroz and Maria Teresa L. M. B. Andresen).[14] And individual chapters discuss material from the medieval period to the present, including a number of time periods in between.

Diverse as all the chapters in this book may be in terms of subject matter and research methods, they also share important commonalities that make the whole of this book add up to more than the sum of its parts. Taken together, these chapters identify two types of roles that representations of animals tend to play in human cultures: they mark off the boundaries between human and nonhuman and between permissible and forbidden behavior, and, paradoxically, they serve as stand-ins for human selves and as sources of self-understanding.

Lynne S. McNeill's chapter, for instance, shows how cat folklore in England and the United States tends to focus on what makes cats different from humans as well as what makes them different from other animals, closer in many ways to the supernatural than the natural. The tales of shapeshifting foxes in China and serpents in Japan that are discussed in Xiaofei Kang's and Ria Koopmans–de Bruijn's chapters both function to highlight the consequences of transgressing established social norms, especially norms involving gender roles. Tonia L. Payne explores how Ursula K. Le Guin also uses shapeshifting to explore the boundaries between human and nonhuman, but from the animal's perspective, with humans sharing or at least coming to understand the experience of animals, especially how it feels to be the "animal Other" in contrast to humans, by reading Le Guin's animal fables. And E. J. W. Hinds shows how the history of Western European taxonomy reveals scientific classification as being less about separating animals from one another than about separating animals from humans.

Shifting to animals as symbols of self, Susan Braden argues that the tigers in Jorge Luis Borges's writings served as symbols of his own psychological evolution. Elisabet Sveingar Amundsen shows how Norwegian hunters saw themselves as "wild and free," like the reindeer they hunted in the wild, but also how their writings about the decline of the reindeer led to voluntary limits on their own hunting practices. Anne Alden's analysis of dog cartoons in the *New Yorker* from 1925 to 2002 demonstrates that these cartoons both reveal changing cultural attitudes to dogs over this time period and demonstrate how *New Yorker* artists used their dog cartoons as vehicles for critical commentaries on their society. And Muffet Jones shows how the postmodern artist Ray Johnson used a bunny head or a snake in his artworks and writings to symbolize himself and sometimes to symbolize others, blurring boundaries among humans and between humans and animals.

Perhaps most important, though, this book identifies potential new directions that we might explore in nurturing animal studies from just another catch-all category into a real discipline. Sometimes leading by example, sometimes highlighting roads not yet taken, *What Are the Animals to Us?* argues for the need to develop a more integrated, truly interdisciplinary approach to animal studies, rather than just an ad hoc cluster of related yet disciplinarily segregated perspectives.

One way to do this would be to move from thinking about what animals mean to us humans to thinking about what animals mean on their own terms. Or, paraphrasing Thomas Nagel's well-known 1974 philosophical essay, to move from studying what humans *think* bats are like to what bats are *really* like. Barring as yet unknown scientific developments or spiritual techniques, there is no way we can conclusively know what it is like to be another animal. Nagel rather pessimistically summed up this state of affairs as follows: "At present we are completely unequipped to think about the subjective character of experience without relying on the imagination—without taking up the point of view of the experiential subject."[15] Yet those of us interested in animal studies could read this in much more positive terms. We could take this as an opportunity to show the powerful role the human imagination can play in reconnecting us to animals, and in according those animals their own individual lives and agencies. Just as the field of women's studies has recovered previously minimized or forgotten roles that women have played in cultures the world over, and thereby catalyzed a profound rethinking of how women ought to be treated, so too could the field of animal studies take as its mission the investigation of animal subjectivity, using the human imagination as a crucial tool in this project. Perhaps, then, we will stop thinking of animals as merely "Other" or "nonhuman" and instead think of them as bats and cockroaches, dogs and bears—as individual "animals," each with their own valuable lives, thoughts, and emotions.[16]

For example, Kenneth J. Shapiro has developed a phenomenological method to investigate animal subjectivity through the use of what he calls kinesthetic empathy.[17] Shapiro argues that we can achieve an intuitive understanding of the "meaning implicit in an animal's postures, gestures, and behavior" through interpretive, empathetic observation of the animal and its behaviors, followed by critical evaluation of those observations through the lenses of social construction, as experienced by both the investigator and the animal in question, and individual history, again of both the investigator and the animal.[18] He persuasively demonstrates the usefulness of this method in studying how the dog Sabaka experiences space and interprets Shapiro's own intentions.

In this volume, Lynne S. McNeill argues that people's observations of the apparent subjectivity of cats, evidenced in behaviors such as staring intently at closed doors or suddenly jumping up and running around the house, have inspired folkloric representations of cats as "permanently liminal" animals who stand outside both normal human and normal animal experience. Susan Carole Roy uses her intuitive understanding of the obsessive-compulsive cocker spaniel Freckles's licking behavior not just to come to terms with Freckles as a thinking, feeling agent in the world but also to reexamine the author's and all animals' roles in relation to one another and to the sacred. And in her introduction to part 2, Marion W. Copeland argues that using anthropomorphism as a literary device can help free our minds and hearts from cultural constraints so that we might more easily explore the lifeways and modes of experience of other animals. Finally, in an extensive afterword, Dave Aftandilian and David Scofield Wilson offer a number of theoretical and practical suggestions for how we as scholars, educators, and individuals might learn to better understand animals in their own rights and to share that understanding with others.

But perhaps the most valuable take-home message from this book for scholars of animal studies and anyone else who cares about animals is simply this: the stories we tell about animals matter, to both our lives and theirs. By studying stories told about animals from a given time or place, then, we can learn about the animals in the stories as well as the people telling them, as you will see demonstrated throughout this book. Furthermore, by changing the stories we tell about animals, we can begin to change the ways we view and treat them. For instance, by recovering forgotten tales of animals from Christian scripture and hagiographic literature and art, Susan Carole Roy and Laura Hobgood-Oster offer contemporary Christians the opportunity to enrich their worship services and personal spirituality with stories of animals who are not just objects of God's care (and therefore worthy of humanity's care as well) but also active participants in communion with the sacred. Viewing animals from this perspective has the potential to radically alter the way we treat them in both sacred contexts and our daily lives.

Before concluding, I should perhaps say a few words about the term "animal studies," which I have used throughout this introduction without ever defining it. By "animal studies," I mean "cultural studies of animals," much as "American studies" means "cultural studies of America" or "disability studies" means "cultural studies of disability" to many scholars.[19] Other terms have, of course, also been used to refer to this same concept. There is "anthrozoology," for instance, which is part of the name of the International Society for Anthrozoology (ISAZ), or "human-animal studies," which the Society and Animals Forum has used in the subtitle of its journal *Society and Animals* since 2000.[20] In his introduction to part 1 of this volume, Boria Sax proposes the term "totemic literature." And as a search using any standard Internet search engine will quickly demonstrate, far and away the most common usage of "animal studies" on web pages is to refer to scientific studies of animals, often in laboratory settings. So why use "animal studies" to refer to cultural studies of animals?

First, because "animal studies" has a nice parallelism with the names of other recently founded disciplines, such as gender studies or museum studies, that take a multidisciplinary approach to a given subject; this parallelism will give anyone familiar with these new disciplines an immediate sense of what "animal studies" might mean. Second, because more and more scholars are using the term in the sense that I described above.[21] And third, because "animal studies" has the virtue of a certain vagueness—a vagueness that will allow the term to encompass research grounded in the humanities, life sciences, or social sciences, and that, I hope, will encourage people to reflect on (and perhaps contest) its meaning.

Because animal studies is young, it has not yet developed a core set of approaches or texts (though some of the works listed in note 7 below are likely to find their way into the animal studies canon eventually). But one characteristic that does seem to define it is a welcoming attitude toward interdisciplinary work, "batty" work that is neither one thing nor the other—work such as the chapters in this volume. I and the other contributors hope that *What Are the Animals to Us?* will help define the field of animal studies, encourage its growth, and introduce new readers and researchers to its tremendous possibilities.

I would like to end with a few words of much-deserved thanks. First and foremost, we owe a debt of immense gratitude to all the people who gave papers at the 2001 NILAS conference; not all of their papers are included here, but they all played a part in making the conference so stimulating. NILAS held this conference jointly with the International Society for Anthrozoology; we are very grateful to ISAZ in general, and to Lynette A. Hart in particular (director of the Center for Animal Alternatives at the University of California–Davis), for their financial, logistical, and personal assistance with the conference. The American Studies program at the University of California–Davis also generously contributed financial assistance to the NILAS conference. David C. Anderson and David Scofield Wilson did a masterful job of attending to the thousand and one tasks, many of them thankless, that must be done to make a conference successful; they performed those tasks with good humor and considerable distinction, and their efforts were very much appreciated by everyone who attended the conference. Boria Sax kept the fire of NILAS burning for many years with his encyclopedic knowledge of animal folklore and tremendous dedication to animal studies; without his largely unsung enthusiasm and scholarly advocacy, neither NILAS nor this book would exist. Finally, we would also like to thank the anonymous reader and Marc Bekoff for their helpful comments on the manuscript; Scot Danforth, Stan Ivester, Karin Kaufman, Stephanie Thompson, Thomas Wells, and everyone else at the University of Tennessee Press who has worked so hard to bring this book from manuscript to print.

In addition to my coeditors Marion W. Copeland and David Scofield Wilson, Michael Bathgate, Sarah F. Rose, and Boria Sax all read earlier drafts of this introduction and provided helpful suggestions. Any faults that remain are, of course, solely my own responsibility.

My mother, Emily Aftandilian (née Harman), first instilled a love of and respect for animals in me. Reading fairy and folktales, walking along the beach, tromping through the edges of my uncle's farm—wherever we went while I was growing up, we looked for the wild things together and learned to care for them as best we could. More recently, I have been deeply moved by my mother's selfless devotion to animal rescue work—work for which she is not paid yet for which she is richly rewarded by her intimate experiences with the animals whose lives she has touched, and who have touched hers.

Finally, I would like to say a word of thanks to the nonhuman animals who inspired each and every chapter in this book. Every beast that slithers or crawls, flies or swims, climbs or trots: it is you that we have written this book about and for. We may not always do our best to show it, but we are grateful for the many things you have done to show us what it means to be human—and to be animal.

Last but not least, I would like to say a special thank-you to some specific animals who have enriched my life. To Adolph and Charger, Luke and Teddy, Aviva and Bo, and so many others with and without names: this batty human thanks you from the bottom of his heart.

Dave Aftandilian
Chicago
December 2005

Notes

1. For a recent English translation of this fable, see Laura Gibbs, *Aesop's Fables* (Oxford: Oxford Univ. Press, 2002), 171–72. A web site connected to that book, www.aesopica.net, includes the full text of four English and six Latin versions; search under Perry index number 566.

2. Joseph Jacobs, ed., *The Fables of Aesop: Selected, Told Anew and Their History Traced* (1894; reprint, New York: Mayflower Books, 1979), 62–63.

3. NILAS is a group of interdisciplinary scholars, storytellers, folklorists, teachers, librarians, and others who share a common interest in trying to understand relationships between humans, animals, and plants through the mediation of stories, poems, legends, artworks, and other cultural products. The organization was founded unofficially in 1989 by Boria Sax and Noel Ortega at Pace University and received official nonprofit status in 1995. For more information on NILAS, see www.h-net.org/~nilas.

4. Kathleen C. Gerbasi, David C. Anderson, Alexandra M. Gerbasi, and Debbie Coultis, "Doctoral Dissertations in Human-Animal Studies: News and Views," *Society and Animals* 10, no. 4 (2002): 339–46.

5. Jonathan Balcombe, "Animals and Society Courses: A Growing Trend in Post-Secondary Education," *Society and Animals* 7, no. 3 (1999): 229–40.

6. Julie Ann Smith, "Review of Academic Conferences," *Society and Animals* 9, no. 3 (2001): 293–97.

7. The number of humanistic and social scientific publications in animal studies has skyrocketed in recent years. Not including studies that focus solely on individual animals or groups of animals, here are some of the many monographs and collections in animals studies published since 1994: Carol J. Adams and Josephine Donovan, eds., *Animals and Women: Feminist Theoretical Explorations* (1995); Salman Akhtar and Vamik Volkan, eds., *Cultural Zoo: Animals in the Human Mind and Its Sublimations* (2005); Arnold Arluke and Clinton R. Sanders, *Regarding Animals* (1996); A. James Arnold, ed., *Monsters, Tricksters, and Sacred Cows: Animal Tales and American Identities* (1996); Steve Baker, *The Postmodern Animal* (2000) and *Picturing the Beast: Animals, Identity, and Representation* (2001); Elizabeth P. Benson, *Birds and Beasts of Ancient Latin America* (1997); Jonathan Burt, *Animals*

in Film (2002); Billie Jean Collins, ed., *A History of the Animal World in the Ancient Near East* (2002); Eileen Crist, *Images of Animals: Anthropomorphism and Animal Mind* (1999); Lorraine Daston and Gregg Mitman, eds., *Thinking with Animals: New Perspectives on Anthropomorphism* (2005); Erica Fudge, *Perceiving Animals: Humans and Beasts in Early Modern English Culture* (2000) and *Animal* (2002); Erica Fudge, ed., *Renaissance Beasts: Of Animals, Humans, and Other Wonderful Creatures* (2004); Jennifer Ham and Matthew Senior, eds., *Animal Acts: Configuring the Human in Western History* (1997); Donna J. Haraway, *The Companion Species Manifesto: Dogs, People, and Significant Otherness* (2003); Mary J. Henninger-Voss, ed., *Animals in Human Histories: The Mirror of Nature and Culture* (2002); Andrew Linzey, *Animal Theology* (1995) and *Animal Gospel* (1998); Andrew Linzey and Dorothy Yamamoto, eds., *Animals on the Agenda: Questions about Animals for Theology and Ethics* (1998); Akira Mizuta Lippit, *Electric Animal: Toward a Rhetoric of Wildlife* (2000); Randy Malamud, *Reading Zoos: Representations of Animals and Captivity* (1998) and *Poetic Animals and Animal Souls* (2003); Aubrey Manning and James Serpell, eds., *Animals and Human Society: Changing Perspectives* (1994); Gail F. Melson, *Why the Wild Things Are: Animals in the Lives of Children* (2001); Robert W. Mitchell, Nicholas S. Thompson, and H. Lyn Miles, eds., *Anthropomorphism, Anecdotes, and Animals* (1997); Brian Morris, *The Power of Animals: An Ethnography* (1998) and *Animals and Ancestors: An Ethnography* (2000); Gene Myers, *Children and Animals: Social Development and Our Connections to Other Species* (1998); Chris Philo and Chris Wilbert, eds., *Animal Spaces, Beastly Places: New Geographies of Human-Animal Relations* (2000); Anthony L. Podberscek, Elizabeth S. Paul, and James A. Serpell, eds., *Companion Animals and Us: Exploring the Relationships between People and Pets* (2000); Mary Sanders Pollock and Catherine Rainwater, eds., *Figuring Animals: Essays on Animal Images in Art, Literature, Philosophy, and Popular Culture* (2005); Louise E. Robbins, *Elephant Slaves and Pampered Parrots: Exotic Animals in Eighteenth-Century Paris* (2002); Nigel Rothfels, *Savages and Beasts: The Birth of the Modern Zoo* (2002); Nigel Rothfels, ed., *Representing Animals* (2002); Joyce E. Salisbury, *The Beast Within: Animals in the Middle Ages* (1994); Nicholas J. Saunders, ed., *Icons of Power: Feline Symbolism in the Americas* (1998); Boria Sax, *The Serpent and the Swan: The Animal Bride in Folklore and Literature* (1998), *Animals in the Third Reich: Pets, Scapegoats, and the Holocaust* (2000), and *The Mythical Zoo: An Encyclopedia of Animals in World Myth, Legend, and Literature* (2001); Paul Shepard, *The Others: How Animals Made Us Human* (1996); Roel Sterckx, *The Animal and the Daemon in Early China* (2002); Jennifer Wolch and Jody Emel, eds., *Animal Geographies: Place, Politics, and Identity in the Nature-Culture Borderlands* (1998); Cary Wolfe, *Animal Rites: American Culture, the Discourse of Species, and Posthumanist Theory* (2003); and Cary Wolfe, ed., *Zoontologies: The Question of the Animal* (2003). Several of these books have appeared in one of several recently founded book series in animal studies, such as Temple University Press's Animals, Culture, and Society series, edited by Arnold Arluke and Clinton R. Sanders; Johns Hopkins University Press's Animals, History, Culture series, edited by Harriet Ritvo; E. J. Brill's Human-Animal Studies series, edited by Kenneth J. Shapiro et al.; and Reaktion's Animal series, edited by Jonathan Burt. Expanding this list to include books in animal welfare and animal rights would add dozens more titles.

8. George E. Lankford, *Native American Legends: Southeastern Legends* (Little Rock, Ark.: August House, 1987), 239–42; Gary F. McCracken, "Folklore and the Origin of Bats," *Bats* 11, no. 4 (1993): 11–13; James Mooney, *Myths of the Cherokee* (1900; reprint, New York: Dover, 1995), 286–87.

9. See, for instance, Jeannette Thomas, Cynthia Moss, and Marianne Vater, eds., *Echolocation in Bats and Dolphins* (Chicago: Univ. of Chicago Press, 2003).

10. Lévi-Strauss first used the term "good to think" in *Totemism* (Boston: Beacon Press, 1963), 89. Two decades later he wrote the following about the difficulty of identifying precisely which species a culture would find "good to think": "Each culture settles on a few distinctive features of its environment, but no one can predict which these are or to what end they will be put. Furthermore, so great is the wealth and diversity of the raw material offered by the environment for observation and reflection that the mind is capable only of apprehending a fraction of it. The mind can put it to use for elaborating one system among an infinity of other, equally conceivable ones: nothing predestines any one among them for a privileged fate." Lévi-Strauss, *The View from Afar* (New York: Basic Books, 1985), 103.

11. Dave Aftandilian, "Bear," in *Encyclopedia of World Environmental History*, ed. Shepard Krech III, J. R. McNeill, and Carolyn Merchant (New York: Routledge, 2004), 119–21; A. Irving Hallowell, "Bear Ceremonialism in the Northern Hemisphere," *American Anthropologist*, n.s., vol. 28, no. 1 (1926): 1–175; Richard K. Nelson, *Make Prayers to the Raven: A Koyukon View of the Northern Forest* (Chicago: Univ. of Chicago Press, 1983), 172–94; David Rockwell, *Giving Voice to Bear: North American Indian Myths, Rituals, and Images of the Bear*, revised ed. (Lanham, Md.: Roberts Rinehart, 2003); Paul Shepard and Barry Sanders, *The Sacred Paw: The Bear in Nature, Myth, and Literature* (New York: Viking Penguin, 1985). When they are skinned or skeletonized, dead bears also look uncannily like dead humans. In northern climates, for instance, each year's spring thaw usually brings many reports from hikers and others of human body parts found in the woods, and in the fall, mutilated hands and feet are often discovered near dumpsters in city alleyways. More often than not, these turn out to be bear parts left over from the fall hunting season and subsequent skinning of the hides. T. D. Stewart, *Essentials of Forensic Anthropology, Especially as Developed in the United States* (Springfield, Ill.: Charles C. Thomas, 1979), 47–52.

12. Marilyn Jorgenson, "Butterflies as Symbols of Transformation in Traditional Folk Narratives," *NILAS Newsletter*, n.s., vol. 1, nos. 3–4 (2002–3): 12–15; Boria Sax, *The Mythical Zoo: An Encyclopedia of Animals in World Myth, Legend, and Literature* (Santa Barbara, Calif.: ABC-CLIO, 2001), 52–56.

13. See, for example, Eileen Crist, *Images of Animals: Anthropomorphism and Animal Mind* (Philadelphia: Temple Univ. Press, 1999) and Robert W. Mitchell, Nicholas S. Thompson, and H. Lyn Miles, eds., *Anthropomorphism, Anecdotes, and Animals* (Albany: State Univ. of New York Press, 1997).

14. For the convenience of Norwegian and Portuguese scholars, the chapters by Amundsen and Queiroz and Andresen in this volume include foreign-language abstracts (at the end of each chapter).

15. Thomas Nagel, "What Is It Like to Be a Bat?" *Philosophical Review* 83, no. 4 (1974): 449.

16. We could make a subtle but significant step in the right direction of according subjectivity to animals simply by changing the relative pronouns we use to refer to animals from "which" or "that" to "who," as I have done throughout this introduction.

17. Kenneth J. Shapiro, "Understanding Dogs through Kinesthetic Empathy, Social Construction, and History," *Anthrozoös* 3 (1990): 184–95; Kenneth J. Shapiro, "A Phenomenological Approach to the Study of Nonhuman Animals," in *Anthropomorphism, Anecdotes, and Animals*, ed. Robert W. Mitchell, Nicholas S. Thompson, and H. Lyn Miles (Albany: State Univ. of New York Press, 1997), 277–95.

18. Shapiro, "Phenomenological Approach," 281–83, 292.

19. Jay Mechling, Robert Merideth, and David Wilson, "American Culture Studies: The Discipline and the Curriculum," *American Quarterly* 25, no. 4 (1973), 368; Paul K. Longmore and Lauri Umansky, "Disability History: From the Margins to the Mainstream," in *The New Disability History: American Perspectives*, ed. Paul K. Longmore and Lauri Umansky (New York: New York Univ. Press, 2001), 13.

20. The Society and Animals Forum was formerly known as Psychologists for the Ethical Treatment of Animals (PSYETA). I am grateful to David C. Anderson for informing me of the date that the Society and Animals Forum changed its journal's subtitle from *Social Scientific Studies of the Human Experience of Other Animals* to *The Journal of Human-Animal Studies*.

21. See, for instance, Charles Bergman, "Making Animals Matter," *Chronicle of Higher Education*, Mar. 23, 2001, B15; Smith, "Review of Academic Conferences," 293–97; and the promotional description on the back cover of Nigel Rothfels, ed., *Representing Animals* (Bloomington: Indiana Univ. Press, 2002). I would like to thank Carmen Lee for calling the Bergman and Smith references to my attention and Chien-hui Li for explaining her rationale for choosing "animal studies" as the name of a theme issue on that topic she guest edited for the Taiwanese journal *Chung-Wai Literary Monthly* in July 2003.

Works Cited

Adams, Carol J., and Josephine Donovan, eds. *Animals and Women: Feminist Theoretical Explorations*. Durham, N.C.: Duke Univ. Press, 1995.

Aftandilian, Dave. "Bear." In *Encyclopedia of World Environmental History*, edited by Shepard Krech III, J. R. McNeill, and Carolyn Merchant, 119–21. London: Routledge, 2004.

Akhtar, Salman, and Vamik Volkan, eds. *Cultural Zoo: Animals in the Human Mind and Its Sublimations*. Madison, Conn.: International Universities Press, 2005.

Arluke, Arnold, and Clinton R. Sanders. *Regarding Animals*. Philadelphia: Temple Univ. Press, 1996.

Arnold, A. James, ed. *Monsters, Tricksters, and Sacred Cows: Animal Tales and American Identities*. Charlottesville: Univ. Press of Virginia, 1996.

Baker, Steve. *Picturing the Beast: Animals, Identity, and Representation*. New ed. Urbana: Univ. of Illinois Press, 2001.

———. *The Postmodern Animal*. London: Reaktion Books, 2000.

Balcombe, Jonathan. "Animals and Society Courses: A Growing Trend in Post-Secondary Education." *Society and Animals* 7, no. 3 (1999): 229–40.

Benson, Elizabeth P. *Birds and Beasts of Ancient Latin America*. Gainesville: Univ. Press of Florida, 1997.

Bergman, Charles. "Making Animals Matter." *Chronicle of Higher Education*, Mar. 23, 2001, B15.

Burt, Jonathan. *Animals in Film*. London: Reaktion Books, 2002.

Collins, Billie Jean, ed. *A History of the Animal World in the Ancient Near East*. Leiden: E. J. Brill, 2002.

Crist, Eileen. *Images of Animals: Anthropomorphism and Animal Mind*. Philadelphia: Temple Univ. Press, 1999.

Daston, Lorraine, and Gregg Mitman, eds. *Thinking with Animals: New Perspectives on Anthropomorphism*. New York: Columbia Univ. Press, 2005.

Fudge, Erica. *Animal*. London: Reaktion Books, 2002.

———. *Perceiving Animals: Humans and Beasts in Early Modern English Culture*. New York: St. Martin's Press, 2000.

———, ed. *Renaissance Beasts: Of Animals, Humans, and Other Wonderful Creatures*. Urbana: Univ. of Illinois Press, 2004.

Gerbasi, Kathleen C., David C. Anderson, Alexandra M. Gerbasi, and Debbie Coultis. "Doctoral Dissertations in Human-Animal Studies: News and Views." *Society and Animals* 10, no. 4 (2002): 339–46.

Gibbs, Laura. *Aesop's Fables*. Oxford: Oxford Univ. Press, 2002.

Hallowell, A. Irving. "Bear Ceremonialism in the Northern Hemisphere." *American Anthropologist*, n.s., vol. 28, no. 1 (1926): 1–175.

Ham, Jennifer, and Matthew Senior, eds. *Animal Acts: Configuring the Human in Western History*. New York: Routledge, 1997.

Haraway, Donna J. *The Companion Species Manifesto: Dogs, People, and Significant Otherness*. Chicago: Prickly Paradigm Press, 2003.

Henninger-Voss, Mary J., ed. *Animals in Human Histories: The Mirror of Nature and Culture*. Rochester, N.Y.: Univ. of Rochester Press, 2002.

Jacobs, Joseph, ed. *The Fables of Aesop: Selected, Told Anew and Their History Traced*. 1894. Reprint, New York: Mayflower Books, 1979.

Jorgenson, Marilyn. "Butterflies as Symbols of Transformation in Traditional Folk Narratives." *NILAS Newsletter*, n.s., vol. 1, nos. 3–4 (2002–3): 12–15.

Lankford, George E. *Native American Legends: Southeastern Legends*. Little Rock, Ark.: August House, 1987.

Lévi-Strauss, Claude. *Totemism*. Translated by Rodney Needham. Boston: Beacon Press, 1963.

———. *The View from Afar*. Translated by Joachim Neugroschel and Phoebe Hoss. New York: Basic Books, 1985.

Linzey, Andrew. *Animal Gospel*. Louisville, Ky.: Westminster John Knox Press, 1998.

———. *Animal Theology*. Urbana: Univ. of Illinois Press, 1995.

Linzey, Andrew, and Dorothy Yamamoto, eds. *Animals on the Agenda: Questions about Animals for Theology and Ethics*. Urbana: Univ. of Illinois Press, 1998.

Lippit, Akira Mizuta. *Electric Animal: Toward a Rhetoric of Wildlife*. Minneapolis: Univ. of Minnesota Press, 2000.

Longmore, Paul K., and Lauri Umansky. "Disability History: From the Margins to the Mainstream." In *The New Disability History: American Perspectives*, edited by Paul K. Longmore and Lauri Umansky, 1–29. New York: New York Univ. Press, 2001.

Malamud, Randy. *Poetic Animals and Animal Souls*. New York: Palgrave, 2003.

———. *Reading Zoos: Representations of Animals and Captivity*. New York: New York Univ. Press, 1998.

Manning, Aubrey, and James Serpell, eds. *Animals and Human Society: Changing Perspectives*. London: Routledge, 1994.

McCracken, Gary F. "Folklore and the Origin of Bats." *Bats* 11, no. 4 (1993): 11–13.

Mechling, Jay, Robert Merideth, and David Wilson. "American Culture Studies: The Discipline and the Curriculum." *American Quarterly* 25, no. 4 (1973): 363–89.

Melson, Gail F. *Why the Wild Things Are: Animals in the Lives of Children*. Cambridge, Mass.: Harvard Univ. Press, 2001.

Mitchell, Robert W., Nicholas S. Thompson, and H. Lyn Miles, eds. *Anthropomorphism, Anecdotes, and Animals*. Albany: State Univ. of New York Press, 1997.

Mooney, James. *Myths of the Cherokee*. 1900. Reprint, New York: Dover, 1995.

Morris, Brian. *Animals and Ancestors: An Ethnography*. New York: Berg, 2000.

———. *The Power of Animals: An Ethnography*. New York: Berg, 1998.

Myers, Gene. *Children and Animals: Social Development and Our Connections to Other Species*. Boulder, Colo.: Westview Press, 1998.

Nagel, Thomas. "What Is It Like to Be a Bat?" *Philosophical Review* 83, no. 4 (1974): 435–50.

Nelson, Richard K. *Make Prayers to the Raven: A Koyukon View of the Northern Forest*. Chicago: Univ. of Chicago Press, 1983.

Philo, Chris, and Chris Wilbert, eds. *Animal Spaces, Beastly Places: New Geographies of Human-Animal Relations*. New York: Routledge, 2000.

Podberscek, Anthony L., Elizabeth S. Paul, and James A. Serpell, eds. *Companion Animals and Us: Exploring the Relationships between People and Pets*. Cambridge, Mass.: Cambridge Univ. Press, 2000.

Pollock, Mary Sanders, and Catherine Rainwater, eds. *Figuring Animals: Essays on Animal Images in Art, Literature, Philosophy, and Popular Culture*. New York: Palgrave Macmillan, 2005.

Robbins, Louise E. *Elephant Slaves and Pampered Parrots: Exotic Animals in Eighteenth-Century Paris*. Baltimore: Johns Hopkins Univ. Press, 2002.

Rockwell, David. *Giving Voice to Bear: North American Indian Myths, Rituals, and Images of the Bear*, revised ed. Lanham, Md.: Roberts Rinehart, 2003.

Rothfels, Nigel. *Savages and Beasts: The Birth of the Modern Zoo*. Baltimore: Johns Hopkins Univ. Press, 2002.

———, ed. *Representing Animals*. Bloomington: Indiana Univ. Press, 2002.

Salisbury, Joyce E. *The Beast Within: Animals in the Middle Ages*. London: Routledge, 1994.

Saunders, Nicholas J., ed. *Icons of Power: Feline Symbolism in the Americas*. London: Routledge, 1998.

Sax, Boria. *Animals in the Third Reich: Pets, Scapegoats, and the Holocaust*. New York: Continuum, 2000.

———. *The Mythical Zoo: An Encyclopedia of Animals in World Myth, Legend, and Literature*. Santa Barbara, Calif.: ABC-CLIO, 2001.

———. *The Serpent and the Swan: The Animal Bride in Folklore and Literature*. Blacksburg, Va.: McDonald and Woodward, 1998.

Shapiro, Kenneth J. "A Phenomenological Approach to the Study of Nonhuman Animals." In *Anthropomorphism, Anecdotes, and Animals*, edited by Robert W. Mitchell, Nicholas S. Thompson, and H. Lyn Miles, 277–95. Albany: State Univ. of New York Press, 1997.

———. "Understanding Dogs through Kinesthetic Empathy, Social Construction, and History." *Anthrozoös* 3 (1990): 184–95.

Shepard, Paul. *The Others: How Animals Made Us Human*. Washington, D.C.: Island Press, 1996.

Shepard, Paul, and Barry Sanders. *The Sacred Paw: The Bear in Nature, Myth, and Literature*. New York: Viking Penguin, 1985.

Smith, Julie Ann. "Review of Academic Conferences." *Society and Animals* 9, no. 3 (2001): 293–97.

Sterckx, Roel. *The Animal and the Daemon in Early China*. Albany: State Univ. of New York Press, 2002.

Stewart, T. D. *Essentials of Forensic Anthropology, Especially as Developed in the United States.* Springfield, Ill.: Charles C. Thomas, 1979.

Thomas, Jeanette, Cynthia Moss, and Marianne Vater, eds. *Echolocation in Bats and Dolphins.* Chicago: Univ. of Chicago Press, 2003.

Wolch, Jennifer, and Jody Emel, eds. *Animal Geographies: Place, Politics, and Identity in the Nature-Culture Borderlands.* New York: Verso, 1998.

Wolfe, Cary. *Animal Rites: American Culture, the Discourse of Species, and Posthumanist Theory.* Chicago: Univ. of Chicago Press, 2003.

——, ed. *Zoontologies: The Question of the Animal.* Minneapolis: Univ. of Minnesota Press, 2003.

Part 1

From Totems to Tales

Folklore, Myth, and Animals

Introduction

Boria Sax

Words have traditionally been a means to conjure, bless, or curse. In the book of Genesis, Adam calls the animals into existence by reciting their names. The Gospel of John begins, "In the beginning was the Word." Today, we academics may say that names are fairly arbitrary linguistic signs, but we hardly act as though we believed that. Words can easily infuriate us or send us into reveries. "Socialism," "fascism," "psychoanalysis," "feminism," "deconstruction," "sociobiology"—such are the banners under which intellectuals march into battle. Like Adam naming the creatures of the earth, air, and sea, scholars must learn to name schools and trends in intellectual life. We use those words at least as much for their magic as for their meaning. Until there is a name for something, it does not seem fully to exist.

Members of the group Nature in Legend and Story (NILAS) trace the changing representations of animals and plants in myth, literature, painting, religion, and other aspects of human culture. When I founded NILAS in 1995, those who took part in the fledgling organization often felt lonely in their work. Judging from the relatively easy time NILAS has had soliciting many fine papers for its conferences, its approach is no longer so much of a novelty.

But until we have labeled what we do, many scholars will not believe that it is real. I recommend, then, the name "totemic literature." The phrase describes, as well as any I can think of, an approach to culture based primarily on understanding the changing bonds that people have with other forms of life that share our planet. "Totemism" is the collective identification of groups of people, especially tribes, with specific kinds of animals or plants. Thus, for example, the raven is an important totem for tribes from the Northwest Coast of North America, while the jaguar is important for those of Central and South America. A legacy of totemism may be found in such forms as national emblems—the American eagle, for example—or even in the mascots of sports teams. On a more serious, though also more elusive, level, it can take such forms as the identification of coastal people with marine life or of fascists with predators.

While the concept of totemism is too rich and complex to be captured in any simple definition, our contemporary understanding of it comes largely from the French anthropologist Claude Lévi-Strauss. Victorian anthropological folklorists such as Edwin Sidney Hartland and James George Frazer had first developed the concept in relation to tales of descent of tribal peoples from birds and beasts.[1] They had, for the most part, understood these tales in very restrictive ways, conjuring up all sorts of exotic, and occasionally lurid, images of people mating with animals. In his book *Le totemisme aujourd'hui* (translated into English as *Totemism*) Lévi-Strauss traced the history of the concept of totemism and argued that it was "the projection outside our own universe, as though by a kind of exorcism, of mental attitudes incompatible with the exigency of a discontinuity between man and nature."[2] He argued that the concept was based on confusions such as that between tribal ancestors and spiritual guardians. Most seriously, he argued that the concept of totemism was based on a strictly literal understanding of many tales that had originally been intended to be metaphoric.

Then, in 1962, Lévi-Strauss himself revived the concept of totemism in his seminal book *La Penseé sauvage* (*The Savage Mind*). He maintained that tribal traditions were not less refined or subtle than those of the industrialized Western world. They differed primarily from ours in that primitive classifications were based on broad associations rather than on hierarchical systems of analysis. People, as both individuals and groups, were classified on the basis of analogies with the natural world simply because tribal peoples lived in an environment where such images came most readily to mind. As Lévi-Strauss put it, the "diversity of species furnishes man with the most intuitive picture he can perceive of the ultimate discontinuity of reality."[3] It was a way of thinking that was more poetic than the literal understanding of either science or fundamentalist religion.

Can totemic literature help people to make sense of the world, not only through isolated insights but also in a sustained way? Can more associative modes of thinking lead us to knowledge or to wisdom? Those modes of understanding are, in any case, being revived on the Internet, where searches are conducted by associations rather than by rigid formulas. Scholars are now being compelled, if they are not to retreat into increasingly narrow specialties, to supplement linear modes of analysis with more fluid ones. The necessity of processing vast amounts of information relatively quickly now forces us to think less in terms of abstractions and more in terms of metaphors. Animals and plants still provide people with the metaphors that are most vivid, most thoroughly integrated into human history and culture.

New abilities such as cloning and genetic manipulation, as well as new problems such as the mass extinction of species, require a rapid response. The practice in scientific communities of constant testing as one gradually builds a consensus can be too slow and cumbersome to provide a very effective answer to the crises we are facing. In any case, it is far from clear that scientists are even moving any closer to a consensus on such questions as how much the mental processes of animals are like our own.[4]

Very often, in periods of especially dramatic social change, the disruptions enable archaic aspects of cultural heritage to emerge. The Renaissance, for example, led to a revival of classical mythology. Romanticism, which accompanied the Industrial Revolution, brought a renewed interest in folklore. In a similar way, the technological and social upheavals of today may have helped to revive totemism. The chapters in part 1 suggest that a fairly systematic intellectual approach to totemic literature may be emerging spontaneously. Though the authors of these chapters did not know one another prior to the NILAS conference, and cite very different sources, there is a remarkable similarity in the ways in which they organize their research.

All of the authors in this section approach one or two animals as totems, organizing human experience around them. Thus Dave Aftandilian's "Frogs, Snakes, and Agricultural Fertility: Interpreting Illinois Mississippian Representations" provides extensive anthropological documentation for the association of frogs and snakes with fertility throughout North America and Mesoamerica. Mythology is, in fact, a largely global tradition that constantly threatens to overwhelm us with its vastness, so the first question for any scholar is how to draw the parameters of his or her investigation. Aftandilian does this by focusing on a limited, if vast, geographic and historical unit, though, as he indicates in his opening paragraph, this symbolism of amphibians and reptiles is probably universal.

Since pre-Columbian peoples left few written records, Aftandilian relies primarily on material culture, but other authors here focus on recorded legends. Xiaofei Kang, in "Spirits, Sex, and Wealth: Fox Lore and Fox Worship in Late Imperial China," for example, explores the connection of foxes with wealth and sexuality in the folklore of China during the early modern period. Both sex and wealth have traditionally been regarded with ambivalence, in China as in the West, and so have foxes. There are many tales of human beings, both women and men, carrying on sexual liaisons with foxes who then provide their families with riches. Kang shows how the tales of fox paramours were used to externalize social and familial tensions. Whether providing a cover for prostitution or simply rationalizing financial success, responsibility could be projected onto the fox.

Ria Koopmans–de Bruijn examines a closely related tradition of animal paramours in "Serpentine Mates in Japanese Folklore." While Kang emphasizes the similarities between animal brides and grooms, Koopmans–de Bruijn stresses the differences. She finds that when the serpent paramours are female, they are represented more positively in many respects. The serpent women tend to initiate relationships out of gratitude, while their masculine counterparts do it out of malice. The amorous relationships, in both cases, however, bring pain to the human beings and destruction to the serpents. Koopmans–de Bruijn concludes that the stories are generally warnings against the violation of social or religious prohibitions.

The chapter here that focuses most intently on a single sort of animal is "The Waving Ones: Cats, Folklore, and the Experiential Source Hypothesis," by Lynne S. McNeill. Since ancient times, authors have remarked on something mysterious—McNeill's word is "liminal"—about cats. McNeill quotes Herodotus, who, in the fifth century B.C.E., called them the "waving ones." This mysterious quality, she believes, attaches to cats because of the way they seem to straddle so many contraries: domestic and wild, lazy and vigilant, nocturnal and diurnal, needy and independent.

All these works of totemic literature show a similarity with respect to both theme and methodology. Much work remains to be done, however, in giving this commonality a more theoretical and universal expression. All of the chapters here vividly describe relationships between certain animals and humans, but all are very cautious about generalizing across lines of culture and species. As explorers of uncharted territory, we are understandably wary. But I think that we are gradually gaining the self-confidence and the tools to move beyond such restricted, though fascinating, themes. The authors tell us what totems meant to people in distant times and places, but what do totems mean to us today?

To even raise such a broad question invites the reproach of being unscientific, but scholars in more established disciplines are also never entirely objective. Folklorists, since they endeavor to preserve and disseminate products of the oral tradition, inevitably become "folk." Scholars of myth often end up creating myths, just as scholars of politics often guide affairs of state. So if scholars of totemic literature often help to perpetuate a totem such as the frog or cat, there is no need to be ashamed.

I think we should be proud!

Notes

1. Edwin Sidney Hartland, *The Science of Fairy Tales: An Inquiry into Fairy Mythology* (London: Scott, 1891); James George Frazer, *Totemism and Exogamy: A Treatise on Certain Early Forms of Superstition and Society* (1910; reprint, Rushden, U.K.: Dawson's, 1968).

2. Claude Lévi-Strauss, *Totemism*, trans. Rodney Needham (Boston: Beacon Press, 1963), 3.

3. Claude Lévi-Strauss, *The Savage Mind* (Chicago: Univ. of Chicago Press, 1966), 137.

4. For a recent discussion of the debate over animal consciousness by a pioneer in this field, see Donald R. Griffin, *Animal Minds: Beyond Cognition to Consciousness* (Chicago: Univ. of Chicago Press, 2001).

Works Cited

Frazer, James George. *Totemism and Exogamy: A Treatise on Certain Early Forms of Superstition and Society*. 1910. Reprint, Rushden, U.K.: Dawson's, 1968.

Griffin, Donald R. *Animal Minds: Beyond Cognition to Consciousness*. Chicago: Univ. of Chicago Press, 2001.

Hartland, Edwin Sidney. *The Science of Fairy Tales: An Inquiry into Fairy Mythology*. London: Scott, 1891.

Lévi-Strauss, Claude. *The Savage Mind*. Chicago: Univ. of Chicago Press, 1966.

———. *Totemism*. Translated by Rodney Needham. Boston: Beacon Press, 1963.

Chapter 1

The Waving Ones
Cats, Folklore, and the Experiential Source Hypothesis

Lynne S. McNeill

> I tell you, cats are queer articles. You never know where
> you are with them. They seem to be different to every
> other class of animals. In the old days there were people
> who worshipped them, and it is not to be greatly won-
> dered at, when you think of the intelligence of cats.
>
> —Mr. Buckley, the tailor, of Cork, Ireland, 1942

In the fifth century B.C.E., the Greek historian Herodotus dubbed cats *ailorous,* or the "waving ones." He was, at the time, referring to their delicately undulating tails, but he also happened to be accurately describing a major characteristic of felines: their ontological impermanence, their ability to wave in and out of the natural world. Buckley the tailor, in his quotation above, accurately sums up how many people feel about cats: they are natural creatures who have some not-so-natural, or "queer," characteristics about them. In the words of historian Robert Darnton, "There is an indefinable *je ne sais quoi* about cats, a mysterious something that has fascinated mankind since the time of the ancient Egyptians."[1]

The Cat in World Folklore

The domestic cat, *Felis catus,* is of the class mammalia, the order carnivora, and the family Felidae, which also includes the lion, tiger, leopard, jaguar, cougar, wildcat, lynx, and cheetah.[2] Today's domestic cat most likely developed from the small European wildcat, *Felis silvestris silvestris,* and the similar small African wildcat, *Felis silvestris lybica,* and although the domestic cat is rapidly becoming the Western world's most popular pet, it was almost the last species to be tamed.[3] While it is possible that humans kept cats as early as the Neolithic period,[4] the first definite evidence of domesticated cats comes thousands of years later, from Egypt. Ancient Egyptian cat skeletons from excavations are difficult to use as a measure of domesticity because domesticated cats and African wildcats were still almost indistinguishable in form, but when cats began to appear in paintings and mosaics, around 2000 B.C.E., the incorporation of felines into both family life and religious life became evident.[5] Most parts of the world have at least one native species of Felidae, and once *Felis catus's* utility and charm were discovered by outsiders, the animals were quickly spread far and wide by travelers and traders and became a fascinating part of cultures around the world. All people who had cats recognized something special about them:

> Evidence has been advanced that Norsemen worshipped cats, and we know that Siamese cats were the royal and sacred temple cats of Thailand. Cats in India became religious symbols, and in Japan they guarded Buddhist temples against rodent invasion—witness the splendid Go-To-Ku-Ji or Temple of the Cat, in Tokyo. In Burma, cats were the adored of the priests and nobility and had their own human attendants.[6]

Cats are also a pervasive motif in folklore, and it takes only a few minutes of browsing through the incredible masses of cat lore that exist around the world to discover that this sense of something mysterious or indefinable about cats is expressed and expanded on in vernacular culture: folklore shows us that cats are considered supernatural creatures. Their roles in stories, legends, and beliefs mirror the roles of other supernatural creatures such as fairies, demons, ghosts, and monsters; the motifs and themes attached to cat lore are the same motifs and themes in other supernatural folklore. The first records of cats as supernatural creatures, or creatures with supernatural power, are from Egypt, roughly three thousand years ago; a carving on a commemorative stone, dating between 1570 and 1075 B.C.E., bears the inscription, "The beautiful cat which endures and endures."[7] As one of the earliest cereal-growing (and storing) cultures in the Middle East, the ancient Egyptians often attracted large rodent populations, which in turn attracted cats, allowing Egyptians to observe the cat at length and place it where they felt it belonged—among the gods. Mildred Kirk explains:

> In Egyptian religion the cat had two distinct roles. The male cat symbolized the Sun-God Ra, and the female cat first represented a mother-goddess called Mut who later became the Cat-Goddess Bast. The myth of the "Great Cat Ra" goes back to earliest dynastic or even pre-dynastic times and is recounted in the "Book of the Dead," a sort of guide book buried with the dead to help them on their journey to the underworld.[8]

Solar eclipses were believed to be reenactments of the battle between the cat Ra and the python Apep, a "titanic combat between darkness and light, evil and good."[9] The successful end to the eclipse always intensified the already passionate veneration for the victorious cat.

Cat beliefs permeated Egyptian life. Cats could control fertility and, as Herodotus reported during a festival at Bubastis (the location of Bast's temple), merrymaking and "general licentiousness" were the rule of the day while the cat-shaped or cat-headed goddess was being revered.[10] Priests at Bubastis carefully tended the cats that lived there, interpreting their movements and sounds to make predictions for the public. When the cats died, they were mummified as humans were; in the 1800s, one excavated temple site yielded three hundred thousand felines (most of which unfortunately became fertilizer). Cats as pets were so loved by families that upon a cat's death, family members would shave off their eyebrows—a moving public enactment and display of the loss of "fur" that one felt especially close to. The punishment for killing a cat in Egypt was death.[11]

In recent years, long after the last Egyptian temple at Bubastis was utilized, we find cats still endowed with supernatural power in folklore. Black cats are bad luck; never let one cross your path. If it does, reverse the bad luck by tipping your hat and saying, "Good evening Mr. Black Cat," and then do it once more when the cat is behind you to ward off the bad luck.[12] This display of respect and formality is common in beliefs about the devil and fairy folk as well; an accidental or unintended insult could bring unwanted attention by a creature whose help is often as dangerous as its anger. White cats, on the other hand, are good luck, but if you travel in England, be prepared to switch that around. If a white cat crosses your path there, turn around completely, spit on the ground, and make the sign of the cross.[13]

Occupational folk beliefs often take the cat's possible bad or good luck quite seriously. Cornish miners will not even mention a cat while underground, and if a cat should appear in a mine, it will be instantly killed.[14] In Japan, sailors kept cats on ships to protect them from ghosts, and English sailors sometimes placed a howling cat under a pot to raise winds.[15] Even on land, cats are renowned weather forecasters. The *Handwörterbuch des Deutschen Aberglaubens* notes:

> Dann gilt die Katze als grober Wetter-prophet. Regen gibt es, wenn sie sich wascht oder sich den Hintern leckt; ebenso, wenn sie Gras fribt. Dreht sie den Schwanz nach dem Ofen oder Herd, dann gibt es Frost.

> (The cat is also said to be a crude weather-prophet. When she washes herself or licks her behind, it is going to rain; this can also happen when she eats grass. When she turns her tail towards the oven or stove, frost is coming.)[16]

The Pennsylvania Dutch place a cat in the empty cradle of a newlywed couple because the cat will grant their wish for children. Cats also aid in fertility in other parts of the United States, India, Egypt, and Scandinavia, but in the Ozarks, keeping black cats can render a young woman an old maid, and many people believe a cat will kill a baby, and sometimes even an adult, by sucking out its breath.[17] In Belgium, if a girl loves cats, she is sure to marry, and in the United States, shaking a cat in a quilt and watching which way it runs when you let it out can determine who will be the next to wed.[18] Welsh girls are supposed to feed their cats well so that they will have a sunny wedding day, and Italians in need of good luck will offer the first portion of every meal to the cat.[19] In Germany, France, and parts of the United States, though, cats are followers of the devil, and bring nothing but bad luck, no matter how well fed.[20]

In Ireland, legend has it that cats gather for meetings, speak a mysterious "cat language," and conduct business.[21] Norwegian legend tells of swarms of black cats overtaking churches when the devil is up to no good, as in the story of Svien Unafraid.[22] Cats were the familiars of witches or the embodiment of Satan himself in medieval Europe.[23] Similarly, in Hopi tradition, sorcerers disguise themselves as cats in order to "roam about at night without uttering a sound."[24] Cats can even create other evil creatures: a cat jumping over a corpse brings a vampire to life.[25] As recently as 1658, cats were described in Edward Topsel's work on natural history as "dangerous to soul and body";[26] these beliefs are not totally forgotten in many places today.

Currently in the United States, people still have strong supernatural beliefs about cats, black cats especially. For example, when I spoke with Kitty White of Logan, Utah, the "cat lady" who at any given time cares for between 50 and 150 cats, over half of her cat population was black. Kitty has trouble giving away black cats; as she says, "people just don't want them." Logan's locally owned pet store, Pet Kingdom, also has difficulties with its black cats. Rumors and legends of local satanist groups keep them from selling their black cats in the fall for fear of brutal and disturbing Halloween ceremonies in which the cats become unfortunate sacrifices. Such legends, like many satanist legends, are of questionable veracity, but even the popular (and well-researched) legend-debunking Internet site Snopes.com classifies them as "undetermined."[27] Cat superstitions clearly live on.

There are many themes in these examples of world folklore about cats that parallel themes in folklore about other supernatural creatures: required formality at encounters (the devil himself often requests formal treatment), power over fertility and death (women thought to be witches were often blamed for—or asked in secret to assist with—situations pertaining to both these issues), and ability to provide luck both good and bad (a common aspect of fairy encounters as well). But cats, unlike these and other supernatural creatures, are not treated with a consistent apprehension by humans. While most people would hesitate to invite the living dead to curl up by their fire or the devil to sleep in their bed, and while folklore clearly indicates that cats can be just as dangerous as these other creatures, we nevertheless welcome the cat into all aspects of our lives.

In fact, cats have had a mutually beneficial, working relationship with humans for roughly thirty-five hundred years now; they catch rodents and protect grain and receive shelter and consistent meals in return.[28] In recent times, the cat has even been considered a symbol of the home and of comfort, often by the very same people who are tipping their hats to black cats on the street to ward off bad luck. Mark Twain expressed the common view that "a home without a cat, and a well-fed, well-petted and properly revered cat, may be a perfect home, *perhaps*, but how can it prove its title?"[29] Twain insightfully targets the cat's ambiguity: homey and comforting but still deserving of the worship the Egyptians gave it and the fear so many other cultures have felt for it. So why are cats regarded as supernatural creatures at all? What is it about this animal that causes us to place it in the supernatural realm when it fits so comfortably in the ordinary, natural world?

The Permanently Liminal Cat and the Experiential Source Hypothesis

Before beginning, I want to acknowledge the common trend, recognized by Carl Lindahl, of modern legends to move from definitively supernatural to simply extraordinary without the obvious spiritual aspect so often encountered in supernatural narratives. Often, legends told nowadays are left open, leaving "questions of the supernatural to be resolved according to personal preference. This 'optional' approach to the supernatural is symptomatic of the modern world's views on belief."[30] You may notice that many cat legends and beliefs are more extraordinary than supernatural. But the presence of unequivocally supernatural cat folklore is so pervasive that I think it is fair to assume that even the nonsupernatural legends are shaped by people's familiarity with the supernatural ones. Cats cannot easily escape this vernacular classification.

To start with, I want to focus on a major characteristic of all things supernatural: *liminality*, the state of being "betwixt-and-between."[31] To be supernatural, to be "above and beyond" the laws of nature,[32] is to be liminal, trapped between the conceptual categories that are so integral to our perception of the natural world. Human beings want to categorize things, and we are uncomfortable when we can't. Susan Stewart, author of *Nonsense: Aspects of Intertextuality in Folklore and Literature*, describes categorical ambivalence as "a threat to the hierarchy of interpretations by talking through two domains at once."[33] Liminality disconcerts us, and luckily, we as humans do not have to spend much time in that uncomfortable position.

Through my research with this subject, I have noticed an interesting phenomenon: liminality attracts liminality. This is perhaps best illustrated by the danger humans face from the supernatural when in a transitory phase of a rite of passage.[34] When we as humans pass from one social category to another (single to married, for example), we enter an in-between stage (engaged, to follow the previous example) and become liminal, but only *temporarily*. During the time we spend in that middle ground, though, we are at a heightened risk of danger from the supernatural. We draw it to us by being similar to it, and superstitions and protective customs cluster around these liminal points of transition in people's lives. It is as though when we become liminal, we have stepped into the supernatural realm and opened ourselves to attack from creatures that hold permanent residency there and usually cannot reach us so easily.

On the subject of supernatural legends, Carl Lindahl observes the significance of "the supernatural being on the scene so swiftly when humans—knowingly or otherwise—cross moral boundaries."[35] I propose that it is not just moral boundaries that need to be crossed to bring the supernatural running—it is any boundary. Anytime a human or nonhuman animal crosses a boundary between two categories, the supernatural is no longer a categorical boundary away, and as folklore shows, supernatural creatures jump at the chance to interact with the unfortunate, temporarily liminal humans.

So while most humans experience this unsettling liminality only temporarily, supernatural creatures are *permanently* liminal. When we perceive this "perpetual liminality" in something, we understand it to be somehow outside of our category-based perception of nature and therefore supernatural. We can see now that cats, which often serve the same function or play the same role in folklore as do more straightforward supernatural creatures, must be liminal in some way at the least and are probably in a permanent state of liminality. The cat's supernatural status is one definite kind of liminality, but we need to seek the source of the liminality that gave the cat its supernatural status in the first place, and that continues to reinforce the connection in current belief traditions.

When studying belief traditions, scholars in the past have proposed different theories about why people would believe in a supernatural event or creature. One theory, the cultural source hypothesis, offers several possible explanations such as "misinterpretations of ordinary events caused by the action of tradition upon the imagination" and "experiences of those who are victim of a hoax by someone who has used the tradition as a model."[36] In other words, if a person claims to have seen a troll, it is probably because his culture has taught him to expect to see trolls and something, a person playing a trick or perhaps simply a pair of blurry glasses, has created the opportunity for traditional expectation to fill in a blank. Sometimes, the believer may not even be given credit for reacting to an actual, albeit misinterpreted, stimulus; without any event that could have been misinterpreted, belief in trolls is perceived as basic ignorance or cultural misguidance. The important thing to note here is that these explanations revolve around the assertion that people are wrong or mistaken in their assessment of a situation. Folklorist Wayland Hand supports the cultural source hypothesis when he refers to folk beliefs as "the vagaries of the human mind," "irrational notions," and "odd human quirks."[37] Though he acknowledges that even educated people may fall prey to folk beliefs—"Superstition is not the preserve of the unlettered only, but is a state of mind or a way of looking at things that may befall even the most sophisticated members of society"—his patronizing tone and obvious assumption that the beliefs are "mental errors" are indications of his lack of respect for the believers' abilities to reason.[38]

Folklorist David Hufford, in several of his works, including *The Terror that Comes in the Night* and "Beings Without Bodies," proposes an alternative approach, the experiential source hypothesis, with regard to memorates (personal, firsthand accounts of supernatural experiences) and traditional spiritual folk beliefs ("spiritual" here meaning not necessarily religious beliefs but simply beliefs in "extra-corporeal beings").[39] This hypothesis proposes that people who have supernatural experiences are not necessarily either mistaken or culturally influenced. Folk belief is not simply a "self-fulfilling process";[40] a person does not necessarily believe in a certain creature or event just because his culture tells him it exists or occurs. Hufford's view affirms a person's ability to reason and to believe in the supernatural at the same time: "The problem is a too-narrow view of what intellectual activity is and who has the capacity to reason soundly."[41] His hypothesis holds that certain elements of traditional supernatural beliefs may be descriptions of non–culturally dictated experiences that people have had, and that belief in supernatural beings and occurrences is often "rationally derived from experience."[42] Hufford's study of the Old Hag tradition, in which sleeping people awake to find themselves unable to move and in the presence of a clearly malicious creature, showed that one community's descriptive legends of being visited by the Old Hag happen to very precisely describe a medical condition—hypnogogic hallucination with sleep paralysis—that many people around the world, even those who have no knowledge of the Old Hag legends, experience.[43]

The experiential source hypothesis holds up well in situations in which people from different cultural backgrounds with different traditional beliefs describe similar supernatural experiences; in such cases, there may be a non-culture-based element of truth in their beliefs. Considering that belief in cats as supernatural creatures or vessels of supernatural power is definitely a "cross-culturally stable pattern,"[44] it is possible that beliefs about cats as supernatural creatures began with and are reinforced by objective experiences that people around the world have had with this animal. We must consider that perhaps the "incident precedes [the] belief."[45]

So is the cat experientially liminal? In answering the question "Why have [people] believed these things [about cats]?" Patricia Dale-Green is quick to point out that most beliefs about cats "have at least a tenuous connexion with the physique and natural habits of the animal."[46] Folklorist Frank De Caro, in his work *The Folktale Cat*, points out that cats are "amalgams of alternate, even opposing qualities."[47] Robert Darnton holds the opinion that cats have an "ambiguous ontological position," that they "straddle conceptual categories."[48] He cites examples such as the "quasi-human intelligence behind a cat's eyes" and the fact that a cat's howl at night can be mistaken for a human scream, "torn from some deep, visceral part of man's animal nature."[49] He also points out, in a chapter on the workers' revolt (during which a group of young Parisian printing apprentices tortured and killed "sackloads" of cats), that cats often become associated with certain humans, representing them symbolically even to the point that murdering the cat delivers a direct blow to the master.[50]

Desmond Morris, a British zoologist, notes in his book *Catwatching* that "the domestic cat is a contradiction."[51] Morris describes some of the most observable liminal traits of cats when he discusses what he calls the animal's "double life." He feels that domestication has changed the cat very little, that "both in anatomy and behavior it is still remarkably like the African wild cat from which it was gradually developed."[52] Biologist John Bradshaw points out that the cat "is neither a man-made species like the dog, nor simply an animal made captive for utilitarian purposes, like the elephant."[53] He later asserts that "in behavioural terms, domestication has probably had less effect on the cat than on any other domestic mammal."[54] Mildred Kirk agrees, offering the term "house cat" in favor of "domestic cat," as the latter does not accurately describe the feline's nature.[55] So people who encounter the cat in daily life may observe that the animal is both domestic and wild, or perhaps somewhere in between.

Cats are also nocturnal; they are designed for active life at night, yet people expect to interact with them during the day. The cats occasionally oblige, though they require roughly sixteen hours of sleep each day, and usually want to roam at night. Cats are therefore reputed to be lazy, while at the same time being admired for their impeccable alertness. Many cat owners will often notice how a sleeping cat always has one ear listening, or one eye only half shut. So again we find the cat at behavioral boundaries: nocturnal and diurnal, lazy and vigilant.

There is also the issue of independence, the trait that many people love and just as many people detest in this animal. Perhaps Kipling's "Cat that Walked by Himself," who slept by the fire and drank warm milk but would not accept human domination as the other animals had, says it best himself: "I am not a friend, and I am not a servant. I am the Cat who walks by himself, and I wish to come into your cave."[56] Cats are aloof, distanced, and self-sufficient yet demand an owner's attention the minute they want something. Kitty White, the cat lady from Utah, cited the cat's independence as one of the reasons people find it mysterious. Folklorist Venetia Newall suggested that the cat's "oddly independent" nature was possibly a factor in its connection to witches,[57] just as it is similarly a factor in its connection to modern-day "crazy cat ladies," older women who live alone (except for their cats) and often stand out in their respective communities as a unique traditional figure.[58] It is even possible to connect the discomfort that many people feel toward both cats and women (and especially "cat ladies") to a perception that they are similar in their impermanence between domesticity and wildness.

The connection of cats to women, a longstanding comparison in many cultures, has many manifestations and, in a way, parallels the connection of cats to the supernatural. The most obvious historic examples of this connection are witches and their familiars; women and cats were often burned together for crimes of witchcraft and sorcery. In fact, the cat familiar appears in one of the first "notable" Elizabethan witch trials at Chelmsford in 1566: "It was a white-spotted creature named Sathan, which sucked blood; it took the form of a toad and caused the death of a man who touched it."[59] While the cat may also be an incarnation of the devil (in 1495, one woman claimed to have learned her spells at a witches' gathering where "Lucifel" was present in the form of a black cat),[60] more often than not the cat was either the familiar of a witch or the witch herself transformed. It is a tenacious connection; forty years after the last official witch trial in Britain, a Bavarian nun was beheaded in 1749 for talking to her three cats, which were judged to be devils.[61] Also in the eighteenth century, John Gay penned "The Old Woman and Her Cats," a poem in which an old woman bemoans her choice to take in the animals: "Had ye been never hous'd and nurst / I, for a witch had ne'er been curst." The cats reply with a similar sentiment: "'Tis infamy to serve a hag; / Cats are thought imps, her broom a nag."[62] While the tale itself does not come from the oral tradition, Gay often used folk references in his work and the poem's assumption of audience understanding clearly reflects the traditional belief of the time that an older, single woman with cats was at risk for persecution for witchcraft. And of course, women today, hundreds of years removed from the legally sanctioned killing of women and cats, are still persecuted for their relationship to this animal; the popular cultural script for the "crazy cat lady" is not exactly complimentary.

This pervasive connection of women and cats is due in large part to the fact that women, like cats, are often perceived as liminal creatures, and I would say this is especially true in a patriarchal society, where "male" is perceived as the status quo, the base gender, and "female" is a deviation from that norm. Johannes Myyra, in a discussion of the ambivalence of motherhood, points out that "our patriarchal culture *needs* to put women in a position of otherness congruent with the imagined and enforced subordinating position of femininity."[63] This can lead to dangers for both women and cats; while the cultural script for women and cats often tends toward collusion, popular narratives about men and cats tend to focus on violence and destruction.[64] I would say that women's "otherness" (which, combined with their obvious "sameness" creates a liminal definition of the gender) could come from physical differences as well. Through pregnancy, women are capable of being both two beings and one being at the same time. Women also bleed regularly but are not hurt and do not die. For a man, bleeding is a sign of being wounded, of losing life. Women can bleed to death as well, but for females bleeding is also a sign of vitality and fertility, another quality that has been associated symbolically with cats. It is interesting to note that the identifying wounds of transformed witches are predominantly bleeding cuts, not bruises or breaks. It was noted earlier that liminality tends to attract liminality, so the connection of cats to women within a culture's world view is understandable. Though "independence" alone is a linking factor between cats and cat ladies, the connection is clearly deeper. Women and cats both, while being very much natural and earthly, still have very debatable ontological positions.[65]

When considering the animal's independent nature, John Bradshaw points out that the lack of a hierarchy in a cat's relationship to a human, as opposed to the obvious hierarchy in a dog's relationship to a human, is one source for the attitude of self-sufficiency that cats can project to their owners; the cat imposes its expected cooperative social structure on its owner rather than seeing the owner as a superior.[66] And yet many cat owners are dragged out of bed at night by a demanding yowl from a hungry feline. To further confuse the owners, studies have shown that owners who try very actively to spend time with their cats actually run the risk of spending less time with them than they would if they put out less of an effort; cat-initiated interaction usually lasts longer than human-initiated interaction.[67] Again the cat is found in between, both needy and independent.

Cat owners also testify to observing unusual behavior: a sleeping pet suddenly leaps into action, tearing about the house, crying out, attacking people, and then just as suddenly falling back asleep, as though nothing out of the ordinary had occurred. This behavior, called "vacuum activity," is due to the fact that the cat is designed to hunt, to sprint after prey, and indoor, domestic cats sometimes spontaneously release their pent-up energy in response to even the slightest stimulus, too subtle for humans to perceive.[68]

The subject of cats' eyes often arises when the cat's "mysteriousness" is discussed. Kirk asserts that the Egyptians were compelled to deify the cat because of observations of its "mysterious changing eyes which could be used symbolically to express mythological or abstract ideas," among other things.[69] Dale-Green supposes the dilation of the cat's eyes causes many people to think of the phases of the moon.[70] Many people have witnessed the eerie glow of a cat's eyes in the dark; this reflection off the "tapetum," a mirrorlike layer inside the animal's eye, helps the cat see in near-total darkness and has fascinated people for centuries.[71] Cats' eyes are also eerie because of the way they use them; a cat's eyes focus differently than a human's do, on slight motion rather than on sharp detail, resulting in the cat often staring fixedly at what appears to humans to be nothing at all.[72] One cat owner I spoke with noted, "You'll look up and they're just staring at you, like they know something. And they won't be the ones to blink first. It's creepy." This "creepy cat stare," as I call it, unnerves many people. My own cats often stare intently at closed doors, and it does indeed seem as though they "know something" that I don't know about what is behind them. But are my culture's beliefs about cats affecting my experience, or is it the other way around?

I argue that while my culture's belief traditions about cats tell me to be wary of them, those folk beliefs originated from culturally removed, firsthand experiences and observations, and the behavior I observe in my cats reinforces my cultural learning on the subject, so that the belief is perpetuated. We see again what Hufford discovered in his study of supernatural assault traditions: "Here [is] a host of traditional beliefs [that] actually seem to be *produced by* a particular kind of experience."[73] Many aspects of the cat's behavior are liminal; they do indeed "straddle categories," as Darnton puts it. The liminal behavior is also permanent, not temporary; it is part of their nature. So like supernatural creatures, cats, too, are "perpetually liminal." Though the cat's ability to defy categorization may be less easily articulated than, say, that of the living dead, cats are undeniably trapped in a permanent liminal state. Just as a human's temporary social liminality can draw the supernatural closer, the cat's permanent physical and behavioral liminality makes for an even closer tie. It makes sense, then, that people's experiences with an observable liminality in this animal's nature lead them to group this animal with other things that they perceive to be perpetually liminal: the supernatural.

Notes

1. Robert Darnton, *The Great Cat Massacre* (New York: Basic Books, 1999), 89.
2. Ernest H. Hart, *The Complete Guide to All Cats* (New York: Charles Scribner's Sons, 1980).
3. Mel Sunquist and Fiona Sunquist, *Wild Cats of the World* (Chicago: Univ. of Chicago Press, 2002), 100.
4. Hart, *Complete Guide to All Cats.*
5. Sunquist and Sunquist, *Wild Cats of the World,* 100.
6. Hart, *Complete Guide to All Cats,* 8.

7. Mildred Kirk, *The Everlasting Cat* (New York: Galahad Books, 1977), 19.

8. Ibid.

9. M. Oldfield Howey, *The Cat in the Mysteries of Religion and Magic* (New York: Castle Books, 1956), 32.

10. Kirk, *Everlasting Cat*, 21.

11. Katharine Briggs, *Nine Lives: The Folklore of Cats* (New York: Pantheon Books, 1980), 2.

12. Wayland Hand Collection of Superstition and Popular Belief, Fife Folklore Archives, Milton R. Merrill Library, Utah State University, Logan, s.v. "cat," 2000 (hereafter cited as Wayland Hand Collection).

13. Ibid.

14. Briggs, *Nine Lives*, 68.

15. *Eyewitness, Cat*, directed by Gavin Maxwell, Dorling Kindersley and BBC Lionheart Television International, 1994, videocassette.

16. E. Hoffman-Krayer, *Handwörterbuch des Deutschen Aberglaubens* (Berlin: Walter de Gruyter, 1931), 1108, my translation.

17. Vance Randolph, *Ozark Magic and Folklore* (New York: Dover, 1947), 205.

18. Wayland Hand Collection.

19. Briggs, *Nine Lives*.

20. Wayland Hand Collection.

21. Henry Glassie, ed., *Irish Folktales* (New York: Pantheon Books, 1985), 177.

22. Reider Christiansen, *Folktales of Norway* (Chicago: Univ. of Chicago Press, 1964), 161.

23. Desmond Morris, *Catwatching* (London: Jonathan Cape, 1986), 10.

24. Ekkehart Malotki, ed., *Hopi Animal Stories* (Lincoln: Univ. of Nebraska Press, 1998), 220.

25. Wayland Hand Collection.

26. Desmond Morris, *Catlore* (London: Jonathan Cape, 1987), 107.

27. Barbara Mikkelson and David P. Mikkelson, "Cat o' Nine Tales," http://www.snopes.com/horrors/mayhem/blackcat.htm, 2001, accessed Dec. 10, 2002.

28. John Bradshaw, *The Behaviour of the Domestic Cat* (Melksham, U.K.: Redwood Press, 1992), 6.

29. F. C. Sillar and R. M. Meyler, *Cats Ancient and Modern* (New York: Viking Press, 1966), 17.

30. Carl Lindahl, "Psychic Ambiguity at the Legend Core," *Journal of Folklore Research* 23, no. 1 (1986): 6.

31. Victor Turner, introduction to *Celebration*, ed. Victor Turner (Washington, D.C.: Smithsonian Institution Press, 1982), 29.

32. *Webster's Encyclopedic Unabridged Dictionary of the English Language*, 1996, s.v. "supernatural."

33. Susan Stewart, *Nonsense: Aspects of Intertextuality in Folklore and Literature* (Baltimore: Johns Hopkins Univ. Press, 1989), 61.

34. For a thorough discussion of rites of passage and liminality, see Arnold Van Gennep, *The Rites of Passage*, trans. Monika B. Vizedom and Gabrielle L. Caffee (Chicago: Univ. of Chicago Press, 1960).

35. Lindahl, "Psychic Ambiguity," 3.

36. David J. Hufford, *The Terror that Comes in the Night* (Philadelphia: Univ. of Pennsylvania Press, 1982), 13.

37. Wayland Hand, introduction to *The Frank C. Brown Collection of North Carolina Folklore* 6, ed. Wayland Hand (Durham, N.C.: Duke Univ. Press, 1961), xix.

38. Ibid., xix–xx.

39. David J. Hufford, "Beings Without Bodies: An Experience-Centered Theory of the Belief in Spirits," in *Out of the Ordinary: Folklore and the Supernatural*, ed. Barbara Walker (Logan: Utah State Univ. Press, 1995), 16.

40. Ibid., 13.

41. Ibid., 40.

42. Ibid., 11.

43. Hufford, *Terror*.

44. Hufford, "Beings Without Bodies," 12.

45. Ibid., 9.

46. Patricia Dale-Green, *The Cult of the Cat* (New York: Weathervane Books, 1963), 141.

47. Frank De Caro, *The Folktale Cat* (Little Rock, Ark.: August House, 1992), 14.

48. Darnton, *Great Cat Massacre*, 89.

49. Ibid.

50. Ibid.

51. Morris, *Catwatching*, 3.

52. Ibid., 4.

53. Bradshaw, *Behaviour of the Domestic Cat*, 6.

54. Ibid., 8.

55. Kirk, *Everlasting Cat*, 18.

56. Rudyard Kipling, "The Cat that Walked by Himself," in *Rudyard Kipling: Stories and Poems*, ed. Roger Green (1902; reprint, London: Everyman's Library, 1970), 75.

57. De Caro, *Folktale Cat*, 15.

58. Lynne McNeill, "The Waving Ones: A Study of Cats in Folklore" (master's thesis, American Studies/Folklore, Utah State Univ.), 2002.

59. George Lyman Kittredge, *Witchcraft in Old and New England* (New York: Russell and Russell, 1956), 178.

60. Ibid., 160.

61. Angela Sayer and Howard Loxton, *Encyclopedia of the Cat* (San Diego: Thunder Bay Press, 1999), 25.

62. Kirk, *Everlasting Cat*, 78.

63. Kaj Bjorkqvist and Pirkko Niemela, *Of Mice and Women* (San Diego: Academic Press, 1992), 264.

64. For further discussion, see Carol J. Adams, "Women-Battering and Harm to Animals," in *Animals and Women: Feminist Theoretical Explorations*, ed. Carol J. Adams and Josephine Donovan (Durham, N.C.: Duke Univ. Press, 1995), 55–84, and McNeill, "Waving Ones."

65. For further discussion of the connection between cats and women, see Katharine Rogers, *The Cat and the Human Imagination* (Ann Arbor: Univ. of Michigan Press, 1998) and McNeill, "Waving Ones."

66. Bradshaw, *Behaviour of the Domestic Cat*, 163.

67. Ibid., 164–65.

68. Morris, *Catlore*, 52.

69. Kirk, *Everlasting Cat*, 18.

70. Dale-Green, *Cult of the Cat*, 141.

71. Morris, *Catwatching*, 61.

72. Ibid., 63.

73. Hufford, "Beings Without Bodies," 14 (emphasis added).

Works Cited

Adams, Carol J. "Women-Battering and Harm to Animals." In *Animals and Women: Feminist Theoretical Explorations*, edited by Carol J. Adams and Josephine Donovan, 55–84. Durham, N.C.: Duke Univ. Press, 1995.

Bjorkqvist, Kaj, and Pirkko Niemela. *Of Mice and Women*. San Diego: Academic Press, 1992.

Bradshaw, John. *The Behaviour of the Domestic Cat*. Melksham, U.K.: Redwood Press, 1992.

Briggs, Katharine. *Nine Lives: The Folklore of Cats*. New York: Pantheon Books, 1980.

Christiansen, Reider. *Folktales of Norway*. Chicago: Univ. of Chicago Press, 1964.

Dale-Green, Patricia. *The Cult of the Cat*. New York: Weathervane Books, 1963.

Darnton, Robert. *The Great Cat Massacre*. New York: Basic Books, 1999.

De Caro, Frank. *The Folktale Cat*. Little Rock, Ark.: August House, 1992.

Eyewitness, Cat. Directed by Gavin Maxwell. Dorling Kindersley and BBC Lionheart Television International, 1994. Videocassette.

Glassie, Henry, ed. *Irish Folktales.* New York: Pantheon Books, 1985.

Hand, Wayland. Introduction to *The Frank C. Brown Collection of North Carolina Folklore* 6:xix–xlvii, edited by Wayland Hand. Durham, N.C.: Duke Univ. Press, 1961.

Hart, Ernest H. *The Complete Guide to All Cats.* New York: Charles Scribner's Sons, 1980.

Hoffmann-Krayer, E. *Handwörterbuch des Deutschen Aberglaubens.* Berlin: Walter de Gruyter, 1931.

Howey, M. Oldfield. *The Cat in the Mysteries of Religion and Magic.* New York: Castle Books, 1956.

Hufford, David J. "Beings Without Bodies: An Experience-Centered Theory of the Belief in Spirits." In *Out of the Ordinary: Folklore and the Supernatural,* edited by Barbara Walker, 9–45. Logan: Utah State Univ. Press, 1995.

———. *The Terror that Comes in the Night.* Philadelphia: Univ. of Pennsylvania Press, 1982.

Kipling, Rudyard. "The Cat that Walked by Himself." In *Rudyard Kipling: Stories and Poems,* edited by Roger Green, 68–75. 1902. Reprint, London: Everyman's Library, 1970.

Kirk, Mildred. *The Everlasting Cat.* New York: Galahad Books, 1977.

Kittredge, George Lyman. *Witchcraft in Old and New England.* New York: Russell and Russell, 1956.

Lindahl, Carl. "Psychic Ambiguity at the Legend Core." *Journal of Folklore Research* 23, no. 1 (1986): 1–21.

Malotki, Ekkehart, ed. *Hopi Animal Stories.* Lincoln: Univ. of Nebraska Press, 1998.

McNeill, Lynne. "The Waving Ones: A Study of Cats in Folklore." Master's thesis, American Studies/Folklore, Utah State Univ., 2002.

Mikkelson, Barbara, and David P. Mikkelson. "Cat o' Nine Tales." Snopes.com. http://www.snopes.com/horrors/mayhem/blackcat.htm. 2001. Accessed Dec. 10, 2002.

Morris, Desmond. *Catlore.* London: Jonathan Cape, 1987.

———. *Catwatching.* London: Jonathan Cape, 1986.

Randolph, Vance. *Ozark Magic and Folklore.* New York: Dover, 1947.

Rogers, Katharine. *The Cat and the Human Imagination.* Ann Arbor: Univ. of Michigan Press, 1998.

Sayer, Angela, and Howard Loxton. *Encyclopedia of the Cat.* San Diego: Thunder Bay Press, 1999.

Sillar, F. C., and R. M. Meyler. *Cats Ancient and Modern.* New York: Viking Press, 1966.

Stewart, Susan. *Nonsense: Aspects of Intertextuality in Folklore and Literature.* Baltimore: Johns Hopkins Univ. Press, 1989.

Sunquist, Mel, and Fiona Sunquist. *Wild Cats of the World*. Chicago: Univ. of Chicago Press, 2002.

Turner, Victor. Introduction to *Celebration*, edited by Victor Turner, 11–30. Washington, D.C.: Smithsonian Institution Press, 1982.

Van Gennep, Arnold. *The Rites of Passage*. Translated by Monika B. Vizedom and Gabrielle L. Caffee. Chicago: Univ. of Chicago Press, 1960.

Wayland Hand Collection of Superstition and Popular Belief. Fife Folklore Archives, Milton R. Merrill Library, Utah State University, Logan. S.v. "cat," 2000.

White, Kitty. Interview by author. Tape recording. Logan, Utah. Mar. 26, 2000.

Chapter 2

Spirits, Sex, and Wealth

Fox Lore and Fox Worship in Late Imperial China

Xiaofei Kang

In 1529, while traveling in a small county of northern China, Lang Ying (1487–1566), a southern scholar, became curious about local lore of fox metamorphosis. Here is what he learned:

> Foxes sneak into the shabby houses of poor families, jump on beds and open their mouths to steal people's breath. When people wake up and smell a fox they will shout in fear: "Beat the fox! Beat the fox!" But by this time the foxes are long gone. Practicing like this for a long time, foxes become able to shrink their bodies and penetrate into the earth even at impenetrable places. After practicing for an even longer time, foxes master the arts of metamorphosis and are therefore able to form illicit relationships with mortal men and women. They will find the opposite sex to engage in sexual intercourse, and they are also skillful in conveying wealth and property [from other places] to benefit their [human] hosts.[1]

Lang's record shows that daily encounters with real foxes provided a breeding ground for fox lore in northern China, and that there was not a clear line between natural and supernatural foxes in the popular imagination. Furthermore, similar to the case of the Japanese serpentine mates that will be discussed by Ria Koopmans–de Bruijn in the next chapter, the relationship between foxes and humans was dominated by two concepts: sex and wealth.

Lang Ying was not alone in exploring local beliefs in fox spirits. From the sixteenth to the early twentieth century, fox spirits proliferated in Chinese anecdotal collections. Like Lang Ying, the compilers of these collections drew on local informants from all walks of life, including their literati friends, maids and servants, concubines, flower vendors, wet nurses, cooks, and farmers. By emphasizing the accuracy and truthfulness of their stories, these collections provide invaluable sources on local fox lore and fox worship.[2] In these stories, foxes appear as women or men, young or old, and visit families rich and poor. Fox shrines were erected in both rural and urban settings, in places that real and imagined foxes frequented, such as door entrances, backyard haystacks, roadsides, farm fields, bedchambers, shops, and temples.[3] Family wealth generated by sexual liaisons with fox spirits becomes a staple of these tales, and throughout northern China, foxes were worshiped as a "Minor God of Wealth" (as compared to the officially celebrated "God of Wealth" in Buddhist and Daoist temples).

This chapter explores Chinese conceptions of the fox, wealth, and gender as they are represented in fox lore and fox worship of late imperial northern China. Current studies of animals and gender in Western cultural contexts recognize an ultimate divide between nature and culture. They criticize the male patriarchal ideology based on the identification of women with nature and with the irrationality particular to animals.[4] In the Chinese tales, however, foxes transgress the boundaries between nature and culture. They do embody female enchantresses similar to the "foxy lady" in contemporary Western cultures,[5] but more than that, the Chinese people construct different relationships between male foxes and female mortals and between female foxes and male mortals and interpret the wealth brought by these relationships in gendered terms. Fox shrines, paradoxically both respected and detested in individual homes, brought to the forefront socially suppressed voices and culturally repressed desires. Straddling boundaries between personal interests and the public good, immoral practices and Confucian moral teachings, the fox spirits served as effective tools for people to use in coping with financial and moral conflicts in their minds and in their real lives.

The Fox Man and the Mortal Woman

In fox tales, women are more likely to engage in sex with fox spirits in exchange for family wealth than men. Fox possession of women was often turned into a source of family fortune, as this sixteenth-century account shows:

> During the Jiajing (1522–1566) period the wife of a Dezhou man, Zhou, was [sexually] deluded by a demonic fox. In the beginning the family suffered bitterly. Later they tried telling the fox what they needed, and the fox always stole things to satisfy them. Because of this the family soon became very wealthy. Therefore they piled two haystacks behind their house and let the fox live there. [When] Zhou's grandson [became the head of the family], he disliked this. He wanted to tear down the haystacks in order to build new houses. The fox became very angry: "I have made your family enjoy wealth and happiness for generations. If you kick me out perfidiously, don't you believe that I can send you back to poverty?" The grandson was deeply terrified. He raised the heaps every year, so much so that they looked like hills from far away. The family remained the richest in the whole prefecture.

Another sixteenth-century account involves a Yuan family:

> In the beginning a fox committed illicit sex with Yuan's daughter-in-law. Yuan found an opportunity to capture the fox in a bag and was about to boil it. The fox pleaded with him, saying: "If you release me I will make you rich. There is gold hidden in such-and-such place,

please go check it first." Yuan dug at the place and indeed found gold, so he let the fox go. The fox then stole more things for him. The man became rich and did not criticize the fox again. Now his family has been several generations, and all women who marry into it have been subject to the fox's wanton desires, yet the family grows richer and richer. People call them "the Money Spinner Yuans." A regional inspector heard of it and disapproved [the way in which the Yuans got rich]. He was about to confiscate the family's wealth. The fox sent him a message in a dream, threatening to ruin his fortunes. So the regional inspector did not dare to take any action.[6]

In these stories, the spirits' attachment to debauchery went hand-in-hand with the riches they bestowed.[7] For many young women who were undergoing psychic and physical tensions brought about by betrothal or marriage to men they hardly knew, ecstatic trance or sexual debauchery provoked by the capricious spirits offered them an efficient strategy to escape from conjugal duties and to disregard social norms in the patriarchal society.[8] Although in the above accounts the two afflicted women remained mute, it is conceivable that fox possession might have lent power to these women in their families, for they were the sole intermediaries through which the patriarchal family heads communicated with the spirits in order to obtain wealth. A seventeenth-century account shows more explicitly that women used fox possession to defy social norms. The daughter of a certain Li in a rural town was possessed by a fox as soon as she became betrothed. When the wedding day approached, her family found that the fox had changed her into a male, and the marriage contract was therefore annulled. When the local official investigated this anomaly, he found that Li's daughter was still a female. Bewildered and agitated, the official threw her in jail. There she was protected by the fox spirit and soon was released. She was later married to a man living far away, but the fox followed her and killed her husband. It was not until she returned to her natal home that the fox finally disappeared.[9]

Women of low status also used fox possession to negotiate their own interests with patriarchal authorities. For example, a maid who had long passed the age of marriage in Zhang Xuan'er's household, a well-known gentry, suddenly went crazy and ran from Zhang's house several times, only to be found asleep under the haystack behind the house. She was allegedly possessed by a fox. Zhang was about to punish the maid for the illicit sex she had committed while being possessed, but the fox laughed at him: "She has passed the age of marriage, yet you have not found her an appropriate mate. Is this the maid's fault alone?" Zhang halted, and the next day he called upon a matchmaker and soon married out all the old maids.[10]

These cases may also tell us about human worshipers. The family head's consent to the sacrifice of the household women and his incessant efforts to keep the fox within the family are revealing, for by so doing he actually violated a publicly upheld moral code of female chastity. This kind of sex-for-wealth deal happened exactly at a time when a cult of female chastity grew to remarkable prominence in Chinese society.[11] In addition, by virtue of fox magic the family head allowed the accumulation of wealth at the expense of other families and thus knowingly pursued selfish interests. Craving for material goods overrode moral concerns in these cases. By consecrating the fox, people's selfish interests might not be morally justified, but they were practically served.

We can also detect an even more subtle and ambiguous attitude toward sexual politics in the part of a third party—those who watched Zhou and Yuan grow rich and spread the stories around. We can only guess their sentiments through the recorders of these cases. No respect was paid to the fox. It was described as "demonic," its sexual advances were "adulterous," and the women they possessed were "deluded." The fox accumulated wealth for its host family mainly by stealing and robbery. Yet locals appeared to have passed no moral judgment. The Zhous were considered "the richest of the whole prefecture." The fox that enriched "the Money Spinners Yuans" even successfully blocked the efforts of a government official. And according to several contemporary observers, "people don't think [these activities of the fox] are strange."[12] Behind the negative features ascribed to the fox, a mixed feeling of both contempt and admiration may have emerged among many onlookers: the immoral means by which one obtained wealth had to be publicly denounced, but to become and stay wealthy could be a wish secretly endorsed by all.

In the eyes of both the fox host's family and the people surrounding them, the fox was a tutelary spirit who served only the private and often selfish interests of the given family. The personal bond between the fox and its human host was exclusive, and the benefit of fox magic would not extend beyond the immediate family of the possessed. Here the relationship between the human family and the tutelary spirit was reciprocal. It was based on a fair exchange of practical favors without any involvement of moral judgment.

Such deals between human families and possessing spirits required a delicate balancing of interests. In both the Zhou and Yuan cases, the family heads demonstrated their initial neglect of and even aversion to the foxes for the disturbance they caused. They showed no fear of the superhuman power of the foxes when the original family's interests suffered. However, when the foxes promised riches, the Zhous and Yuans started to treat the foxes with extreme care. The Zhous "renovated" the fox's abode unfailingly every year. All women of the Yuan household were subject to "whatever the fox wantonly desired." The sharp contrast between attitudes people held before and after they reached agreements with foxes indicate a businesslike relationship between foxes and humans.

The interest-driven reciprocity between the fox and the human family could be so practical that it might affect the ways in which the fox was worshiped in the domestic arena. A proper shrine was not always necessary.[13] The fox was satisfied with a den made of straw in the backyard of the Zhou family. This kind of fox den was common in rural homes of northern China until the twentieth century. Content, rather than formality, seems to be important. The above cases and many other accounts of this time all lack elaboration on ritual manners but specify the particulars of material offerings: wine, fruits, eggs, and chicken—all expensive delicacies yet available to normal farmers in northern China. An obnoxious spirit serving selfish interests of the human family, the fox was conceived of as useful but not necessarily respectable. By satisfying the fox's demands and attentively propitiating it, human worshipers showed their confidence in gaining an equal footing in negotiating with the fox and exploiting its power for their own personal ends. The simplicity and practicality of the shrines also indicate that the fox's magical powers could be personally invoked by a wide array of people, even by the poorest of the poor.

The Fox Woman and the Mortal Man

Like the Japanese serpents discussed in the next chapter, Chinese foxes also approached mortal men in female forms. The following story illustrates the differences between fox women and fox men:

> A certain Li from Henan emigrated to Suzhou (northern Anhui). He was utterly destitute and earned his livelihood as a hired laborer. One day a beautiful woman called to him from the field ditch. Li did not dare to respond. The woman said: "I am a fox. The predestined fate of our past life brings us together, so I venture to be my own matchmaker. I am not the kind that harms you." Li was suspicious of her bewitchment but fascinated by her beauty, so he brought her home, and they lived together thereafter. She suggested Li move to another village and build big houses. In a few years Li's properties and farms extended for miles. The whole place looked up to the Lis and came to be called Li Village. The fox was virtuous in nature. She did not produce any heir, so she bought a concubine for Li and raised the concubine's son as her own. Having lived like this for a long time she started to introduce the art of guiding energies to Li and to exhort him to abstain from sexual life. She urged Li to sleep alone, and that the concubine should not be in his company. Li's relatives therefore believed that she was a monstrous apparition wielding bewitching arts and should be exorcised. Persuaded by his relatives Li beguiled her into shrinking her body and entering a bottle. Li then sealed the bottle with a charm and boiled it. A while later, only a few drops of blood were left in the water. Li's family soon declined: Li and his concubine died, followed by the untimely death of their son.[14]

The fox woman in this story is also a source of wealth, but here the means by which the fox woman brought in wealth is not specified, and she is depicted as a wife of beauty and virtue. With the gender switch between the fox and the mortal, the illicit sex in earlier cases is replaced by legitimate marriage, and the wealth the mortal man thus obtains is morally justifiable. Moreover, in such a marital relationship the fox is no longer the cause of sexual indulgence but a woman who avoids procreation and advocates sexual abstinence. She also personifies female virtues: making unconditional contributions to family welfare, getting her husband a concubine to secure an heir, and raising the concubine's child as her own. These virtues make her a model woman who serves her husband's best interests and assures male authority over family wealth. Hierarchy, instead of exchange on equal terms, characterizes the relationship between the mortal man and the fox woman.

The image of fox women as passionate lovers and caring wives was the most extensively written about and most aspired to by men, especially the literati. Among the eighty-three stories about fox spirits in the famous seventeenth-century collection *Tales of the Strange from the Studio of Leisure* (*Liaozhai zhiyi*), for example, thirty-six involve romances between mortal men and fox women, and in as many as thirty of them, the fox women are young, beautiful, and benevolent. In many of these tales, fox heroines were given names that invoked literary imagery, such as Blue Phoenix (Qingfeng), Green Plum (Qingmei), or Lotus Scent (Lianxiang). These fox women were depicted as eager to shake off their supernatural features and attain identities as human beings. Allan Barr has keenly observed that the author, Pu Songling (1644–1715), adopted a strict male perspective to delineate these women. Sexual liaisons between these fox women and mortal men were morally justified by either legitimate marriage or predestined fate (*yuan*). In marrying mortal men, the fox women committed themselves to traditional values and strove to be fully integrated into human families. Fox women who came to men by predestined fate, on the other hand, associated themselves with mortal men only for a short period and were bound to leave when the allotted time expired. As transient beings in human society, these women often violated conventional expectations, most notably by refusing to have children. But they never harmed mortal families, and they even sought to conform to traditional moral codes by arranging for appropriate mortal women to marry mortal men in order to produce male heirs.[15]

Such fox women were well accepted not only as products of literary creation or objects of male fantasy but also as wives and concubines in real life. Fox heroines in Pu Songling's long stories are generally considered to be literary creations, but anecdotal writers of this time also recorded their personal experiences with fox women in real life. An admirer of Pu Songling, Xu Kun (b. 1715), for example, recounts that his close friend and neighbor, Wang Peng, married a fox woman. She bore him a son and helped the Wang family win a lawsuit against a local bully. When Xu and Wang traveled together, Xu even shared with Wang the cookies made by his "fox sister-in-law."[16] Another famous scholar-official, Ji Yun (1724–1805), records several times that men in his hometown had fox wives or concubines. Among them was one member from a prominent local gentry family. The man once asked his fox concubine whether her *yin* qualities would harm him, and she explained that "foxes maintain sexual relations with mortals either by bewitchment or by predestined fate. Men who are bewitched lose their *yang* to replenish the fox's *yin*. They fall ill and die when the *yang* is exhausted. Those who come together by predestined fate follow the natural course; their energies respond to each other spontaneously, and the *yin* and *yang* exchange normally. Therefore their relationship can last long and peacefully."[17]

While authors of fox tales consciously elaborated oral materials to suit their own literary tastes, the recurrent appearances of these benign fox women in different types of anecdotal collections suggests that folklore and literati writings shared and mutually reinforced similar perceptions of fox women. Female power was recognized and even exemplified by fox heroines who were satisfied with short-term romances with men without family burdens. However, behind the common acclamation of foxes as model women, there perhaps also lay uneasy feelings of a male-dominant society about constant challenges to such model images by mortal women in real life, as Pu Songling colorfully depicts elsewhere in his collection.[18] The wider appeal of fox women, therefore, still lay in their complementary roles within the patriarchal society. Their supernatural powers had to be restrained within the limits of secular male authority.

Foxes, Wealth, and Gender

Northern China during late imperial times was second only to the Lower Yangzi region in population density but was lower in levels of urbanization and rural commercialization than all other regions. Except for Beijing, Tianjin, and some other cities along the Grand Canal, it was a poor and self-sufficient rural hinterland.[19] Population growth consumed commercial profits from the household handicraft production, and small-scale peasant family farming persisted, accompanied by insulated villages and general poverty among the peasants.[20] For most families in the northern China plain, who lived on the margin of subsistence, wealth was simply beyond reach. Village elites, a small number of "managerial farmers," were unable to accumulate lineage corporate land as a stable source of income, nor could they gain greater wealth from commerce and public offices. They managed to get rich through certain commercial activities, but they were rich only compared with their poor neighbors and could barely maintain the wealth for more than a generation or two. Their heavy reliance on cash crops made them extremely vulnerable to natural disasters, bad harvests, and other unpredictable accidents—factors easily attributed to fate. More important, the wealth of these families quickly dissipated under the customary practice of family division, *fenjia*, which often, with a single partition, "drove a rich household down to middle or poor peasant status."[21] Richard von Glahn notes that

> in popular perceptions, the temporary and fluctuating nature
> of family wealth was sometimes explained in terms of exclusive
> relationships between a fox spirit and a single family member. Such
> spirit connections could be with women as well as men, and the
> ephemeral wealth brought by foxes could be viewed both positively
> and negatively. The two types of fox/human relationships, between
> the fox man and the mortal woman and between the fox woman

and the mortal man, reflected popular conceptions of wealth as well
as gender in late imperial times.[22]

Women and women's bodies had economic values for many late imperial
Chinese families.[23] Exploiting female members, such as by selling and renting
wives, daughters, or daughters-in-law, became increasingly common and was an
important survival strategy for the poor.[24] Ji Yun, for example, records many such
incidents in his home area, Cangzhou, and it seems common for men to live on
the income from their wives' sexual service to other men. In one account, a family sold their daughter-in-law to a rich household to gain handsome pay. Another
family sold the household wife out of poverty.[25] A village hoodlum lost his family property, and his livelihood therefore depended on his wife's prostitution.[26]
A cousin of Ji Yun even provides an anecdote that a local man used the income
from his wife's prostitution to support a fox mistress.[27] Such practices were generally considered dishonorable, but frequently concerns for actual profits overrode
moral ideals, and these practices were ordinarily conducted by "those who chose
to accumulate money rather than honor, or by the merely poor."[28] In some places,
popular attitudes toward prostitution outside marriage were not harsh and sometimes were even encouraging when there was an economic necessity.[29]

In giving tacit consent to the "illicit" sex between the fox and the young female
members of the family, the male family heads in fact chose to accumulate money
rather than honor. The fox man who sexually defiled a mortal woman might serve
as, to borrow a Freudian term, a "projection" of the household men who gave up
moral principles to pursue monetary gains. Such a projection in religious practices
indicates "the unconscious attribution to other people of thoughts, feelings, and
acts of our own which would otherwise be felt as unpleasurable—perhaps feelings
of guilt or inferiority."[30] By attributing both the illicit sex and the wealth to the
fox, the male members of the family could legitimately enjoy the wealth brought
in by the fox/woman without bearing blame for sacrificing honor for practical
profits. Moral tensions in real life, through projection onto the fox, were ritually
mitigated. Furthermore, worshiping the fox spirit allowed these men to convert
the threatening spirit into a helpful deity. In propitiating the fox they might sub-
jugate the potential power of female family members, who might use spirit possession to achieve goals unattainable through ordinary means. By making the fox
an object of worship and establishing an equal exchange relationship with it, men,
or society as a whole, which assumed male perspectives, were able to mediate the
moral and immoral, the ideal and real, and male dominance and female resistance
in everyday life.

The fox woman as a source of wealth, on the other hand, often embodied
female virtue. The moral overtone of the second type of story might be associated
with women's capability to bring wealth into the family through marriage or other
acceptable means in real life. The family wealth produced by women included not
only income from household production but also dowry and the male heirs they
bore. Unlike the fox man who, as an outsider, claimed someone's wife, the fox
woman assumed the role of a mortal woman who was supposed to be submissive

to the man in both social and financial standing. The supernatural power of the fox woman in the family was perceived as controllable by the established moral order. If it grew uncontrollable, it had to be suppressed and eliminated. It was exactly at the moment when Li's wife stepped out of the role of a model woman, by asking her husband to withdraw from sexual life against his wish, that she met her fatal destruction. Few such fox women appeared as objects of worship in these stories, because worshiping these women would formally acknowledge female power in the male-centered family settings and therefore undermine male control over the family fortune. However, the ultimate death of Li's family does imply that female power was still well recognized in informal ways, just as women in real life improved families' economic life without being given legal rights or official recognition.[31] The principle of divine retribution counterbalanced the dominant male-centered ideology and proved that women in patriarchal families might be invisible but by no means negligible.

There are counterexamples. In bringing wealth, foxes also formed same-sex friendships with the mortals. One fox man, for instance, was not made an object of worship even though he brought in considerable wealth for the human family he was affiliated with. He came into the family through a connection to a mortal man. The two men became bosom friends over many nights of drinking and talking. Feeling sympathy for the mortal's modest life, the fox revealed hidden treasures to the man and advised his family to grow different crops according to market fluctuations. Genuine friendship cast the fox/man interaction in a positive light, and the fox disappeared soon after the man's death.[32] In the second case, a female spirit granted financial favors to the family by communicating with the wife. Unlike the wife of Li, who married a mortal man, this fox woman had no secular position in the mortal family. The wealth she generated for the family bore an immoral imprint: the money she generously distributed among the family members was stolen from others. She also misused her power to help the husband to pay his gambling debt. To maintain this lavish source of income, however, the husband and wife emptied a room for the fox and made daily offerings to her.[33] These two stories reverse the gender roles illustrated in earlier cases, but they retain the innate connection between moral justifications and worship of foxes, and they still emphasize personal reciprocity between the fox and the mortal.

Fox spirits came to Chinese people with two faces: they could do harm as well as provide divine help and assume both male and female forms. Like their Japanese serpent counterparts described in Koopman–de Bruijn's chapter in this volume, foxes as benign spirits were more likely imagined as female and helped reassert common morality and dominant values, but they appeared as wives, not mothers, and as such they rarely became objects of worship. Generating wealth on morally gray ground, they were worshiped as male deities and signified people's attempts to undermine the established order for their private good. Family wealth, as well as the moral value of the wealth, were perceived in gendered terms, and women's roles in family life were expressed in the gendered construction of the fox's magic power.

For the Chinese, the fox spirit has long been "betwixt and between": it roams in the wild and remains untamable for domestic uses, yet it preys on domestic fowl, builds dens in human settlements, and demonstrates quasi-human intelligence. With their ambiguities and gender flexibility, fox spirits and fox shrines provided ample choices for families in late imperial China to deal with the complexities and the contradictions in everyday life and to find a balance between the public good and their private needs, between unorthodox practices and official ideologies. The fox lore and fox worship of late imperial China exemplifies how an animal had gained symbolic meanings to convey people's perceptions of the world and their own place in it.

Notes

This is a revised version of a chapter in *The Cult of the Fox: Power, Gender, and Popular Religion in Late Imperial and Modern China* by Xiaofei Kang. © 2005 Columbia University Press. Reprinted with permission of the publisher.

1. Lang Ying, *Qixiu leigao*, 1775 ed., University of Toronto East Asian Rare Book Collection, 48.9b–11a. Unless otherwise noted, all translations from original Chinese sources are by the author.

2. On Chinese fox tales, see, among others, Leo Tak-hung Chan, *Discourse on Foxes and Ghosts: Ji Yun and Eighteenth-Century Literati Storytelling* (Honolulu: Univ. of Hawaii Press, 1998); Rania Huntington, *Alien Kind: Foxes and Late Imperial Chinese Narrative* (Cambridge, Mass.: Harvard Univ. Asia Center, 2003); and Xiaofei Kang, *The Cult of the Fox: Power, Gender, and Popular Religion in Late Imperial and Modern China* (New York: Columbia Univ. Press, 2005). All these works discuss the different uses of fox tales by literati compilers.

3. The fox also features in both Japanese folklore and popular worship in a similar manner. On Japanese folklore and fox worship, see Karen Smyers, *The Fox and the Jewel: Shared and Private Meanings in Contemporary Japanese Inari Worship* (Honolulu: Univ. of Hawaii Press, 1999) and Michael R. Bathgate, *The Fox's Craft in Japanese Religion and Folklore: Shapeshifters, Transformations, and Duplicities* (New York: Routledge, 2004).

4. See, for example, Josephine Donovan and Carol J. Adams, introduction to *Animals and Women: Feminist Theoretical Explorations*, ed. Carol J. Adams and Josephine Donovan (Durham, N.C.: Duke Univ. Press, 1995), 1–8.

5. Joan Dunayer points out that the ambivalence of the Foxy Lady in Western culture is based on the vixens as prey for hunters and trappers who are mostly male. Joan Dunayer, "Sexist Words, Speciesist Roots," in *Animals and Women: Feminist Theoretical Explorations*, ed. Carol J. Adams and Josephine Donovan (Durham, N.C.: Duke Univ. Press, 1995), 11.

6. Both stories are from Xu Changzuo (fl. 1602), *Yanshan conglu*, seventeenth-century ed., Rare Book Collection of Beijing National Library, 8.4a.

7. The fox in northern China had a southern parallel, the Wutong spirits, capricious deities whose sexual appetite for women made them popular gods of wealth. On the cult of Wutong, see Richard von Glahn, "The Enchantment of Wealth: The God Wutong in the Social History of Jiangnan," *Harvard Journal of Asiatic Studies* 51, no. 2 (1991): 651–714.

8. On the use of spirit possession by women to defy social norms, see Ioan M. Lewis, *Ecstatic Religion: A Study of Shamanism and Spirit Possession*, 2d ed. (New York: Routledge, 1989), 100–126. Von Glahn also pointed out this feature in the worship of the Wutong spirits; von Glahn, "Enchantment of Wealth," 698–701.

9. Wang Tonggui (fl. 1530–1608), *Xinke ertan* (The new edition of tales overheard), 1603 ed., "Hushu nü bian nanzi (A woman changed into a man by fox magic)," Rare Book Collection of Beijing National Library, 16b–17a.

10. Ji Yun, *Yuewei caotang biji* (Chongqin: Chongqin Chubanshe, 1996), 422.

11. Von Glahn, "Enchantment of Wealth," 685. On the cult of female chastity, see T'ien Ju-k'ang, *Male Anxiety and Female Chastity: A Comparative Study of Chinese Ethical Values in Ming-Ch'ing Times* (Leiden: E. J. Brill, 1989); Mark Elvin, "Female Virtue and the State in China," *Past and Present* 104 (1984): 111–52; and Katherine Carlitz, "The Social Uses of Female Virtue in Late Ming Editions of Lienü Zhuan," *Late Imperial China* 12, no. 2 (1991): 117–52.

12. Lang, *Qixiu leigao*, 48.9b–10a.

13. Von Glahn notes that from the early sixteenth century onward, "a small yet magnificently embellished Wutong shrine could be found in nearly every courtyard, usually inside the gate leading to the street" in south China. See von Glahn, "Enchantment of Wealth," 678–79.

14. Wang Jian (fl. 18th century), *Qiudeng conghua*, 1777 ed., Rare Book Collection of Shekeyuan Library, Beijing, 9.22b–24a.

15. Allan Barr, "Disarming Intruders: Alien Women in *Liaozhai zhiyi*," *Harvard Journal of Asiatic Studies* 49, no. 2 (1989): 501–17.

16. Xu Kun, *Liuya waibian*, 1792 ed., Rare Book Collection of Beijing National Library, 4. 1a–2a, "Xiaonian."

17. Ji, *Yuewei caotang bij*, 89–90. It is possible that Ji Yun is using the fox story to make a moral point about the goodness of following one's predestined fate. I thank the editor, Dave Aftandilian, for bringing this point to my attention. The didacticism of Ji Yun's fox stories is most extensively discussed in Chan, *Discourse on Foxes and Ghosts*.

18. Barr, "Disarming Intruders," 517. He gives a summary of the many different kinds of mortal women in the *Tales of the Strange*:

> The power that [mortal] women exercise over their husbands or other women, their resourcefulness in protecting and promoting their own

interests, are themes common to many of these tales. We see how a teenage
girl quickly brings her unruly husband to heel, and maintains her supremacy
into old age (9.1272–73); how a shrewish wife subjects her spouse to one
humiliation after another (6.861); how a jealous wife will beat a concubine
so as to provoke a miscarriage (6.723), or mount an insidious campaign to
terrorize her rival and drive her to suicide (7.883–84); how a woman can
be a tyrant towards her daughter-in-law, only to be dominated herself by
the wife of her second son (10.1409–11); and how husbands are so often
helpless or acquiescent in the face of female assertiveness (7.902–4, 8.1112,
10.1409–11, 11.1564).

19. G. William Skinner, "Regional Urbanization in Nineteenth-Century China" and
"Cities and the Hierarchy of Local Systems," in *The City in Late Imperial China*,
ed. G. William Skinner (Stanford, Calif.: Stanford Univ. Press, 1977), 211–49,
275–351.

20. Philip C. C. Huang, *The Peasant Economy and Social Change in North China* (Stanford, Calif.: Stanford Univ. Press, 1985), 69–71.

21. Ibid., 69–121. The quote is on 78.

22. In pursuing the connection between acquisition of wealth and spirit possession of
women, von Glahn argues that in the volatile market economy of late imperial Jiangnan (Lower Yangzi region), wealth was perceived similarly to women, as being "alluring but inconstant and fickle, pregnant with destructive power." Robert P. Weller
discusses a similar cult, that of the Eighteen Lords, which rose up in modern-day
Taiwan amid economic opportunities. Von Glahn, "Enchantment of Wealth," 694,
711; Robert P. Weller, *Resistance, Chaos, and Control in China: Taiping Rebels, Taiwanese Ghosts and Tiananmen* (Seattle: Univ. of Washington Press, 1994), 113–53.
The case of the fox shows that such marginal cults also thrived in northern China,
an area ecologically and economically very different from late imperial Jiangnan or
modern-day Taiwan.

23. Hill Gates, "The Commoditization of Chinese Women," *Signs* 14, no. 4 (1989):
799–832. See also Francesca Bray, *Technology and Gender: Fabrics of Power in
Late Imperial China* (Berkeley and Los Angeles: Univ. of California Press, 1997),
173–272. Bray shows that the economic expansion and the new division of labor of
this time marginalized women's prominent position in household production, but
elite discourse continued to emphasize the productive capability of women. In the
meantime, the value of a woman hinged more on her reproductive capability.

24. Gates, "Commoditization of Chinese Women," 813–19. Matthew Sommer, *Sex,
Law, and Society in Late Imperial China* (Stanford, Calif.: Stanford Univ. Press,
2000), 243–47, 282–87. For his book, Sommer used many legal cases in this regard from Shuntian Prefecture in Hebei, an area plagued with fox worship.

25. Ji, *Yuewei caotang biji*, 37, 528.

26. Ibid., 356.

27. Ibid., 509.

28. Gates, "Commoditization of Chinese Women," 816. See also Susan Mann, *Precious Records: Women in China's Long Eighteenth Century* (Stanford, Calif.: Stanford Univ. Press, 1997), 41–44.

29. Susan Gronewold, *Beautiful Merchandise: Prostitution in China, 1860–1936* (New York: Institute for Research in History and Haworth Press, 1982), 34–50.

30. Victor Turner, "Encounter with Freud: The Making of a Comparative Symbologist," *Blazing the Trail: Way Marks in the Exploration of Symbols*, ed. Edith Turner (Tucson: Univ. of Arizona Press, 1992), 25.

31. This female predicament in Chinese history is best summarized by Rubie S. Watson: "Women may be property holders but have few or no legal rights to property, they may be decision makers without the authority to make decisions, they may have physical mobility but are socially and economically constrained, they may exercise the power of an emperor but have no right to the imperial title." See Rubie S. Watson, "Marriage and Gender Inequality," in *Marriage and Inequality in Chinese Society*, ed. Rubie Watson and Patricia Ebrey (Berkeley and Los Angeles: Univ. of California Press, 1991), 348.

32. Pu Songling, *Liaozhai zhiyi huijiao huizhu huiping ben* (Shanghai: Shanghai guji chubanshe, 1978), 2.217–18, "Jiu you."

33. Fang Yuankun, *Liangpeng Yehua*, 1839 ed., 1.16b–18a, "Gulou hu."

Works Cited

Barr, Allan. "Disarming Intruders: Alien Women in *Liaozhai zhiyi*." *Harvard Journal of Asiatic Studies* 49, no. 2 (1989): 501–17.

Bathgate, Michael R. *The Fox's Craft in Japanese Religion and Folklore: Shapeshifters, Transformations, and Duplicities*. New York: Routledge, 2004.

Bray, Francesca. *Technology and Gender: Fabric of Power in Late Imperial China*. Berkeley and Los Angeles: Univ. of California Press, 1997.

Carlitz, Katherine. "The Social Uses of Female Virtue in Late Ming Editions of Lienü Zhuan." *Late Imperial China* 12, no. 2 (1991): 117–52.

Chan, Leo Tak-hung. *Discourses on Foxes and Ghosts: Ji Yun and Eighteenth-Century Literati Storytelling*. Honolulu: Univ. of Hawaii Press, 1998.

Donovan, Josephine, and Carol J. Adams. Introduction to *Animals and Women: Feminist Theoretical Explorations*, edited by Carol J. Adams and Josephine Donovan, 1–8. Durham, N.C.: Duke Univ. Press, 1995.

Dunayer, Joan. "Sexist Words, Speciesist Roots." In *Animals and Women: Feminist Theoretical Explorations*, edited by Carol J. Adams and Josephine Donovan, 11–31. Durham, N.C.: Duke Univ. Press, 1995.

Elvin, Mark. "Female Virtue and the State in China." *Past and Present* 104 (1984): 111–52.

Fang Yuankun. *Liangpeng yehua.* 1839 ed.

Gates, Hill. "The Commoditization of Chinese Women." *Signs* 14, no. 4 (1989): 799–832.

Gronewold, Susan. *Beautiful Merchandise: Prostitution in China, 1860–1936.* New York: Institute for Research in History and Haworth Press, 1982.

Huang, Philip C. C. *The Peasant Economy and Social Change in North China.* Stanford, Calif.: Stanford Univ. Press, 1985.

Huntington, Rania. *Alien Kind: Foxes and Late Imperial Chinese Narrative.* Cambridge, Mass.: Harvard Univ. Asia Center, 2003.

Ji Yun. *Yuewei caotang biji* (Random jottings at the cottage of close scrutiny). Chongqing: Chongqing Chubanshe, 1996.

Kang, Xiaofei. *The Cult of the Fox: Power, Gender, and Popular Religion in Late Imperial and Modern China.* New York: Columbia Univ. Press, 2005.

Lang Ying. *Qixiu leigao.* (A seven-time edited classified manuscript). 1775 ed. Univ. of Toronto East Asian Rare Book Collection.

Lewis, Ioan M. *Ecstatic Religion: A Study of Shamanism and Spirit Possession.* 2d ed. New York: Routledge, 1989.

Mann, Susan. *Precious Records: Women in China's Long Eighteenth Century.* Stanford, Calif.: Stanford Univ. Press, 1997.

Pu Songling. *Liaozhai zhiyi huijiao huizhu huiping ben* (Tales of the strange from the studio of leisure: The edition with a collection of annotations and comments). Edited by Zhang Youhe. Shanghai: Shanghai guji chubanshe, 1978.

Skinner, G. William. "Cities and the Hierarchy of Local Systems." In *The City in Late Imperial China,* edited by G. William Skinner, 275–351. Stanford, Calif.: Stanford Univ. Press, 1977.

———. "Regional Urbanization in Nineteenth-Century China." In *The City in Late Imperial China,* edited by G. William Skinner, 211–49. Stanford, Calif.: Stanford Univ. Press, 1977.

Smyers, Karen. *The Fox and the Jewel: Shared and Private Meanings in Japanese Inari Worship.* Honolulu: Univ. of Hawaii Press, 1999.

Sommer, Matthew. *Sex, Law, and Society in Late Imperial China.* Stanford, Calif.: Stanford Univ. Press, 2000.

T'ien, Ju-k'ang. *Male Anxiety and Female Chastity: A Comparative Study of Chinese Ethical Values in Ming-Ch'ing Times.* Leiden: E. J. Brill, 1989.

Turner, Victor. "Encounter with Freud: The Making of a Comparative Symbologist." In *Blazing the Trail: Way Marks in the Exploration of Symbols,* edited by Edith Turner, 1–28. Tucson: Univ. of Arizona Press, 1992.

von Glahn, Richard. "The Enchantment of Wealth: The God Wutong in the Social History of Jiangnan." *Harvard Journal of Asiatic Studies* 51, no. 2 (1991): 651–714.

Wang Jian. *Qiudeng conghua* (Conversation at the autumn lamp). 1777 ed. Rare Book Collection of Shekeyuan Library, Beijing.

Wang Tonggui. *Xinke ertan* (The new edition of tales overheard). Rare Book Collection of Beijing National Library.

Watson, Rubie S. "Marriage and Gender Inequality." In *Marriage and Gender Inequality in Chinese Society*, edited by Rubie Watson and Patricia Ebrey, 231–55. Berkeley and Los Angeles: Univ. of California Press, 1991.

Weller, Robert P. *Resistance, Chaos, and Control in China: Taiping Rebels, Taiwanese Ghosts and Tiananmen*. Seattle: Univ. of Washington Press, 1994.

Xu Changzuo. *Yanshan conglu* (Collective anecdotes from Mount Yan). Rare Book Collection of Beijing National Library.

Xu Kun. *Liuya waibian* (Unauthorized compilations of Willow Cliff). 1792 ed. Rare Book Collection of Beijing National Library.

Chapter 3

Serpentine Mates in Japanese Folklore

Ria Koopmans–de Bruijn

> Once upon a time there was a farmer whose rice fields
> had dried up as a result of a severe drought. Distraught,
> the farmer exclaimed, "I would give one of my daughters
> in marriage to anyone who manages to irrigate my fields
> and save my crop!" A serpent overheard the farmer, and
> liked the idea of a pretty human bride. Since serpents
> have power over water, the serpent easily irrigated the
> farmer's fields and the crops were saved. Hereupon the
> serpent came forward to claim his price. The farmer
> realized that he had to keep his word, although he did
> not relish the thought of having to give up one of his
> daughters to a serpent. He went home and pleaded
> with the girls. The two eldest were appalled at the very
> thought of being asked to consider such a fate. But the
> youngest, who loved her father very much, agreed to go
> in order to save her father's honor. Before she set off,
> however, she asked her father for a dowry of one hun-
> dred gourds and one hundred needles. When she came
> to the pond where her husband-to-be lived she threw
> the gourds and needles into the water and told him "I will
> come to you as soon as you have sunk these gourds and
> floated these needles." The serpent set to work at once,
> the sooner to have his bride with him. He tried and tried,
> until he died of exhaustion. Then the girl was free to go
> back home again.
>
> —Retelling based on tale type # 312B,
> "Snake Husband Killed," in Ikeda,
> *Type and Motif Index*

In the previous chapter, Xiaofei Kang discussed Chinese fox lore of the late imperial period, highlighting issues of morality as well as the gendered character of the
tales under discussion. In this chapter, the focus will be on Japanese folktale types
involving serpents, particularly tales in which serpents pursue "marital" relationships with humans, and the consequences of such relationships.[1] Despite the fact

that Kang deals with tales from a particular historical period, whereas most tales discussed in this chapter have their origin in a less defined (but historically much earlier) period, and despite the essentially divine character of the foxes in the Chinese tales (an element mostly absent in the Japanese serpent context), in several respects the Japanese serpent tales display comparable characteristics. In particular, the interpretation of the tales as symbolic representations of human morality and the prevalence of gendered distinctions are equally present in both Chinese fox lore and Japanese serpent lore.

Although some folktales seem to exist purely for entertainment, and others have a religious character, I suggest that tales of the types discussed here are "encoded sociology,"[2] that is, they have didactic or moralistic aspects to them and the animals in them symbolize social values. This need not exclude either the entertainment potential or the religious aspects of these tales. I contend that the serpents really represent humans, and the message conferred by the tales is meant as a warning not to break a social taboo—in the "Snake Husband" case, not to get involved with the wrong human mate. I further argue that the imagery of the serpent in place of one of the human partners is merely used to emphasize the moral lesson.

In a sense, what follows is an exercise in folklore interpretation. The reading I give here is not the only possible interpretation. Contrary to what is often assumed, folktales are very complex narratives, and it is this very complexity that demands multiple readings. Since many folktales have, in more recent times, evolved into children's literature, and many tales are now best known in the versions included in storybooks for the young, it is frequently assumed that these tales are simplistic stories with no depth.[3] The fact that they have a long history and were not originally developed as entertainment for toddlers, even if they can be adapted for that purpose, is often too easily overlooked.

At face value it may be tempting to try to use current literature on human-animal relations to help interpret these folktales. However, that literature typically refers to real relations between humans and real-life animals, whereas this chapter deals with metaphoric relations between humans and "others" represented by serpents as symbols, not real-life snakes. The serpents' "animality" is simply a tool to create the necessary distance to allow for easy absorption of the underlying meaning of the tale. Particularly when current literature refers to human-animal relations in a gendered context, the human-animal dualism is frequently equated to male-female dualism—a poor fit for the interpretation of the tales under discussion here.[4] Feminist literature on animals and animality is frequently a response to what is perceived as the male-oriented perspective represented in evolutionary speciesism, which is seen as according inferior status to animals, and by extension to women, by equating them to animals.[5] However, such male-female dualism hardly applies to the Japanese serpent tales. Where the issue of gender is brought into the discussion in current literature, it is frequently in the context of (eco)feminism and animal rights (women and animals as fellow victims).[6] However, although in the tales discussed here some form of victimization may be included, it is of a very different kind and affects males as much, if not more, than females. The harm happens to a metaphorical other rather than a real-life animal. It is the otherness, not the species or gender, that matters in these traditional folktales.

The essence of a folktale, as the name already implies, is that the tale belongs to the folk. A folktale does not have a known author, nor is there one single authoritative version of a tale. Transmission is traditionally oral, although particularly since the nineteenth century many tales have been recorded in writing. Not the exact wording, but the motifs included, are what make up the essence of a folktale. I have, therefore, chosen not to cite one particular recorded version of the tales I discuss in this chapter but to "assemble" my own retellings based on the recognized motifs as they are listed in Hiroko Ikeda's *Type and Motif Index of Japanese Folk-literature.*[7] This *Index*, by its very nature, is not a collection of tales but of tale types and the motifs and variant versions associated with them. It provides an overview of the tale types and their variants and invaluable insight into the essence of each tale type. In her *Index*, Ikeda identifies five major folktale types with serpent-human marital relationships as their main motif. Together these five types amount to hundreds of variants. "Snake Husband Killed" (*Hebi Muko*), the tale type retold at the start of this chapter, is the largest tale type of this kind in the *Index*, with as many as 130 variants. This figure represents only the variants identified by Ikeda in the 1960s, when she was compiling the *Index*; many more variants may well exist.

Serpents and Their Symbolism

The concept of the serpent can be divided into two basic aspects: the biological creature and the metaphor. In the context of this study, I am particularly concerned with the latter. It is, however, important to remember that the metaphorical serpent derives from people's perceptions of the physical and behavioral characteristics of the biological serpent. Serpents occur almost everywhere in the world, yet even in regions such as Ireland and Iceland, where no live serpents are to be found outside zoos, serpent lore persists. This can reasonably be ascribed to migration. The Celts, for instance, originated from the European mainland before settling in Ireland, introducing into the island elements of their mainland culture, including their folklore. While it is thus important not to lose sight of the connection between the biological serpent and its metaphorical equivalent, we do have to be careful not to view them as one and the same. As Weston La Barre puts it, "As biological scientists we agree on what snakes are and do. As anthropological scientists we must report what informants 'think' snakes are and do."[8]

Although their number has substantially diminished in recent years, many serpent varieties existed in Japan in ancient times. Anyone living in the mountains, woods, and rural areas would have been habitually exposed to their presence, their characteristic behavior and appearance, and their occasional threat. As in any culture, this exposure, combined with humanity's fertile imagination, conspired to turn a mere grass snake into a deity and a regular viper (mamushi) into a fire-breathing demon. It is clear from the frequency with which serpents are represented in Jōmon period (c. 10,000 to 300 B.C.E.) pottery that Japanese fascination with serpents, and use of serpent imagery and symbolism, have been an inherent part of Japanese culture since very early times.[9]

Animals in general figure prominently in many Japanese folktales. Frequently appearing creatures include raccoons, foxes, dogs, cranes, and monkeys, as well as the imaginary *tengu* and *kappa*.[10] There are, however, few animals that represent as broad a range of symbolic functions as does the serpent. Many creatures fall into this category. The terminology used to refer to these creatures in the various versions of the tales I am concerned with here is broad and has changed over the centuries. What binds them together, however, is their serpentine character. For the purposes of this chapter, therefore, I will use the term "serpent" throughout. But this term should be understood to include not only snakes but also any snakelike monsters, such as dragons. In its various forms, the serpent represents an astonishingly large portion of Japanese animal tales. The meaning of the serpent as symbol is extensive, sometimes contradictory, and frequently ambiguous. Rather than discuss the full range of possible symbolic aspects of the serpent,[11] I will focus on just a few such functions, all interrelated—namely, the serpent as didactic tool, as symbol of a moral code, and as representative of a taboo.

Japanese serpent lore contains a substantial number of tales that deal with marital relationships between serpents and humans. The example at the beginning of this chapter illustrates this type of folktale—in this particular case, the prospect of a relationship between a serpent and a human rather than an actual relationship. This "Snake Husband Killed" type contains a number of characteristic motifs that also occur in several of the tale types to be discussed shortly. The initial encounter with the serpent, for instance, is a frequently repeated stock motif, as is the use of trickery to save oneself from actual involvement with the serpent. In the above case, the girl is not the one to initiate the relationship; it is the father who allows himself to be tempted into putting his daughter at risk. Although the risk involved in such a relationship is not specified, the idea that such a relationship involves risk and is undesirable is clearly present.[12] The very use of the serpent imagery is enough to imply this.

Humans have an almost instinctive fear of and fascination with serpents, and it is this fear and fascination that makes the serpent effective as symbol. Both Qiguang Zhao and David E. Jones suggest that the primate's fear of serpents is related to prehistoric experiences of predation, and that the elements about serpents that induce fear are based on the primate's mental image of the physical characteristics of the serpent.[13] Jones cites particularly the "sudden, writhing movement" as a fear-inducing element.[14] Balaji Mundkur is more specific and detailed in his enumeration of physical characteristics that inspire our fascination with the serpent; he mentions the "limbless motion," the "flickering tongue, the fixed gaze of its lidless eyes, the slithering, undulating form of its body, and the violence of its feeding habits" as well as its "voicelessness" and, in the case of some species, its venom.[15] To these basic physical traits Boria Sax further adds a number of less tangible characteristics that have inspired symbolic connotations in the human mind. Among other things he highlights the serpent's role as symbol of fertility, its association with rebirth represented by the shedding of the skin, and the flickering red tongue suggestive of a dragon's fire breathing.[16] Freudians would also add reference to the obvious phallic shape of the serpent, itself suggestive of multiple interpretations. Taken together, all these characteristics make the serpent a powerful and complex metaphor. By focusing on a single narrow aspect, the interpretation in the current chapter only scratches the surface of the variety of symbolic meanings of the serpent, and yet this one aspect is in itself already quite complex.

Even though the girl in "Snake Husband Killed" recognizes the risk involved in an association with a serpent, she cares too much about her father and his honor not to comply with his plea. However, she prepares herself by taking the precaution of asking for the unusual dowry. The moral of the tale suggests that one should not involve either oneself or a loved one in a relationship that is cause for potential danger.[17] Although the girl's trickery turns out to be effective, and she manages to save herself, it was a gamble.[18] What if the serpent had figured out that he was being tricked?

Such trickery is again at play in the tale type identified by Ikeda as "Stork's Eggs":

> Once upon a time there was a man who saw a serpent who was about to swallow a frog. The man felt sorry for the frog, and told the serpent "If you spare the life of that frog, I will marry you." The serpent complied and the man married her. After the wedding the man fell ill, and no medicine seemed to exist that could heal him. Then, one day, a fortuneteller came to the house and predicted that the medication the man needed was to be found in stork's eggs. In order to more easily climb the tree in which the storks had built their nest, the serpent wife then took on her original, serpentine form to get such eggs for her husband. When she reached the nest she was pecked to death by the storks, and the man was miraculously healed. It turned out that the fortuneteller was really the grateful frog in disguise.[19]

We find several motifs in this tale type that are comparable to those in "Snake Husband Killed." Both tale types start, for instance, with a serpent being promised a human mate. Repetition of a limited repertoire of standard motifs in multiple tales was a common practice in the transmission of oral tales. As Albert Lord has explained in the context of Slavic epic songs, it would have been virtually impossible for the singers to remember the extremely long songs they performed if they had not had a formula, including such elements as rhythm and repetition.[20] Rhythm, for instance, functioned as a cue of what was to come next. Likewise storytellers need cues—a formula—to memorize the stories they perform. A limited number of motifs, applied where appropriate, serve well for this purpose.

As we have seen in the examples quoted thus far, the Japanese folk serpent, like Kang's Chinese fox, can be either male or female. Although the tale types representing the most variants seem to involve more male serpents, variants of either sex exist for most tale types, and in the tale types represented by fewer variants the serpent is as likely to be male as female. A marked difference in this context is the initial outcome of the relationship. Whereas in the "Snake Husband Killed" example, with a male serpent, the relationship was never fully achieved, in the "Stork's Eggs" example, a marriage does take place. This is a noticeable pattern that repeats itself in many tale types on this theme, although examples of the reverse do exist. For instance, in variants of "Stork's Eggs" with a male serpent we again find a person offering his daughter in marriage, just as in "Snake Husband Killed." In this case, a marriage takes place and the girl gets pregnant. The resolution in this context is that stork's eggs are proclaimed to be much-needed nourishment for the pregnant girl. When the serpent husband has been disposed of by the storks in the same manner as his female counterpart was, the girl's pregnancy is miraculously terminated and she is no longer burdened by having to carry the serpent's offspring. As this motif will appear again in later examples, we will see that the question of offspring is not necessarily always interpreted as a bad thing.

The frog/fortuneteller in "Stork's Eggs" represents yet another motif that appears in many tale types—the grateful animal motif. As another example of a serpent suitor tale involving grateful animals we can look at the tale type identified by Ikeda as "Grateful Crabs":

> Once upon a time a girl found a crab in mortal danger. She saved
> the crab's life and took good care of it. Years later, the girl is pursued
> by a huge serpent. Terrified, she locks herself into a building. How-
> ever, the enraged serpent twirls himself around the building several
> times while continuously hammering the door with his tail. Eventually
> the hammering stops and the girl's people go out to find out what is
> going on. They find that the grateful crab of the past has come out
> with thousands of its friends, and that they have killed the serpent in
> gratitude for the girl's kindness to the crab so many years ago.[21]

The grateful animal motif can be interpreted as good karma: an illustration of the moral that goodness (saving a creature in distress) can save one from evil (the serpent). Note that in this example we again find a male serpent pursuing a female human but ultimately failing to achieve a relationship. Once again the serpent, representing a trespassing human, is the loser and gets punished for his inappropriate behavior.

The image of a huge serpent twirling itself around a large object in which the pursued human is hiding can be found also in a tale called "Dōjōji." In it a female lusts after a young itinerant monk. As the monk tries to flee from her, she pursues him with great intent, growing ever more enraged. Eventually her rage causes her to transform into a serpent (her true form). The monk reaches the Dōjōji temple, where he hides under a great temple bell. The local monks lower the bell to the ground thinking the serpent will not be able to reach the monk that way. The serpent then twirls herself around the bell, and her rage makes her breathe fire, which turns the entire bell red hot. She then slides away to a mountain river. When the bell has cooled off and is raised, nothing but a small heap of ashes is left of the monk underneath. Though some of the motifs in this tale correspond to the tales under discussion here, it is different in a number of ways, the opposite outcome—the serpent overcoming the human—being the least of it. This tale is, emphatically, a Buddhist tale, a category I do not include in my current observations. The tales discussed here have much older roots (Buddhism was not introduced in Japan until the sixth century c.e., was not universally adopted until much later, and certainly did not at first influence the existing folklore). The Dōjōji tale is also a much more literary tale. The tale summary here given corresponds to its adaptation as a Nō play, which is, at this point, the more popularly known version.[22] The Buddhist version of this tale is substantially more complex and has a lengthy ending that deals with the ultimate enlightenment of the woman/serpent.[23]

The Telling of Tales

Tales of the kind discussed in this chapter come in many forms. Sometimes, as in the example of the "Grateful Crabs," they amount to barely more than a brief anecdote; at other times they are presented as elaborate narratives full of detail. How they are presented depends to a great degree on the style of the storyteller.[24] There is no single authoritative version of folktales, and therefore there is no wrong way of telling them, provided that the core motifs are included. Obviously, it is possible to embroider a great deal on many of the details in a tale, but such details do not affect the essence of the tale's theme.

Variations can also influence the version told at any given time. For example, for most tale types presented in this chapter, both male and female versions exist. This influences how the tale evolves; for instance, a man cannot get pregnant. Age is another factor, and many of these tales have a very long history. Already in the *Kojiki* (Tales of ancient matters, 712 c.e.) and the *Nihongi* or *Nihonshoki* (Chronicles of Japan, 720 c.e.), the oldest extant "histories" of Japan, many tales, either in full or in part, are quoted—generally as true history.[25] A good example of this is the tale Ikeda identifies as "Snake Paramour":

> Once upon a time there was a distinguished family which had a beautiful young daughter. Every night the girl was visited by a mysterious lover, and in due course she got pregnant. Her nurse advised her to stick a needle with a long thread in the seam of her lover's robe before he left. The following morning they found that the thread led through a hole in the door, out into the mountains to a spot where there was a deep pool. Hiding between the bushes the girl and her nurse overheard a conversation between a serpent dying from iron poisoning as a result of a needle stuck in his throat and his serpent mother. The mother serpent scolded her son for getting involved with a human at the cost of his life. The serpent son

> assured his mother, saying: "I don't mind dying, because the girl is already carrying my offspring." The mother serpent, however, told him that humans know that if the girl would only drink sake on festival days, the pregnancy would be terminated. Hereupon the girl and her nurse went home and followed this remedy, the pregnancy was promptly terminated, and the girl's reputation was saved.[26]

The tale as told here follows the same pattern we find in those presented earlier in this chapter: the serpent inflicts an unwelcome situation on the human mate, but the human manages to reverse the situation through trickery. However, in other variants—including the version as it appears in the *Kojiki*—the outcome is dramatically different. There the tale is told as a legend, to explain the ancestry of a famous warrior or priest. Sometimes it is also told to explain the descent of a family or even an entire village population.[27] In those variants, the tale usually ends with the dying serpent predicting that the girl will bear such special offspring. Offspring was an important matter. Not only was there always an urgent need for workers in the fields, as well as for caretakers for the elderly and very young, but it also was considered very important to carry on the family name (particularly among the higher classes). Pride of descent also came into play, as becomes clear in the version of this tale as told in the *Kojiki*, where the divine character of the serpent plays an important role. Descent from a divinity is not to be sneered at, after all.

In some of these tales, particularly in "Snake Paramour," we see a practice which until the nineteenth century was quite common in Japan. This practice, which came to be called "night-crawling" in Western literature, involved the nightly visits of sexual partners, without permanent cohabitation.[28] As in most societies, until relatively recent times in Japan the concept of a formal marriage was a ritual largely reserved for the upper classes (where such alliances frequently were more practical or more political affairs than unions of the heart). Sexual partnering did not automatically lead to the sharing of a joint household. This change often did not take place until the relationship had proven fruitful, that is, when viable offspring had been born.[29]

It is interesting to note that secrecy plays an important role in many of these tales. When the identity of the serpent is not known at the outset—as is the case in "Snake Paramour"—a seemingly well-functioning relationship can develop between the serpent and the human. Once the identity becomes known, however, disaster is the result, particularly for the serpent. When the identity of the serpent is known from the start, a relationship is frequently avoided altogether. The following, final example—"Snake Wife" in Ikeda's *Index*—is another variation on this theme:

> Once upon a time a man was walking along the beach when he saw some boys who were about to kill a serpent. He chased the boys away and set the serpent free. Some time after this a beautiful woman came to the man's house and insisted on becoming his wife.

They were very happy together and eventually the woman became pregnant. When the delivery time had come the woman withdrew herself in the parturition hut, as was the habit in those days, but before doing so she warned her husband not to look inside the hut on any account while she was in there. However, the man was too curious and despite his wife's warnings peeped inside the hut. There he saw a huge serpent coiled around a little baby. After the customary seven days of confinement were over the wife came out of the hut. She looked very sad, and giving the baby to her husband said: "I am the serpent you saved on the beach a while ago. Out of gratitude for your kindness, I had come to provide you with a nice life, but now that you know my real form I can no longer stay with you. Take good care of our son." As she said this, she pulled out one of her eyeballs and gave it to her husband so he could nourish the baby on it. Then she disappeared to a pond up in the mountains. The husband lost the eyeball to the overlord who thought it was a precious jewel. Not knowing what to do, he went to the pond where his wife now lived and told her what had happened. She gave him her other eyeball, and told him to take their son and move away. As soon as the man and baby were out of the area, the serpent caused a huge earthquake, followed by major flooding, which destroyed the wicked overlord's land.[30]

Like several of the previous examples, this tale shows that knowledge of the true identity of the serpent is crucial information. The relationship between the serpent and the human seems to be working well until the identity of the serpent becomes known. After that, this relationship, too, is doomed. Also, in this tale we come across other, by now familiar motifs, such as the man saving a creature in distress and the grateful animal. Contrary to all the previous examples, and for obvious reasons, this tale type has no variants with a male serpent.

In all the examples above, there is a distinct difference in the course these tales take, running almost exactly along gender lines. As I explained earlier, this difference does not represent inferiority of one or the other, as feminist literature would have it. In fact, female serpents' roles tend to be portrayed as more positive; they frequently act out of gratitude. Furthermore, they are more successful in winning their chosen human mates, even if the relationships do not last. Also, in most cases, their identity is not initially known. Male serpents, on the other hand, are more frequently portrayed as aggressively pursuing such relationships and subsequently being frustrated in their efforts. Their identity is generally known from the outset. Contrary to the Chinese fox examples cited by Kang in the previous chapter, Japanese serpent-human relationships never become permanently legitimate. Even if for a while they seem to work, eventually they are terminated—usually with dire consequences for the serpent partner. The human mate may initially suffer through illness, fright, or pregnancy, but in the end he or she typically survives intact.

The thread that runs through all these tales is a warning to avoid breaking taboos. Placing morality in evolutionary terms, Frans de Waal emphasizes the human "tendency to develop social norms and enforce them" while highlighting our basic "unalterable needs and desires."[31] The friction between these elements serves as the basis of the moral framework represented by the tales discussed here. Japanese society has traditionally been very hierarchical; a rigid social structure existed, and this greatly influenced the choice of marital partners, regardless of individual needs and desires. One's entire reputation could easily be destroyed by affiliation with the wrong person. Possibly even more important here, such a liaison could destroy the entire family by association. In such a context, it is easy to understand how society would go to great lengths to ensure that everyone understood the rules and lived up to the social norms. This did not just concern the "upper classes" but needed to be clear to those below as well. The members of the elite needed to preserve their status; the lower rungs of society needed to be discouraged from ambitions beyond their station. This societal objection to mixing (of class, race, or any perceived "otherness") is not unique to Japan. Paul Shepard, for instance, refers to "the theme of purity of type" as it is presented, again using animal imagery, in the biblical prohibition against "crossing horses with asses or creating other hybrids."[32] The tales here presented were orally transmitted over the course of many centuries and were familiar to all. Rather than explicitly spelling out societal rules, they use the distance created by the animal imagery to hint at them. Every member of society, from high to low, understood the rules and standards and could, therefore, understand the symbolic meaning behind these tales.

As Kang also alludes to in the previous chapter, many animals in folklore—and Japanese folklore is a prime example of this—are ascribed the capacity of transforming themselves at will. The serpents in these tales are not enchanted humans, however, as we might see in Western tales. Rather, they symbolize humans, but humans of a different social status from the human mates they seek. The imagery of the animal "beings, that is, who are recognizably our own kind but not yet, not quite," merely provides a measure of distance from reality, which helps the human consumer of the tale to internalize the tale's message that (socially) inappropriate courting and mating will have consequences.[33] Whereas in the current discussion the particular animal is a serpent, variants with other animals are also known for many of these tales. For instance, the "Snake Wife" tale type has variants involving a crane, a fish, a frog, and a fox.[34]

As suggested at the beginning of this chapter, the above is one interpretation of tales of this kind. I am not suggesting that it is the only possible interpretation. Contrary to what is frequently assumed, folktales are very complex stories, typically with many layers to them. They can be read at many different levels and retold in a great variety of ways. In the description of the tales above, I hinted at a variety of motifs. I have not addressed most of these motifs in depth here but instead have chosen to focus on only one such motif, leading to the current interpretation. If my focus had been on, for instance, the frequent occurrence of the saving of creatures in distress, a very different interpretation might have presented itself, as would have been the case if I had focused on the grateful animal motif. It would be a fruitful exercise to reinterpret these tales from those perspectives—to unearth those layers of the tales, so to speak—just as it would be fascinating to make a comparison between these tales and comparable tales from very different cultures. I am certain that such reinterpretations would result in very different readings of these same tales. This does not invalidate the reading I have given but, on the contrary, merely proves the true complexity inherent in folktales as it confirms the many layers a single brief tale can hold.

Notes

I would like to express my appreciation to Gregory Pflugfelder, whose invitation to speak about my work in his seminar on animals in Japanese history gave me the push I needed to get back to my research on this subject after too long a hiatus.

1. The term "marital" will be used here with a very broad meaning. Any tale about a male-female relationship, or pursuit of such a relationship, in which one of the partners is a serpent and the other a human qualifies for inclusion in this study. Although "marital" is not always fully accurate in the context of some of the tales, it is difficult to truly capture the full range of folktales discussed here with a single, unambiguous term. In a 1975 article on the subject, F. J. Daniels uses the terms "wives" and "lovers" by not taking any of the tales involving male serpents into account, as I do, thus circumventing this dilemma to some degree; see F. J. Daniels, "Snakes as Wives and Lovers in Japanese Myth, Legend and Folk-tale," *Japan Society of London, Bulletin* 4, no. 20 (1975): 12–21. As we will see in this study, though "wife" is generally accurate in the case of female serpents, "husband" or "groom"— the terms most frequently encountered in this context—do not reflect the actual status of male serpents very well. I have, therefore, chosen to avoid naming the serpents' status (except on occasion in the tales themselves) and focus instead on the (intended) relationship.

2. Boria Sax, *The Serpent and the Swan: The Animal Bride in Folklore and Literature* (Blacksburg, Va.: McDonald & Woodward, 1998), 9.

3. Whether this is a fair assessment of children's literature is an entirely different discussion. Although I am inclined to disagree with the notion, this subject falls outside my area of expertise and I will not further consider it here.

4. Illustrative of this approach are such writings as Ronnie Zoe Hawkins's "Ecofeminism and Nonhumans: Continuity, Difference, Dualism, and Domination," *Hypatia* 13, no. 1 (1998): 158–97; Joan Dunayer's "Sexist Words, Speciesist Roots," in *Animals and Women: Feminist Theoretical Explorations*, ed. Carol J. Adams and Josephine Donovan (Durham, N.C.: Duke Univ. Press, 1995), 11–31; and Lynda Birke, Mette Bryld, and Nina Lykke's "Animal Performances: An Exploration of Intersections between Feminist Science Studies and Studies of Human/Animal Relationships," *Feminist Theory* 5, no. 2 (2004): 167–83.

5. In this context, see Dunayer's "Sexist Words, Speciesist Roots" and Lynda Birke's "Intimate Familiarities? Feminism and Human-Animal Studies," *Society & Animals: Journal of Human-Animal Studies* 10, no. 4 (2002), http://www.psyeta.org/sa/sa10.4/birke.shtml.

6. See, for instance, Carol J. Adams's "Women-Battering and Harm to Animals," in *Animals and Women: Feminist Theoretical Explorations*, ed. Carol J. Adams and Josephine Donovan (Durham, N.C.: Duke Univ. Press, 1995), 55–84.

7. Ikeda bases her *Index* to a large degree on *The Types of the Folk-tale*, a classification of tale types and their motifs first published by Antti Aarne and revised and updated by Stith Thompson; see Antti Aarne, *The Types of the Folk-tale: A Classification and Bibliography*, 2d rev. ed., trans. and enlarged by Stith Thompson, FF Communications, No. 184 (Helsinki: Suomalainen Tiedeakatemia, 1964). Ikeda adjusts the classification where necessary to better reflect the Japanese context, using Keigo Seki's "Types of Japanese Folktales," *Asian Folklore Studies* 25 (1966): 1–220.

8. Weston La Barre, *They Shall Take Up Serpents: Psychology of the Southern Snake-handling Cult* (New York: Schocken Books, 1969), 90.

9. Balaji Mundkur, *The Cult of the Serpent: An Inter-disciplinary Survey of Its Manifestations and Origins* (Albany: State Univ. of New York Press, 1983), 46.

10. A *tengu* is a fictional creature from Japanese folklore. It is a long-beaked and winged half-human/half-bird mountain creature, particularly feared as an abductor of humans. The *kappa* is another fictional creature from Japanese folklore. It is a little water demon with a saucerlike skull that preys on humans and animals for their livers. It can lure entire horses into the water, but is said to lose its power if the liquid is removed from its saucer skull.

11. I have done so in the past and fully expect to continue to do so in the future. My graduation thesis at the Center for Japanese and Korean Studies, Leiden University, for instance, was a survey of the serpentine symbol in Japanese folklore; see Ria Koopmans–de Bruijn, "Schurk en Minnaar: Het slangensymbool in Japanse volks-verhalen" (Villain and lover: The serpent symbol in Japanese folktales), thesis (in Dutch), Center for Japanese and Korean Studies, Leiden Univ., 1986.

12. This idea of the animal as a symbol, or Freudian "projection," of a moral digression is discussed in the previous chapter by Kang as well. However, whereas in the cases Kang discusses the digression is very specific—pursuing monetary gain at the cost of moral principles—in Japanese serpent tales, the represented digression is not specified. Instead, there is merely the suggestion of a wrong.

13. Both Zhao and Jones are specifically concerned with the dragon, although their definitions of what constitutes a dragon differ to some degree. See Qiguang Zhao, *A Study of Dragons, East and West*, vol. 11 of *Asian Thought and Culture* (New York: Peter Lang, 1992) and David E. Jones, *An Instinct for Dragons* (New York: Routledge, 2000).

14. Jones, *Instinct for Dragons*, 84.

15. Mundkur, *Cult of the Serpent*, 2.

16. Sax, *Serpent and the Swan*, 58.

17. In a different reading of this same tale, the moral could conceivably be interpreted as representing the notion that "clever girls win."

18. The fate of the serpent is less benign, as is the case in all these tales. Since the serpent is the embodiment of a wrong, its predicament apparently does not warrant our sympathy.

19. This retelling is based on Ikeda's tale type # 411A, "Stork's Eggs" (*Kō-no-tori no Tamago*).

20. Albert Lord, *The Singer of Tales* (Cambridge, Mass.: Harvard Univ. Press, 1969), 30–33.

21. This retelling is based on Ikeda's tale type # 411B, "Grateful Crabs" (*Kami Hōon; Kanima Dera*).

22. For a translation of the play, see Donald Keene's *Twenty Plays of the Nō Theatre* (New York: Columbia Univ. Press, 1970).

23. A version of the longer, Buddhist tale can be found in the *Konjaku Monogatari shu*, compiled around 1120 C.E. A partial translation of this classical work was published by Marian Ury as *Tales of Times Now Past: Sixty-Two Stories from a Medieval Japanese Collection* (Berkeley and Los Angeles: Univ. of California Press, 1979). The work is divided into four sections: Tales of India, Tales of China, Tales of Buddhism in Japan, and Secular Tales of Japan. The Dōjōji tale appears in the third section.

24. Or of the compiler in the case of printed versions. The concept of recording verbatim is a rather new concept, which only really became possible after electronic recording devices had been developed.

25. For English translations of these works, see Basil Hall Chamberlain, trans., *The Kojiki: Records of Ancient Matters* (Rutland, Vt.: Charles E. Tuttle, 1981) and W. G. Aston, trans., *Nihongi: Chronicles of Japan from the Earliest Times to AD 697* (Rutland, Vt.: Charles E. Tuttle, 1972). Like some other ancient cultures, the Japanese recorded their creation myths early on. The *Kojiki* and *Nihon shoki* are different interpretations of the same myths. Although both entire works are presented as true history, only their final few chapters can really claim any approximation of true fact.

26. This retelling is based on Ikeda's tale type # 411C, "Snake Paramour" (*Miwayama*).

27. The belief that some people were descended from serpents survived into the twentieth century. For example, Morris Opler recorded such accounts during his interviews with Japanese Americans living in U.S. internment camps during World War II; Morris Edward Opler, "Japanese Folk Belief Concerning the Snake," *Southwestern Journal of Archaeology* 1 (1945): 249–59.

28. We can, for example, find multiple descriptions of this practice in Murasaki Shikibu's *The Tale of Genji*. This famous lengthy romance has been translated in full into English by no less than three different scholars. The earliest translation was by Arthur Waley in the 1930s; the second translation, by Edward Seidensticker, appeared for

the first time in the mid-1970s; and recently Royall Tyler published a third translation. Incidentally, Tyler is also well known for his publication *Japanese Tales* (New York: Pantheon Books, 1987).

29. Traditional Japanese mating and marriage practices are described in a number of publications, among them Joy Hendry's *Marriage in Changing Japan: Community and Society* (London: Croom Helm, 1981) and Kunio Yanagida, ed., *Japanese Manners and Customs in the Meiji Era* (Tokyo: Ōbunsha, 1957).

30. This retelling is based on Ikeda's tale type # 413C, "Snake Wife" (*Hebi Nyōbo*).

31. Frans de Waal, *Good Natured: The Origins of Right and Wrong in Humans and Other Animals* (Cambridge, Mass.: Harvard Univ. Press, 1996), 39.

32. Paul Shepard, *The Others: How Animals Made Us Human* (Washington, D.C.: Island Press, 1996), 61.

33. Barbara Herrnstein Smith, "Animal Relatives, Difficult Relations," *Differences: A Journal of Feminist Cultural Studies* 15, no. 1 (2004): 1.

34. Another instance is the tale type here presented as "Snake Husband Killed," which is also told with a *kappa*, or a mud snail, in the husband role, while the "Grateful Crab" tale type is also told in a grateful frog variation.

Works Cited

Aarne, Antti. *The Types of the Folk-tale: A Classification and Bibliography. Antti Aarne's Verzeichnis der Märchentypen*. FF Communications, No. 3. 2d rev. ed. Translated and enlarged by Stith Thompson. FF Communications, No. 184. Helsinki: Suomalainen Tiedeakatemia, 1964.

Adams, Carol J. "Woman-Battering and Harm to Animals." In *Animals and Women: Feminist Theoretical Explorations*, edited by Carol J. Adams and Josephine Donovan, 55–84. Durham, N.C.: Duke Univ. Press, 1995.

Aston, W. G., trans. *Nihongi: Chronicles of Japan from the Earliest Times to AD 697*. Rutland, Vt.: Charles E. Tuttle, 1972.

Birke, Lynda. "Intimate Familiarities? Feminism and Human-Animal Studies." *Society & Animals: Journal of Human-Animal Studies* 10, no. 4 (2002). http://www.psyeta.org/sa/sa10.4/birke.shtml. Accessed June 8, 2005.

Birke, Lynda, Mette Bryld, and Nina Lykke. "Animal Performances: An Exploration of Intersections between Feminist Science Studies and Studies of Human/Animal Relationships." *Feminist Theory* 5, no. 2 (2004): 167–83.

Chamberlain, Basil Hall, trans. *The Kojiki: Records of Ancient Matters*. Rutland, Vt.: Charles E. Tuttle, 1981.

Daniels, F. J. "Snakes as Wives and Lovers in Japanese Myth, Legend and Folk-tale." *Japan Society of London, Bulletin* 4, no. 20 (1975): 12–21.

Dunayer, Joan. "Sexist Words, Speciesist Roots." In *Animals and Women: Feminist Theoretical Explorations,* edited by Carol J. Adams and Josephine Donovan, 11–31. Durham, N.C.: Duke Univ. Press, 1995.

Hawkins, Ronnie Zoe. "Ecofeminism and Nonhumans: Continuity, Difference, Dualism, and Domination." *Hypatia* 13, no. 1 (1998): 158–97.

Hendry, Joy. *Marriage in Changing Japan: Community and Society.* London: Croom Helm, 1981.

Herrnstein Smith, Barbara. "Animal Relatives, Difficult Relations." *Differences: A Journal of Feminist Cultural Studies* 15, no. 1 (2004): 1–23.

Ikeda, Hiroko. *A Type and Motif Index of Japanese Folk-literature.* FF Communications, No. 209. Helsinki: Suomalainen Tiedeakatemia, 1971.

Jones, David E. *An Instinct for Dragons.* New York: Routledge, 2000.

Keene, Donald. *Twenty Plays of the Nō Theatre.* Records of Civilization, Sources and Studies, No. 85. UNESCO Collection of Representative Works. Japanese Series. New York: Columbia Univ. Press, 1970.

Koopmans–de Bruijn, Ria. "Schurk en Minnaar: Het slangensymbool in Japanse volksverhalen" (Villain and lover: The serpent symbol in Japanese folktales). Thesis, Center for Japanese and Korean Studies, Leiden Univ., 1986.

La Barre, Weston. *They Shall Take Up Serpents: Psychology of the Southern Snakehandling Cult.* New York: Schocken Books, 1969.

Lord, Albert. *The Singer of Tales.* Cambridge, Mass.: Harvard Univ. Press, 1960.

Mundkur, Balaji. *The Cult of the Serpent: An Inter-disciplinary Survey of Its Manifestations and Origins.* Albany: State Univ. of New York Press, 1983.

Murasaki Shikibu. *The Tale of Genji.* Translated with an introduction by Edward Seidensticker. New York: Alfred A. Knopf, 1979.

———. *The Tale of Genji.* Translated by Royall Tyler. New York: Viking, 2001.

———. *The Tale of Genji: A Novel in Six Parts.* Translated from the Japanese by Arthur Waley. New York: Modern Library, 1960.

Opler, Morris Edward. "Japanese Folk Belief Concerning the Snake." *Southwestern Journal of Archaeology* 1 (1945): 249–59.

Sax, Boria. *The Serpent and the Swan: The Animal Bride in Folklore and Literature.* Blacksburg, Va.: McDonald & Woodward, 1998.

Seki, Keigo. "Types of Japanese Folktales." *Asian Folklore Studies* 25 (1966): 1–220.

Shepard, Paul. *The Others: How Animals Made Us Human.* Washington, D.C.: Island Press, 1996.

Tyler, Royall. *Japanese Tales.* New York: Pantheon Books, 1987.

Ury, Marian. *Tales of Times Now Past: Sixty-Two Stories from a Medieval Japanese Collection.* Berkeley and Los Angeles: Univ. of California Press, 1979.

Waal, Frans de. *Good Natured: The Origins of Right and Wrong in Humans and Other Animals.* Cambridge, Mass.: Harvard Univ. Press, 1996.

Yanagida, Kunio, ed. *Japanese Manners and Customs in the Meiji Era.* Tokyo: Ōbunsha, 1957.

Zhao, Qiguang. *A Study of Dragons, East and West.* Vol. 11 of *Asian Thought and Culture.* New York: Peter Lang, 1992.

Chapter 4

Frogs, Snakes, and Agricultural Fertility

Interpreting Illinois Mississippian Representations

Dave Aftandilian

For thousands of years, in cultures around the world, frogs and toads have symbolized water, fertility of people and agricultural plants, and renewal.[1] Anyone who has stood outside before or after a heavy rain or seasonal flood of a river and listened carefully will understand why frogs might be associated with water, because the calling of frogs in great numbers is often associated with rain and floods. Frogs and toads are also "notoriously fecund creatures" whose females often deposit thousands of eggs at a time in large masses just under the water's surface,[2] which helps explain why some peoples connect these creatures with fertility.

This chapter will explore some of the many Native American sacred stories,[3] rituals, and artworks from Mesoamerica, the Southwestern United States, and the Eastern Woodlands (from the Mississippi River to the Atlantic Ocean) that link frogs with water and agricultural fertility, together with related material on snakes.[4]

The Rattler Frog Pipe and Its Contexts

I first became interested in this topic when I came across the Rattler Frog pipe (fig. 4.1), which was found in the late 1800s in a precontact Native American burial mound on the bluffs opposite East St. Louis in St. Clair County, Illinois.[5] This blood-red stone pipe, made from flint clay quarried nearby,[6] is an exquisite piece of art, elegantly carved with smooth curves and a shiny finish that bring its amphibian subject to vivid life. The frog is depicted in a naturalistic pose, squatting on its haunches. Two large holes are drilled in the center of the frog's back, one serving as the bowl to hold tobacco and the other the hole through which smoke is drawn (through a short stem, separate from the pipe; see below). The frog's eyes are large and prominent and give the piece a watchful feel, as if it were waiting for something important to happen. Its left forelimb curves in front of the frog's body, bracing it against the ground. But the real surprise is grasped in the frog's right forelimb: a gourd rattle, an object from the human world, from which descend a number of curving lines that some have identified as streamers or fringes but that might also represent falling rain.[7]

Beautiful as this pipe is, it is also maddeningly enigmatic. What does it mean? Why did the Illinois Mississippians who made it put so much effort into carving this gorgeous image of a large frog?[8] And why did they put a gourd rattle

Fig. 4.1. Rattler Frog pipe (ISM 800/519) from a mound on the bluffs opposite East St. Louis in St. Clair County, Illinois. Three-quarters front view. Photo by the author. Courtesy of the Illinois State Museum.

in its right "hand"? The rest of this chapter will take us on a journey in search of answers to these questions. We will start in Illinois, then travel to the Southwest, the Southeast, and finally come back to Illinois for the conclusion of our quest.

Let us begin where this pipe began: with a frog. What kind of frog? According to Christopher A. Phillips, curator of amphibians and reptiles for the Illinois Natural History Survey, the frog depicted on the Rattler Frog pipe is a southern leopard frog, *Rana sphenocephala* (pers. comm., June 2001).[9] This species is native to Illinois and is also found throughout much of the Southeast, but no farther west than the eastern portions of Texas and Oklahoma.[10]

In terms of their natural history, leopard frogs may have been interesting to the Illinois Mississippians who made this pipe for a number of reasons. To begin with, they are one of the first frogs to emerge from hibernation in the spring[11] and begin breeding as early as late February.[12] Leopard frogs, therefore, might have been viewed by the Illinois Mississippians as calling spring into being with their mating cries. Southern leopard frogs are also widely distributed throughout the southern half of Illinois (and, indeed, are one of the most common frogs throughout the eastern United States), so they would have been a familiar animal to the Illinois Mississippians.[13] More to the point in terms of agriculture, leopard frogs often wander far from waterways to feed during the summer months in grassy fields and gardens; they eat a wide variety of terrestrial insects, including many that would likely have been unwanted visitors to Illinois Mississippian agricultural fields.[14] It is quite possible that Illinois Mississippians would have noticed a decrease in insect pests in their fields when leopard frogs were present and would have seen them as a farmer's friend and ally, as giant toads (*Bufo marinus*) are known today throughout the Caribbean and Pacific.[15] Finally, as their common name suggests, leopard frogs are spotted, and spots are often seen by Native Americans of the Plains and Eastern Woodlands as markers of spiritual power.[16]

So now we know why the frog depicted on this pipe might have intrigued the Illinois Mississippians. But why did they show it holding a gourd rattle? As Thomas E. Emerson, Guy Prentice, and others have pointed out, gourd rattles are intimately identified with priests and shamans throughout the Eastern Woodlands; indeed, the rattle, as Emerson put it, "was considered so emblematic of the shaman that it was occasionally substituted as a symbol for them and served as a badge of office."[17] Therefore, it is possible that the Rattler Frog pipe may represent a priest or shaman transformed into the shape of a frog, or a frog who acted as a priest or shaman for the frog people.[18]

Now that we know a bit more about the Rattler Frog pipe and what it may represent, we need to place it in its archaeological context. The area where the Rattler Frog pipe was found lies just outside the borders of a prehistoric city named Cahokia, which was home to thousands of people about 1100 c.e. but was suddenly abandoned just a few hundred years before the first European explorers visited the site in the 1600s.[19] It is likely that the Cahokians made and used the Rattler Frog flint clay pipe.[20] Cahokia is located near the conjunction of the Mississippi and Illinois Rivers, on the border between eastern Missouri and southwestern Illinois, just east of St. Louis. The Illinois Mississippians who lived at Cahokia were heavily dependent on maize for their subsistence and planted it intensively in the seasonally inundated flood plains alongside the major rivers and their tributaries.[21] Like all the Native Americans of the Eastern Woodlands, the Illinois Mississippians needed the right amounts of rain at the right times.[22] Seasonal floods brought new, rich soil to these early farmers[23] but could also devastate their crops if they came at the wrong time—a point to which we will return later. Too little rain could spell drought, also causing the crops to fail.

Given the likely concern of the Terminal Late Woodland and Mississippian peoples (c. 900–1400 c.e.) of Illinois with flooding and drought, it is interesting that so many of the pipes and other art objects they made portrayed frogs—creatures which, as we have noted above, are often associated with rain and agricultural fertility. In addition to the Rattler Frog, there are a number of other large sandstone, limestone, or siltstone frog pipes from this time period in Illinois—for instance, the Sutter, St. Louis, and Calhoun County frog pipes.[24] Indeed, few nonhuman animals other than frogs are depicted on Late Woodland and Mississippian pipes from Illinois, which is a stark shift from the preceding Middle Woodland period (200 b.c.e. to 400 c.e.), when dozens of species of animals were portrayed in a naturalistic style on stone platform pipes.[25]

Although fully naturalistic frog images seem to occur exclusively on pipes in precontact Illinois, frogs are also depicted in a more stylized fashion on several other types of Mississippian, but not Middle Woodland, objects. For instance, a number of small Mississippian pottery jars from Fulton County in central Illinois

Fig. 4.2. Tridactyl jar (D181) from the Dickson Mounds site in Fulton County, Illinois. Compare foot depicted here to the left front foot of the Rattler Frog pipe in figure 4.1. Photo by the author. Courtesy of the Illinois State Museum.

have a "tridactyl" design consisting of three long toes, incised or in low relief, that strongly resembles a frog's or tadpole's forefoot (fig. 4.2). This tridactyl design is normally placed below the two handles on opposite sides of the jar, with the back of the "foot" oriented toward the top of the jar.[26] Frogs modeled in relief also occur on Mississippian pottery bowls from southern Illinois and the American Bottom; the head, forelimbs, and hindlimbs of a frog are represented, although often quite schematically (fig. 4.3). I have seen one example of this kind of bowl from the James Ramey Mound at Cahokia and several from Union County in southern Illinois.[27]

Frog imagery during the Mississippian period is not confined to Illinois; there are a number of examples from other areas, which indicates that frogs likely played important ritual and mythological roles throughout the Mississippian world. Pottery bowls or jars with frogs modeled in relief had a relatively wide distribution during Mississippian times, for instance, and have been found fairly frequently in Missouri, Arkansas, Mississippi, and Alabama.[28] One bowl or jar from the Moundville site in Alabama even bears a tridactyl design somewhat similar to those described above from Fulton County, Illinois.[29] Mississippian frog pipes seem to be less common, and perhaps more restricted in their geographic distribution, than frog pottery vessels, but large sandstone frog pipes have been found in Missouri, Kentucky, and Mississippi.[30]

While frogs and toads *were* represented in artworks during the earlier Middle Woodland period, such as finely carved stone platform pipes from Lincoln County,

Fig. 4.3. Frog effigy bowl with appendages in relief, from Union County, Illinois: (a) front view; (b) right side view. Collections of the Field Museum, Anthropology object #55593. Photos by the author. Courtesy of the Field Museum.

Missouri[31] or Pike County, Illinois,[32] frogs become much more common in Late Woodland and Mississippian artworks. I am only aware of two or three frog and/ or toad depictions in total from the Middle Woodland period in Illinois, while I have seen several dozen from the Terminal Late Woodland and Mississippian periods.

Frogs among the Southwestern and Southeastern Tribes

To understand why frogs become much more important in Illinois Mississippian art, and presumably associated beliefs and rituals, than they had been previously, we need to travel to the Southwest. As Gayle J. Fritz, Bruce D. Smith, Patty Jo Watson, and other archeologists have demonstrated, maize probably came to the Mississippian peoples of the Eastern Woodlands from the Southwest via the Plains; the peoples of the Southwest, in turn, had learned about maize from

Mesoamerican groups.[33] Although small quantities of maize were present in Illinois during the Middle Woodland period at a few sites, it did not become a staple food there until the end of the Late Woodland and the beginning of the Mississippian period[34]—precisely the time when frog images begin to appear in large numbers in artworks. As Florence Ellis, Karl Taube, and others have noted, it is extremely unlikely that just maize seeds were traded between the Mesoamericans, the Puebloans, and the Late Woodland peoples of the Eastern Woodlands; the techniques for growing maize would also have been passed on, including the rituals needed to make the maize prosper.[35] And the prominent role that frogs play in some of these rituals and related sacred stories among the Hopi, Zuni, and other Pueblo peoples of the Southwest provides an important clue to why frogs may have been especially important to the Illinois Terminal Late Woodland and Mississippian peoples as well.[36]

A wealth of Hopi beliefs and ritual images of frogs connect them with rain and agricultural fertility both directly and indirectly. These beliefs and images can be divided into two main categories: frogs themselves as bringers of rain and fertility (direct connections) and frogs as intermediaries between humans and supernatural powers that can bring rain and agricultural fertility (indirect connections). In terms of the frogs themselves, the Hopi honor frogs as sacred beings because they constantly pray for rain with their croaks and calls.[37] Small wonder, then, that the sounds of frogs (or flowing water) were seen as good omens after a ceremony.[38] Similar connections among frog calls, rainmaking, and agricultural ceremonies are reflected in the lyric of a Hopi women's song from the Oaqöl harvest-season ceremony at Oraibi Pueblo: "He is croaking / The water frog, / About big corn ears."[39] Contemporary Hopi author and ceremonial participant Alph Secakuku calls this ceremony Owaqölt and says that it "expresses the concept of healthy impregnation and reinforces maternal idealism."[40] So in addition to the obvious connection of frogs and agricultural fertility in the song lyrics, the overall subject matter of the ceremony suggests that frogs might also be associated with human fertility through this ceremony.

A number of Hopi stories, images, and rituals also discuss frogs as being associated with supernatural beings that bring rain and agricultural fertility or serving as intermediaries between the human world and the world of the supernaturals, carrying prayers for rain from people to the supernaturals. According to Alexander Stephen, for instance, the Hopi see frogs as the pet animals of the clouds or kachinas (supernatural beings who bring rain and other blessings to the Pueblos).[41] A story recorded by Ruth Benedict also demonstrates the close connection between frogs and kachinas; in this story, a frog wins a race (and a bride) by convincing the kachinas to send rain.[42] Frogs were also associated with the Plumed or Horned Water Serpent, another (more powerful) supernatural being that was believed to bring rain and agricultural fertility (for more about this serpent, see the next section). On the kilt worn during the Snake-Antelope dance for rain and agricultural fertility, a frog's track is depicted inside that of the horned water serpent, according to one of Stephen's informants; see the angular mark in the middle of the

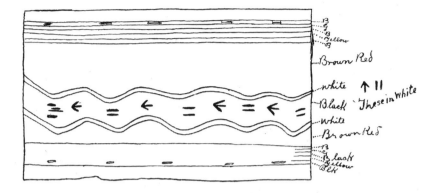

Fig. 4.4. Hopi snake kilt design. The broad central zigzag panel represents the Horned Water Serpent; the angular marks in the center of that panel represent frog's track. From Stephen, *Hopi Journal of Alexander M. Stephen*, pt. 1, 650, fig. 355. Copyright © 1936 by Columbia University Press. Reprinted with permission of the publisher.

kilt in figure 4.4 (compare to tridactyl frog design from precontact Illinois in fig. 4.2).[43] And during the Hopi agricultural ceremony of Palülükoñti (or Añkwañti), the Festival of the Great Plumed Serpent, which he observed at Walpi in 1900, Jesse Walter Fewkes saw a framework used as a backdrop for the performance that included semicircular symbols for rain clouds; each of the rain cloud symbols also had representations of frogs (and birds) painted on them.[44] Fewkes describes Palülükoñti as a "theatrical performance or mystery play, illustrating the growth of corn; its purpose is the production of rain."[45] In this ceremony, which is the second major agricultural ceremony of the Hopi winter calendar,[46] frogs are again directly associated with rain, and thus with agricultural fertility.

In terms of material culture, a stone or clay frog effigy was sometimes present on Hopi altars constructed for various ceremonies. For instance, both Alexander Stephen and Jesse Walter Fewkes saw a "rude stone frog" that was used during a winter solstice ceremony to call for rain and other blessings. Fewkes's account suggests that the frog served as an intermediary in either carrying the prayers for blessings to the supernaturals, bringing back the blessings in response, or both.[47] And a ceremonial pottery bowl that Stephen saw was decorated in the interior with clouds, frogs, and tadpoles,[48] again demonstrating that the Hopi associated frogs (and tadpoles) with rain.

Like the Hopi, the Zuni, too, see frogs as having direct and indirect connections to rain and agricultural fertility, with frogs sometimes seen as bringing rain themselves (direct connections) and sometimes as associated with other supernatural beings that send rain and agricultural fertility to the people (indirect connections). According to Frank Hamilton Cushing, the Zuni Frog Clan held the "Medicine Seed of Water . . . without the administration of which the world would dry up."[49] Perhaps this is why the songs of the men of the Frog Clan were so highly valued in terms of their ability to produce rain, as Matilda Coxe Stevenson recorded.[50] Stevenson also describes a ritual object used by the Zuni rain priests to call for rain, one part of which included a hollow reed in which lived a small toad.[51] She also relates the sacred story of when the Zunis were leaving the Underworld to find their home and the children carried on the backs of the first group of women to cross the river pinched and bit so hard that the women dropped them into the water. There the children turned into tortoises, water snakes, frogs, and tadpoles and eventually became the Council of the Gods.[52] The Zuni people later prayed to these gods for rain and agricultural fertility.

In addition to bringing rain themselves, frogs are thought by the Zuni to be intimately connected to other supernatural powers that blessed the people with rain and agricultural fertility. For instance, this song lyric from the Zuni Good Kachina calls the frog a child of the rain-makers:

> "Guess, younger brother,
> Whose fine tracks go all about here?
> All over my water-filled field
> He has walked about.
> Can you not guess?"
> Thus he said to his younger brother,
> "The child of the rain-makers,
> The water frog,
> Goes about hurrying his fathers, the rain-makers."[53]

Like the Hopi, then, the Zuni also see the frog as a go-between who can convince the supernatural powers to send rain to water agricultural fields. Many Zuni stepped prayer bowls also have a frog in their center, in the part that is often filled with water;[54] such bowls are often used in agricultural ceremonies intended to bring rain and fertility to the crops.

Frogs are also associated with water and agricultural fertility among other Pueblo peoples. For instance, Elsie Clews Parsons mentions the Big Water Man of the Taos Pueblo, a monstrous frog that caused landslides and floods.[55]

Considering the high esteem in which the frog was held as a caller of rain among the Hopi, Zuni, and other Pueblo peoples of the late nineteenth and early twentieth centuries, and in which it is still held today (rain being the most important ingredient for raising maize in a dry land), it is not surprising that there are a number of representations of frogs found at prehistoric sites in the Southwest as well. For instance, a beautiful Anasazi frog carved from jet and inlaid with turquoise was found at Pueblo Bonito in Chaco Canyon, New Mexico, and dates to around 1000 c.e.[56] A Mesa Verde black-on-white pottery pitcher from about the same time period has a base made in the shape of a frog or toad; it was found in the Holmes Group, San Juan Region, New Mexico.[57] And a number of Mimbres black-on-white pottery bowls from the eleventh century c.e. depict frogs, toads, or lizards laid out centrally in the bottom of the bowl with their limbs in bent position.[58] These Mimbres representations of frogs and toads are especially interesting, since they date to about the same time period that frogs began to become common in Illinois Mississippian imagery.

If the peoples of the Southwest thought so highly of frogs as rainmakers and bringers of agricultural fertility, and for so long (likely at least one thousand years, judging from the precontact representations of frogs discussed above), we might expect that the peoples of the Southeast also would have a number of beliefs linking frogs, rain, and agricultural fertility. Indeed, they might even have more, since the peoples of the rainy, swampy Southeast likely saw a lot more frogs than did the peoples of the arid Southwest. However, Native American tribes of the Southeast actually have said remarkably little about frogs in their sacred stories, folklore, and rituals, especially in comparison to the voluminous material about frogs that has been recorded from Southwestern tribes.

That having been said, various tribes of the Southeast do have scattered sacred stories, images, and dances that directly and indirectly connect frogs with rain and flooding. The Alabama tribe, for instance, tell a sacred story in which a frog predicted the great flood that drowned the world; a man saved it from the fire, and because of the man's kindness, the frog not only warned the man about the flood but also taught him how to build a raft that saved his family.[59] As with Hopi and Zuni beliefs, we see the frog associated with water in this Alabama story, although in this case with flooding and, specifically, surviving it. Recall that flooding was likely a leading concern of the Illinois Mississippian agriculturalists who made the Rattler Frog image as well.

The Yuchi of Georgia and South Carolina also represented frogs in their art, specifically on the bowls of some of their pipes (as did the Illinois Mississippians); the stems of these pipes were decorated with serpent designs. According to Frank Speck, these images refer to a sacred story of the Yuchi god Wind, in which the god used a pipe that had a frog for a bowl and a snake for the stem.[60] Again drawing on our survey of Pueblo frog beliefs, we might suggest that the Yuchi saw frogs and snakes as beings connected with the supernatural powers, in this case Wind, which bring life-giving rain for crops (through Wind's role in bringing storms); their frog- and snake-decorated pipes, then, would have been used to convey their requests for the blessings of rain and agricultural fertility to Wind and the other powers—perhaps not unlike how the Rattler Frog pipe might have been used by the Illinois Mississippians (see below). This interpretation is also consistent with the widespread Southeastern tribal associations of serpents and Under World powers that were seen to bring rain and agricultural fertility (see below). Indeed, as Charles Hudson has pointed out, a number of tribes had sacred stories about Under World beings who wore rattlesnakes around their necks and wrists instead of necklaces and bracelets.[61] The Yuchi story related above clearly has similar roots, with a powerful supernatural being using a real frog and snake for his pipe bowl and stem instead of the stone and wood that normal people use for these items.[62]

Finally, the Eastern Cherokee of Tennessee and North Carolina performed a dance modeled after the tree frog, or spring peeper.[63] Although at the time it was recorded this was a social dance that could be performed in any season, we might speculate that perhaps it used to be held in the spring, to welcome and perhaps hasten the arrival of the spring rains, and again we might wonder if the Illinois Mississippians had a similar ritual, since the southern leopard frog they represented on the Rattler Frog pipe is one of the first to emerge from hibernation in Illinois in the spring.

These interesting references notwithstanding, when you compare the frog-related lore of any one Southeastern tribe with any one of the Pueblo tribes of the Southwest, the Southeastern tribes have much less to say about frogs than the Pueblo tribes—or at least much less good to say about them. The Cherokee, for instance, about whose belief systems we know more than almost any other tribe of the Southeast, view frogs and toads as "relatively weak and unimportant little animals"[64] and accordingly say "very little" about them in their folklore and sacred stories.[65] One of the few Cherokee stories associated with frogs cast them in a negative light for their role in solar and lunar eclipses, which were said to be caused by great frogs swallowing the sun or moon; these celestial frogs had to be frightened away with loud drumming and gunshots.[66] The Creek had a similar belief,[67] as did the Yuchi, for whom the moon-swallower was a toad.[68] Among the Southeastern tribes more generally, frogs were classed as "vermin" associated with the chaotic, dangerous Under World.[69] But it should also be noted that creatures of the Under World were seen by Southeastern tribes to be closely linked to thunder, rain, and water,[70] which of course are crucial for agricultural fertility.

As for why tribes of the Southeast in general seem not to accord frogs the close connections with life-giving rain and agricultural fertility that the Pueblo tribes do, we can only speculate. Vernon James Knight Jr., James A. Brown, and George E. Lankford have suggested that Southeastern tribes experienced "a significant loss of astronomical lore . . . since Mississippian times," so perhaps they also experienced a similar loss in their amphibian lore.[71] Or perhaps they associated rain and agricultural fertility with a different sort of Under World creature—a creature they considered quite powerful and about which they had much to say in their folklore: a serpentine creature known as the Horned or Plumed Water Serpent, or Uktena (and perhaps other more mundane serpents who were its servants).

Plumed Serpents, Horned Water Serpents, and Agricultural Fertility

We have one more stop to make before circling back to Illinois to reconsider the mystery of the Rattler Frog pipe. Connected with many of these stories and images of frogs among the Pueblo peoples are beliefs concerning a Horned or Plumed Water Serpent, a creature that bears many striking similarities to the well-known Quetzalcoatl from Mesoamerica, whose name literally translates as "the Plumed Serpent."[72] As Jonathan Reyman points out, the Hopi origin story of Pala'tkwabi explicitly states that the Great Horned Water Serpent, together with his associated ceremonies, frog and tadpole effigies and motifs, as well as maize, beans, and

Fig. 4.5. The Plumed Serpent Quetzalcoatl on the mural of the Lower Temple of the Jaguars in Chichen Itza. From Florescano, *Myth of Quetzalcoatl*, 159, fig. 4.35. © 1999 The Johns Hopkins University Press. Reprinted with permission of The Johns Hopkins University Press.

shell, came to the Hopi from the "Red Land of the South," which Reyman convincingly identifies as northern Mexico.[73]

The parallels between Plumed or Horned Water Serpent images and stories among the Pueblos are very striking, as M. Jane Young has demonstrated at length,[74] and suggest a common origin for both these serpents. Among the

Hopi, this creature is known as Palölökong; the Zuni know it as Kolowisi. In each case, the figure is connected with rain, serpents, and fertility, and the images constructed of it for ceremonial use have goggle eyes filled with seeds of crop plants; these traits are all connected with Quetzalcoatl among the Aztecs. The Mayan and Toltec city of Chichen Itza in Mexico has produced many examples of elaborately carved Plumed Serpents in stone.[75] Compare the Mesoamerican Plumed Serpent illustrated in figure 4.5 with the drawing in figure 4.6 of a Zuni Kolowisi ritual object that dates to the early twentieth century;[76] note the plumes or feathers attached to the head of the serpent in both examples. During the Coming of Kolowisi ceremony, both water and seeds are spilled from an object like this one, according to Elsie Clews Parsons,[77] demonstrating this serpent's connec-

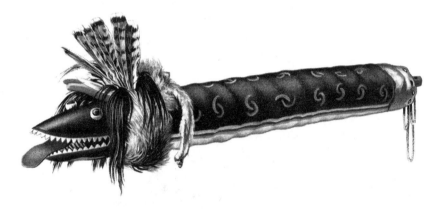

Fig. 4.6. Zuni Kolowisi (Plumed Serpent) effigy image, used in the Coming of Kolowisi ceremony. From Stevenson, *Zuñi Indians*, 94–95, plate 13.

tion to both rain and agricultural fertility. Among all the Pueblos, the Plumed or Horned Water Serpent is thought to cause floods, earthquakes, and landslides; some groups believed that child sacrifices to the Water Serpent were required to calm the floodwaters.[78]

Crossing the Mississippi River once again, we find a large number of representations of Plumed, Horned, and/or Underwater Serpents in art and sacred stories. Because such representations are extremely rare east of the Mississippi River before the Mississippian period,[79] they were probably part of a set of new beliefs about rain, flooding, and agricultural fertility that arrived along with maize agriculture around this time. For instance, at the Mississippian period Moundville site in west-central Alabama, Plumed and Horned Serpents are represented on a variety of pottery vessels; these depictions bear a close resemblance to the Plumed Serpent images from Mesoamerica and the Southwest (fig. 4.7).[80] And four winged, spotted, feline-headed serpents wind their way around an engraved conch shell cup found in the Craig mound at the Spiro site in LeFlore County, Oklahoma, another major Mississippian site (fig. 4.8). Although the appearance of these feline-headed creatures does not have as much in common with the Plumed Serpents from Mesoamerica and the Southwest as do the ones from Moundville, the association of wings with serpent creatures on the Spiro examples indicates that a similar concept is probably being expressed. In addition, some of the Plumed Serpents depicted on the Moundville pots, and all of the serpents depicted on the Spiro cup, had spots along their bodies, which also suggests they were referring to the same creature. Furthermore, a number of the historic tribes of the Southeast, such as the Cherokee, Creek, and Yuchi, shared sacred stories of various serpent monsters associated with water, flooding, and fertility, including not just the Horned Water Serpent but also the Underwater Panther, Tie-Snake, and Uktena.[81] George E. Lankford has written that the different names by which these monstrous water serpents are known in different tribes "may just be different ways of describing a standard family of Under World beings,"[82] such as the Plumed or Horned Water Serpents we have already encountered in Mesoamerica and the Southwest.

Fig. 4.7. Plumed or Horned Serpents from the Moundville site in west-central Alabama. Both images were originally engraved on pottery bottles. Top image is about two-thirds actual size; bottom is about half size. From Moore, "Moundville Revisited," 374–75, figs. 58 and 61.

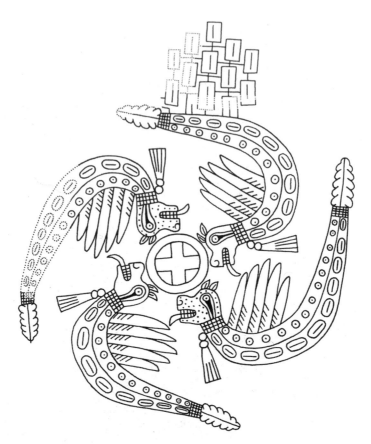

Fig. 4.8. Feline-headed Plumed or Horned Serpents engraved on a shell cup from the Spiro site, Oklahoma. Plate 229 drawing from Phillips and Brown, *Pre-Columbian Shell Engravings*, 228. Copyright ©1984 by the President and Fellows of Harvard College. Courtesy of the Peabody Museum Press.

Among Illinois Mississippians, at least, snakes without horns or plumes also seem to be connected with agricultural fertility beliefs. For instance, consider the Birger figurine (fig. 4.9). This flint clay carving was found at the BBB Motor site near Cahokia in Illinois and dates from around the same time as the Rattler Frog pipe.[83] The figurine depicts a woman holding a feline-headed serpent with her left hand, while with her right hand she hoes the back of the serpent. The serpent's body splits into two vines, each of which bears gourds as they travel around the woman's body and up her back. Based on a comprehensive survey of related sacred stories and images of various Native American peoples of the Plains and Eastern Woodlands, Guy Prentice has convincingly argued that this image represents an Earth Mother figure, obviously connected with agriculture and fertility.[84] Three other fragmentary flint clay figurines from the nearby Sponemann site, known as

Fig. 4.9. Birger figurine from the BBB Motor site, Madison County, Illinois. Photos are of a cast of the figurine (ISM c817/720a): (a) left side; (b) right side. Photos by the author. Courtesy of the Illinois State Museum.

the Sponemann, West, and Willoughby figurines, bear similar imagery linking women, snakes, and agricultural plant parts.[85]

The Rattler Frog Pipe and Its Use

At long last, we return to the Rattler Frog pipe (fig. 4.1) with which we began this excursion into the uses of frogs and snakes as symbols of agricultural fertility among Native Americans past and present. Now we can see the Rattler Frog pipe as one in a long line of Native American images and beliefs connecting frogs, snakes, and agricultural fertility through their mutual association with rivers, springs, and other water sources. When maize came to the Late Woodland and Mississippian peoples of the Eastern Woodlands from the Pueblo peoples of the Southwest, so too did rituals and beliefs associated with it, including instructions on how to avert natural disasters such as flooding or drought through proper behaviors and ceremonies. In most of the Southeast, the serpent in the form of a Horned or Plumed Water Serpent seems to be the main being controlling the waters. In precontact Illinois, however, frogs seem to have had that charge—or perhaps one monstrous frog, such as the Big Water Man of Taos Pueblo. As potential formal (artistic) evidence supporting this identification, consider the rather sinister expression of the Rattler Frog (see fig. 4.1). Such an image seems intended to evoke awe and perhaps even fear in its viewers, which would make sense if the Rattler Frog image represented a supernatural being with the power to send devastating floods as well as life-giving waters.

We should also consider how the Rattler Frog pipe might have been used by the Illinois Mississippians. First, generally speaking, pipes are one of the main means that Native Americans use to communicate with the spirit world.[86] Often pipes are smoked to ask the gods for blessings. The tobacco (or other substances) smoked in the pipe are given as offerings to the gods, who are expected to respond with the requested blessings. Among the Hopi, for instance, pipes are smoked ritually to ask for rain, fertility, and good health; "ritual smoking is perhaps the most common mode of prayer for Hopi men," as John D. Loftin has written.[87] On the one hand, the tobacco smoke is intended as an offering, which the Hopi expect will be reciprocated with rain. Indeed, clouds of ritual smoke are often compared to rain clouds by Pueblo peoples. In this sense, the act of smoking helps directly bring about the desired result (rain clouds), partly because the participants puff out their breath along with the smoke. Breath, in turn, is intimately connected with spirits, souls, and creation among many Native American tribes, including the Hopi. So through the act of breathing out smoke through a pipe, a ritual participant contributes some of her or his own spiritual essence to the ceremony.[88]

In the case of the Rattler Frog pipe, we might hypothesize, based on the ethnographic analogies presented above, that the requested blessings were rain, agricultural fertility, and the prevention of damaging floods. The frog depicted on the pipe might have been the supernatural entity being prayed to for these blessings. But because frogs are more often described in Native American ethnographic information as helper spirits for the rain gods, perhaps the frog on this pipe served a similar purpose, helping carry the smoke offerings from the pipe to the gods. Putting this idea in aesthetic perspective, recall the rather watchful expression of the Rattler Frog; perhaps what the frog was depicted as watching for was rain, which the people who used this pipe hoped the Rattler Frog (or the transformed priest acting out the role of the Rattler Frog; see below) would help draw down from the heavens for them with its gourd rattle and its croaking prayers for rain.

We might then wonder who used this pipe, and on what sorts of occasions. Some evidence is provided by the pipe itself. It is large, quite heavy, and awkward to hold, so we might assume that it was not held in the hands while smoked but placed flat on some surface. This assumption is supported by images on other, similar pipes, which depict men smoking pipes just like the Rattler Frog pipe (for instance, the Frog Smoker pipe from the Spiro site in Oklahoma):[89] they lean over the pipe, which is placed on a flat surface, and insert a short, thick stem into the more posterior of the two holes on the top of the pipe (the other hole holds the tobacco) to smoke it. Because the smoker is *behind* the pipe, she or he would not see the image of the frog, which is on the front of the pipe, while smoking it. This, in turn, suggests that more than one person would be involved in ceremonies during which the Rattler Frog pipe was smoked—one person to actually smoke the pipe and one or more others to observe and pray while the pipe was being smoked. Again drawing on ethnographic analogies, it would seem most likely that the people involved in smoking the Rattler Frog pipe would have been priests—perhaps members of a formalized weather-controlling priesthood.[90] The Rattler Frog pipe might then have been buried with a leading priest when he died.

A New Method for Studying Archaeological Images of Animals

This chapter has demonstrated a new interdisciplinary method I have developed that could be productively applied to help interpret other precontact or prehistoric animal effigies from archaeological or art historical collections. The method involves the following steps: formal, functional, and material analysis; contextual analysis; natural history; ethnographic and ethnohistoric analogy; and, finally, interpretation.[91] We begin with formal description of the object being studied because this description provides the primary data for our study. For instance, the fact that the Rattler Frog pipe shows its amphibian subject holding a gourd rattle is crucial to interpreting the meaning of this artifact. Knowing that this object is a pipe gives us some clues about the ritual contexts within which it might have been used. And the fact that the material of which the Rattler Frog pipe is made was quarried locally tells us that the object was most likely both made and used in the Cahokia area rather than imported from elsewhere.

Next, we need to consider the relevant archaeological and comparative art historical contexts. Starting with local contexts: Where was the object found? For instance, did it come from a house or a grave? If the object was found with a burial, was it found with a man or woman? An adult or a child? What other objects were found in association with it? Moving to broader comparative contexts: Where have objects bearing similar images been found? How widely are they distributed? For certain types of animal images, it may also be useful to draw on the insights of archaeologists who study animal bones to determine how the animal portrayed in the artwork was used for purposes other than art. Was it used as a food? As a source of clothing or tools? Because we know so little about the local contexts within which the Rattler Frog pipe and other similar Illinois Mississippian frog pipes have been found, I have not stressed this step in this chapter, but it is nevertheless a vital one for interpreting what these objects and their imagery meant to their makers.

By investigating the natural history of the animal represented on a given item, one can uncover features of the animal's appearance or behavior that might have been especially interesting to the people who made the item. These features, in turn, may help explain the cultural meanings of the representation. It helps to identify the species of the animal represented, of course, which can be quite a challenge when a representation is not particularly detailed. But even knowing just the general type of animal, such as "a duck," can be helpful. In this chapter, for instance, we learned from the natural history of southern leopard frogs that they are one of the first species to emerge from hibernation in the spring; therefore, the Illinois Mississippians might well have seen these frogs as bringers of spring, along with its warmth and life-giving rains.

From natural history we move to ethnohistory: How did other historical or contemporary peoples view the animal in question? What roles did the animal play in each people's subsistence, society, ritual, and cosmology? Applying ethnographic and ethnohistoric data recorded from historic and/or contemporary peoples to help understand archaeological data is known as ethnographic analogy (see note 36 below). For this research project, I mainly used analogies with Southwestern peoples, since I wanted to explore what religious beliefs and rituals might have been transmitted from them to Late Woodland and Mississippian peoples along with maize. However, throughout most of the larger research project of which this chapter is a part, I have been focusing on peoples who were most likely descended from or in close interaction with Illinois Mississippian peoples, including a number of Southeastern tribes (who were likely descended from other Mississippian groups) and especially the Siouan-speaking tribes[92] of the central Plains and Great Lakes region, such as the Osage, Omaha, Ponca, Oto, Missouri, Ioway, and Ho-chunk (Winnebago).[93]

Finally, we end with interpretation. Once we have completed the formal, functional, and material analysis of the item, investigated its various archaeological and art historical contexts, surveyed the natural history of the animal it depicts, and explored ethnohistoric analogies with the beliefs of other peoples, we put all that information together to come up with the most plausible interpretation(s) of what the animal and its representation meant to the people who made the animal effigy in question.

Some say that animal effigies like the Rattler Frog pipe made by peoples long dead cannot speak to us. I suggest that they can, if only we can learn how to listen. Key to that listening is an interdisciplinary method such as the one I just described. Only by adopting such an approach can we hope to make the conceptual leap from representations of animals on archaeological objects to an understanding of the roles those animals played in the lives of the people who made the objects.

Notes

I would like to thank Kenneth B. Farnsworth, Sarah F. Rose, and the anonymous reviewer from the University of Tennessee Press editorial board for their helpful comments on earlier versions of this chapter. Thanks also to Columbia University Press, the Field Museum, the Illinois State Museum, the Johns Hopkins University Press, and the Peabody Museum Press for their kind permission to reproduce images for this chapter.

1. Robert M. DeGraaff, *The Book of the Toad: A Natural and Magical History of Toad-Human Relations* (Rochester, Vt.: Park Street Press, 1991), 87; Alison Bailey Kennedy, *"Ecce Bufo:* The Toad in Nature and in Olmec Iconography," *Current Anthropology* 23, no. 3 (1982): 275; Laura C. Martin, *Wildlife Folklore* (Old Saybrook, Conn.: Globe Pequot Press, 1994), 146–48.

2. Kennedy, *"Ecce Bufo,"* 275.

3. By "sacred stories," I mean stories of the timeless time at the beginning of creation during which the gods walked the earth, when the boundaries between humans and other animals were more fluid than they are today and different species could communicate with each other and even change shapes. While some call these stories "myths," I prefer the term "sacred stories," which emphasizes the fact that the Native Americans and other peoples who tell such stories believe them to be true and powerful, able not just to instruct the listener in tribal history or religion or culturally appropriate behavior but also to literally recreate the sacred time before time in the present while the tales are being told. Joseph Epes Brown with Emily Cousins, *Teaching Spirits: Understanding Native American Religious Traditions* (Oxford: Oxford Univ. Press, 2001), 55–56. As Sam D. Gill explains, "From the modern Native American point of view, the word *myth* has the meaning the word bears in common usage: it refers to a misconception or a story without base. To many Native Americans, *myth* is a pejorative term that indicates insensitivity and misunderstanding on the part of those who apply it to their stories." Sam D. Gill, "Mythic Themes," in *Native American Religions: North America*, ed. Lawrence E. Sullivan (New York: Macmillan, 1989), 158.

4. Throughout this chapter, precontact Native American objects bearing intentionally worked representations of animals will be referred to as "artworks" or "art objects." While some might question the application of Western notions of what is and is not art to the precontact Native American context, the problem is not insurmountable. As Franz Boas first suggested more than seventy years ago (Franz Boas, *Primitive Art* [1928; reprint, New York: Dover, 1955], 10–13), two common elements are

shared by "art" the world over: intentional shaping by human agency (form) and association of certain ideas with the forms thus produced (meaning). These criteria are certainly met by the objects under discussion here.

5. William McAdams, *Records of Ancient Races in the Mississippi Valley* (St. Louis: C. R. Barns, 1887), 45–46; Thomas E. Emerson, *Mississippian Stone Images in Illinois*, Illinois Archaeological Survey Circular No. 6 (Urbana: Illinois Archaeological Survey, 1982), 33; Thomas E. Emerson, "Materializing Cahokia Shamans," *Southeastern Archaeology* 22, no. 2 (Winter 2003): 138–39. According to McAdams, other items found in the grave with the Rattler Frog pipe included a copper and pearl headdress and two ceramic vessels.

6. Emerson, "Materializing Cahokia Shamans," 138; Thomas E. Emerson and Randall E. Hughes, "Figurines, Flint Clay Sourcing, the Ozark Highlands, and Cahokian Acquisition," *American Antiquity* 65, no. 1 (2000): 79–101.

7. See Emerson, *Mississippian Stone Images*, 33, for the streamer identification; see Emerson, "Materializing Cahokia Shamans," 141, for the fringe identification. There are several other stone pipes from the Mississippian period, made of Missouri flint clay from the Cahokia region (see below), that represent either a frog or a human with a gourd rattle in its hand (Emerson, "Materializing Cahokia Shamans," 138–41). One represents a frog holding a rattle, the Gahagan Frog pipe from Red River Parish in northwestern Louisiana. Three others represent humans holding a gourd rattle: the Macoupin Creek pipe from the lower Illinois River Valley, the Gilcrease Rattler pipe from the Spiro site in Oklahoma, and the WPA Rattler, also from the Spiro site. Kenneth B. Farnsworth has suggested to me that all of these pipes might represent the same individual, such as a powerful priest or supernatural being whose spiritual helper was a frog (pers. comm., June 2005).

8. The term "Mississippian" refers to an archaeological time period, to the cultures and societies of the precontact Native Americans who lived during that time period, and to those people themselves. For clarity, I will use "Mississippian" or "Mississippian period" to refer to time, and "Mississippians" or "Mississippian peoples" to refer to people. And when speaking specifically of precontact peoples who lived in the region of present-day Illinois during the Mississippian period, I will refer to them as "Illinois Mississippians."

9. Because the Rattler Frog does not have toe pads depicted, we know it is not a tree frog. John L. Behler and F. Wayne King, *National Audubon Society Field Guide to North American Reptiles and Amphibians* (New York: Alfred A. Knopf, 1997), 15. We might, though, wonder if it could be a bullfrog (*Rana catesbeiana*), which is also found in Illinois. Bullfrogs are the largest frogs in North America and are also fearsome predators for their size, eating other frogs, small snakes, and sometimes even small birds (ibid., 372), so they might well have been of interest to the Illinois Mississippians. However, after comparing photographs of bullfrogs and southern leopard frogs, it seems unlikely that the Rattler Frog was a bullfrog. For one thing, bullfrogs are massively built, with a large, rounded body relative to the size of their limbs, especially their forelimbs. But the Rattler Frog's body is fairly slender, and its

limbs are large relative to the size of its body, making it resemble a southern leopard frog much more than a bullfrog. Furthermore, the single most distinguishing characteristic of a bullfrog's head is its very large external eardrums, depressed circular areas behind the eyes that are actually larger than its eyes. But no eardrums are depicted on the Rattler Frog at all, which suggests that a species with a less prominent external eardrum is being depicted. Southern leopard frogs have small external eardrums which are cryptically colored (and thus much less noticeable than those of a bullfrog) and smaller than its eyes, suggesting again, as Christopher Phillips said, that the Rattler Frog represents a southern leopard frog.

10. Behler and King, *National Audubon Society Field Guide*, 379–80.

11. Paul W. Parmalee, *Amphibians of Illinois*, Story of Illinois Series, No. 10 (Springfield: Illinois State Museum, 1954), 34.

12. Illinois Natural History Survey, "*Rana sphenocephala*—Southern Leopard Frog," http://www.inhs.uiuc.edu/cbd/herpdist/species/ra_sphenoc.html, last updated Apr. 6, 2004.

13. Behler and King, *National Audubon Society Field Guide*, 380; Philip W. Smith, "Amphibians and Reptiles of Illinois," *Illinois Natural History Survey Bulletin* 28, no. 1 (1961): 108.

14. James H. Harding, *Amphibians and Reptiles of the Great Lakes Region* (Ann Arbor: Univ. of Michigan Press, 1997), 156–57; Parmalee, *Amphibians of Illinois*, 34; Smith, "Amphibians and Reptiles of Illinois," 104.

15. Kennedy, "*Ecce Bufo*," 175.

16. For instance, the powerful serpent monster known to the Cherokee as the Uktena was described as having "rings or spots of color along its whole length." James Mooney, *Myths of the Cherokee* (1900; reprint, New York: Dover, 1995), 297. The Uktena will be discussed in greater detail later in this chapter.

17. Emerson, "Materializing Cahokia Shamans," 141–42; Guy Prentice, "Origins of Plant Domestication in the Eastern United States: Promoting the Individual in Archaeological Theory," *Southeastern Archaeology* 5, no. 2 (1986): 112–13.

18. Native American sacred stories frequently describe animal shamans who help heal their people and defend them from harm. For citations to a number of examples involving beaver shamans, see Dave Aftandilian, "Earth Diver Comes to Illinois? The Meaning of the Beaver to the Illinois Mississippians" (paper presented at the 81st Annual Central State Anthropological Society meeting, Milwaukee, Apr. 15–18, 2004).

19. George R. Milner, *The Cahokia Chiefdom: The Archaeology of a Mississippian Society* (Washington, D.C.: Smithsonian Institution Press, 1998); Timothy R. Pauketat, *Ancient Cahokia and the Mississippians* (Cambridge, Mass.: Cambridge Univ. Press, 2004), 106; Timothy R. Pauketat and Thomas E. Emerson, "Introduction: Domination and Ideology in the Mississippian World," in *Cahokia: Domination and Ideology in the Mississippian World*, ed. Timothy R. Pauketat and Thomas E. Emerson (Lincoln: Univ. of Nebraska Press, 1997), 1–29; Timothy R. Pauketat and Neal H.

Lopinot, "Cahokian Population Dynamics," in *Cahokia: Domination and Ideology in the Mississippian World*, ed. Timothy R. Pauketat and Thomas E. Emerson (Lincoln: Univ. of Nebraska Press, 1997), 103–23; Biloine Whiting Young and Melvin L. Fowler, *Cahokia: The Great Native American Metropolis* (Urbana: Univ. of Illinois Press, 2000).

20. Timothy R. Pauketat and Brad Koldehoff, "Cahokian Ritual and the Ramey Field: New Insights from Old Collections," *Southeastern Archaeology* 21, no. 1 (2002): 88.

21. By Middle Mississippian times (1050–1150 c.e.), better than 50 percent of nutrients in the diet of Illinois Mississippians came from maize, according to carbon isotope studies of human bone from the Dickson Mounds site in west-central Illinois; see Jane E. Buikstra, Jerome C. Rose, and George R. Milner, "A Carbon Isotopic Perspective on Dietary Variation in Late Prehistoric Western Illinois," in *Agricultural Origins and Development in the Midcontinent*, ed. William Green (Iowa City: Univ. of Iowa, 1994), 155–70. These trends are confirmed by the increasing presence of maize cobs at the Mississippian site of Cahokia over time; during the Early Mississippian period (1000–1050 c.e.), maize cobs are found in 45 percent of archeological deposits examined at Cahokia; during the Middle Mississippian, they are found in 83.3 to 93.8 percent of the deposits; and during the Late Mississippian (1150–1250 c.e.), maize cobs are found in *all* such deposits. Neal H. Lopinot, "A New Crop of Data on the Cahokian Polity," in *Agricultural Origins and Development in the Midcontinent*, ed. William Green, Office of the State Archaeologist Report 19 (Iowa City: Univ. of Iowa, 1994), 137. The use of large fields planted with rows of crops also becomes evident for the first time in Illinois during the Mississippian period; see Melvin L. Fowler, "Middle Mississippian Agricultural Fields," *American Antiquity* 34, no. 4 (1969): 365–75; Lopinot, "New Crop of Data," 135; and Patty Jo Watson, "Prehistoric Gardening and Agriculture in the Midwest and Midsouth," in *Interpretations of Culture Change in the Eastern Woodlands during the Late Woodland Period*, ed. Richard W. Yerkes, Occasional Papers in Anthropology No. 3 (Columbus: Ohio State Univ., 1988), 45–46.

22. Charles Hudson, *The Southeastern Indians* (Knoxville: Univ. of Tennessee Press, 1976), 337–38.

23. Historians disagree on whether Native Americans in New England used fish to fertilize their fields before contact with Europeans or whether they learned that practice from the colonists; see the discussion in Amy D. Schwartz, "Colonial New England Agriculture: Old Visions, New Directions," *Agricultural History* 69, no. 3 (1995): 461. Charles Hudson states that "we have no evidence that the Southeastern Indians fertilized their fields" (Hudson, *Southeastern Indians*, 290–91). (Southeastern Native American groups are believed by many scholars to be descended from Mississippian peoples related to those who lived at Cahokia.) Hudson suggests that the rich, easily tilled, well-drained floodplain soil in which Southeastern Native American groups planted their crops was crucial to their agricultural system, in part because its fertility was replenished quickly by new soil deposited by the rivers while the land was left fallow.

24. See Emerson, *Mississippian Stone Images*, figures 19 and 20, for photos of these pipes. Other Late Woodland and Mississippian period frog pipes from Illinois that I have viewed in museum collections or read about include two from Calhoun County (both different from the one from this county illustrated in Emerson's *Mississippian Stone Images*; one is from the Golden Eagle site, the other from an unidentified site), two from Fulton County (one from the Crable site and one from an unidentified site), two from unidentified sites in Jersey County, one from the Kane Village site in Madison County, two from St. Clair County (one from the Range site; see Joyce A. Williams, "Patrick Phase Lithics," in *The Range Site: Archaic through Late Woodland Occupations (11-S-47)*, ed. John E. Kelly et al., American Bottom Archaeology: FAI-270 Site Reports, vol. 16 [Urbana: Univ. of Illinois Press, 1987], 306–10, 336, 338; and one from the Halliday site; see Thomas E. Emerson, Brad Koldehoff, and Timothy R. Pauketat, "Serpents, Female Deities, and Fertility Symbolism in the Early Cahokian Countryside," in *Mounds, Modoc, and Mesoamerica: Papers in Honor of Melvin L. Fowler*, ed. Steven R. Ahler, Scientific Papers, vol. 28 [Springfield: Illinois State Museum, 2000], 511–22), one from the Cahokia site in St. Clair and Madison Counties (Pauketat and Koldehoff, "Cahokian Ritual"), and one unfinished example each from the Larson site in Madison County and the Orendorf site in Fulton County.

25. Based on objects I have observed or read about, other animals depicted on Late Woodland or Mississippian pipes found in or near Illinois are largely limited to humans, owls, rabbits, felines, and squirrels. One pipe from the Pete Klunk site in Calhoun County represents a nonraptorial bird (Gregory Perino, "The Late Woodland Component at the Pete Klunk Site, Calhoun Country, Illinois," in *Late Woodland Site Archaeology in Illinois I: Investigations in South-Central Illinois*, ed. James A. Brown, Bulletin No. 9 [Urbana: Illinois Archaeological Survey, 1973], 70–73, 77), and another from Jersey County likely depicts a crow or raven (Paul F. Titterington, "Certain Bluff Mounds of Western Jersey County, Illinois," *American Antiquity* 1 [1935]: 26–27). One pipe from the Mississippian Orendorf site in Fulton County may represent a bird torso, and another from the same site perhaps represents a reptilian head.

26. In many cases, as in the example in figure 4.2, two low, rounded triangular projections are also modeled at the top of the handles of jars with tridactyl designs; these projections might represent the tops of two frog eyes as they would look if the rest of the frog's body were submerged in water. A similar tripartite design bearing some resemblance to a horizontally oriented bird track occurs on other pots and pipes from Illinois dating to the Late Woodland, Mississippian, or Oneota periods. Duane Esarey and Kelvin Sampson have suggested that this design may represent a generic symbol for the Underworld (pers. comm., July 2001). Also see figure 4.4 for a tripartite, horizontally oriented symbol on a Hopi snake kilt that is intended to represent frog's track.

27. Three kinds of animals are modeled very similarly in relief on Illinois Mississippian bowls: frogs, beavers, and fish. All three of these animals spend much of their time

in or near water, so perhaps these bowls were used in ceremonies involving water. Another possibility is that the animals on these bowls each represented a different clan—frog clan, beaver clan, and so on. The bowls would have then been used by members of that clan in clan or tribal ceremonies. See Aftandilian, "Earth Diver Comes to Illinois?" for further discussion of a possible Illinois Mississippian beaver clan.

28. David S. Brose, James A. Brown, and David Penney, *Ancient Art of the American Woodland Indians* (New York: Harry N. Abrams, 1985), plate 87; Emma Lila Fundaburk and Mary Douglass Foreman, *Sun Circles and Human Hands: The Southeastern Indians Art and Industries* (Luverne, Ala.: Emma Lila Fundaburk, 1957), plates 123 and 124; Roy Hathcock, *Ancient Indian Pottery of the Mississippi River Valley*, 2d ed. (Marceline, Mo.: Walsworth, 1988), 134–36, figs. 348–53 and 355–56; Clarence B. Moore, "Certain Aboriginal Remains of the Black Warrior River," *Journal of the Academy of Natural Sciences of Philadelphia* 13 (1905): 184–85, fig. 78; Clarence B. Moore, "Moundville Revisited," *Journal of the Academy of Natural Sciences of Philadelphia* 13 (1907): 360–61, figs. 29 and 30.

29. Moore, "Moundville Revisited," 362, fig. 33.

30. Cottie Burland, *North American Indian Mythology* (New York: Tudor, 1965), 124; Fundaburk and Foreman, *Sun Circles and Human Hands*, plate 103; Frederic Ward Putnam, "The Swallow Collection: Pottery and Stone Artifacts from Mounds near New Madrid, Missouri," 1875, in *The Archaeological Reports of Frederic Ward Putnam* (New York: AMS Press, 1973), 5.

31. David W. Penney, *Native Arts of North America* (Paris: Terrail Editions, 1998), 24.

32. Kenneth B. Farnsworth and Karen A. Atwell, *Documentation of Human Burials and Mortuary Remains Recovered from Test Excavations at Naples-Russell Mound #8, Ray Norbut Conservation Area, Pike County, Illinois*, Technical Report Submitted to the Illinois Historic Preservation Agency and the Illinois Department of Transportation, 2001.

33. Gayle J. Fritz, "'Newer,' 'Better' Maize and the Mississippian Emergence: A Critique of Prime Mover Explanations," in *Late Prehistoric Agriculture: Observations from the Midwest*, ed. William I. Woods, Studies in Illinois Archaeology 8 (Springfield: Illinois Historic Preservation Agency, 1992), 28; Bruce D. Smith, *The Emergence of Agriculture* (New York: Scientific American Library, 1998), 184; Watson, "Prehistoric Gardening," 45.

34. David L. Asch, "Aboriginal Specialty-Plant Cultivation in Eastern North America: Illinois Prehistory and a Post-Contact Perspective," in *Agricultural Origins and Development in the Midcontinent*, ed. William Green, Office of the State Archaeologist Report 19 (Iowa City: Univ. of Iowa, 1994), 29; Lopinot, "New Crop of Data," 135; Thomas J. Riley, Gregory R. Walz, Charles J. Bareis, Andrew C. Fortier, and Kathryn E. Parker, "Accelerator Mass Spectrometer (AMS) Dates Confirm Early Zea Mays in the Mississippi River Valley," *American Antiquity* 59, no. 3 (1994): 490–98; Smith, *Emergence of Agriculture*, 200–201; Watson, "Prehistoric Gardening," 44.

35. Florence Ellis, cited in M. Jane Young, "The Interconnection between Western Puebloan and Mesoamerican Ideology/Cosmology," in *Kachinas in the Pueblo World*, ed. Polly Schaafsma (Albuquerque: Univ. of New Mexico Press, 1994), 108; Karl Taube, "Lightning Celts and Corn Fetishes: The Formative Olmec and the Development of Maize Symbolism in Mesoamerica and the American Southwest," in *Olmec Art and Archaeology in Mesoamerica*, ed. John E. Clark and Mary E. Pye, Studies in the History of Art 58 (Washington, D.C.: National Gallery of Art, 2000), 297.

36. Using stories, religious beliefs, or documentary evidence recorded during the nineteenth and twentieth centuries to interpret the meanings of archaeologically recovered materials dating to an earlier period is known as ethnographic or ethnohistoric analogy. While the limitations of this approach are obvious, one has little choice but to use it if one hopes to decode the meanings of objects made by peoples who lived and died centuries ago. As Gordon R. Willey puts it, "There are some aspects of past life, principally those in the ideological realm, that can be satisfactorily explained only with the aid of specific historical analogy" (i.e., ethnohistoric analogy). Gordon R. Willey, "Mesoamerican Art and Iconography and the Integrity of the Mesoamerican Ideological System," in *New World Archaeology and Culture History: Collected Essays and Articles* (Albuquerque: Univ. of New Mexico Press, 1990), 303. The ethnohistorian Patricia K. Galloway offers a very useful set of caveats and advice on how to critically apply ethnohistoric analogy in her article on "The Direct Historical Approach and Early Historical Documents: The Ethnohistorian's View," in *The Protohistoric Period in the Mid-South: 1500–1700*, ed. David H. Dye and Ronald C. Brister, Archaeological Report No. 18 (Jackson: Mississippi Department of Archives and History, 1986), 14–23.

37. Alexander M. Stephen, *Hopi Journal of Alexander M. Stephen*, ed. Elsie Clews Parsons, Columbia Contributions to Anthropology, vol. 23 (New York: Columbia Univ. Press, 1936), pt. 1, 707.

38. Ibid., pt. 2, 806.

39. Elsie Clews Parsons, *Pueblo Indian Religion* (Chicago: Univ. of Chicago Press, 1939), 1:409.

40. Alph H. Secakuku, *Following the Sun and Moon: Hopi Kachina Tradition* (Flagstaff, Ariz.: Northland Publishing and the Heard Museum, 1995), 99.

41. Stephen, *Hopi Journal*, pt. 1, 306–7.

42. Ruth Benedict, *Zuni Mythology* (New York: Columbia Univ. Press, 1935), 1:129–30.

43. Stephen, *Hopi Journal*, pt. 1, 650 and plate 19.

44. Jesse Walter Fewkes, *Hopi Katcinas* (1903; reprint, New York: Dover, 1991), 47. Alexander Stephen calls Palülükoñti the "Horned Water Serpent Dance" (*Hopi Journal*, pt. 1, 287).

45. Fewkes, *Hopi Katcinas*, 22.

46. Stephen, *Hopi Journal*, pt. 1, 289.

47. Ibid., 53; Fewkes, *Hopi Katcinas*, 31, 56; see also Parsons, *Pueblo Indian Religion* 1:334, 336. Fewkes writes, "At or near the winter solstice . . . the Winter Sun prayer-stick making takes place. . . . The only fetish employed is a rude stone frog, over which is stretched a string extended along a line of meal on the floor, symbolic of the pathway of blessings" (*Hopi Katcinas*, 31).

48. Stephen, *Hopi Journal*, pt. 1, 515.

49. Frank Hamilton Cushing, "Creation and the Origin of Corn," *Millstone* 9, no. 1 (1884): 1–3, http://www.public-domain-content.com/books/native_american/zuni/cushing/cush07.shtml, accessed June 20, 2005.

50. Matilda Coxe Stevenson, *The Zuñi Indians: Their Mythology, Esoteric Fraternities, and Ceremonies*, Annual Report of the U.S. Bureau of American Ethnology, vol. 23, 1901–2 (Washington, D.C.: U.S. Bureau of American Ethnology, 1904), 200.

51. Ibid., 163.

52. Ibid., 33.

53. Parsons, *Pueblo Indian Religion* 1:409–10.

54. For photos of several contemporary examples by Zuni potter Quanita Kalastewa, see Milford Nahohai and Elisa Phelps, *Dialogues with Zuni Potters* (Zuni, N.M.: Zuni Ashiwi, 1995), 12.

55. Parsons, *Pueblo Indian Religion* 2:937.

56. Linda S. Cordell, *Ancient Pueblo Peoples* (Montreal: St. Remy Press; Washington, D.C.: Smithsonian Books, 1994), 101; John C. McGregor, *Southwestern Archaeology*, 2d ed. (Urbana: Univ. of Illinois Press, 1965), 278–95.

57. Robert H. Lister and Florence C. Lister, *Anasazi Pottery: Ten Centuries of Prehistoric Ceramic Art in the Four Corners Country of the Southwestern United States* (Albuquerque: Maxwell Museum of Art and Univ. of New Mexico Press, 1978), 50–51.

58. J. J. Brody, *Anasazi and Pueblo Painting* (Albuquerque: Univ. of New Mexico Press, 1991), 49.

59. John R. Swanton, *Myths and Tales of the Southeastern Indians* (1929; reprint, Norman: Univ. of Oklahoma Press, 1995), 121.

60. Frank G. Speck, *Ethnology of the Yuchi Indians* (1909; reprint, Lincoln: Univ. of Nebraska Press, 2004), 99.

61. Hudson, *Southeastern Indians*, 127. One example is the Cherokee story of Untsaiyi, the Gambler, and the Under World power of Thunder; see Mooney, *Myths of the Cherokee*, 311–15.

62. This interpretation does put us in the somewhat uncomfortable position of suggesting that the Yuchi saw Wind as an Under World power, rather than as an Upper World power, as most other tribes did and do. Still, the similarities in the sacred stories and images discussed in the text are too powerful to ignore. Also, the Cherokee, at least, saw Thunder as an Under World power, even though many Plains

Indians saw it as an Upper World power; see previous note. So perhaps it is not as much of a stretch to suggest that the Yuchi saw Wind as an Under World power as it might at first appear.

63. Frank G. Speck, Leonard Broom, and Will West Long, *Cherokee Dance and Drama* (1951; reprint, Norman: Univ. of Oklahoma Press, 1983), 76.

64. Arlene Fradkin, *Cherokee Folk Zoology: The Animal World of a Native American People, 1700–1838* (New York: Garland, 1990), 328.

65. Mooney, *Myths of the Cherokee*, 306.

66. Ibid., 257, 306.

67. Ibid., 257.

68. Speck, *Ethnology of the Yuchi Indians*, 110. The Tunica of southeastern Arkansas and northeastern Louisiana may also have linked the frog and the moon. One of the "household gods" of this tribe was said to be a frog, and the other was said to be a woman. John R. Swanton thinks that "if . . . the sun is feminine in Tunica, the woman referred to was very likely the solar goddess, but it is hard to understand what connection there could have been between the sun and the frog." John R. Swanton, *Indian Tribes of the Lower Mississippi Valley and Adjacent Coast of the Gulf of Mexico* (1911; reprint, Mineola, N.Y.: Dover, 1998), 318. Perhaps, since the Cherokee, Creek, Yuchi, and likely other tribes of the Southeast associated frogs with the moon, the Tunica did as well. If so, the Tunica frog image may have represented a lunar deity, and the frog and woman "household gods" together may then have represented the celestial duo of sun and moon (the pairing of sun and moon as consorts being fairly common in folklore the world over).

69. Hudson, *Southeastern Indians*, 128.

70. Thomas E. Emerson, "Water, Serpents, and the Underworld: An Exploration into Cahokian Symbolism," in *The Southeastern Ceremonial Complex: Artifacts and Analysis*, ed. Patricia Galloway (Lincoln: Univ. of Nebraska Press, 1989), 59; Hudson, *Southeastern Indians*, 128.

71. Vernon James Knight Jr., James A. Brown, and George E. Lankford, "On the Subject Matter of Southeastern Ceremonial Complex Art," *Southeastern Archaeology* 20, no. 2 (2001): 138.

72. Zuni artist Gabriel Paloma has drawn on these beliefs to create a colorful contemporary rendering of a stepped prayer bowl depicting a Plumed Serpent together with a frog in the bottom of the bowl; see Nahohai and Phelps, *Dialogues with Zuni Potters*, 77.

73. Jonathan E. Reyman, "Pala'tkwabi: Red Land of the South," in *The Grand Chichimeca: Essays on the Archaeology and Ethnohistory of Northern Mesoamerica*, ed. Jonathan E. Reyman, 320–35 (Brookfield, Vt.: Avebury, 1995).

74. Young, "Interconnection."

75. Enrique Florescano, *The Myth of Quetzalcoatl*, trans. Lysa Hochroth (Baltimore: Johns Hopkins Univ. Press, 1999), 159, 163.

76. Stevenson, *Zuñi Indians*, plate 13.

77. Parsons, *Pueblo Indian Religion* 1:448.

78. Ibid., 185–86.

79. I only know of one horned serpent effigy from the Eastern Woodlands that was made before Mississippian times, a boatstone carving from the Turner site in Hamilton County, Ohio, that dates to 200–400 c.e. See Brose, Brown, and Penney, *Ancient Art*, 56, plate 43, for a photograph of this object.

80. See also Fundaburk and Foreman, *Sun Circles and Human Hands*, 71, plate 34, for more images.

81. See Emerson, "Water, Serpents, and the Underworld," 58–61, and Hudson, *Southeastern Indians*, 144–45, for overviews. See George E. Lankford, *Native American Legends, Southeastern Legends: Tales from the Natchez, Caddo, Biloxi, Chickasaw, and Other Nations* (Little Rock, Ark.: August House, 1987), 83–96, for an annotated collection of relevant stories from various Southeastern Indians, and see Mooney, *Myths of the Cherokee*, 297–301, for Cherokee beliefs about the Uktena.

82. Lankford, *Native American Legends*, 92.

83. Emerson, *Mississippian Stone Images*, 3–5; Emerson and Hughes, "Figurines."

84. Guy Prentice, "An Analysis of the Symbolism Expressed by the Birger Figurine," *American Antiquity* 51, no. 2 (1986): 239–66.

85. Thomas E. Emerson, *Cahokia and the Archaeology of Power* (Tuscaloosa: Univ. of Alabama Press, 1997), 199–203; Andrew C. Fortier, "Stone Figurines," in *The Sponemann Site 2: The Mississippian and Oneota Occupations (11-Ms-517)*, by Douglas K. Jackson, Andrew C. Fortier, and Joyce A. Williams (Urbana: Univ. of Illinois Press, 1992), 277–303.

86. Jordan Paper, *Offering Smoke: The Sacred Pipe and Native American Religion* (Moscow: Univ. of Idaho Press, 1988), 5.

87. John D. Loftin, *Religion and Hopi Life*, 2d ed. (Bloomington: Indiana Univ. Press, 2003), 38.

88. Ibid.

89. See Emerson, "Materializing Cahokia Shamans," 139, fig. 1c, for a photo of this pipe.

90. Thomas E. Emerson has suggested that the being depicted on the Rattler Frog pipe, and its likely user, would have been a shaman rather than a priest (Emerson, "Materializing Cahokia Shamans"). Because shamans are most commonly found among small-scale groups of gatherer-hunters, it seems unlikely to me that the highly stratified Illinois Mississippian societies, with their likely divisions into nobles, priests, warriors, and commoners, would have supported independent-minded religious practitioners such as shamans. I find it much more likely instead that there would have been a religious hierarchy composed of several overlapping, well-organized priesthoods. Regardless of whether its smoker was a priest or a shaman, however,

the use of the Rattler Frog pipe to call for the blessings of rain and agricultural fertility would likely have been the same.

91. For a more detailed description and demonstration of this method, see Dave Aftandilian, "Animals, Art, and Prehistoric Religion: A Methodological Perspective" (paper presented at the Midwest American Academy of Religion annual meeting, Chicago, Apr. 8–9, 2005).

92. Many Native American tribes (i.e., the Ioway, Omaha, and Osage), in addition to the Sioux themselves, speak Siouan dialects. For a helpful map of the current distribution of Siouan-speaking tribes and a complete list of those tribes, see Carl Waldman, *Atlas of the North American Indian,* rev. ed. (New York: Facts on File, 2000), 77 and 79.

93. The Siouan-speaking tribes of the central Plains and Great Lakes shared similar lifeways, with a mix of agriculture, gathering, and hunting, like the Illinois Mississippians; they also all had patrilineal clan structures, formalized priesthoods, and similar religious rituals. Quite likely all these similarities derived from a common source— the Illinois Mississippians and related Mississippian peoples. See Garrick A. Bailey, ed., *The Osage and the Invisible World: From the Works of Francis La Flesche* (Norman: Univ. of Oklahoma Press, 1995), 28–29, 284; J. Owen Dorsey, "Mourning and War Customs of the Kansas," *American Naturalist* 19, no. 7 (1885): 673; James H. Howard, "The Persistence of Southern Cult Gorgets among the Historic Kansa," *American Antiquity* 21, no. 3 (1956): 301–3; James H. Howard, *The Ponca Tribe* (1965; reprint, Lincoln: Univ. of Nebraska Press, 1995), 4–5; and William E. Unrau, *The Kansa Indians: A History of the Wind People, 1673–1873* (Norman: Univ. of Oklahoma Press, 1971), 15–16.

Works Cited

Aftandilian, Dave. "Animals, Art, and Prehistoric Religion: A Methodological Perspective." Paper presented at the Midwest American Academy of Religion annual meeting, Chicago, Apr. 8–9, 2005.

———. "Earth Diver Comes to Illinois? The Meaning of the Beaver to the Illinois Mississippians." Paper presented at the 81st Annual Central States Anthropological Society Meeting, Milwaukee, Apr. 15–18, 2004.

Asch, David L. "Aboriginal Specialty-Plant Cultivation in Eastern North America: Illinois Prehistory and a Post-Contact Perspective." In *Agricultural Origins and Development in the Midcontinent,* edited by William Green, 25–85. Office of the State Archaeologist Report 19. Iowa City: Univ. of Iowa, 1994.

Bailey, Garrick A., ed. *The Osage and the Invisible World: From the Works of Francis La Flesche.* Norman: Univ. of Oklahoma Press, 1995.

Behler, John L., and F. Wayne King. *National Audubon Society Field Guide to North American Reptiles and Amphibians.* New York: Alfred A. Knopf, 1997.

Benedict, Ruth. *Zuni Mythology*. Vols. 1 and 2. Columbia University Contributions to Anthropology, vol. 21. New York: Columbia Univ. Press, 1935.

Boas, Franz. *Primitive Art*. 1928. Reprint, New York: Dover, 1955.

Brody, J. J. *Anasazi and Pueblo Painting*. A School of American Research Book. Albuquerque: Univ. of New Mexico Press, 1991.

Brose, David S., James A. Brown, and David Penney. *Ancient Art of the American Woodland Indians*. New York: Harry N. Abrams, 1985.

Brown, Joseph Epes, with Emily Cousins. *Teaching Spirits: Understanding Native American Religious Traditions*. Oxford: Oxford Univ. Press, 2001.

Buikstra, Jane E., Jerome C. Rose, and George R. Milner. "A Carbon Isotopic Perspective on Dietary Variation in Late Prehistoric Western Illinois." In *Agricultural Origins and Development in the Midcontinent*, edited by William Green, 155–70. Office of the State Archaeologist Report 19. Iowa City: Univ. of Iowa, 1994.

Burland, Cottie. *North American Indian Mythology*. New York: Tudor, 1965.

Cordell, Linda S. *Ancient Pueblo Peoples*. Montreal: St. Remy Press; Washington, D.C.: Smithsonian Books, 1994.

Cushing, Frank Hamilton. "Creation and the Origin of Corn." *Millstone* 9, no. 1 (1884): 1–3. http://www.public-domain-content.com/books/native_american/zuni/cushing/cush07.shtml. Accessed June 20, 2005.

DeGraaff, Robert M. *The Book of the Toad: A Natural and Magical History of Toad-Human Relations*. Rochester, Vt.: Park Street Press, 1991.

Dorsey, J. Owen. "Mourning and War Customs of the Kansas." *American Naturalist* 19, no. 7 (1885): 670–80.

Emerson, Thomas E. *Cahokia and the Archaeology of Power*. Tuscaloosa: Univ. of Alabama Press, 1997.

———. "Materializing Cahokia Shamans." *Southeastern Archaeology* 22, no. 2 (Winter 2003): 135–54.

———. *Mississippian Stone Images in Illinois*. Illinois Archaeological Survey Circular No. 6. Urbana: Illinois Archaeological Survey, 1982.

———. "Water, Serpents, and the Underworld: An Exploration into Cahokian Symbolism." In *The Southeastern Ceremonial Complex: Artifacts and Analysis*, edited by Patricia Galloway, 45–92. Lincoln: Univ. of Nebraska Press, 1989.

Emerson, Thomas E., and Randall E. Hughes. "Figurines, Flint Clay Sourcing, the Ozark Highlands, and Cahokian Acquisition." *American Antiquity* 65, no. 1 (2000): 79–101.

Emerson, Thomas E., Brad Koldehoff, and Timothy R. Pauketat. "Serpents, Female Deities, and Fertility Symbolism in the Early Cahokian Countryside." In *Mounds, Modoc, and Mesoamerica: Papers in Honor of Melvin R. Fowler*, edited by Steven R. Ahler, 511–22. Scientific Papers, vol. 28. Springfield: Illinois State Museum, 2000.

Farnsworth, Kenneth B., and Karen A. Atwell. *Documentation of Human Burials and Mortuary Remains Recovered from Test Excavations at Naples-Russell Mound #8, Ray Norbut Conservation Area, Pike County, Illinois*. Technical Report Submitted to the Illinois Historic Preservation Agency and the Illinois Department of Transportation, 2001.

Fewkes, Jesse Walter. *Hopi Katcinas*. 1903. Reprint, New York: Dover, 1991.

Florescano, Enrique. *The Myth of Quetzalcoatl*. Translated by Lysa Hochroth. Baltimore: Johns Hopkins Univ. Press, 1999.

Fortier, Andrew C. "Stone Figurines." In *The Sponemann Site 2: The Mississippian and Oneota Occupations (11-Ms-517)*, by Douglas K. Jackson, Andrew C. Fortier, and Joyce A. Williams, 277–303. Urbana: Univ. of Illinois Press, 1992.

Fowler, Melvin L. "Middle Mississippian Agricultural Fields." *American Antiquity* 34, no. 4 (1969): 365–75.

Fradkin, Arlene. *Cherokee Folk Zoology: The Animal World of a Native American People, 1700–1838*. New York: Garland, 1990.

Fritz, Gayle J. "'Newer,' 'Better' Maize and the Mississippian Emergence: A Critique of Prime Mover Explanations." In *Late Prehistoric Agriculture: Observations from the Midwest*, edited by William I. Woods, 19–43. Studies in Illinois Archaeology 8. Springfield: Illinois Historic Preservation Agency, 1992.

Fundaburk, Emma Lila, and Mary Douglass Foreman. *Sun Circles and Human Hands: The Southeastern Indians Art and Industries*. Luverne, Ala.: Emma Lila Fundaburk, 1957.

Galloway, Patricia K. "The Direct Historical Approach and Early Historical Documents: The Ethnohistorian's View." In *The Protohistoric Period in the Mid-South: 1500–1700*, edited by David H. Dye and Ronald C. Brister, 14–23. Archaeological Report No. 18. Jackson: Mississippi Department of Archives and History, 1986.

Gill, Sam D. "Mythic Themes." In *Native American Religions: North America*, edited by Lawrence E. Sullivan, 157–66. New York: Macmillan, 1989.

Harding, James H. *Amphibians and Reptiles of the Great Lakes Region*. Great Lakes Environment Series. Ann Arbor: Univ. of Michigan Press, 1997.

Hathcock, Roy. *Ancient Indian Pottery of the Mississippi River Valley*. 2d ed. Marceline, Mo.: Walsworth, 1988.

Howard, James H. "The Persistence of Southern Cult Gorgets among the Historic Kansa." *American Antiquity* 21, no. 3 (1956): 301–3.

———. *The Ponca Tribe*. 1965. Reprint, Lincoln: Univ. of Nebraska Press, 1995.

Hudson, Charles. *The Southeastern Indians*. Knoxville: Univ. of Tennessee Press, 1976.

Illinois Natural History Survey. "*Rana sphenocephala*—Southern Leopard Frog." INHS Amphibian and Reptile Collections. http://www.inhs.uiuc.edu/cbd/herpdist/species/ra_sphenoc.html. Last updated Apr. 6, 2004.

Kennedy, Alison Bailey. "*Ecce Bufo*: The Toad in Nature and in Olmec Iconography." *Current Anthropology* 23, no. 3 (1982): 273–90.

Knight, Vernon James, Jr., James A. Brown, and George E. Lankford. "On the Subject Matter of Southeastern Ceremonial Complex Art." *Southeastern Archaeology* 20, no. 2 (2001): 129–41.

Lankford, George E. *Native American Legends, Southeastern Legends: Tales from the Nat-chez, Caddo, Biloxi, Chickasaw, and Other Nations.* American Folklore Series. Little Rock, Ark.: August House, 1987.

Lister, Robert H., and Florence C. Lister. *Anasazi Pottery: Ten Centuries of Prehistoric Ceramic Art in the Four Corners Country of the Southwestern United States.* Albuquerque: Maxwell Museum of Anthropology and Univ. of New Mexico Press, 1978.

Loftin, John D. *Religion and Hopi Life.* 2d ed. Bloomington: Indiana Univ. Press, 2003.

Lopinot, Neal H. "A New Crop of Data on the Cahokian Polity." In *Agricultural Origins and Development in the Midcontinent,* edited by William Green, 127–53. Office of the State Archaeologist Report 19. Iowa City: Univ. of Iowa, 1994.

Martin, Laura C. *Wildlife Folklore.* Old Saybrook, Conn.: Globe Pequot Press, 1994.

McAdams, William. *Records of Ancient Races in the Mississippi Valley.* St. Louis: C. R. Barns, 1887.

McGregor, John C. *Southwestern Archaeology.* 2d ed. Urbana: Univ. of Illinois Press, 1965.

Milner, George R. *The Cahokia Chiefdom: The Archaeology of a Mississippian Society.* Washington, D.C.: Smithsonian Institution Press, 1998.

Mooney, James. *Myths of the Cherokee.* 1900. Reprint, New York: Dover, 1995.

Moore, Clarence B. "Certain Aboriginal Remains of the Black Warrior River." *Journal of the Academy of Natural Sciences of Philadelphia* 13 (1905): 125–244.

———. "Moundville Revisited." *Journal of the Academy of Natural Sciences of Philadelphia* 13 (1907): 335–405.

Nahohai, Milford, and Elisa Phelps. *Dialogues with Zuni Potters.* Zuni, N.M.: Zuni Ashiwi, 1995.

Paper, Jordan. *Offering Smoke: The Sacred Pipe and Native American Religion.* Moscow: Univ. of Idaho Press, 1988.

Parmalee, Paul W. *Amphibians of Illinois.* Story of Illinois Series, No. 10. Springfield: Illinois State Museum, 1954.

Parsons, Elsie Clews. *Pueblo Indian Religion.* Vols. 1 and 2. Chicago: Univ. of Chicago Press, 1939.

Pauketat, Timothy R. *Ancient Cahokia and the Mississippians.* Cambridge, Mass.: Cambridge Univ. Press, 2004.

Pauketat, Timothy R., and Thomas E. Emerson. "Introduction: Domination and Ideology in the Mississippian World." In *Cahokia: Domination and Ideology in the Mississippian World,* edited by Timothy R. Pauketat and Thomas E. Emerson, 1–29. Lincoln: Univ. of Nebraska Press, 1997.

Pauketat, Timothy R., and Brad Koldehoff. "Cahokian Ritual and the Ramey Field: New Insights from Old Collections." *Southeastern Archaeology* 21, no. 1 (2002): 79–91.

Pauketat, Timothy R., and Neal H. Lopinot. "Cahokian Population Dynamics." In *Cahokia: Domination and Ideology in the Mississippian World,* edited by Timothy R. Pauketat and Thomas E. Emerson, 103–23. Lincoln: Univ. of Nebraska Press, 1997.

Penney, David. W. *Native Arts of North America*. Paris: Terrail Editions, 1998.

Perino, Gregory. "The Late Woodland Component at the Pete Klunk Site, Calhoun County, Illinois." In *Late Woodland Site Archaeology in Illinois I: Investigations in South-Central Illinois*, edited by James A. Brown, 58–89. Bulletin No. 9. Urbana: Illinois Archaeological Survey, 1973.

Phillips, Philip, and James A. Brown. *Pre-Columbian Shell Engravings from the Craig Mound at Spiro, Oklahoma*. Paperback ed., pt. 2. Cambridge, Mass.: Peabody Museum Press, 1984.

Prentice, Guy. "An Analysis of the Symbolism Expressed by the Birger Figurine." *American Antiquity* 51, no. 2 (1986): 239–66.

———. "Origins of Plant Domestication in the Eastern United States: Promoting the Individual in Archaeological Theory." *Southeastern Archaeology* 5, no. 2 (1986): 103–19.

Putnam, Frederic Ward. "The Swallow Collection: Pottery and Stone Artifacts from Mounds near New Madrid, Missouri." 1875. In *The Archaeological Reports of Frederic Ward Putnam*, 3–31. New York: AMS Press, 1973.

Reyman, Jonathan E. "Pala'tkwabi: Red Land of the South." In *The Gran Chichimeca: Essays on the Archaeology and Ethnohistory of Northern Mesoamerica*, edited by Jonathan E. Reyman, 320–35. Brookfield, Vt.: Avebury, 1995.

Riley, Thomas J., Gregory R. Walz, Charles J. Bareis, Andrew C. Fortier, and Kathryn E. Parker, "Accelerator Mass Spectrometer (AMS) Dates Confirm Early Zea Mays in the Mississippi River Valley." *American Antiquity* 59, no. 3 (1994): 490–98.

Schwartz, Amy D. "Colonial New England Agriculture: Old Visions, New Directions." *Agricultural History* 69, no. 3 (1995): 454–81.

Secakuku, Alph H. *Following the Sun and Moon: Hopi Kachina Tradition*. Flagstaff, Ariz.: Northland Publishing and the Heard Museum, 1995.

Smith, Bruce D. *The Emergence of Agriculture*. New York: Scientific American Library, 1998.

Smith, Philip W. "The Amphibians and Reptiles of Illinois." *Illinois Natural History Survey Bulletin* 28, no. 1 (1961): 1–298.

Speck, Frank G. *Ethnology of the Yuchi Indians*. 1909. Reprint, Lincoln: Univ. of Nebraska Press, 2004.

Speck, Frank G., Leonard Broom, and Will West Long. *Cherokee Dance and Drama*. 1951. Reprint, Norman: Univ. of Oklahoma Press, 1983.

Stephen, Alexander M. *Hopi Journal of Alexander M. Stephen*, Pts. 1 and 2. Edited by Elsie Clews Parsons. Columbia Contributions to Anthropology, vol. 23. New York: Columbia Univ. Press, 1936.

Stevenson, Matilda Coxe. *The Zuñi Indians: Their Mythology, Esoteric Fraternities, and Ceremonies*. Annual Report of the U.S. Bureau of American Ethnology, vol. 23, 1901–2. Washington, D.C.: U.S. Bureau of American Ethnology, 1904.

Swanton, John R. *Indian Tribes of the Lower Mississippi Valley and Adjacent Coast of the Gulf of Mexico*. 1911. Reprint, Mineola, N.Y.: Dover, 1998.

———. *Myths and Tales of the Southeastern Indians*. 1929. Reprint, Norman: Univ. of Oklahoma Press, 1995.

Taube, Karl. "Lightning Celts and Corn Fetishes: The Formative Olmec and the Development of Maize Symbolism in Mesoamerica and the American Southwest." In *Olmec Art and Archaeology in Mesoamerica*, edited by John E. Clark and Mary E. Pye, 296–337. Studies in the History of Art 58. Washington, D.C.: National Gallery of Art, 2000.

Titterington, Paul F. "Certain Bluff Mounds of Western Jersey County, Illinois." *American Antiquity* 1 (1935): 6–46.

Unrau, William E. *The Kansa Indians: A History of the Wind People, 1673–1873*. Norman: Univ. of Oklahoma Press, 1971.

Waldman, Carl. *Atlas of the North American Indian*. Rev. ed. New York: Facts on File, 2000.

Watson, Patty Jo. "Prehistoric Gardening and Agriculture in the Midwest and Midsouth." In *Interpretations of Culture Change in the Eastern Woodlands during the Late Woodland Period*, edited by Richard W. Yerkes, 39–67. Occasional Papers in Anthropology No. 3. Columbus: Ohio State Univ., 1988.

Willey, Gordon R. "Mesoamerican Art and Iconography and the Integrity of the Mesoamerican Ideological System." In *New World Archaeology and Culture History: Collected Essays and Articles*, by Gordon Randolph Willey, 297–303. Albuquerque: Univ. of New Mexico Press, 1990.

Williams, Joyce A. "Patrick Phase Lithics." In *The Range Site: Archaic through Late Woodland Occupations (11-S-47)*, by John E. Kelly, Andrew C. Fortier, Steven J. Ozuk, and Joyce A. Williams, 305–46. American Bottom Archaeology: FAI-270 Site Reports, vol. 16. Urbana: Univ. of Illinois Press, 1987.

Young, Biloine Whiting, and Melvin L. Fowler. *Cahokia: The Great Native American Metropolis*. Urbana: Univ. of Illinois Press, 2000.

Young, M. Jane. "The Interconnection between Western Puebloan and Mesoamerican Ideology/Cosmology." In *Kachinas in the Pueblo World*, edited by Polly Schaafsma, 107–20. Albuquerque: Univ. of New Mexico Press, 1994.

Part 2

Real Toads in Imaginary Gardens

Animals in Literature and History

Introduction

Marion W. Copeland

In "Poetry," Marianne Moore announced that we would have no genuine poetry until "the poets among us" are able to "present / for inspection, imaginary gardens with real toads in them."[1] Poet Mary Oliver went further in *A Poetry Handbook*, claiming that the power of poetry comes from both mental inquiry and figurative language, "the very mud and leaves of the world. Without this mud and leaves—and fish and roses and honeybees—the poem would be as dull as a mumble."[2] Animals have been at the heart of human art and story ever since humans began making art and telling stories. Sometimes, when the story only focuses on things human, animals serve the artist as image or symbol. But traditionally, human artists have slipped the boundaries of human experience to inhabit the worlds of wild and domestic animal neighbors, and the animals themselves—"real toads"—are the subjects of the "imaginary gardens" of art and story.

Despite that, little attention is paid by either literary critics or historians to the poet/shamans who make journeys into the worlds of other animals possible. Only students of children's literature have taken them seriously, perhaps because no one objects to the prominence of animals in stories intended for children.[3] The objection comes when the imaginary gardens are clearly intended for adult audiences. "Real toads," say the literary scholars and critics, "do not talk." So stories in which they do talk (or wear clothes or subscribe to Martha Stewart's guides to home decoration) can neither depict real toads nor claim serious adult attention. The "nature faker" controversy of the early twentieth century clearly demonstrates that anthropomorphism, endowing nonhumans with qualities assumed to be solely human, is only palatable to critics in stories intended for the nursery. Thus the turn-of-the-century animal fantasies or animal biographies of such "nature fakers/fakirs" as Ernest Thompson Seton, William Long, or Charles G. D. Roberts, although aimed at young adults, alarmed the critics, perhaps because so many adults also read, enjoyed, and believed them. That contemporary critics have remained more sanguine about the audience appeal of recent crossover novels by J. K. Rowling (Harry Potter series) and Phillip Pullman (His Dark Materials series) suggests the evolving sophistication of the field.[4]

Scholars of animal studies have been, since the field's inception, determined to overcome this cultural, ageist, and speciesist bias, and with it the assumption it supports that humans are qualitatively rather than quantitatively different from—better than, more important than—the other animals. These scholars see anthropomorphism as, at the very least, an essential literary device for translating the ways of nonhumans for human audiences and, at most, an immersion in a world view like those of many indigenous peoples who see the boundary between the human and nonhuman animal as permeable, with each capable of shapeshifting into the other.[5]

In the view of scholars such as Calvin Luther Martin, Randy Malamud, and Barbara Noske, anthropomorphism works to liberate the imagination from domination by what Daniel Quinn's *Ishmael* calls the "Western culture story," freeing it to explore the worlds and ways of other than human beings.[6] Perhaps no literary scholar has said it as well as did the visionary naturalist Henry Beston in *The Outermost House*, his journal of a year on what is now the Cape Cod National Seashore:

> We need another and a wiser and perhaps a more mystical concept of animals. Remote from universal nature, and living by complicated artifice, man in civilization surveys the creature through the glass of his knowledge and sees thereby a feather magnified and the whole image in distortion. We patronize them for their incompleteness, for their tragic fate of having taken form so far below ourselves. And therein we err, and greatly err. For the animal shall not be measured by man. In a world older and more complete than ours they move finished and complete, gifted with extensions of the senses we have lost or never attained, living by voices we shall never hear. They are not our brethren, they are not underlings; they are other nations, caught with ourselves in the net of life and time, fellow prisoners of the splendour and travail of the earth.[7]

Stories in which anthropomorphism works its enchantment, although they may also be satires or allegories useful in helping us view our human selves and culture more clearly, are radical in intent. Toad helpers inhabit these gardens, ready and able to guide us beyond the boundaries most of us have assumed define the real into a closer relationship not only with the earth and its nonhuman animal peoples—or "nations," as Henry Beston called them—but also with our own dimly remembered past, when we too were shapeshifters like all hunter-gatherer humans. The chapters in this section are examples of steps in that direction.

We begin with E. J. W. Hinds's "The Nature and Culture of Species" because it clarifies just how strongly Euro-American culture has objected to anything, artistic or scientific, that questioned the superiority and dominance of the human species. Hinds concludes that the history of taxonomy—the so-called scientific classification of species—"amounts to a story of drawing the lines between human and nonhuman." Despite our widespread acceptance of the theory of evolution and our relative sophistication about our genetic relationship to the other creatures that inhabit the Earth with us, the evidence points to the reality that "the legend of humanity's unchallenged spot at the top of the chain of being remains" at the root of our culture story.

Hinds begins her chapter by observing that it is poets such as Jorge Luis Borges who provide alternative systems of classification that are held less captive by our anthropocentrism and ends with a discussion of the animals, human and nonhuman, found in the imaginary worlds of novels by Thomas Pynchon and Andrew Miller. Both novelists, Hinds contends, use hybridization to confound the prevailing system of classification and to "remind us that, after all, it is the animal qualities—pain, pleasure, pure physicality—that provide the human with humanity." History must include the information about us provided by the nonhuman as well as by the human story. With that perspective in mind, she concludes her chapter with one of Steven Wise's guiding rules for scientific and legal inquiry—one which is obviously just as crucial to the historian and literary critic: "We must be at our most skeptical when we evaluate arguments that confirm the extremely high opinion that we have of ourselves."

Elisabet Sveingar Amundsen finds an equally challenging story in the relationship between Norwegian sportsmen and the reindeer they hunted from 1850 to 1950. Drawing on the sportsmen's own descriptions of reindeer in journals, memoirs, and fiction by writer/sportsmen such as Henrik Ibsen, she traces the changing perceptions of reindeer and the interrelations between the sportsmen's views of the reindeer and of themselves. Initially, Norwegian sportsmen reveled in seeing themselves and their quarry as creatures of the wild, free and unfettered. This vision was largely drawn from the Leatherstocking Tales of James Fenimore Cooper, whose novels inspired new generations of Norwegian sportsmen to get "in touch with nature" and modeled "qualities and values the sportsmen wanted to be a part of their lives." Ironically, however, the fate of the American bison by the turn of the twentieth century had become, along with deforestation, "a worldwide symbol of how nature was destroyed by civilization," providing a caution that discipline in hunting and wildlife management were needed if the reindeer were to avoid the same fate. Thus Amundsen reveals the unresolved dichotomy between an "ethos of discipline and management" and an ideal "spirit of the free, unfettered" hunter and game that characterizes both Norwegian and American thought, undoubtedly to the detriment of humans and game species alike.

Ana Isabel Queiroz and Maria Teresa L. M. B. Andresen's study of the birds in the twentieth-century novels of Portuguese writer Aquilino Ribeiro reveals that these literary works, as much as the sportsmen's observations in Amundsen's study, provide environmental histories for periods and places in which studies in environmental matters are scarce or nonexistent. Earlier literary critics have interpreted Ribeiro's novels, as well as the novels of writers in other countries, equally as observant of the natural world, only in anthropocentric terms. What Queiroz and Andresen demonstrate is the deep connections between humans and the lands they inhabit in these works and how deeply the animals, wild and domestic, who also share that land affect both the environment and its human inhabitants. Ribeiro observes the birds with the eye and knowledge of a naturalist, making them, as Moore suggested they must be, "real toads . . . in imaginary gardens," fit subjects for novelist, biologist, and environmentalist alike.

The animals in the fictions discussed by Susan Braden and Tonia L. Payne function in related ways but serve as well to illustrate two old and venerable functions of animals in human story. Braden's tiger, studied in the works of Borges, becomes not only a "real toad"—the animal valued for itself—but also a symbol for the writer's psychic and psychological evolution. The two functions come together in what Braden points to as Borges's "most famous" works, his "fantastic short stories" in which "the lines between fictional reality and the ordinary"— and between human and animal—"are ruptured." Because Borges believed that man cannot be fully human without identifying himself as a part of the animal world, he produces "imaginary gardens" in which human and animal become one by breaking the boundary separating the two. Thus, by the end of her chapter, Braden's reader, like Borges's reader, is ready to be concerned that the tiger benefit from its relationship with humanity as much as humanity has benefited from its relationship with the tiger. The animal's status as an endangered species suggests how far we are from achieving that attitude in the real world.

Payne's study of the "imaginary gardens" of Ursula K. Le Guin focuses on Le Guin's reconfiguration of the traditional animal fable in order to emphasize the writer's thematic concern with the status of the Other. Le Guin's Others can be human as well as nonhuman, but it is with the latter that Payne concerns herself. Whereas Borges and the tiger become one as the poet/writer uses the creature as a symbol, Le Guin shifts our viewpoint by "placing her readers in a situation in which we become the other." We learn, thereby, not only how it feels to be othered but also how it feels to be nonhuman, to be wolf, coyote, "dark brother," and "shadow soul." In some of her tales, Le Guin makes the shapeshifting literal, as in "The Wife's Tale." In others, as in *Buffalo Gals*, the shifting is from the human to the nonhuman world. Myra, having lost an eye in the accident that strands her in this magic world, acquires a new, "animal" eye that allows her to achieve a new vision, a nonanthropocentric point of view. She finds herself able to talk with the animals on whom her life now depends—clearly Le Guin's reminder of how all human life depends on the well being of the other animals, a lesson learned in part from the indigenous peoples her ethnographer parents studied.[8]

All of these chapters strive, as Le Guin does, not only to teach readers new rules to the game of life but also to introduce them to a new/old game that levels the playing field for all players, human and nonhuman. Payne concludes: "Through the experiences [of the 'real toads'] in ['the imaginary gardens' of] Le Guin's animal stories, the reader is implicitly urged to reconsider her or his own relationship with the natural world, with the other." That magic, at the heart of human art and story from their beginning, can transport us into a world larger and richer than the walled-off garden Western humans have constructed to separate themselves from the Others, a world in which humans count themselves as one species among many, rather than as a solitary alien—a home rather than a prison.

Notes

1. Marianne Moore, "Poetry," in *Observations*, by Marianne Moore (New York: Dial Press, 1924), 30–31.

2. Mary Oliver, *A Poetry Handbook* (New York: Harcourt, Brace, 1994), 107.

3. Although there are many such scholars well worth citing, the pioneering works of Jonathan Cott and Ann Swinfen exemplify how "children's" animal novels, particularly animal fantasy, benefit from sophisticated criticism: Jonathan Cott, *Piper at the Gates of Dawn: The Wisdom of Children's Literature* (New York: Random House, 1981); Ann Swinfen, *In Defence of Fantasy: A Study of the Genre in English and American Literature since 1945* (London: Routledge & Kegan Paul, 1984). More recently, a number of valuable anthologies and special issues of journals have been published that focus on or include scholarly treatments of such novels. To mention only a few: Arien Mack, ed., "In the Company of Animals," *Social Research* 62, no. 3 (Fall 1995); Jennifer Ham and Matthew Senior, eds., *Animal Acts: Configuring the Human in Western History* (New York: Routledge, 1997); and Sidney I. Dobrin and Kenneth B. Kidd, eds., *Wild Things: Children's Culture and Ecocriticism* (Detroit: Wayne State Univ. Press, 2004).

4. For the "nature faker" controversy, see Ralph H. Lutts, *The Nature-Fakers: Wildlife, Science, and Sentiment* (Golden, Colo.: Fulcrum Press, 1990) and Ralph H. Lutts, ed., *The Wild Animal Story* (Philadelphia: Temple Univ. Press, 1998). For response to contemporary crossover novels, particularly crossover animal fantasies, see Marion W. Copeland, "Crossover Animal Fantasy Series: Crossing Cultural and Species as Well as Age Boundaries," *Society & Animals* 11, no. 3 (2003): 287–98.

5. For more on this topic, see Barbara Noske, *Beyond Boundaries: Human and Animal* (Montreal: Black Rose Press, 1997); Calvin Luther Martin, *In the Spirit of the Earth: Rethinking History and Time* (Baltimore: Johns Hopkins Univ. Press, 1992); and Calvin Luther Martin, *The Way of the Human Being* (New Haven: Yale Univ. Press, 1999). Many other thinkers and scholars (Max Oelschlaeger and David Rains Wallace come immediately to mind) as well as writers and artists too numerous to list here are presently engaged in helping audiences reach toward an understanding of the world views of others, human and nonhuman. Literary scholars as well are lending support to the effort; see particularly Randy Malamud's *Poetic Animals and Animal Souls* (New York: Macmillan Palgrave, 2003).

6. Martin, *Spirit of the Earth*; Martin, *Way of the Human Being*; Malamud, *Poetic Animals*; Noske, *Beyond Boundaries*; Daniel Quinn, *Ishmael* (New York: Bantam/Turner, 1992).

7. Henry Beston, *The Outermost House* (1928; reprint, New York: Ballantine Books, 1971), 19–20.

8. Le Guin's parents were Alfred L. Kroeber and Theodora Covel Brown Kracaw Kroeber, who held a joint appointment at the University of California–Berkeley.

Works Cited

Beston, Henry. *The Outermost House.* 1928. Reprint, New York: Ballantine Books, 1971.

Copeland, Marion W. "Crossover Animal Fantasy Series: Crossing Cultural and Species as Well as Age Boundaries." *Society & Animals* 11, no. 3 (2003): 287–98.

Cott, Jonathan. *Pipers at the Gates of Dawn: The Wisdom of Children's Literature.* New York: Random House, 1981.

Dobrin, Sidney I., and Kenneth B. Kidd, eds. *Wild Things: Children's Culture and Eco-criticism.* Detroit: Wayne State Univ. Press, 2004.

Ham, Jennifer, and Matthew Senior, eds. *Animal Acts: Configuring the Human in Western History.* New York: Routledge, 1997.

Lutts, Ralph H. *The Nature Fakers: Wildlife, Science, and Sentiment.* Golden, Colo.: Fulcrum Press, 1990.

———, ed. *The Wild Animal Story.* Philadelphia: Temple Univ. Press, 1998.

Mack, Arien, ed. "In the Company of Animals." *Social Research* 62, no. 3 (Fall 1995).

Malamud, Randy. *Poetic Animals and Animal Souls.* New York: Macmillan Palgrave, 2003.

Martin, Calvin Luther. *In the Spirit of the Earth: Rethinking History and Time.* Baltimore: Johns Hopkins Univ. Press, 1992.

———. *The Way of the Human Being.* New Haven: Yale Univ. Press, 1999.

Moore, Marianne. "Poetry." In *Observations,* by Marianne Moore, 30–31. New York: Dial Press, 1924.

Noske, Barbara. *Beyond Boundaries: Human and Animal.* Montreal: Black Rose Press, 1997.

Oliver, Mary. *A Poetry Handbook.* New York: Harcourt, Brace, 1994.

Quinn, Daniel. *Ishmael.* New York: Bantam/Turner, 1992.

Swinfen, Ann. *In Defence of Fantasy: A Study of the Genre in English and American Literature since 1945.* London: Routledge & Kegan Paul, 1984.

Chapter 5

The Nature and Culture of Species
Eighteenth-Century and Contemporary Views

E. J. W. Hinds

Many readers will recall Michel Foucault's famous allusion to an imaginary taxonomy in Borges, which invents a "certain Chinese encyclopaedia" where it is written that

> "animals are divided into (a) belonging to the Emperor, (b) embalmed, (c) tame, (d) sucking pigs, (e) sirens, (f) fabulous, (g) stray dogs, (h) included in the present classification, (I) frenzied, (j) innumerable, (k) drawn with a very fine camelhair brush, (l) *et cetera*, (m) having just broken the water pitcher, (n) that from a long way off look like flies." In the wonderment of this taxonomy, the thing we apprehend in one great leap, the thing that, by means of the fable, is demonstrated as the exotic charm of another system of thought, is the limitation of our own, the stark impossibility of thinking *that*.[1]

This is how Foucault opens his study of the epistemic shifts in taxonomies in the modern era, *The Order of Things*, to point to their basic manipulability. Indeed, we have long since recognized the folly of classification schemes. Or we think we have. Keith Thomas notes that taxonomists since Aristotle have classified plants and animals according to their usefulness to humans, often with bizarre results. Thus "John Parkinson in 1640 used such categories for plants as 'sweet-smelling,' 'purging,' 'venomous, sleepy and hurtful' and 'strange and outlandish.'" "Even today," Thomas writes, "English lawyers impose human criteria upon animals by dividing species into 'dangerous' and 'nondangerous,' though admitting that 'such a division is not to be found in nature.'"[2] Perhaps Borges was fabricating less than one might imagine.

In this chapter, I will look at the history of such classifications—the history of natural history—to try to make out a relationship between the originating moment of natural history and our current views of animals in Euro-American culture. This history is, among other things, a legend of relentless progress toward increasingly fine divisions in nature, using increasingly mature technologies, toward a goal of increasingly pure taxonomies. Taking as my test case the phenomenon of the hybrid—both officially registered and imaginary crossed species—I suggest that eighteenth-century taxonomies codified under the Linnaean system relegated hybrids to provinces of popular culture under the sign of "scientific" classification. Natural history exhibits in Europe displayed hybrids early in the eighteenth century as *exemplars* of taxonomies, as did those in the United States as late as Charles Willson Peale's museum, founded in 1786. By century's end, however, hybrids were almost always regarded as "freaks of nature," outside official taxonomy. In this early modern shift in perspective, a mechanized definition of all animal species had been ratcheted up several notches. Currently, we have entered a new age of mechanization in taxonomy; now, however, the materialism at the bottom of species definition resides at the molecular level in DNA mapping. And once again, with our new technologies of mechanization, the boundaries between species—and alongside them, the reclassification of hybrids—are shifting.

While Swedish botanist Carl von Linné (1707–1778), better known as Carolus Linnaeus, was not the first taxonomist of species, it was his classification in the mid-eighteenth century that formed the international language by which species are still known today. His magisterial *Systema Naturae* (1735–68) revolutionized taxonomy with the "sexual system" of classification, under which plants and animals were to be known by their reproductive systems. Linnaeus's work followed centuries of natural history that had been approaching purely physical definitions. Although as early as Aristotle's *Historia Animalium*, species were seen to share physical features, most premodern systems, such as medieval bestiaries, saw non-human species as merely allegories of the human condition: "The world was a cryptogram full of hidden meanings for man," Thomas writes.[3] Yet Linnaeus's institutionally recognized system, and alongside it the views of the Frenchman the Comte de Buffon, the Italian Andrea Cesalpino, and the Englishmen John Ray and even John Locke, shifted species classification into a purely mechanical set of criteria.

What was distinct about Linnaeus's system was the same empiricism that drove the many other "classifying" projects of eighteenth-century science—Boyle's experiments with gases, for example, or Franklin's with electricity, which required visual observation—just as it was enabled by improved technologies such as magnifying glass. Such empiricism attempted to jettison the more fabulous aspects of earlier classifications of nature. No longer were species to be tainted with mystical, spiritual, or religious significance; indeed, as Paul Lawrence Farber notes, the philosophes in France, among them Buffon, led the ideology of the new naturalism and "sought to replace a traditional Christian worldview with a naturalistic one based on human reason," that is, based on the concept of natural laws governing the physical world.[4] Importantly, this new system incorporated historical perspective, with the view that to understand present species, one had to understand species change over time, including hybridizations.

The hybrid served both to threaten and to confirm newly empirical taxonomies, because it had long been the kind of nonclassifiable category which, by virtue of its borderline status, had been infused with marvelous, spiritual, even religious significance. Popular interest in and display of "monsters," rare hybrids or hybrid individuals thought to represent monstrous species, as Dennis Todd, Harriet Ritvo, and others have pointed out, was more common than might be imagined for an era so taxonomically obsessed.[5] I would argue, in fact, that it was the very pressure on hybridity "from above"—the official scramble to create order out of hybridity by classification—that fueled a continued interest, among popular and sometimes learned cultures, in the rather traditional view of hybrids as "monsters," what Allison Pingree helpfully describes as "various types of 'in-betweenness'" included in both the period's "extensive taxonomies" and popular display.[6] As "hybrids" displaced "monsters" within the scientific community during the eighteenth century, "monsters" came to be the sole province of popular culture; this shift in fundamental understandings was represented in the proliferation of displays at fairs in England and in the growing "scientific" natural history community in the United States.

"From antiquity through the nineteenth century," Karyn Valerius writes, "*monster* was the term used by scholars and surgeons and common folk alike to refer to human births marked by death or deformity, as well as to abnormal plant or animal formations."[7] Yet an important shift in the *interpretation* of "monsters" came, throughout the eighteenth century, to produce a split between scientific and popular cultures on the subject. As Katherine Park and Lorraine Daston explain,

> In the early years of the Reformation, the tendency to treat monsters as prodigies—frightening signs of God's wrath dependent ultimately or solely on his will—was almost universal. By the end of the seventeenth century only the most popular forms of literature—ballads, broadsides, and the occasional religious pamphlet—treated monsters in this way. For the educated layman, full of Baconian enthusiasm, and even more for the professional scientist of 1700, the religious associations of monsters were merely another manifestation of popular ignorance and superstition, fostering uncritical wonder rather than the sober investigation of natural causes.[8]

What I see as the "hybridization" of monsters among scientists relegated "monsters" to popularity: hybrids "now belonged wholly to natural history, the products of wholly natural causes or 'general rules.' . . . Although the 'miracles of nature,' including monsters and the rest of the prodigy canon, could be 'comprehended under some Form or fixed Law,' for Bacon they nonetheless constituted a coherent category rather than a miscellaneous collection of phenomena."[9] Theories of extinction, for example, were revolutionizing Western understanding such that hybrids could be viewed as manifestations of change over time, not as signs from God; but these theories were acceptable only among some, notably scientific, communities.

That the several Linnaean taxonomic projects focused interest on the monstrous is confirmed by Dennis Todd, who explains that the "sheer volume of this literature of monsters was immense, spanning everything from popular ballads and broadsides to recondite treatises," the latter increasingly suspicious of "monstrosity" as a serious category.[10] In England, popular interest in monsters was to be seen in the proliferation of exhibitions at fairs, both cause and symptom of the monster mania. Giants and dwarfs made up a large number of exhibitions, but "the third popular attraction at the Fair were creatures which blurred the distinction between men and beasts. Apes and monkeys were taught to mimic human actions, and other animals were trained so that they appeared to have the skills or intelligence of men: an elephant that could raise a flag and shoot a gun, a troop of eight dancing dogs, dressed in the newest French fashions, who appeared at the Southwark Fair in the early eighteenth century and later performed before Queen Anne."[11] Furthermore, "at the other end of the spectrum were human beings who seemed to have degenerated into animals": the Northumberland Monster, who sported the head of a horse and the body of a man; a boy covered in fish scales; and a boy covered in bristles all over, like a hedgehog, among a number of unnamable human hybrids.[12]

These displays were not new to the eighteenth century, though they were newly popular on a large scale. Pliny the Elder's *Historia Naturalis* (77 c.e.) was widely popular throughout medieval Europe, serving as source book for the well-circulated *Travels* of Sir John Mandeville, which in turn informed travelers such as Columbus. Equally well known were such Latin texts as the seventh-century *Etymologiae* of Isidorus, bishop of Sevilla, while the late Middle Ages had offered the *De Imagine Mundi* of Honorius Augustodunensis (c. 1220), as Peter Mason describes.[13] What these works were concerned to describe were, early on, *species* of monstrous creatures, oddities ranging from the often-reported dog-headed men, to men with their faces in their chests, to—always the last extreme—anthropophagi (cannibals), who only sometimes were described as actual hybrids. As several histories attest, these "races" of monsters were almost always reported to the recorder secondhand; they are said to live just over the next mountain, for instance, a few islands over, or even right next door, but in each case, the reporter has not *seen* the monster himself: they lived in cultural memory only.

As Mason writes about the histories of Pliny and Isidorus, "The monstrous human races are part of a system of roughly concentric circles with their centre in the region of Italy or Greece. The further one progresses from the centre, the wilder the inhabitants become."[14] That Columbus and others "found" so much monstrosity to report in the New World comes, therefore, as little surprise. Columbus, for instance, in a 1493 letter to Luis de Santegel, reported hearing about a region "where the people with the tails are born," even though he is at this point describing a portion of his journey during which his interpreters were absent and he very likely misunderstood his informants.[15] Marc Lescarbot represented the natives of Canada as "sitting on their tails like apes."[16]

Ambroise Paré's sixteenth-century *Des Monstres et Prodiges* carried on the medieval view that monstrous species are included in "the perfections of the whole, which represents the great body of the universe."[17] In other words, monsters simply defined the outside limits of God's creation. During the seventeenth century, study of monstrous species gave way to study of monstrous individuals, the "condition" coming to be viewed as biological pathology. As Karyn Valerius informs us, "Seventeenth-century science initiated the investigation of monsters as natural rather than supernatural phenomena."[18] As a result, treatises like Paré's were studied with suspicion: the "second edition of *Des Monstres et Prodiges* in 1575 provoked a vigorous attack by the Faculty of Medicine at Paris on the author's competence and integrity. . . . Details of this condemnation furnish informative examples of the new 'scientific' attitude, which eschewed 'wonder' for fact."[19] Paré's "condemnation by the intellectual establishment of the time reveals the beginnings of the tendency to exile to the ranks of the popular the monstrous representations that once functioned at the highest levels of intellectual discourse."[20]

Indeed, as scientific *and* popular communities enforced the increasingly "official" and therefore respectable with the Latinate binomials associated with Linnaean taxonomy, the reality of species themselves was confirmed by such naming. As Harriet Ritvo explains,

> Like any system of classification, that of Linnaeus required an associated terminology; and, as with any system, the elation between categorization and naming was so close as to make it difficult to distinguish between them. Yet, from the beginning, naturalists were inclined to perceive Linnaean nomenclature as somewhat independent of the taxonomic scheme to which it ostensibly belonged.[21]

But, naturally, official circles—the higher "class" of natural history—ridiculed and rejected the use of Latinate binomials by those among the popular orders, particularly those who would attempt to legitimate the discourse of monstrosity at, perhaps, the expense of the "scientific" hybrid. Since "naming constituted a strong, if metaphoric, claim to possession," then an "energetically enforced standard of nomenclatural propriety would embody and reinforce hierarchical order both inside the zoological community and in the larger society," she explains. "Consequently, the errors and eccentricities in nomenclature that attracted the most severe and protracted criticism . . . were those that most clearly associated their perpetrators with groups considered obnoxious for political or social reasons."[22] Those ordinary citizens who would, for instance, name species they discovered using this nomenclature could be, by the nineteenth century, condemned by the likes of Charles Darwin; they were merely "species-mongers," creating a *"vast amount of bad work,"* wanting to "have their vanity tickled."[23] Hybrids under the new scientism remained hybrids, evacuated of any claim to meaningful monstrosity as the power even to name species remained firmly with the government- and organization-sponsored scientists. The shift of monstrosity to suspicious popularity is most usefully summarized by Rosemarie Garland Thomson, who writes that "a movement from a narrative of the marvelous to a narrative of the deviant" signals the "collective cultural transformations into modernity."[24]

Modernity, inclusive of Linnaean-style classification, renewed popular fascination with definitions of nature. Todd makes the case that such fascination centered on a freshly felt puzzlement about the boundaries of bodies, which I would see as a popular result of taxonomic efforts in botany and the animal sciences.

Popular interest in "monstrous births," such as the succession of rabbits Mary Toft famously "birthed" over several months in 1726, exemplified this new fascination about species via a longstanding, indeed ancient, belief that "the imagination was the faculty that mediated the transactions between the body and the mind." So a pregnant woman's imagination, for example, could result in a cross-species birth, since that "faculty" allowed for transference from the nonmaterial mind to the physical body.[25] Ritvo describes, to give one example, the "case of trans-specific maternal impression": a hairy-backed girl whose hybridity was "attributed to prenatal fright by an organ grinder's monkey."[26] It isn't a stretch, following this reasoning, to allow for similar transfers from species to species, the body providing only, as Francis Bacon called it, a "narrow Suture" by way of boundary to cross.[27] Todd concludes that the "puzzlement" over the mechanism by which these boundaries may be crossed "indicates how thoroughly the eighteenth century was living amidst the wreckage of explanation."[28]

Rather than succumb to the wreckage, scientists now preferred to classify and arrange. What with the vulgar classes embracing the mysterious, perhaps even supernatural, spectacle of monstrosity, the scientific community turned to hybridity—taxonomically possible as *exceptions* to general rules of species: "the collection and display of monsters occurred during a readjustment," Peter Mason writes, "to scientific investment in singularity from an attention to objects and bodies themselves to an emergent focus on the ways in which such 'ethnographic subjects' conformed to taxonomies."[29] Much of the taxonomic practice among scientists, in fact, grew out of a class bias. Thomas notes, for example, that common, traditional names for plants and animals were viewed as not only scientifically incorrect but also downright vulgar by the likes of Sir Thomas Browne. The common "hound's piss" plant comes to mind as a perhaps legitimate example, along with "pissabed" (dandelion) and "maidenhair."[30] Encouragement of Latin terminology further widened the divide between learned and popular discourse about species; "those who wish to remain ignorant of the Latin language," according to John Berkenhout in 1789, "have no business with the study of botany."[31] In short, "monsters," like the common names among the vulgar, came to belong within the boundaries of popular culture as scientists invented categories and "laws" to demystify hybrids.

The popularizing of monsters, with the concomitant rift between scientific and popular cultures, could not have been more fully played out than in the various Peale's museums in the United States. American-born, London-trained portrait painter Charles Willson Peale opened the first American museum in 1786 in Philadelphia—a museum devoted to natural and cultural history, with an increasing number of displays of animals, vegetables, and minerals over the thirty-five years it remained open. Peale's most famous exhibit was his "mastodon," the complete and reconstructed skeleton of a mammoth he and a crew excavated in upstate New York. Among his thousands of displays were "a large collection of minerals, four thousand species of insects, ninety species of stuffed quadrupeds, and over seven hundred mounted birds."[32] And among these exhibits, Peale displayed oddities of all sorts, including a one-eyed hog, an "orang-utan," and a supposed unicorn. His museum appealed both to current scientific discourse and to use by an "industrious middling population," who stood to benefit from the education such a museum might provide, as "an institutional form derived from aristocratic precedents, but adapted to fulfill a particularly American and republican goal: a universally educated public."[33] Using a Linnaean classification system from 1794 on, Peale also made the museum attractive to women, with special "ladies'" rates, and to the working class, by keeping the museum open on weeknights.

By ordering "natural curiosities" alongside "legitimate" species with no apparent distinctions made among them, his collection "deliberately exploited" the effect of "wonder" from an earlier, less taxonomically obsessed time, which gave him the image of a "showman" and his museum the aura of a theater—both coming under some suspicion by many scientists as being rather vulgar.[34] European visitors would offer a variety of responses, ranging from John Bernard's comment that "no traveller has entered [Philadelphia] without awarding the proprieter his due meed of praise," to John M. Duncan's quip that "a good deal [of the museum] is worth seeing, mingled with many miscellaneous monstrosities which are not worth house-room."[35] American Frances Wright spoke for many in a comment stinging with wounded class and political propriety:

> The State-house, state-house no longer in any thing but name, is an interesting object to a stranger, and, doubtless, a sacred shrine in the eyes of Americans. I know not but that I was a little offended to find stuffed birds, and beasts, and mammoth skeletons filling the place of senators and sages. It had been in better taste, perhaps, to turn the upper rooms of this empty sanctuary into a library, instead of a museum of natural curiosities, or a mausoleum of dead monsters.[36]

On display in museums, fairs, and other points of performance in the eighteenth century were monstrous bodies whose very existence defied taxonomy. In their slippage between categories, these creatures likewise defied both anthropomorphism and allegorization, being individual instances pitted against the abstract "species" offered by science; to some degree, they increasingly defied class sensibilities, as Frances Wright's comment attests. Once accepted as part of a divine natural order, hybrids became, by the late eighteenth century, suspiciously "unnatural," outside of taxonomy's rule. This change from symbolic and portentous to purely physical, from official to popular culture, played out in eighteenth-century scientific taxonomy as species came to be defined as pure mechanism, a view which only widened during the nineteenth century.

My purpose here is not to trace the history of natural history from the eighteenth century to the present, however, but to compare the current scientific era with natural history's originating moments. What we find now is not a coherent *scientific* field for comparison but rather a renewed interest in the boundaries of species scattered across the *cultural* terrain of the West, just as eighteenth-century popular culture took up the question of species during that earlier era of reclassification. With new technologies enabling DNA mapping to parallel earlier enabling improvements, there is once again pressure to redraw the lines between species, to redesign what is considered pure and what is regarded as hybrid.

Steven Wise, for instance, the foremost animal rights lawyer in the United States, makes the case that chimpanzees and bonobos should be legally reclassified due to their genetic similarity to humans.[37] Sharing 98.7 percent of their DNA profile with *Homo sapiens*, chimpanzees belong, Wise argues, more properly in the genus *Homo* and should enjoy legal rights commensurate with their status as both conscious and sentient. Stephen Jay Gould more eloquently puts the point: humans "cannot represent a separate family, lest we commit the genealogical absurdity of uniting two more-distant forms (chimps and gorillas) in the same family and excluding a third creature (humans) more closely related to one of the two united species. I surely cannot claim," he goes on, "to be more closely related to my uncle than to my brother, but we make exactly such a statement when we argue that chimps are closer to gorillas than to humans."[38]

Morris Goodman argues that now-traditional taxonomy is a holdover of a pre-Darwinian Great Chain of Being idea, simply confirming with little mechanical evidence that *Homo sapiens* rules.[39] The question now is as always: do the links in the chain specify clear *distinctions* between related species or do they indicate clear *relations* between them? Naturally, the controversy over these issues is fierce. Marc Hauser, to take only one example, argues that, for all of our shared physical characteristics, behaviorally speaking, even the most advanced animals like chimps "have no role to play in shaping the moral community because they have an impoverished capacity for inhibition and conceptual change."[40] He is arguing specifically against those such as Wise and Masson, as did Julian Huxley earlier in the twentieth century, who took the view that evolution has led humanity to a level of moral and aesthetic values inconceivable by nonhuman animals.[41] If Wise's inclination to reconsider taxonomic boundaries takes newer technologies into consideration —"reliance on DNA, its relative objectivity and lack of arbitrariness"—those in favor of more traditional taxonomies are forced into new criteria for confirming human dominance.[42] David Barash, for example, claims that "we are not only *part* of nature, but strangely *outside* it as well, creatures who in many ways have transcended our organic selves, to think and do things that no other animal ever thinks or does."[43] Culture, in Barash's mind quite distinct from nature, is the evolutionary step that nonhuman animals cannot take. Now that our genetics hints at uncomfortably close likeness to other species, the new taxonomy simply slides the argument over to different criteria—the moral sense, culture—to draw the lines in the same old places. What these positions regarding culture do not consider is the growing evidence that nonhuman animals *do* participate in their own and sometimes human culture, as evidenced by the research and meta-analysis of Jeffrey Moussaieff Masson in *When Elephants Weep*; his observations of elephant culture alone, with its elaborate rituals and friend, kin, and adopted kind relationships, should be enough to move the sliding scale of animal nature-culture back toward the human.[44]

As did eighteenth-century taxonomists, some latter-day thinkers such as Hauser project onto scientific "objectivity" a fundamental queasiness about crossing the lines between human and nonhuman animal. As a result of these new shifts, the hybrid, scientifically problematic, is once again perceived to be acceptable only on popular culture's terms. Jan Bondeson, for instance, a medical historian, brands hybridity with a view of popular culture as liminal—indeed, as "vulgar" as his eighteenth-century counterparts in the Royal Society would construe both hybrids and the strata of culture in which they were deemed acceptable: "Various oddballs and political extremists do their best to supply explanations—from their own warped minds—of . . . freaks of nature."[45] He then proceeds to place hybridity firmly in a *cultural* history, parsing it as only a fantastic category.

As biologists study genetic structure, the hybrid seems naturalized only within popular cultural terms. Katharine Park and Lorraine Daston explain that the elitism that split official and popular culture over the matter of taxonomy is as much a reality now as it was then: hybrids "are frankly popular; indeed, they are so popular as to border on the undignified. . . . 'Serious' journalists scorn the tabloids, 'serious' novelists shun science fiction, and their readers often follow suit."[46] And yet popular culture, a diverse array of discursive and visual practices, does not itself overwhelmingly accept the hybrid as natural, nor is any one facet of popular culture always separated across a firm divide from the more staunchly taxonomic view of scientists. Any quick check of the news over the past several years will reveal a near-obsession with the creation and use of transgenic creatures—plants and animals, unrelated in nature, blended scientifically by crossing strands of DNA. While the benefits of these products to humanity are hawked even in television commercials (improved medical care, for instance, and "improved" food sources), popular discussion, including that of ethicists, often looks on transgenic cross-breeding as unnatural, potentially dangerous, even immoral.

Donald Griffin summarizes a view that confuses attention to nonhuman species with a kind of philosophical contamination by hybridity, prominent though not exclusively held in scientific circles:

> Much of twentieth-century science gradually slipped into an attitude that belittles nonhuman animals. Subtle but effective nonverbal signals to this effect emanate from much of the scientific literature. Physical and chemical science is assumed to be more fundamental, more rigorous, and more significant than zoology. Modern biology revels in being largely molecular, and this inevitably diverts attention from the investigation of animals for their own sakes. Part of this mechanomorphic trend may be due to an unrecognized reaction against the deflation of human vanity by the Darwinian revolution. The acceptance of biological evolution and the genetic relationship of our species to others was a shattering blow to the human ego from which we may not have fully recovered. It is not easy to give

up a deep-seated faith that our kind is completely different in kind
from all other living organisms.[47]

Cultural treatments of the same issues can either entertain hybridity as legitimate
or relegate it to the threatening conceptual universe of the in-between, varying
according to genre and approach. Science fiction—both in film and literature—
may legitimate the hybrid by treating it (them? him? her?) as worthy of rights and
as an entity in its own right, as in the film *An American Werewolf in London*, but
may also question its position as "natural," as in, for instance, *The Fly*, in which the
only choice for the hybrid is either to become either human or insect, or die.

New attention to the boundaries between species produced in 1997 two literary explorations of hybridity set, significantly, in the eighteenth century—the
first paradigm shift regarding taxonomy in the modern era. In the United States,
Thomas Pynchon's magisterial novel *Mason & Dixon* rounds out a landscape that
covers much of the globe (England, South Africa, Europe) with hybrid and meta-
morphosing creatures. Pynchon engages the taxonomic enterprise by representing
species as hybrid and transforming, with several talking dogs, a man who morphs
into a beaver during the full moon, and Vaucanson's mechanical duck. Hybrids
other than purely animal appear in this novel as well: a teenaged boy who changes
not into a werewolf during a full moon but into a well-dressed and well-behaved
young fop; giant, sentient vegetables appear in a scene reminiscent of "Jack and the
Beanstalk"; golems both large and "kitchen-sized" appear;[48] and in South Africa,
even clocks take on personality and talk. With these hybrids, Pynchon recon-
figures, as he also represents, eighteenth-century species debates that were both
scientifically progressive and anachronistically enchanted within popular culture.
Mason & Dixon is both an accurate representation of a populist eighteenth century—one which viewed many species as fluid and interchangeable—and a critique of the generalizing classification schemes that finally disenchanted the study
of species at the same time taxonomy participated in imperialism and supported
slavery in a once-promising New World.

Andrew Miller's *Ingenious Pain* offers an English counterpart to Pynchon's
discourse on hybridity. This novel seamlessly combines various cultures of
eighteenth-century England: it features the medical world, progressive psycho-
therapeutic practices, and experiments with Boyle's air pump while we are treated
to a background and foreground peopled with less "officially" recognized members of the cultural terrain—a mermaid, a cabinet of wonders, table-top-sized
automata, and a hermaphroditic doctor who collects human oddities for medical experiments. James Dyer, born without the capacity to experience pain, is an
oddity of a protagonist in that he is himself a "monster," used, in fact, at one point
in his life as a sort of sideshow freak for the demonstration and sale of a cure-all
"medicine." This novel of wonders has a landscape that is all but enchanted: there
are so many hybrids and oddities that they make up the warp and woof of the
ordinary. Animals are as present as people in this nature, both hybrid and otherwise, and they insist that, after all, it is the animal qualities—pain, pleasure, pure

physicality—that provide the human with humanity. Both *Ingenious Pain* and *Mason & Dixon* are clear about how the animal and the hybrid creature are to be taken: if the joy of the tactile that James Dyer lacks represents the soul he also lacks, both novels explore, fundamentally, what it means to be human.

Such renewed attention to taxonomy and hybridity, even in contemporary fictions, signals a cultural anxiety regarding species. Even J. M. Coetzee's magnificent *The Lives of Animals*, an otherwise thoughtful exploration of the potentially "soft" boundary between human and nonhuman, has the most animal-sympathetic character say, "Hybrids are, or ought to be, sterile. . . . [They are] monstrous thinking devices mounted inexplicably on suffering animal bodies."[49] Conceived as neither/nor, the hybrid as culturally rendered remains as mysterious and monstrous as the medieval bestiary would have it; post-Enlightenment culture has worked, however, to root out that in-between-ness, to draw ever-finer lines between species in order to close the gap between the species.

My point is not so much about hybrids per se except insofar as they provide a limit case of eighteenth-century and current species discussion. Attitudes toward hybridity demonstrate exclusivity and purity that were and are the goals of empirical classification. The history of taxonomy amounts to a story of drawing the lines between human and nonhuman. As we redraw them now, our criteria have changed, but the legend of humanity's unchallenged spot at the top of the chain of being remains. Now, as then, scientific taxonomy can be blind to its own cultural motivations, no less than cultural explanations fail to address often glaring scientific evidence. I will end, then, with one of Steven Wise's guiding questions for scientific and legal inquiry, or Wise's Rule Number 2: "We must be at our most skeptical when we evaluate arguments that confirm the extremely high opinion that we have of ourselves."[50]

Notes

1. Michel Foucault, *The Order of Things* (New York: Vintage Books, 1970), xv.

2. Keith Thomas, *Man and the Natural World: Changing Attitudes in England, 1500–1800* (New York: Oxford Univ. Press), 53, 57.

3. Ibid., 64.

4. Paul Lawrence Farber, *Finding Order in Nature: The Naturalist Tradition from Linnaeus to E. O. Wilson* (Baltimore: Johns Hopkins Univ. Press, 2000), 17.

5. Dennis Todd, *Imagining Monsters: Miscreations of the Self in Eighteenth-Century England* (Chicago: Univ. of Chicago Press, 1995); Harriet Ritvo, *The Platypus and the Mermaid and Other Figments of the Classifying Imagination* (Cambridge, Mass.: Harvard Univ. Press, 1997).

6. Allison Pingree, "America's 'United Siamese Brothers': Chang and Eng and Nineteenth-Century Ideologies of Democracy and Domesticity," in *Monster Theory*, ed. Jeffrey Jerome Cohen (Minneapolis: Univ. of Minnesota Press, 1996), 95.

7. Karyn Valerius, "The Monstrous Genealogy of Assisted Reproduction," in *Playing Dolly: Technocultural Formations, Fantasies, and Fictions of Assisted Reproduction,* ed. E. Ann Kaplan and Susan Merrill Squier (New Brunswick, N.J.: Rutgers Univ. Press, 1999), 174.

8. Katharine Park and Lorraine J. Daston, "Unnatural Conceptions: The Study of Monsters in Sixteenth- and Seventeenth-Century France and England," *Past and Present* 92 (1981): 24.

9. Ibid., 43.

10. Todd, *Imagining Monsters,* 44.

11. Ibid., 147.

12. Ibid.

13. Peter Mason, *Deconstructing America: Representations of the Other* (New York: Routledge, 1990).

14. Ibid., 79.

15. Quoted in Mason, *Deconstructing America,* 102.

16. Ibid.

17. Quoted in David Williams, *Deformed Discourse: The Function of the Monster in Mediaeval Thought and Literature* (Montreal: McGill-Queen's Univ. Press, 1996), 325. See Ambroise Paré, *On Monsters and Marvels, 1573–1585,* trans. Janis L. Pallister (Chicago: Univ. of Chicago Press, 1982), for an English translation of Paré's book.

18. Valerius, "Monstrous Genealogy," 174.

19. Williams, *Deformed Discourse,* 325–26.

20. Ibid., 325.

21. Ritvo, *Platypus and the Mermaid,* 51.

22. Ibid., 61.

23. Quoted in Ritvo, *Platypus and the Mermaid,* 64.

24. Rosemarie Garland Thomson, "Introduction: From Wonder to Error—A Genealogy of Freak Discourse in Modernity," in *Freakery: Cultural Spectacles of the Extraordinary Body,* ed. Rosemarie Garland Thomson (New York: New York Univ. Press, 1996), 3.

25. Todd, *Imagining Monsters,* 52–53.

26. Ritvo, *Platypus and the Mermaid,* 112.

27. Quoted in Todd, *Imagining Monsters,* 59.

28. Ibid., 119.

29. Mason, *Deconstructing America,* 150.

30. Thomas, *Man and the Natural World,* 82.

31. Quoted in ibid., 87.

32. Christophe Irmscher, *The Poetics of Natural History: From John Bartram to William James* (New Brunswick, N.J.: Rutgers Univ. Press, 1999), 57.

33. David R. Brigham, *Public Culture in the Early Republic: Peale's Museum and Its Audience* (Washington, D.C.: Smithsonian Institution Press, 1995), 18, 2.

34. Ibid., 53.

35. Ibid.

36. Quoted in ibid., 56.

37. Steven M. Wise, *Rattling the Cage: Toward Legal Rights for Animals* (Cambridge, Mass.: Perseus Books, 2000), 134–41.

38. Stephen Jay Gould, *The Panda's Thumb* (New York: Norton, 1980), 398–99.

39. Morris Goodman, "Epilogue: A Personal Account of the Origins of a New Paradigm," *Molecular Phylogenetics and Evolution* 5, no. 1 (Feb. 1996): 269.

40. Marc D. Hauser, *Wild Minds: What Animals Really Think* (New York: Henry Holt, 2000), 234.

41. See Farber, *Finding Order in Nature*, 106.

42. Wise, *Rattling the Cage*, 140.

43. David P. Barash, *The Hare and the Tortoise: Culture, Biology, and Human Nature* (New York: Viking, 1986), 2.

44. Jeffrey Moussaieff Masson and Susan McCarthy, *When Elephants Weep: The Emotional Lives of Animals* (New York: Dell, 1995), especially chaps. 3, 4, and 8. See also Luke Rendell and Hal Whitehead, "Culture in Whales and Dolphins," *Behavioral and Brain Sciences* 24, no. 2 (2001): 309–82, and Sharon Levy, "The Cultural Cetacean," *National Wildlife* 41, no. 6 (2003), http://www.nwf.org/nationalwildlife/article.cfm?articleId=830&issueId=64.

45. Jan Bondeson, *The Two-Headed Boy and Other Medical Marvels* (Ithaca, N.Y.: Cornell Univ. Press, 2000), xxi.

46. Katharine Park and Lorraine J. Daston, *Wonders and the Order of Nature, 1150–1750* (New York: Zone Books, 1998), 366.

47. Donald R. Griffin, *Animal Minds: Beyond Cognition to Consciousness*, rev. ed. (Chicago: Univ. of Chicago Press, 2001), 270.

48. Thomas Pynchon, *Mason & Dixon* (New York: Henry Holt, 1997), 481.

49. J. M. Coetzee, *The Lives of Animals* (Princeton, N.J.: Princeton Univ. Press, 1995), 30.

50. Wise, *Rattling the Cage*, 121.

Works Cited

Barash, David P. *The Hare and the Tortoise: Culture, Biology, and Human Nature.* New York: Viking, 1986.

Bondeson, Jan. *The Two-Headed Boy and Other Medical Marvels*. Ithaca, N.Y.: Cornell Univ. Press, 2000.

Brigham, David R. *Public Culture in the Early Republic: Peale's Museum and Its Audience*. Washington, D.C.: Smithsonian Institution Press, 1995.

Coetzee, J. M. *The Lives of Animals*. Princeton, N.J.: Princeton Univ. Press, 1999.

Farber, Paul Lawrence. *Finding Order in Nature: The Naturalist Tradition from Linnaeus to E. O. Wilson*. Baltimore: Johns Hopkins Univ. Press, 2000.

Foucault, Michel. *The Order of Things*. New York: Vintage Books, 1970.

Goodman, Morris. "Epilogue: A Personal Account of the Origins of a New Paradigm." *Molecular Phylogenetics and Evolution* 5, no. 1 (Feb. 1996): 269–85.

Gould, Steven Jay. *The Panda's Thumb*. New York: Norton, 1980.

Griffin, Donald R. *Animal Minds: Beyond Cognition to Consciousness*. Rev. ed. Chicago: Univ. of Chicago Press, 2001.

Hauser, Marc D. *Wild Minds: What Animals Really Think*. New York: Henry Holt, 2000.

Irmscher, Christophe. *The Poetics of Natural History: From John Bartram to William James*. New Brunswick, N.J.: Rutgers Univ. Press, 1999.

Levy, Sharon. "The Cultural Cetacean." *National Wildlife* 41, no. 6 (2003). http://www.nwf.org/nationalwildlife/article.cfm?articleId=830&issueId=64.

Mason, Peter. *Deconstructing America: Representations of the Other*. New York: Routledge, 1990.

Masson, Jeffrey Moussaieff, and Susan McCarthy. *When Elephants Weep: The Emotional Lives of Animals*. New York: Dell, 1995.

Miller, Andrew. *Ingenious Pain*. New York: Harcourt, Brace, 1997.

Paré, Ambroise. *On Monsters and Marvels, 1573–1585*. Translated by Janis L. Pallister. Chicago: Univ. of Chicago Press, 1982.

Park, Katharine, and Lorraine J. Daston. "Unnatural Conceptions: The Study of Monsters in Sixteenth- and Seventeenth-Century France and England." *Past and Present* 92 (1981): 20–54.

———. *Wonders and the Order of Nature, 1150–1750*. New York: Zone Books, 1998.

Pingree, Allison. "America's 'United Siamese Brothers': Chang and Eng and Nineteenth-Century Ideologies of Democracy and Domesticity." In *Monster Theory*, edited by Jeffrey Jerome Cohen, 92–114. Minneapolis: Univ. of Minnesota Press, 1996.

Pynchon, Thomas. *Mason & Dixon*. New York: Henry Holt, 1997.

Rendell, Luke, and Hal Whitehead. "Culture in Whales and Dolphins." *Behavioral and Brain Sciences* 24, no. 2 (2001): 309–82.

Ritvo, Harriet. *The Platypus and the Mermaid and Other Figments of the Classifying Imagination*. Cambridge, Mass.: Harvard Univ. Press, 1997.

Thomas, Keith. *Man and the Natural World: Changing Attitudes in England, 1500–1800.* New York: Oxford Univ. Press, 1983.

Thomson, Rosemarie Garland. "Introduction: From Wonder to Error—A Genealogy of Freak Discourse in Modernity." In *Freakery: Cultural Spectacles of the Extraordinary Body,* edited by Rosemarie Garland Thomson, 1–19. New York: New York Univ. Press, 1996.

Todd, Dennis. *Imagining Monsters: Miscreations of the Self in Eighteenth-Century England.* Chicago: Univ. of Chicago Press, 1995.

Valerius, Karyn. "The Monstrous Genealogy of Assisted Reproduction." In *Playing Dolly: Technocultural Formations, Fantasies, and Fictions of Assisted Reproduction,* edited by E. Ann Kaplan and Susan Merrill Squier, 172–88. New Brunswick, N.J.: Rutgers Univ. Press, 1999.

Williams, David. *Deformed Discourse: The Function of the Monster in Mediaeval Thought and Literature.* Montreal: McGill-Queen's Univ. Press, 1996.

Wise, Steven M. *Rattling the Cage: Toward Legal Rights for Animals.* Cambridge, Mass.: Perseus Books, 2000.

Chapter 6

Wild Animals in a Free Man's World?

North American References in Norwegian Sportsmen's
Descriptions of Reindeer, 1850–1950

Elisabet Sveingar Amundsen

> Have you seen or
> been on Gjendin ridge before?
> Two miles long, perhaps, or more,
> stretching like a scythe's sharp blade.
> Down past glacier, slope and slide
> you could see where grey screes made
> mirrors of the tarns that cower
> black and heavy, some thirteen or
> fourteen hundred metres lower. —
>   Along the ridge we raced together,
> slicing through the wind and weather.
>   What a colt to ride—amazing!
> As we started on our run
> it was just like suns were blazing.
> Eagles, brown-backed every one,
> hung in the space between us there
> and the way-down watery reaches, —
> specks of dust upon the air.
>
> —Henrik Ibsen, *Peer Gynt* (trans. John Northam)

Into a landscape of stone and water, ice and solitude, a figure of mere fiction—the stag-jockey—flung himself or was flung. Peer Gynt followed a hunter's lust regardless of the fact that it was the busiest harvest season. What did he care? While the high mountains offered no grain, there was a plenitude of fish and meat, and more: there was excitement for restless bodies and escapades for dreamy minds. There was a sense of personal freedom. The traditional hunting legends of the southern Norwegian mountain areas captured the imagination of the playwright Henrik Ibsen (1828–1906) and his bourgeois audience, as did the hunt itself.

The hunting stories told in the evenings by the fire, or read at bedtime, were mostly nonfiction: lively, vivid, and minute descriptions of nature, animals, and human life in nature. The life of free men in God's free nature was the fervent essence of the stories. It kindled a spark and haunted many a young boy's fantasy, until one early summer or autumn morning the young boy-turned-man lay, a rifle at his side, looking through his binoculars at a terrain of rock, stones, and water, mountain birch and willow, and vast fields of moss, heather, and grass (fig. 6.1). A new adventure began:

> Ahead of me lay an ancient realm, as I saw it, quite untouched. The great lakes and the rivers between them, the small tarns in the fields—all were full of fish. Among the willow shrubs lay broods of grouse, one right next to the other, everywhere I looked. Across the fields, over hills and bogs, the wild reindeer roamed in herds of thousands.[1]

Fig. 6.1. Binoculars and telescopes were the wild reindeer hunter's most important equipment, here with a view of Hardangervidda's lakes and high mountain plains. "Bjørnesfjorden" by Anders Beer Wilse (1864–1949). Courtesy of Norsk Folkemuseum—the Norwegian Museum of Cultural History.

These were the hunting grounds of a Norwegian officer, Johannes Dahl (1872–1960), who spent most vacations fishing and hunting. His description of Hardangervidda, northern Europe's largest high mountain plateau and one of several reindeer areas in southern Norway, gives us a portrait of a landscape that is not Peer Gynt's. It borrows colors from similar landscapes visualized in previous and contemporary literature, and it evokes this landscape and encourages the mind to drift toward another continent, across the sea—to America.

For over a hundred years, Norwegian sportsmen drew upon many other sources than their own nation's stories, history, poetry, and mountain mythol-

ogy in describing Norwegian nature. I wondered why. In his writings, Johannes
Dahl has provided me with one answer: what he found in North American literature was a form he could use to express his personal impressions. However
personal this answer may be, it reflects a broad collective influence found in a
variety of written, public sources that can be called a *testament of hunters*: scientific
and political treatises on natural history and wild game management; preliminary
work on legislation; reports from lectures, meetings, and organization work; field
reports and statistics; and biographies and personal narratives.

Parts of this testament were published in the Norsk Jæger- og Fisker-Forening
(Norwegian Hunters' and Anglers' Association) magazine. When the association
was formed in 1871, it followed an international pattern of organizations that
worked for the promotion of what was referred to as "rational" (*rasjonell*) wild game
management based on the wise or "sensible" (*fornuftig*) use of wild game resources.
Its magazine informed and entertained its members, sometimes with articles and
abstracts reprinted from European and North American sport and hunting magazines. It gave access to world events in the field, news—and ideologies.

The influence foreign organizations, magazines, and books had on Norwegian sportsmen cannot be reduced to copying a form but became meaningful to
each individual who dedicated his life to a common cause. Inherent in the hunters' testament are their own explanations, intentions, and ideals—content and
context to help understand their choice of form. Here is not only one form, but
several forms of action, expression, and genres of literature, containing apparent
contradictions.

While Norwegian hunters' writings on wild game from 1850 to 1950 have an
ethos of discipline and management, the spirit of the free, unfettered hunting life
in remoteness and solitude remained the main ingredient of the reindeer stalkers'
personal narratives. The sportsmen's perceptions are therefore as intriguing to me
as the way these perceptions were expressed.

I wish to address questions of form and meaning in the world of the hunting
sportsman, using sportsmen's descriptions of reindeer and the hunt as my sources.
The prey is the first topic of my investigation. Not only are hunters' attentions held
by the prey, but their concept of the wild animal can also be important for research
on the culture of the time.[2] Hunting is more than the relationship between the
animal, its habitat, and its hunter. Because of the hunter, hunting—and thus the
prey—stands in relation to personal, social, and historical circumstances. In this
case, the animal is obviously not just prey to the hunting sportsman but also an
object in a leisure activity built on a foundation of longings and ideals in which
management also plays a part. The descriptions of the wild reindeer focus on certain qualities sportsmen recognized in this animal that correspond with values
shared among the hunters themselves. The relationship between these qualities
and values remained the same between 1850 and 1950, even though reports from
the field spoke of declining reindeer numbers. This paradox leads to the second
topic of my investigation, the consistency of forms and the nature of the hunters'
testament, and to the final question: What did the free man's world have to offer

when describing wild animals, landscapes, and hunting? Is there something here that can tell us more about Norwegian sport hunters' relation to nature and what the wild reindeer meant to them?

Wild Reindeer

About 1850, groups and individuals from the middle classes, both citizens and foreigners, began to roam the fells of Norway. Their purpose was to challenge their own ability to endure physical strain, and for some, to test their huntsmanship.

Fig. 6.2. Wild reindeer (*Rangifer tarandus tarandus*), the only big game in the Norwegian high mountain areas. Illustration by Johan Fredrik Eckersberg (1822–70), *Illustrered Nyhedsblad* (1852).

These two tasks could be accomplished in one quest by going after wild reindeer (*Rangifer tarandus tarandus*), the only big game in the Norwegian high mountain areas (fig. 6.2). It took great skill and experience for a man to get within shooting range of these shy animals and, preferably, to take a stag, the *bukk*. While stag-riding belongs to the sphere of legend and poetry, the reindeer hunt provided food for the skillful hunter and good sport for all those who rose to the challenge—and it nurtured stories.

It was the Norwegian colleague of the Grimm brothers, Peter Christen Asbjørnsen (1812–85), who, during the 1840s, first brought the legends of Peer Gynt to a broader audience. Asbjørnsen's interests were soon to be focused on forestry and the rational management of natural resources. His "Vildrenen" ("The Wild Reindeer"), published in the *Illustrered Nyhedsblad* (illustrated newsletters) in 1852, was one of the first articles on wild reindeer and the hunt in Norway.

Besides collecting fairy tales and legends, Asbjørnsen belonged to the pioneer group of passionate hunters and anglers who wrote for an ever-increasing audience interested in the whole spectrum of nature and wildlife literature. In "Vildrenen," his material included both older and more recent writings by Scandinavian officials and zoologists, in addition to farmers' and his own observations from the field.

"Vildrenen" has a steady flow of formal descriptions of the animal up to its conclusion, where Asbjørnsen wrote: "It is the pride and the adornment of the high mountain areas; without the reindeer, the high mountain solitude would be even more oppressive and intolerable."[3] Asbjørnsen did not praise solitude in the same way sportsmen after him would, but the two traits that he identified, pride and adornment, or beauty, followed wild reindeer in debates, reports, and personal narratives for another century. In addition, as is revealed elsewhere in "Vildrenen," and also in a statement from 1889 made by the young law student Hugo Mowinckel (1868–1949), reindeer were seen as a resource: "Wild reindeer are not just an adornment for our mountains, but also an asset of considerable use for the districts that possess them."[4] Resource, beauty, and pride—let us see these three qualities attributed to the wild reindeer at work.

First of all, Norwegian sportsmen often praised the natural advantages of the reindeer. No other big game was so well adjusted to a life in harsh nature. It was, according to one hunter, "that game that seems especially created for the high mountain fields of Norway."[5] Another hunter wrote, "Wild reindeer are completely harmless; . . . they do no damage to property."[6] On the contrary, sportsmen had in mind "what the reindeer and the hunt add of tangible and intangible assets to our country," as another remarked in 1912.[7] And many took great pleasure in observing the animal: "All hunters who get to know the ways of the wild reindeer will admire its agile grace, its refined sense of smell, its swift escape with a stride-winning, elegant gait."[8] Johannes Dahl became one of these hunters: "I still remember how we admired its light, agile and elastic movements. The free and proud carriage of its head especially distinguished it from the lazy, stoop-shouldered animals that I had often seen in tame reindeer herds."[9] He saw wild reindeer in his dreams: "Proud and free in the soft, wonderful light of the evening sun."[10] Here Dahl maintained a literary tradition of portraying the wild reindeer as an elegant creature with a proud, "self-conscious look," which made one sportsman exclaim, "The reindeer is an animal that loves freedom!"[11] According to some, a "prouder" wild animal was not to be found in the fells of Norway, nor in the whole of northern Europe.[12] As one sportsman concluded, "We should be proud of such magnificent game, enjoy it and do everything possible for it."[13]

Clearly, wild reindeer held an important position in the minds of many Norwegian sportsmen. Most of their descriptions of this animal contained one or more of these three elements—resource, beauty, pride—in one way or another, thereby bringing the spheres of economy, aesthetics, and ethics in relation to the animal and the hunt.

The wild reindeer represented a valuable resource in two ways: the hunt provided both meat and recreation. While the meat was of importance to the local small-scale farmer, modern sportsmen would travel a long way for the sake of the sport, spending money along the way—their contribution to the national economy, according to the rational sportsmen: "Rational reindeer hunting could provide significant income."[14]

The economic aspects of the hunt have a clear, although less prominent, place in the sportsmen's personal narratives. Most of all, a strong admiration of the animal was expressed. Its elegance and more human traits, such as a free and proud carriage of its head, its prideful, self-conscious nature, and its love of freedom, were used to anthropomorphize the animals' movements and manner. Its natural qualities provided it with advantages and abilities to survive for thousands of years. These survival skills were, however, challenged beginning in the late nineteenth century.

Since the 1880s, sportsmen have recognized that reindeer management was not moving in the right direction. "On the contrary," wrote one hunter, "the open hunt for this animal compared to the restrictive elk hunt seems to point clearly enough in the direction one must take if one is to secure the reindeer for game in the future."[15] In 1918, a sportsman warned that "there is no doubt that if we continue as we have begun, and as we have done for decade after decade, there will come a day when reindeer will not be found in the mountains, just like the buffalo in America."[16]

The different spheres of economy, aesthetics, and ethics also came into play in descriptions in which the wild reindeer meets other animals, practically or metaphorically. When a comparison was made between reindeer and other animals, such as the domestic reindeer, the bison, and the elk, qualities and values appear in three different modes—*contrast, parable,* and *model.*

Domestic Reindeer

In Johannes Dahl's description, the proud and free reindeer had its counterpart: the domestic, tame reindeer, "lazy" and "stoop-shouldered." The domesticated animals had initially been kept by nomadic families of the Saami people of the North. During the 1800s, a number of families migrated farther south, seeking new pastures, while Saami herdsmen were employed by Norwegian landowners who took an interest in industrial reindeer herding.[17] "But with what right do tame reindeer pasture in these areas, where the hunter has never met tame reindeer before?" asked the sportsman.[18] In debates about how mountain land ought to be developed, sportsmen drew a line between what was wild and what was tame, and it is clear where their sympathies lay.

Compared to domestic reindeer, sportsmen thought, wild reindeer were better proportioned, taller, larger, stronger, and held their heads higher; they were also more stalwart and vigorous.[19] The domestic reindeer was all that the wild animal was not: stoop-shouldered and lazy, males castrated, females bred like cattle.[20] The similarities to cattle were accentuated by cuts in their ears, a mark of ownership akin to brands, like "slave-marks," a sport hunter commented.[21] The domestic

Fig. 6.3. It is at the moment of death that the contrast between herding tame reindeer and the wild reindeer hunt is the greatest. Representatives from the police are present while the animals are butchered. "Renslagtning paa Vidda" ("Reindeer butchered at Vidda") (1932) by Anders Beer Wilse. Courtesy of Norsk Folkemuseum—the Norwegian Museum of Cultural History.

reindeer had all the signs of being confined and enslaved; it was even physically smaller. "It is a well known fact," claimed a hunter living in northern Norway, "that while animals, tamed and maintained by man through generations, may be improved, the opposite is the case for reindeer."[22] The contrast between tame and wild reindeer was supposedly greatest in the ways that they died, something that was very evident at places where domestic reindeer were butchered (fig. 6.3).

The wild reindeer was "the original inhabitant of our high mountains."[23] Now it was about to lose its customary sovereignty to a pitiable creature. Where the mountain land should be reserved for wild reindeer, the "home" of this shy animal was "invaded"; its peace and solitude disturbed, the original mountain dweller "superseded" and turned into a "homeless outlaw."[24] In the eyes of the sportsmen, domestic reindeer represented a modern element, a threat that disturbed the natural order of the ancient realm, together with new roads, telephone wires, magazine rifles, and all the new cabins built for an increasing number of tourists and hunters.

As the wild reindeer faced its only competitor for high-altitude pasture, the domestic reindeer caused problems for reindeer hunters, too, who were obliged to compensate the owner for the loss of livestock during the hunt.[25] The more experienced herdsman or Saami could point out to the hunter a wild animal in the herd. "But is this hunting?" remarked the sportsman.[26]

The North American Bison

Observant readers of *Skandinavisk Fauna* (Scandinavian fauna), such as Asbjørnsen, noted that herds of thousands of reindeer were a common sight in the 1820s. Such a sight was compared to the herds of bison (*Bison bison*) on the North American prairies by the Swedish zoologist Sven Nilsson (1781–1883).[27] In his comparison, the two continents meet. A few decades later, it occurred again, this time embedded in descriptions of a Norwegian equivalent to Eldorado, a sportsman's paradise soon to be lost.[28]

From the 1870s, echoes of a warning cry could be heard across the country: the mountains' bounty was neither "unlimited nor inexhaustible."[29] In 1885, some said that "the end will come."[30] In certain areas, hunters had already lost sight of their favorite prey. "How desolate the mountain plateaus will be," prophesied Mowinckel in 1908, as Asbjørnsen had in 1852.[31] In 1918, "desolate" is exactly what the fields had become in the eyes of reindeer hunters, in spite of serious efforts to prevent such a gloomy prophecy from coming true.[32]

Since 1890, sportsmen had read the occasional report on the buffalo's fate from Yellowstone.[33] A shared use of the word "extermination" (*utryddelse*) became at the turn of the century an explicit comparison. Abundance had become scarcity.

Massive efforts to prevent the decline in the number of reindeer were made during an eight-year period that began in 1901, when Mowinckel proposed a five-year total ban on reindeer hunting. On this occasion, he reminded the national assembly of "the national loss that Americans suffered on the extermination of the bison."[34] Mowinckel got his ban on hunting reindeer. But the result? After the ban, from 1902 to 1906, a Norwegian-American expressed a wish that the wild reindeer should never suffer a fate similar to the tragic destiny of the buffalo in Yellowstone National Park.[35] He had good reason to worry.

When the hunt opened again, "non-hunters" used magazine rifles to fire at flocks of reindeer from a great distance, turning the glorious hunt into "a scene of slaughter" and "shamelessly" injuring several animals at a time (after 1909, these rifles were declared illegal).[36] This is the antagonistic picture a responsible, cunning sportsman would draw to defend stalking—the safe, humane culling of one to three individuals.[37] As in the case of domestic reindeer, attention was directed to the methods used to kill the animals. The wild reindeer should die as its dignity demanded—one by one, and not by random, brutal slaughter as a result of certain people's reckless actions. Sportsmen had strong arguments to promote their own huntsmanship. The rational hunt was an unbeatable combination of discipline and science: one must not harvest more of the flock than its natural growth dictated or the game would disappear.

At the turn of the century, the destiny of the North American bison had, next to deforestation, gained status as a worldwide symbol of how nature was destroyed by civilization. The bison was the first example, the prototype of extinction, and hunting magazines issued a warning: "When such a species of animal has decreased until it consists of some few individuals, nothing can save it from total extinction."[38] According to a Norwegian forester, the near-extinction of the species was due to a "human lust for destruction" encouraged by the gun industry.[39] The desperately needed protection provided by national parks was not convincing. Though the parks were called "nature-sanctuaries" by a Norwegian observer in 1910, the animals did not thrive there.[40] Why? Obviously because they felt "confined and under guard all the time," because the bison had a marked disposition for "wanderlust"—and just like the wild reindeer, this was due to "an ungovernable thirst for liberty."[41]

When receiving gloomy reports from the mountains, reactions of loss were both individual and public. With the reindeer gone, the high mountain landscape would become desolate. A depressing solitude would take its place, its general sentiment lost. But of most concern was the inevitable fact that the hunt would no longer be possible. This was a personal loss; sportsmen were grieving. They felt powerless, yet they wanted to act "to defy any comparison to the North American bison."[42] They agitated for governmental action while pointing out what failure would lead to. If a civilized nation such as Norway proved unable to manage its wild game, the loss of the reindeer would be a "national loss,"[43] bringing "great shame" upon the nation.[44] The damage would be both tangible and intangible, whether economic, aesthetic, or moral. A "heavy responsibility" rested on the shoulders of the nation.[45]

The European Elk

Sportsmen supported rational wild game management, and alternating periods of preservation and shooting was not considered a very rational way of managing the stock. The decrease in reindeer numbers was said to be due to open hunting, "the unfettered legal right to hunt" wild reindeer—compared to the hunting of elk (*Alces alces*), which was restricted by law in Norway.[46] A regulation from 1900 allowed the reindeer hunter to shoot three animals for a fee, but this did not have the same effect as restrictions on elk hunting, which were based on units of property.

Forests were either private or state property, and the law entitled the owner or the user of each registered, taxable property unit to shoot one elk each year. Thus the home of the elk had been considered an economic asset for decades. This was not the case for the home of the reindeer. On the contrary, land situated higher than the timber line was either in the hands of nearby farmers or belonged to nobody or everybody, until officials in 1908, after a long period in which they regarded high mountain areas as of no value at all, finally decided to draw up property lines.

Despite this administrative measure, the wild reindeer's roaming habits ill fitted the rules of elk management. The free reindeer fell prey to public hunting and an increasing number of hunters. Laws were needed; there was agreement about this among all those concerned. Sportsmen, some of them accomplished lawyers, looked to the laws of other countries, including, during the 1870s, the hunting and fishing acts from twenty-one American states.[47] These were presented to show that there was no open access in "the land of freedom."[48] Here, Norwegian sports-men found an ally in protecting property rights. For decades, Euro-Americans proved to be "practical"; they used a more efficient rifle caliber and their laws were more restrictive and were more fully enforced.[49] Americans had come to terms with the fact that "if one ever has had a need for administration, so it must be in the face of the various attempts to create something useful out of such practical material as a hunting act gives," as one Norwegian lawyer put it in 1901.[50]

Norwegian attempts to enforce the wild game laws in the "vast wilderness" were, for a time, doomed to fail.[51] Lack of surveillance allowed the unlawful hunter to do as he pleased. The sportsmen complained. If only there could be some per-sonal interest in keeping a sustainable stock.[52] Pride should be taken in wild game, in the same way pride was taken in property. Privatization could be one solution, or in a situation in which there was nothing to denationalize, the government should take its management obligations more seriously, as it had for the elk.[53]

Free Creatures of Nature

Sport hunters' descriptions of the wild reindeer indicate strong emotional bonds to the animal. A personal interest might benefit the management of the stock, but their glowing enthusiasm reveals deep affection rather than just cool calculation. This animal had a profound significance in their lives. It played a part in their activities; a culture revolved around it.

Sportsmen's descriptions were in part the result of cognitive processes that were imbued with their culture's contemporary values. The presence of these values makes it difficult to distinguish between formal description and politi-cal statement, especially when literary devices such as anthropomorphism and rhetoric are used. In either case, it is likely that sportsmen's descriptions of these animals represented core values of the sport hunter's culture.

The hunters' prey represented ideas of wildness and liberty, described by words such as "natural," "original," "untamed," "ungovernable," "unrestricted," and "free," reflecting a view in which, compared to agriculture, hunting represents ancient, natural connections with wildlife and life in the wild. This view became important for what was thought of as recreation, and it affected the ideals and val-ues of many modern men.

Sportsmen's descriptions also reveal a particular position with respect to nature and certain preferences with respect to international debate on the dilem-mas inherent in wild game management. The wild reindeer could be capitalized like the tame reindeer. It could be conserved in some areas, not preserved as was needed in the case of the bison, or it could be privatized like the elk. North Ameri-can wild game management provided some of the answers.

Norwegian hunters' descriptions of animals, landscapes, and people share similarities with contemporary sportsmen's narratives to the extent that they must belong to the same ethos of discipline and management. Can this ethos also include a concept of freedom?

The Hunters' Testament

The hunting sportsmen have left behind a written record of scientific observations, political arguments, and enriching impressions of outdoor activities. Their descriptions of the prey operate within a context of administration and management, the long-term goal set by Norsk Jæger- og Fisker-Forening in 1871, a goal which became more and more important concerning the wild reindeer as the decades went by. It is this context that makes the descriptions' content puzzling. Whether compared to tame reindeer, the North American bison, or the European elk, the sportsmen's attention was on what was free or what was not free—legally or emotionally—in terms of the comparison or contrast of qualities. The hunt was no exception.

The Free Hunting Life

Naturalists and explorers, from Asbjørnsen in the 1850s to Fridtjof Nansen (1861–1930) and his contemporaries, celebrated "the most free, unfettered life" of the hunter.[54] Among them, Knut Dahl (1871–1951), Johannes Dahl's older brother, claimed that "the Norwegian mountains have most to give to the fellow who can pack up and take off, turning his back to the rest of the world. He can go his own way for as long and as far as he wants, alone or in company. . . . He will always find a way. He will live where others die."[55] Most of all, zoologist Knut Dahl described a search for the nature within:

> We can never reach greater heights than when we set body and soul in tune with bygone eras and earlier stages of harmony with nature. We have been separated from this ancient immediate interdependence. But deep within us lies a yearning to walk, hungry, by silent trout lakes in primeval forests, as our inner selves remind us we did long ago, and remind us with pain. It is this pain that cannot be stopped. It can only be soothed. And only a few people can afford to soothe it in places on our earth that remain the same as they were in the past. Most of us must search for it closer to home. Illusion comes to our assistance. Without it, not many of us would have been Indians.[56]

Seeking interdependence and harmony with nature, a longing that lies dormant in every man, the Norwegian sportsman turned to a native man—not a Saami, the native of his own country, but a Native American. Where the Saami and their reindeer herds seem to represent problems too close to home, the image of Native Americans had a strong appeal, perhaps due to its distance from the sportsman's everyday life. They were distant, but not unfamiliar to Norwegian sportsmen.

In addition to Native Americans, sportsmen would refer to Natty Bumppo and other characters from James Fenimore Cooper's (1789–1851) series of Leatherstocking Tales—five novels published during the years 1823–41.[57] In the sportsmen's biographies, one local hunter looks like the Native American chiefs in a photograph, while his character and cabin are just like Leatherstocking's.[58]

Fig. 6.4. Jo Gjende (1794–1883) was a Norwegian who made his living as a hunter in the high mountain area of Jotunheimen and was compared with Cooper's protagonist, Leatherstocking. "John Gjendin," photographer unknown, *Norsk Jæger- og Fisker-Forenings Tidsskrift* 1899, p. 137.

Another takes off in a canoe-like boat the same way Pathfinder would.[59] A third moves like an Indian, "lean and tanned," looking for reindeer tracks.[60]

Jo Gjende (1794–1883) (fig. 6.4), who resembled Leatherstocking, lived near Peer Gynt's Gjendin ridge. Jacob Bøckmann Barth (1822–92), a forester and pioneer in the field of wild game management in Norway, explained in 1873 how it was possible for him to compare Jo Gjende to a fictitious American figure. He pinned down the mechanisms that made the rhetoric work: "Ignore the incidental and inessential differences in external conditions and circumstances, and rather concentrate on truly essential similarities. The similarities of character and thought."[61] What really mattered was found in the ideal of the hunter, which the sportsmen recognized in Cooper's writings.

The complexity of Cooper's hunter is captured by American literary historian George Dekker:

Cooper understood that the boastfulness of the hunter might
disguise the essential humility of the man who accepted his own
limitations and made the most of his talents; that the hunter's dislike
of interference and respect for privacy might be an expression, not
merely of the "habits of secluded life" (the explanation given in *The
Prairie*), but of a specialist's sense that each man should have his
own job and the freedom to get on with it; and that the simple integrity of such a man, in the conformity between what he is and what
he possesses, may be the true measure of the just man.[62]

Dekker's description suits Natty Bumppo well. He made the most of his talents
and became a just man. Perhaps he was the son of a frontier hunter somewhere
in Delaware country, as Cooper's daughter Susan Fenimore Cooper (1813–94)
indicated in her introduction to the 1876 household edition of *The Deerslayer*.[63]
But the character has a strongly appealing dimension in addition to that of the
hunter: he had Indians as playmates and as a youth he became part of the tribe.
And just like Peer Gynt, Jo Gjende, and Norwegian sportsmen, he felt best when
he was out in nature.

A Product of Modernity

The way the hunter in the Leatherstocking tales is described applies to the Norwegian sportsman, who preferred to live the life of a hunter, freed from the bonds
of civilization—the same civilization that threatened his Eldorado. Fredrik
Oscar Guldberg (1848–1905) was a headmaster and an avid reindeer huntsman.
Implicit in his 1883 narrative, the damned lumberjacks of *The Prairie* (1827) were
the domestic reindeer and their herders:

Yet the tame reindeer's antlers are already visible both to the east
and to the west, and it probably will not be long until Norway's
largest and best mountain plain once again is "peopled," or rather
"cattled," with thousands of tame, lazy, bred reindeer, hired Lap-
landers and so-called sportsmen with a Baedecker's travel guide
in their pocket and a servant with a rifle beside them. Yes, that is
the future.[64]

But in the end, it was in civilized, rational progress the sportsmen put their trust.
Thus, their ideology had to embrace progress as well as reactions to progress,
making their testament a genuine product of modernity, in which change and
adaptation are important ingredients.

While turning his back on civilization for a couple of glorious weeks a year,
Johannes Dahl admits that at the turn of last century, there were no untouched
realms to write about. Still he did, and with gratitude:

When I previously have described the high mountain plain, Vidda,
as a "new realm," so to speak untouched, it was to give a personal
impression form. It was not so, it just felt that way. I felt this way

because I had been fortunate enough to befriend the Vidda at a
remarkable period of transition in its life.[65]

Meeting wildlife and the people of the high mountain areas of Norway
awoke feelings that could be recreated and communicated to a broader audience
by means of familiar rhetoric about open landscapes, once free-roaming herds,
human solitude, and the life of the hunter. Somehow, it is as if some Norwegian
sportsmen found more satisfaction in foreign ideals, names, and phrases than in
national poetry. At the same time, these are descriptions of the reindeer, its habitat, and the Norwegian hunter, who experienced decline in the herds as progress
made its way into the mountains. Obviously, the Norwegian heritage lacked what
the sportsmen were looking for—something that could express their feelings and
opinions. The story of Natty Bumppo and his hunting grounds had the right elements and was close to the hearts and imagination of Norwegian sportsmen. The
Leatherstocking Tales were among the sources that gave the sportsmen a stable
framework for their descriptions of Norwegian nature, people, and artifacts in
times of change. They contributed to the formation of the Norwegian hunting
literature.

The opposition of nature to culture, freedom to boundaries, and abundance
to decline are important elements in these descriptions. And behind these por-

Fig. 6.5. The title the photographer gave this photo of a reindeer corpse at Hardangervidda corresponds with the sober tone of the sportsmen's texts. Wilse was himself an
experienced wild reindeer hunter. "Viddens saga" ("The Saga of Vidda") (1914) by
Anders Beer Wilse. Courtesy of Norsk Folkemuseum—the Norwegian Museum of
Cultural History.

traits of life's forces, there is always the fear of losing what is dear. In the narratives, as in real life, doing and being move along the axis of time in two different ways: one is reoccurring with nature's seasons while the other is heading toward a dead end. The disappearing wild reindeer represented a decline. The happy hunting days, the free and unfettered life of the mountains would soon belong to the sagas (fig. 6.5); that was the sportsmen's litany of the 1890s.[66] The time of the old hunters is gone, and "no paragraphs, no politics can bring them back to life," according to a statement made in 1916.[67] But it was still possible, decades later, to recall and relive that freedom by stalking reindeer. We are reminded that a sense of freedom is most of all a feeling. It will survive changing conditions. Illusion wasn't necessary for this—not much fantasy was required. The landscape, the animal, and the hunter provided elements for a scenario in which ancient traditions were reenacted as though it was the first dawn.

The conditions for expressing this feeling of freedom have remained remarkably persistent in form, as has the threat against this feeling. In the sportsmen's descriptions, wild game is crowded out by domestic animals and tourists or otherwise wiped out by reckless hunters. What remained was the sport hunter as a heroic, self-reliant man in a harsh environment. What we have is a testament, which can easily be misinterpreted. It comes in the form of rhetoric and the myths that it created. By using the old rhetoric, the myths are recreated, a point which must be taken into consideration in the discussions of historical connections in literature, perceptions, and legislation concerning wild animals. The information in such sources does not necessarily reflect nature objectively. On the other hand, it brilliantly reflects the player's relationship with the natural world and the animals in it.

Wild Animals in a Free Man's World

For Norwegian sportsmen, hunting, reading, and writing went hand in hand. What came first was difficult to say. Not only are their own writings autobiographical, but they also seek to live the lives they have read about in books. The same was true for North American sportsmen. According to Daniel Justin Herman in *Hunting and the American Imagination*, the Leatherstocking Tales had a place in the boyhood reading of many American sport hunters. In fact, an 1889 source promoted Natty Bumppo as one of the popularizers of outdoor sports in America.[68]

Literature brought new generations in touch with nature and thus contributed to the modeling of qualities and values the sportsmen wanted to be a part of their lives. These values are reflected in the descriptions of wild animals and their habitats, or descriptions of good and bad huntsmanship, and in sportsmen's wish for improved management. In *American Sportsmen and the Origins of Conservation*, first published in 1975, John F. Reiger listed a representative selection of "Americans whose hunting or fishing experiences seemed to have shaped, at least to a degree, their desire to preserve some aspects of the natural world."[69] James

Fenimore Cooper is on that list. We are on the trail of a sport hunter culture shared among Norwegian and U.S. sportsmen. The research of Cooper specialists, in addition to the work of the historians Reiger and Herman, provides a good basis for understanding why American references appear in Norwegian sportsmen's narratives.

A Free Man's World?

Both in fact and fiction, the free man's world—understood here as nature—is contrasted with the civilized sphere of the community. Sportsmen stood between the two. They experienced the progress of civilization as negative when it came in conflict with wild game but positive when it benefited management of this resource. A similar duality in relation to civilization is found in *The Prairie*. Henry Nash Smith pointed this out in the introduction to the 1963 edition, and Orm Øverland, a Norwegian specialist on *The Prairie*, summarizes it thus: "Civilization, which is bad, defiles nature, which is good." Yet civilization is also good; the westward movement brings social progress. "These two propositions are reflected in the two contrasting scales—one 'white,' one 'red.' . . . Outside of this scheme, and embodying the underlying unresolved tensions, stands Natty Bumppo," adds Øverland.[70]

Natty Bumppo may have been a skilled hunter before he became a member of the tribe, but he developed an entirely different relationship to nature than other white men moving west. Another Cooper expert, Wayne Franklin, notes that he is "familiar with hidden places and paths, has a subtle feel for his immediate surroundings and evinces an accumulated depth of experience that he wears like a costume."[71] Natty Bumppo belonged to nature and nature belonged to him, whereas "white tenderfoots" were "in the woods without belonging there," Franklin declares.[72] As a hunter, Natty Bumppo knew nature, just like the Native Americans he represented nature, thus "mediating between the red world and the white."[73]

There is much to suggest that Norwegian sport hunters perceived themselves and other hunters as a similar connecting link between nature and civilization— red and white—in their own communities. They were like the Indians, as Knut Dahl formulated it, interdependent with nature, taking part in a collective consciousness linked to life in nature. Herman notes that North American sportsmen "laid claim to Indianness without having any biological relation to Indians."[74] This claim to Indianness also entailed laying a claim to the Indian's customary hunting rights, his knowledge and experience. Behind these claims we find a fascination for the *naturalness* of hunting and a need to belong.

In addition to this, Norwegian sportsmen would claim that reindeer stalking made a man independent and a good member of society. Many of them also became well known in their communities. Thus the sportsmen represented both spheres: on the one side, the free man's world—nature; on the other side, being a player in a free, democratic society—a society that resembled Jefferson's republican America. "In the Jeffersonian view," Herman explains, "republicanism translated into unfettered individualism and grassroots political participation. In this world every man would be a hunter insofar as every man could claim the rights, liberties, and privileges that only elite hunters held in England."[75]

As American historian Harriet Ritvo has pointed out in *The Animal Estate*, there are symbolic bonds between the hunter, the animal, and the land, just as there is a bond between the individual and the nation.[76] While the British at one point were demonstrating the glory of their empire by hunting fierce big game, Americans—and Norwegians—were celebrating democracy. The reindeer hunt was unique in northern Europe, not merely in terms of its prey, but because it was more or less public; the democratic hunt for the reindeer would result in even more independent men, good members of society. Thus the hunt for this shy animal represented valuable experience for the individual as well as for this young nation. But how should public hunting be organized?

While Natty Bumppo came in conflict with the landowner's new hunting laws in *The Pioneers*, sportsmen on both sides of the Atlantic were prepared to approve and follow new hunting laws if they were built on rational wild game management. Thus the Norwegian association Norsk Jæger- og Fisker-Forening had one main concern: to regulate hunting in terms of rational management and recreation. For wild game management to succeed, the hunt needed the support of rational laws and effective surveillance. As a result, the legendary free hunter was "fenced in" by laws and regulations, as one lawyer and passionate reindeer stalker pointed out.[77] Reading such statements, it is hard to miss how the hunter expressed his ambivalent feelings toward these laws and regulations in much the same way that he thought wild animals in national parks would feel, confined and under guard.

A Key to Freedom

One thing is certain. People imbue animals with concepts, and for the Norwegian sportsman between 1850 and 1950, these concepts were the opposite of what a slave mark of domestication implied.

Throughout the sportsmen's descriptions, the concept of freedom was used in all its positive and negative forms. Its counterpart is what can be managed—in all aspects of private and social affairs. But mastery, as in huntsmanship or wild game management, could be combined with it in such a way that did not cause conflict with the concept of freedom. Through the hunt, the animal became manageable without losing its natural wildness or freedom. Game could recuperate by means of the hunters' recreation.

To the ethos of discipline and management belongs a notion of the relationship between animals and people. This is most strongly expressed in protests against preserving animals in national parks. One of the slogans against preservation was "The hunter is the best protector of wild game."[78] In a situation where game was threatened, the sportsman assumed the responsibility to protect the wild animal. By means of his interdependence with nature, his knowledge, experience, and actions, he considered himself to be the right man for the job. It was a duty and a right he had as a hunter in a civilized society. Sportsmen were "nature's noblemen," as Herman calls them.[79]

Reiger's goal has been to show how the combination of sport and management gave birth to the conservation movement: "The fact that only a minority of Americans were the upper-middle and upper-class 'gentleman sportsmen' who founded conservation associations and worked for state, and later national, wildlife legislation does not take away their key contribution to the making of the first conservation movement."[80]

I have shown that the sport hunter's culture also played a part in Norwegian society. It did more than lay the foundation for a game management regime that has maintained the reindeer stocks up to today. It was deeply rooted in the experience of the facts and fictions of hunting. The Norwegian source material clearly suggests that the impact of the sportsman's message lay mainly in economic and scientific argumentation, while the force of an individual's political engagement was inspired by life in nature, which fostered experience, self-reliance, endurance, and joy.

Another fruit of conservation work on Norwegian soil was continuation of the wild reindeer hunt, which, due to the wild reindeer's needs, was an activity that demanded large areas of land and thus could easily come into conflict with other needs in society. The motive for allowing the animal to become a part of government administration has a twofold basis that cannot be undermined. On the one hand, the wild reindeer needed protection, if not through privatization then through public, state-controlled hunting. On the other hand, hunting projected the image of the mountains of southern Norway as an Eldorado and a free man's world.[81] In essence, the wild animal was in many ways the only creature that could save the image of the free man's world, thus keeping man free.

Epilogue

The United Nations Convention on Biological Diversity (1992) has increased interest in wild reindeer.[82] Norway has Europe's only viable stock of wild reindeer, which makes its management an important responsibility for the Norwegian state. In 2004, a report on measures to ensure sustainable management of wild reindeer was released: *Villrein & Samfunn. En veiledning til bevaring og bruk av Europas siste villreinfjell* (Wild reindeer and society: A guide to the protection and use of Europe's last wild reindeer mountains), edited by Reidar Andersen and Håkon Hustad of the Norwegian Institute for Nature Research.

The rhetoric of the free and proud reindeer is no longer present, but in many ways this report reflects the old sportsmen's views. It speaks of the wild reindeer as the first inhabitants of Norwegian mountains and "the most Norwegian of all animals," but the "pride" of the sportsmen's rhetoric has become "veneration" (*ærefrykt*).[83] Genetic analysis has shown that the wild reindeer in Hardangervidda and the surrounding areas are wilder than expected.[84] In addition, the wild reindeer is the last living descendant of the animal that was the key resource for Cro-Magnon man, and afterward for the first Nordic people who followed the reindeer flocks north after the last Ice Age.[85] In other words, wild reindeer laid "the basis for the development of European culture."[86]

Domestic reindeer are still considered dangerous to the wild herds, but the most important threats to the wild reindeer, one of Norway's most land-demanding species, are development and the resulting increase in traffic in its habitat.[87] Among the measures proposed to address these threats are national wild reindeer areas, differentiated land management, strategies for traffic in the mountains, uniform monitoring systems, and promoting Norway's international responsibility.[88] All of these are measures that the old sportsmen would wholeheartedly support.

The authors of the report encourage the precedence of a multidimensional societal perspective over a one-dimensional wild reindeer perspective.[89] Wild reindeer management must also be a part of general land management, and thus the wild reindeer mountains are focused upon as landscape:[90] "Landscape is personal and inclusive, because we perceive it on the basis of memories, associations and knowledge. It is this personal experience that gives the landscape its cultural and social values, in addition to the environmental and economic values."[91] The sportsmen's notion of a landscape's position in their lives is now the rock upon which the new land management scheme will be built.

Because of their close association, the high mountain landscape would lose something precious if the reindeer disappear. Today, the wild reindeer is promoted as a "harbinger of quality" (kvalitetsbudbringer), a guarantor that Norwegian mountain landscape offers genuineness, quietude, and a sufficient amount of the untouched, which remain qualities in demand in the leisure industry.[92]

This was how the sportsmen's testament was honored in 2004. However, Andersen and Hustad argue that wild reindeer management must be run by more than what they call "the parish," the approximately ten thousand wild reindeer hunters in the country.[93] The hunter is no longer the only player on the wild reindeer mountain. Still, hunting is acknowledged as the most important tool to attain game management goals.[94] Last, but not least, the hunter is the caretaker of European history, the wild reindeer "our foremost bearer of culture."[95] "For thousands of years, the wild reindeer hunt has formed both the animal and the hunter," the authors claim.[96]

One fact is neglected—the important shift in attitudes toward the natural world in modern times as new cultures shape their cultural and social values while hunting animals. Though sport hunters for more than a century have connected their hunting practice with bygone eras, there cannot be much prehistoric tradition left in their huntsmanship. The old sportsmen started a process by including the wild reindeer in Norwegian state administration. In the relatively short period of time that has passed, the free creature of nature is now conceived of as a product of culture. The interest in ancient forms of human-animal interaction remains, but the Indianness or naturalness of it has been relegated to the background. Culture—European culture—has taken over as the reference frame.

Sammendrag

Utgangspunktet for denne artikkelen er norske sportsjegeres beskrivelser av villrein i perioden 1850–1950. I en tid da villreinjakt var innslag i et nasjonalt bevisst samfunnsliv, brukte sportsjegerne amerikanske eksempler og litterære talemåter for å beskrive dyret, jegeren og jaktterrenget.

Vi følger sportsjegernes arbeid for å bedre villreinforvaltningen. Ord som 'inntekt', 'pryd' og 'stolthet' knyttet villreinen til økonomi, estetikk og etikk. Det kommer til uttrykk i sammenligninger med tamrein, bison og elg, bygd på kunnskap og forestillinger om kontraster, likheter og bestemte forvaltningsmodeller, blant annet hentet fra amerikansk viltforvaltning. I tillegg stod begrepet frihet sentralt, en kjerneverdi i sportsjegernes kultur og en viktig dimensjon ved jakta.

Bisonen ble en parallell til villreinen, slik også jakta i det norske høyfjellet kunne oppleves som parallelt med jegerlivet på den amerikanske prærien, omtalt i James Fenimore Coopers romanseire om Lærstrømpe. Gjennom amerikansk retorikk formidlet sportsjegerne følelser og personlige inntrykk. Både for norske og amerikanske sportsjegere ble indianerne og Lærstrømpe forbildet på et liv i frihet og samhørighet med naturen, en natur truet av sivilisasjonen. Samtidig lå det håp i en sivilisert behandling av dyret. Det la bånd på jegerne, og forhindret at jakt ble 'en saga'.

I sportsjegernes møte med en viltbestand i nedgang vokste bevisstheten om at jegerne var dyrets beste beskytter. Det la grunnlag for et naturvern som vektlegger bevaring gjennom bruk. Denne forvaltningsideologien var rotfestet i den enkeltes liv, i jakt og jaktlitteratur. Viltforvaltningen kom ikke i konflikt med det frie jegerlivet. Med fantasi og retorikk til hjelp kunne sportsjegerne oppleve og siden beskrive en frihetsfølelse, selv om det moderne samfunnet innhentet villmarka. Det ville dyret ble nøkkelen til frihet.

Notes

1. In the original: "Her lå det for meg et eldgammelt rike, som var så å si uberørt. De svære sjøene og elvene mellom dem, alle småtjønnene utover flakene, var fulle av fisk. I vierbeltene lå rypekullene tett i tett overalt hvor jeg så. Over flyer, fjellsider og myrer streifet villreinen i flokker på tusener." Johannes Dahl, *Hardangervidda: Viddas eget liv* (Oslo: Johan Grundt Tanum, 1944), 18.

2. An important Scandinavian contribution to this research approach was introduced by the Swedish ethnologist Orvar Löfgren. Here anthropology, social history, and the history of ideas are combined to study animal symbolism in bourgeois thought. See Orvar Löfgren, "Our Friends in Nature: Class and Animal Symbolism," *Ethnos* 50 (1985): 184–213. Hunting has, however, not been a main topic for Scandinavian researchers, but a similar research approach is found in the work done outside of Scandinavia. See, for example, how hunting is treated in Harriet Ritvo, *The Animal Estate: The English and Other Creatures in the Victorian Age* (Cambridge, Mass.: Harvard Univ. Press, 1987), 243–88, and Daniel Justin Herman, *Hunting and the American Imagination* (Washington, D.C.: Smithsonian Institution Press, 2001).

3. In the original: "Den er Høifjeldets Stolthed og Pryd; uden Renen skulde Høifjeldets Ensomhed være endnu mere trykkende og utaalelig." Peter Christen Asbjørnsen, "Vildrenen," reprint in *Illustreret Nyhetsblad* (1852): 28.

4. In the original: "Vildrenen er ikke blot en Pryd for vore Fjelde, men ogsaa en Herlighed til adskillig Nytte for de Distrikter, som besidder den." Hugo Mowinckel, "Erklæring fra Norsk Jæger- og Fisker-Forenings bestyrelse i anledning af forslag til lov om vildrenens fredning, og den i henhold hertil emanerede lov af 29 Juni 1889," *Tidsskrift* 18 (1889): 115. See also Louis de B. Saxlund, "Bør man søge at forbedre vildtbestanden i Sverige, Norge og Danmark ved overføring af vildt fra andre lande?" *Tidsskrift* 33 (1904): 266; "Fra renjagten i Jotunheimen 1911" (H. P.), *Tidsskrift* 41 (1912): 29; "Renjagt—økonomi," *Tidsskrift* 45 (1916): 22.

5. In the original: "det vildt, som syntes særlig skabt for Norges højfjeldsmarker." "Gemsen i Norge: Et fortidigt og fremtidigt akklimatiseringsforsøg," *Tidsskrift* 17 (1888): 11.

6. In the original: "Vildrenen er absolut uskadelig; . . . den gjør ingen skade paa eiendom." Hugo Mowinckel, "Om vildrenen," *Tidsskrift* 37 (1908): 43. See also Saxlund, "Bør man søge at forbedre vildtbestanden," 266.

7. In the original: "hvad renen og renjagten kan bringe vort land av materielle og immaterielle værdier." "Fra renjagten i Jotunheimen," 29.

8. In the original: "Alle jægere, som er kommet nærmere ind paa vildrenenes levesæt, beundrer dens smidige ynde, dens overmaade fine lugtesans, dens hurtige flugt med det skridtvindende elegante trav." Mowinckel, "Om vildrenen," 43.

9. In the original: "Jeg husker ennå hvor vi beundret dens lette, smidige og elastiske bevegelser. Særlig den fri, stolte reisningen av hodet skilte den fra de dorske, duknakkete dyrene jeg ofte hadde sett i tamreinflokkene." J. Dahl, *Hardangervidda*, 91.

10. In the original: "Stolte og fri i det umåtelige himmelblå riket i kveldssolens bløte, vidunderlige lys." Johannes Dahl, *Drømmen om Vidda: Fortellinger om fiske og jakt på Hardangervidda* (Oslo: Johan Grundt Tanum, 1953), 17. See also J. Dahl, *Drømmen om Vidda*, 60, 68, and J. Dahl, *Hardangervidda*, 94.

11. In the original: "Renen er et dyr, som elsker frihed!" Axel Hagemann, "Vildren i Vestfinmarken," *Tidsskrift* 20 (1891): 6–7.

12. Thorvald Heiberg, "Jagt og beite," *Tidsskrift* 46 (1917): 135; Hans Bruun, "Vildrensjagten," *Tidsskrift* 47 (1918): 42.

13. In the original: "Et så prægtigt vildt skulde vi være stolte af, glæde os over og gjøre alt muligt for!" "Gemsen i Norge," 11. See also Hans Bruun, "Dyregrave i høifjeldet," *Tidsskrift* 26 (1897): 180; "Fra renjagten i Jotunheimen," 29.

14. In the original: "En rationelt ordnet vildrenjagt kunne gi meget betydelige indtægter." "Renjagt—økonomi," 22.

15. In the original: "Tvertimod synes den frie Jagt efter dette Vildt stillet i Forhold til den lovbundne Jagt efter Elgen, at pege tydelig nok i den Retning, man har at gaa, hvis man vil beholde Renen som fremtidigt Vildt." "Aarsoversigt," *Tidsskrift* 14 (1885): 251.

16. In the original: "det er ikke tvil om, at hvis vi holder paa fremdeles som vi har beg-yndt, og som vi har fortsat 10-aar efter 10-aar, saa vil der komme den dag, da der ikke findes ren tilbake i fjeldet, akkurat paa samme maate som med bisonoksen i Amerika." Bruun, "Vildrensjagten," 43.

17. "Mere om Sport paa Statens Grund" (H.), *Meddelelser* 4 (1875): 177–78; "Årsover-sigt," *Tidsskrift* 17 (1888): 228; Johannes L. Aga, "Hardangervidden," *Tidsskrift* 21 (1892): 120.

18. In the original: "Men med hvilken ret beiter enkelte tamren i trakter, hvor jægeren aldrig har truffet tamren." Hans Bruun, "Vildtaaret: Vosse- Sogne- Hardanger-fjeldene," *Tidsskrift* 27 (1898): 142.

19. Hagemann, "Vildren i Vestfinmarken," 5–15; "Årsoversigt," *Tidsskrift* 22 (1893): 228.

20. Fredrik Oscar Guldberg, *Kringom Peisen: Jagtminder fra det søndenfjeldske Norge* (Kristiana [Oslo]: Jacob Dybwads Forlag, 1891), 187; J. Dahl, *Hardangervidda*, 91.

21. Hans Bruun, "Vildrenjagten paa Hardangervidden," *Tidsskrift* 28 (1899): 126.

22. In the original: "Det er en kjendsgjerning, at medens de andre dyr, som mennesket tæmmer og underholder, gjennem generationer ligesom forædles, er det omvendte tilfældet med renen." Hagemann, "Vildren i Vestfinmarken," 6–7.

23. In the original: "den oprindelige beboer av alle vore høifjelde." Heiberg, "Jagt og beite," 135.

24. "Fældede elgsdyr og vilde rensdyr i Norge i året 1889," *Tidsskrift* 19 (1890): 160; Aga, "Hardangervidden," 120; "Årsoversigt 1894," *Tidsskrift* 23 (1894): 239–40; Bruun, "Vildrenjagten paa Hardangervidden," 124; "Fældede elgsdyr, vildren og hjort i Norge 1900," *Tidsskrift* 30 (1901): 234–35. See also Mowinckel, "Erklæring," 114–15; Bruun, "Vildtaaret," 142–45; and Ludvig Lumholtz, "Renjagten i østre Jotunheimen," *Tidsskrift* 29 (1900): 218–19.

25. Ludvig Lumholtz, "At skyde merket ren," *Tidsskrift* 22 (1893): 201–3; "Årsoversigt," *Tidsskrift* 22 (1893): 228; Bruun, "Vildtaaret," 142, 144–45; Hans Bruun, "Rens-sak," *Tidsskrift* 43 (1914): 114–15.

26. In the original: "Men er sligt jagt?" Bruun, "Vildrenjagten paa Hardangervidden," 126.

27. Sven Nilsson, *Skandinavisk Fauna*, 2d ed. (Lund, 1847), cited in Asbjørnsen, "Vil-drenen," 3.

28. Fredrik Oscar Guldberg, "En Renjagt paa Hardangervidden, Sommeren 1879," *Meddelelser* 10 (1881): 176.

29. "Mere om Sport," 178.

30. In the original: "Engang kommer Enden!" "Aarsoversigt," *Tidsskrift* 14 (1885): 251.

31. In the original: "Hvor øde blir vidden." Mowinckel, "Om vildrenen," 43.

32. Bruun, "Vildrensjagten," 113.

33. "Den amerikanske bisonokses udryddelse," reprinted from *Naturen, Tidsskrift* 19 (1890): 202–7.

34. In the original: "det nationaltab, som amerikanerne led ved udryddelsen af bisonen." Hugo Mowinckel, "Fredning af vildren," *Tidsskrift* 30 (1901): 67.

35. "Bison i Yellowstone Park," *Tidsskrift* 36 (1907): 200.

36. "Militærrifler og jagtrifler" (P.), *Tidsskrift* 37 (1908): 168.

37. Mowinckel, "Aarsoversigt," *Tidsskrift* 25 (1896): 244.

38. In the original: "Naar en saadan dyreart er skrumpet ind til kun at indeholde nogle faa individer, kan intet redde den fra total undergang." "Den amerikanske bisonokse," *Tidsskrift* 33 (1904): 119.

39. Saxlund, "Bør man søge at forbedre vildtbestanden," 266. See also Ritvo, *Animal Estate*, 283.

40. "Yellowstone-parken" (H. W.), *Tidsskrift* 39 (1910): 157.

41. In the original: "saa føler bisonen med sin utæmmelige frihetstrang og sin tvingende vandrelyst sig allikevel indestængt og bevogtet." Ibid., 157–58.

42. Ludvig Lumholtz, "Et par jagtspørgsmaal," *Tidsskrift* 30 (1901): 117.

43. Mowinckel, "Fredning," 67.

44. Bruun, "Dyregrave i høifjeldet," 180.

45. "Gemsen i Norge," 11; "Aarsoversigt," *Tidsskrift* 26 (1897): 244.

46. In the original: "den ubegrænsede Jagtfrihed." Jacob Bøckmann Barth, "Lidt af Hvert om og med Foranledning af Jagtforholdene i Gudbrandsdalen og Valdres i 1881," *Meddelelser* 10 (1881): 209. See also "Aarsoversigt," *Tidsskrift* 14 (1885): 251.

47. "Amerikanske Love om Jagt og Fiskeri," *Meddelelser* 1 (1872): 130–50.

48. "I det frie Amerika," *Tidsskrift* 25 (1896): 271; Ludvig Lumholtz, "Hvorledes bør man arbeide for at faa jagtlovens bestemmelser bedre overholdte?" *Tidsskrift* 33 (1904): 186.

49. Ibid.; "Litt om riflecaliber" (J. W.), *Tidsskrift* 38 (1909): 36; "Yellowstone-parken," 156; Hugo Mowinckel, "Landsmøtet for sportsjagt og sportsfiske i Bergen 1.–4. juli 1910," *Tidsskrift* 39 (1910): 175; Ludvig Lumholtz, "Norsk Jæger- og Fisker-Forenings 43de aarsberetning 1914," *Tidsskrift* 44 (1915): 73.

50. In the original: "skal man nogengang have brug for en administration, saa maa det vel være ligeoverfor de spredte forsøg paa at skabe noget brugbart ud af en saa praktisk materie som en jagtlov." Lumholtz, "Et par jagtspørgsmaal," 116.

51. "Fældede elgsdyr, vildren og hjort i Norge 1901," *Tidsskrift* 32 (1903): 38.

52. Jacob Bøckmann Barth, "Om de principer, på hvilke en hensigtsmæssig ordning af jagten alene kan bygges," *Tidsskrift* 16 (1887): 147.

53. "Mere om Sport," 180–81; "Jagtpoliti i statens høifjeld: Rensdyrjagten, officielle skrivelser," *Tidsskrift* 37 (1908): 37–41; Bruun, "Norsk Jæger- og Fiskerforenings 38te aarsberetning," 283.

54. In the original: "det frieste, det mest ubundne Liv."(Asbjørnsen, "Vildrenen," 25). See also Bruun, "Vildrenjagten paa Hardangervidden," 126; Fridtjof Nansen,

"Friluftsliv (1921)," in *Nansens røst: Artikler og taler (1916–1930)*, vol. 3 of *Nansens røst: Artikler og taler (1884–1930)* (Oslo: Jacob Dybwads Forlag, 1945), 587; Knut Dahl, *Villmarksliv og friluftsferder*, 3d ed. (Oslo: J. W. Cappelens Forlag, 1943), 125–26; J. Dahl, *Hardangervidda*, 11, 43, 50, and J. Dahl, *Drømmen om Vidda*, 52.

55. In the original: "mest gir vel Norges fjell den 'uvane' kar, som kan snøre sin sekk og la jernteppe falle mellom seg og verden. Han kan vandre sin egen vei så langt og så lenge han vil, alene eller i selskap. . . . Han finner alltid utvei, han greier seg. Han lever hvor andre vilde dø." K. Dahl, *Villmarksliv og friluftsferder*, 125–26. See also Bruun, "Vildrensjagten," 42; Ludvig Lumholtz, *Jægerliv* (Oslo: Johannes Bjørnstads Forlag, 1926), 66; and J. Dahl, *Hardangervidda*, 176–77.

56. In the original: "Vi kan aldri nå større høyder enn når vi kan stemme legeme og sjel inn i svunne tidsaldrers, i tilbakelagte stadiers samhørighet med naturen. Vi er skilt fra denne gamle umiddelbare samhørighet. Men dypt i oss ligger lengselen etter å gå sulten langs urskogens stille ørretvann, slik som vårt indre minnes vi gjorde i fjerne tider, og minnes med smerte. Det er denne smerte som ikke kan stilles. Den kan bare lindres. Og få er de som har råd til å lindre den på steder av vår jord som ennå er samtidige med vår fortid. De fleste av oss må søke den stilt nærmere. Derfor blir illusjonen vår hjelp. Uten den var ikke mange av oss indianere." K. Dahl, *Villmarksliv og friluftsferder*, 111.

57. The Leatherstocking Tales by year of publishing: *The Pioneers* (1823), *The Last of the Mohicans* (1826), *The Prairie* (1827), *The Pathfinder* (1840), and *The Deerslayer* (1841). Scandinavian translations appeared shortly after the originals.

58. Jacob Bøckmann Barth, "John Gjendin: En biographisk Skitse," *Meddelelser* 2 (1873): 34–37, 51.

59. K. Dahl, *Villmarksliv og friluftsferder*, 75.

60. Johan Nikolay Lieske Blytt, *Reinsdyrjakter og Friluftsliv* (Oslo: Gyldendal Norsk Forlag, 1935), 55.

61. In the original: "Naar man herved ser bort fra den tilfældige og uvæsentlige Forskjel i ydre Forholde og Omstændigheder, og derimod fæster sig ved den egentlige væsentlige Lighed. Lighed i Karakter og Tænkemåde." Barth, "John Gjendin," 34–35.

62. George Dekker, *James Fenimore Cooper: The American Scott* (New York: Barnes & Noble, 1967), 89.

63. Susan Fenimore Cooper, Introductions to *Household Edition of the Works of J. Fenimore Cooper* (New York: Houghton, Mifflin, 1876–84), http://external. oneonta.edu/cooper, xxiv–xxix.

64. In the original (emphasis added): "Dog tamrenen stikker allerede sine horn i veiret baade i øst og vest, og *det varer kanske ikke længe, før Norges største og herligste fjeldvidde atter er befolket* eller 'befæet' med tusender af—tamme, lade, paasatte reinsdyr, leiede finner og 'sportsmænd' med Baedecker i lommen og en 'dreng' med en rifle ved siden. Ja, det er fremtiden." Guldberg, *Kringom Peisen*, 187. "And *it will not be long afore an accursed band of choppers and loggers will be following on their heels to*

humble the wilderness which lies so broad and rich on the western banks of the Mississippi, and then the land *will be a peopled desert* from the shores of the Maine sea to the foot of the Rocky Mountains, fill'd with all the abominations and craft of man and stript of the comfort and loveliness it received from the hand of the Lord." James Fenimore Cooper, *The Prairie* (1827; reprint, New York: Oxford Univ. Press, 1999), 187–88.

65. In the original: "Når jeg i det foregående har omtalt Vidda som et 'nytt rike,' som var 'så å si uberørt,' er det for å gi et personlig inntrykk en form. Det var ikke så, jeg bare følte det slik. Denne følelsen fikk jeg fordi jeg hadde den lykke å bli venn med Vidda i en merkelig overgangstid i dens liv." J. Dahl, *Hardangervidda,* 23.

66. Aga, "Vildrenen på Hardangervidden," 182; Bruun, "Vildrenjagten paa Hardangervidden," 126.

67. "Renjagt—økonomi," 22.

68. Herman, *Hunting and the American Imagination,* 118.

69. John F. Reiger, *American Sportsmen and the Origins of Conservation,* 3d ed. (Corvallis: Oregon State Univ. Press, 2001), 61–62.

70. Orm Øverland, *James Fenimore Cooper's* The Prairie (New York: Humanities Press, 1973), 153.

71. Wayne Franklin, *The New World of James Fenimore Cooper* (Chicago: Univ. of Chicago Press, 1982), 223.

72. Ibid.

73. Ibid., 227.

74. Herman, *Hunting and the American Imagination,* 118.

75. Ibid., 78. There were probably many more republicans among Norwegians than the 69,264 (26.7 percent of the population) who voted for the republic on the dissolution of the union between Norway and Sweden in 1905.

76. Ritvo, *Animal Estate,* 243–88.

77. Lumholtz, "Et par jagtspørgsmaal," 118.

78. In the original: "Jægeren er Vildtets bedste Beskytter." Mowinckel, "Erklæring," 114. See also H. Huitfeldt-Kaas, "Vaarmøtet," *Tidsskrift* 48 (1919): 113.

79. Herman, *Hunting and the American Imagination,* 119.

80. Reiger, *American Sportsmen,* 65.

81. J. Dahl, *Hardangervidda,* 17. See also Guldberg, "En Renjagt," 176, and K. Dahl, *Villmarksliv og friluftsferder,* 125–26.

82. United Nations Environment Programme, "Convention on Biological Diversity," June 5, 1992, http://www.biodiv.org/convention/articles.asp, accessed June 11, 2005.

83. Reidar Andersen and Håkon Hustad, eds., *Villrein & Samfunn: En veiledning til bevaring og bruk av Europas siste villreinfjell,* NINA Booklet no. 27 (Trondheim: Norwegian Institute for Nature Research, 2004), 11.

84. Ibid., 24.

85. Ibid., 6, 11, 24, 65.

86. Ibid., 5.

87. Ibid., 25, 27–32, 46.

88. Ibid., 70, 76.

89. Ibid., 51.

90. Ibid., 9, 77.

91. In the original: "Landskap er personlig og inkluderende, fordi vi skaper vår egen opplevelse av det på grunnlag av minner, assosiasjoner og kunnskap. Det er disse personlige opplevelsene som gir landskapet dets kulturelle og sosiale verdier, i tillegg til de miljømessige og økonomiske." Ibid., 42. Cf. Council of Europe, "European Landscape Convention," Oct. 20, 2000, http://conventions.coe.int/Treaty/en/Treaties/Html/176.htm, accessed June 11, 2005.

92. Andersen and Hustad, Villrein & Samfunn, 65.

93. Ibid., 46.

94. Ibid., 22.

95. Ibid., 5.

96. Ibid., 27.

Works Cited

Abbreviations

Meddelelser = Meddelelser fra Norsk Jæger- og Fisker-Forening (1872–1881)

Tidsskrift = Norsk Jæger- og Fisker-Forenings Tidsskrift (1882–1936)

"Aarsoversigt." Tidsskrift 14 (1885): 250–57.

"Årsoversigt." Tidsskrift 17 (1888): 222–36.

"Årsoversigt." Tidsskrift 22 (1893): 226–34.

"Aarsoversigt." Tidsskrift 26 (1897): 242–52.

"Årsoversigt 1894." Tidsskrift 23 (1894): 237–49.

Aga, Johannes L. "Hardangervidden." Tidsskrift 21 (1892): 118–23.

———. "Vildrenen på Hardangervidden." Tidsskrift 20 (1891): 182.

"Amerikanske Love om Jagt og Fiskeri." Meddelelser 1 (1872): 130–50.

Andersen, Reidar, and Håkon Hustad, eds. Villrein & Samfunn: En veiledning til bevaring og bruk av Europas siste villreinfjell. NINA Booklet no. 27. Trondheim: Norwegian Institute for Nature Research, 2004. Also available online at http://www.nina.no.

Asbjørnsen, Peter Christen. "Vildrenen." Reprinted in Illustreret Nyhetsblad (1852).

Barth, Jacob Bøckmann. "John Gjendin: En biographisk Skitse." *Meddelelser* 2 (1873): 33–51.

———. "Lidt af Hvert om og med Foranledning af Jagtforholdene i Gudbrandsdalen og Valdres i 1881." *Meddelelser* 10 (1881): 209.

———. "Om de principer, på hvilke en hensigtsmæssig ordning af jagten alene kan bygges." *Tidsskrift* 16 (1887): 144–58.

"Bison i Yellowstone Park." *Tidsskrift* 36 (1907): 200.

Blytt, Johan Nikolay Lieske. *Reinsdyrjakter og Friluftsliv.* Oslo: Gyldendal Norsk Forlag, 1935.

Bruun, Hans. "Dyregrave i høifjeldet." *Tidsskrift* 26 (1897): 179–81.

———. "Norsk Jæger- og Fiskerforenings 38te aarsberetning." *Tidsskrift* 38 (1909): 279–85.

———. "Rens-sak." *Tidsskrift* 43 (1914): 112–15.

———. "Vildrenjagten paa Hardangervidden." *Tidsskrift* 28 (1899): 124–26.

———. "Vildrensjagten." *Tidsskrift* 47 (1918): 42–55, 97–113. Comments by Johan Anker and H. Kristoff.

———. "Vildtaaret: Vosse- Sogne- Hardangerfjeldene." *Tidsskrift* 27 (1898): 140–45.

Cooper, James Fenimore. *The Deerslayer.* Edited with an introduction by H. Daniel Peck. Oxford World's Classics. 1841. Reprint, New York: Oxford Univ. Press, 1999.

———. *The Last of the Mohicans.* Edited by John McWilliams. Oxford World's Classics. 1826. Reprint, New York: Oxford Univ. Press, 1998.

———. *The Pathfinder; or The Inland Sea.* Introduction and notes by William P. Kelly. Oxford World's Classics. 1840. Reprint, New York: Oxford Univ. Press, 1999.

———. *The Pioneers.* Edited by James D. Wallace. Oxford World's Classics. 1823. Reprint, New York: Oxford Univ. Press, 1999.

———. *The Prairie.* Edited with an introduction by Donald A. Ringe. Oxford World's Classics. 1827. Reprint, New York: Oxford Univ. Press, 1999.

Cooper, Susan Fenimore. Introductions to *Household Edition of the Works of J. Fenimore Cooper.* New York: Houghton Mifflin, 1876–84. http://external.oneonta.edu/cooper.

Council of Europe. "European Landscape Convention," Oct. 20, 2000. http://conventions. coe.int/Treaty/en/Treaties/Html/176.htm. Accessed June 11, 2005.

Dahl, Johannes. *Drømmen om Vidda: Fortellinger om fiske og jakt på Hardangervidda.* Oslo: Johan Grundt Tanum, 1953.

———. *Hardangervidda: Viddas eget liv.* Oslo: Johan Grundt Tanum, 1944.

Dahl, Knut. *Villmarksliv og friluftsferder,* 3d ed. Oslo: J. W. Cappelens Forlag, 1943.

Dekker, George. *James Fenimore Cooper: The American Scott.* New York: Barnes & Noble, 1967.

"Den amerikanske bisonokse." *Tidsskrift* 33 (1904): 117–20.

"Den amerikanske bisonokses udryddelse." Reprinted from *Naturen. Tidsskrift* 19 (1890): 202–7.

Franklin, Wayne. *The New World of James Fenimore Cooper.* Chicago: Univ. of Chicago Press, 1982.

"Fra renjagten i Jotunheimen 1911." (H. P.) *Tidsskrift* 41 (1912): 25–29.

"Fældede elgsdyr og vilde rensdyr i Norge i året 1889." *Tidsskrift* 19 (1890): 156–65.

"Fældede elgsdyr, vildren og hjort i Norge 1900." *Tidsskrift* 30 (1901): 222–35.

"Fældede elgsdyr, vildren og hjort i Norge 1901." *Tidsskrift* 32 (1903): 27–39.

"Gemsen i Norge: Et fortidigt og fremtidigt akklimatiseringsforsøg." *Tidsskrift* 17 (1888): 1–20.

Guldberg, Fredrik Oscar. "En Renjagt paa Hardangervidden, Sommeren 1879." *Meddelelser* 10 (1881): 175–97.

———. *Kringom Peisen: Jagtminder fra det søndenfjeldske Norge.* Kristiania (Oslo): Jacob Dybwads Forlag, 1891.

Hagemann, Axel. "Vildren i Vestfinmarken." *Tidsskrift* 20 (1891): 5–15.

Heiberg, Thorvald. "Jagt og beite." *Tidsskrift* 46 (1917): 121–36.

Herman, Daniel Justin. *Hunting and the American Imagination.* Washington, D.C.: Smithsonian Institution Press, 2001.

Huitfeldt-Kaas, H. "Vaarmøtet." *Tidsskrift* 48 (1919): 112–13.

Ibsen, Henrik. *Peer Gynt: A Dramatic Poem.* Translated by John Northam. 1867. Reprint, Oslo: Scandinavian Univ. Press, 1995.

"I det frie Amerika." *Tidsskrift* 25 (1896): 271.

"Jagtpoliti i statens høifjeld: Rensdyrjagten, officielle skrivelser." *Tidsskrift* 37 (1908): 37–41.

"Litt om riflecaliber." (J. W.) *Tidsskrift* 38 (1909): 36–37.

Löfgren, Orvar. "Our Friends in Nature: Class and Animal Symbolism." *Ethnos* 50 (1985): 184–213.

Lumholtz, Ludvig. "At skyde merket ren." *Tidsskrift* 22 (1893): 201–3.

———. "Et par jagtspørgsmaal." *Tidsskrift* 30 (1901): 113–120.

———. "Hvorledes bør man arbeide for at faa jagtlovens bestemmelser bedre overholdte?" *Tidsskrift* 33 (1904): 174–99. Comments to Alexander Nansen.

———. *Jægerliv.* Oslo: Johannes Bjørnstads Forlag, 1926.

———. "Norsk Jæger- og Fisker-Forenings 43de aarsberetning 1914." *Tidsskrift* 44 (1915): 63–74.

———. "Renjagten i østre Jotunheimen." *Tidsskrift* 29 (1900): 211–19.

"Mere om Sport paa Statens Grund." (H.) *Meddelelser* 4 (1875): 168–81.

"Militærrifler og jagtrifler." (P.) *Tidsskrift* 37 (1908): 168–79.

Mowinckel, Hugo. "Aarsoversigt." *Tidsskrift* 25 (1896): 237–48.

————. "Erklæring fra Norsk Jæger- og Fisker-Forenings bestyrelse i anledning af forslag til lov om vildrenens fredning, og den i henhold hertil emanerede lov af 29 Juni 1889." *Tidsskrift* 18 (1889): 114–17.

————. "Fredning af vildren." *Tidsskrift* 30 (1901): 67.

————. "Landsmøtet for sportsjagt og sportsfiske i Bergen 1.–4. juli 1910." *Tidsskrift* 39 (1910): 170–80. Comments to Hans Bruun.

————. "Om vildrenen." *Tidsskrift* 37 (1908): 41–45.

Nansen, Fridtjof. "Friluftsliv (1921)." In *Nansens røst: Artikler og taler (1916–1930)*. Vol. 3 of *Nansens røst: Artikler og taler (1884–1930)*, 584–88. Oslo: Jacob Dybwads Forlag, 1945.

Nilsson, Sven. *Skandinavisk Fauna*, 2d ed. Lund, 1847.

Øverland, Orm. *James Fenimore Cooper's* The Prairie. New York: Humanities Press, 1973.

Reiger, John F. *American Sportsmen and the Origins of Conservation*, 3d ed. Corvallis: Oregon State Univ. Press, 2001.

"Renjagt—økonomi." *Tidsskrift* 45 (1916): 21–22.

Ritvo, Harriet. *The Animal Estate: The English and Other Creatures in the Victorian Age.* Cambridge, Mass.: Harvard Univ. Press, 1987.

Saxlund, Louis de B. "Bør man søge at forbedre vildtbestanden i Sverige, Norge og Danmark ved overføring af vildt fra andre lande?" *Tidsskrift* 33 (1904): 262–78.

United Nations Environment Programme. "Convention on Biological Diversity." June 5, 1992. http://www.biodiv.org/convention/articles.asp. Accessed June 11, 2005.

"Yellowstone-parken." (H.W.) *Tidsskrift* 39 (1910): 156–60.

Chapter 7

Wild Birds in Aquilino Ribeiro's Writings
Using Literature as a Source for Environmental History

Ana Isabel Queiroz and Maria Teresa L. M. B. Andresen

Nature-Writing in Aquilino Ribeiro's Works

Aquilino Ribeiro (1885–1963) was born in Carregal, municipality of Sernancelhe, Beira Alta, Portugal (see fig. 7.1). He is among the most famous and prolific Portuguese writers of the twentieth century, with more than fifty books published during his lifetime. One of Ribeiro's dominant traits is his faithfulness to his rural heritage from Beira Alta. He sensitively explores rural problems and people's characters, making an intense use of regional wording and vocabulary. Beira Alta's Lapa and Leomil highlands and its small villages situated in the mountains provide the main settings of his novels, in which the action often revolves around the use and exploitation of natural resources, including agriculture, forestry, hunting, poaching, and mining. Ribeiro wrote that he was above all "an annotator," which framed his literature in the constraints of realism. Ensuring the opportunity to analyze their literal contents, the verisimilitude of his texts also allows us to explore his "experience of landscape," investigating the subjective dimension of his descriptions.

Ribeiro's literature, both fiction and nonfiction, matches the conditions elaborated by Lawrence Buell as ingredients of an environmentally oriented work:

1. The nonhuman environment is present not merely as a framing device but as a presence that begins to suggest that human history is implicated in natural history;
2. The human interest is not understood to be the only legitimate interest;
3. Human accountability to the environment is part of the text's ethical orientation;
4. Some sense of the environment as a process rather than as a constant or a given is at least implicit in the text.[1]

In the first half of the twentieth century, studies on life or social sciences in Portugal are scarce. Particularly for the region of Beira Alta, there is not much other written information concerning the relationship between humans and nature or wildlife inventories. Because of their landscape descriptions and references

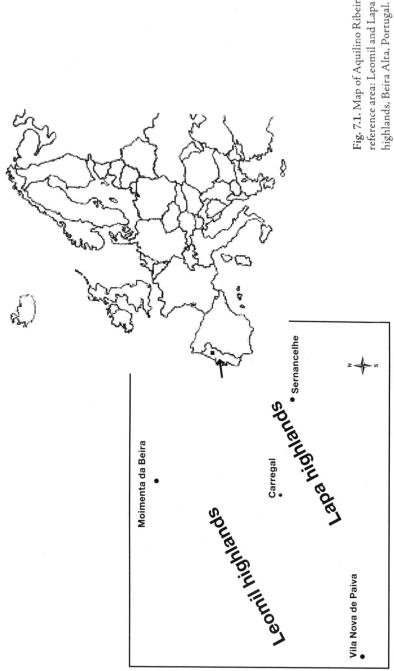

Fig. 7.1. Map of Aquilino Ribeiro's reference area: Leomil and Lapa highlands, Beira Alta, Portugal.

and comments about wildlife, Ribeiro's writings might serve as a major source on the environmental history of Beira Alta.

Birds and Literature

An interest in birdwatching and the use of birds in literature and folklore can be found throughout the world. For instance, at the Dionysos Festival in 414 A.C.E., Aristophanes presented the Greek comedy *The Birds* about a kingdom created in the skies, among birds, that challenged the previous one on earth and the power of gods.[2] Some species that are widely distributed, such as owls, have inspired remarkably diverse cultural responses.[3] But even the hummingbirds, which live only in the Western Hemisphere, have inspired folklore among the Mayans, Aztecs, Chayma people of Trinidad, North American Indians (e.g., Navajo, Cherokee, Apache), and more.[4] *De Beestiis et Aliis Rebis*, the twelfth-century book written by Hugo de Folieto (a monk from Saint Nicolas of Remy, Amiens, France), follows the tradition of interpreting symbolically and allegorically the nature of animals (including birds), fabulous creatures, rocks, and so on.[5] In 1765, John Aikin argued in "An Essay on the Application of Natural History to Poetry" that the study of natural history could serve descriptive poets admirably in achieving novelty in imagery and language.[6] Of all animals, birds seemed to him central. Several canonical writers used birds (and natural elements) as source of inspiration. For instance, D. H. Lawrence (1885–1930) wrote a whole book of poems on *Birds, Beasts and Flowers* (1923),[7] and according to Jeremy Hooker, Edward Thomas (1878–1917) had the "sense of the divine in Nature" and associated lyric poetry with the songs of birds.[8] Artist and naturalist John James Audubon (1785–1851) produced an extraordinary set of paintings and texts on the *Birds of America* (1827–38, 4 volumes, 435 plates).[9] His books called the attention of his contemporaries to the wonders of nature, thereby furthering the cause of early conservationism.[10]

Among other writers of the nineteenth and twentieth centuries, Aquilino Ribeiro was considered one of the Portuguese poets and prose writers leading the modern environmental conscience.[11] Besides this contribution, his writings are also potential material sources for complementing historical scientific studies. He used birds to compose literary scenarios but his references, which appeared in a literal or figurative sense, are always biologically informative.

In general, Portuguese historical studies in ornithology are scarce and restricted to particular issues. The first list of birds of Portugal was published with 193 species,[12] and later 44 more species were added.[13] In the beginning of the twentieth century, Charles of Braganza, king of Portugal (who was a birdwatcher and also a painter), prepared an *Illustrated Catalogue of Portuguese Birds*, in which he planned to include 292 species. Only two volumes of this work, with twenty species each, were published during his lifetime, but his work was recently rediscovered and made available in full.[14] Between 1920 and 1945 a few studies were published.[15] Beyond inventories based in certain locations where their authors lived or worked, unfortunately never our area of reference, these works nevertheless have useful descriptions and data about migration, breeding, habitat, behavior patterns, and relations between humans and birds.

Objectives

This chapter presents part of a study of wildlife in Ribeiro's writings. We focus on wild birds, the group of animals most frequently mentioned by Ribeiro and for which he showed a clear preference. Our main objectives are (1) to describe a method for the analysis of literary writings on the basis of nature descriptors (taxonomic and thematic), which could be replicated by those who want to research "birdwatching in literature"; (2) to evaluate Ribeiro's writings as a material source for local environmental history. This contributes to a more elaborate study of recent changes in Portuguese land use and landscapes.

Methodology

The Literary Writings

Because of their environmental focus and setting in Beira Alta, twelve writings were chosen for analysis from among the many published by Ribeiro. (We are aware of the possibility and profit of enlarging this study to other writings of this author.) Analyzed books were written between 1918 and 1954. They include nine novels, *A Via Sinuosa* (1918), *Terras do Demo* (1919), *O Malhadinhas* (1922), *Andam Faunos pelos Bosques* (1926), *O Homem que matou o Diabo* (1930), *Volfrâmio* (1944), *Cinco Reis de Gente* (1948), *Quando os Lobos Uivam* (1958), and *Mina de Diamantes* (1958), and three essays, *Aldeia* (1946), *Geografia Sentimental* (1951, only chapters I and XVI), and *O Homem da Nave* (1954).

Of these, *Quando os Lobos Uivam* (*When the Wolves Howl*) is the only work that, so far as we know, has been translated into English.[16] This novel centers on the people's negative reaction against forestry policy: the massive pine tree afforestation in the Portuguese commons that was implemented in the middle of the twentieth century.

Nature Descriptors

For this study, each of these works was carefully read and systematic notes were taken of all references to wild birds. Excerpts were defined as an extract in which at least one such reference occurred. The beginning and the end of each excerpt were arbitrarily established, but respecting full sentences and the complete text for the ideas' expression. Each bird species was recorded by its common name (a taxonomic descriptor) and each excerpt was classified according to the information it provided (the thematic descriptors). From the list of common names, a tentative list of equivalent scientific (Latin) names was elaborated, using the comprehensive list of vernacular Portuguese names for the Palearctic birds.[17] Translated English names are from Lars Svensson et al.'s *Collins Bird Guide*.[18]

In addition to the identification of the taxonomic units, the selected excerpts were also organized according to the following thematic descriptors:

Biological aspects: (1) Morphology, (2) Habitat, (3) Songs and calls, (4) Diet, (5) Migration, (6) Nesting, (7) Other behavior patterns

Timetable and calendar: (8) Daily cycle, (9) Annual cycle

Relation between humans and nature: (10) Damages to crops, (11) Hunting, (12) Poaching

Literary aspects: (13) Proverbs, (14) "The wild man" (in which the writer compared human personalities with the animals and plants with which they lived).

Results and Discussion

Analysis of Literary Writings on the Basis of Nature Descriptors

Taxonomic Descriptors

Using the above-described methodology, we selected 270 excerpts in which 488 bird citations are included. Table 7.1 summarizes the results of the content analysis that concern the taxonomic descriptors.

From the writings, we identified sixty-six different taxonomic units, much of which correspond to the species level—whenever the common name is distinctive enough (e.g., *Gallinula chloropus* for *galinha-de-água*) or a single species of the group occurs with those features (e.g., *Turdus viscivorus* for *tordo*, the sole thrush present all year around). Despite that, in some cases, a common name could be attributed to a set of species from one or more genuses, such as *coruja*—in English, the owl—which corresponds, at least, to *Tyto alba* and *Strix aluco*. Other difficulties were cases in which more than one common name corresponds to only one species, such as *marantéu* and *papa-figos*—in English, the golden oriole, *Oriolus oriolus*—or to different species of the same genus, such as *boeirinha* and *alvéola*—in English, the wagtail, *Motacilla alba*, *M. cinerea*, and *M. flava*. Other examples can be found in the tentative list of taxonomic units. There are also a few species whose corresponding Latin names would be impossible to find without additional field research, such as *peneirinha* or *peneireiro dos Bosques*.

Some of the taxonomic units are more frequently cited than others, especially the turtle dove (n = 53), the red-legged partridge (n = 52), the jay (n = 25), the sparrow (n = 24), the common cuckoo (n = 18), the Eurasian blackbird (n = 18), the crow (n=18), the golden oriole (n = 17), the owl (n = 17), and the hoopoe (n = 16). We will discuss later in the article why we think Ribeiro mentioned some species of birds more often than others.

Of the total 270 excerpts, in 68 percent only one taxon was mentioned (n = 184); the maximum number of taxa per excerpt was eleven (in only one). This suggests that Ribeiro more often discussed birds at the species level (or the population) than the community level. Nevertheless, there were only four taxa units that were ever mentioned alone in an entire book (rather than just in an excerpt): the common crane, the black-winged kite, the lesser kestrel, and the European greenfinch, all of them with a low contribution to the total number of excerpts (n = 9).

Table 7.1
Bird Taxonomic Units Identified in Ribeiro's Writings

Ribeiro's Names	English Common Names	Scientific Names	Total Citations
Abetarda	Great bustard	Otis tarda	2
Açor	Northern goshawk	Accipiter gentilis	2
Águia	Eagle	Gen. Aquila, Circaetus, Circus, Hieratus, and Buteo	2
Alcaravão, Perluis	Stone curlew	Burhinus oedicnemus	2
Alvéola, Boeirinha	Wagtail	Motacilla cinerea and/or M. alba	4
Andorinha	House martin or swallow	Fam. Hirundinidae	12
Calhandra, Calandra	Lark	Gen. Melanocorypha and/or Calandrella brachydactila	3
Carriça	Northern wren	Troglodytes troglodytes	9
Cartaxo	Common stonechat	Saxicola torquata	5
Codorniz	Common quail	Coturnix coturnix	6
Corcolher	Crested lark	Galerida cristata and/or G. theklae	5
Coruja, Mocho	Owl	Order Strigiformes	17
Corvo	Crow	Corvus corax	18
Cotovia	Woodlark	Lulula arborea	12
Cuco	Common cuckoo	Cuculus canorus	18
Escrevedeira	Bunting	Gen. Emberiza	3
Estorninho	Common starling	Sturnus unicolor	12
Falcão	Falcon	Gen. Falco	1
Falcão Peneireiro	Kestrel	Falco tinnunculus	1
Gerifalte	Gyrfalcon	Falco rusticolus	4
Francelho	Lesser kestrel	Falco naumanni	6
Nebri	Peregrine falcon	Falco peregrinus	4
Folexa, Folecha, Folosa	Warbler	Fam. Sylvidae	6
Gaio	Jay	Garrulus glandarius	25
Galinha-de-água	Common moorhen	Gallinula chloropus	1
Galinhola	Woodcock	Scolopax rusticola	5
Ganso	Goose	Gen. Anser	1
Gavião	Sparrowhawk	Accipiter nisus	7
Gralha	Carrion crow	Corvus corone	5
Grou	Common crane	Grus grus	4
Guincho	Common starling	Apus apus	1

Laverca	Skylark	*Alauda arvensis*	1
Maçarico	Lapwing	*Vanellus vanellus*	2
Maranteu, Papa-figos	Golden oriole	*Oriolus oriolus*	17
Meigengra, Mejengra	Tit	Fam. *Paridae*	6
Melro	Blackbird	*Turdus merula*	18
Melro dos rochedos	Rock thrush	*Monticola saxatilis* and/or *M. solitarius*	2
Milhafre	Red kite	*Milvus migrans* and/or *M. milvus*	8
Milheira	Serin	*Serinus serinus*	2
Narceja	Common snipe	*Gallinago gallinago*	1
Noitibó	Nightjar	*Caprimulgus europaeus* and/or *C. ruficolis*	7
Pardal	Sparrow	*Passer domesticus, P. hispaniolensis* and/or *P. montanus*	24
Pato-bravo	Duck	*Anas platyrhincos*	2
Pedreiro	Swift	*Phoenicurus ochrurus*	2
Pega	Common magpie	*Pica pica*	5
Peneireiro dos bosques, Peneirinha			3
Perdiz	Red-legged partridge	*Alectoris rufa*	52
Peto, Peto real, Peto-rinchão, Cavalinho	Green woodpecker	*Picus viridis*	10
Pica-peixe	Common kingfisher	*Alcedo atthis*	2
Picanço	Great grey shrike	*Lanius excubitor* and/or *L. senator*	2
Pintarroxo	Linnet	*Carduelis cannabina*	1
Pintassilgo	Goldfinch	*Carduelis carduelis*	3
Pisco	Robin	*Erithacus rubecula*	3
Pombo-bravo	Wood pigeon	*Columba palumbus*	9
Poupa	Hoopoe	*Upupa epops*	16
Rola	Turtle dove	*Streptopelia turtur*	53
Rouxinol	Nightingale	*Luscinia megarhynchos* and/or *Cettia cettia*	10
Sombria	Ortolan bunting	*Emberiza hortulana*	1
Tajasno	Wheatear	*Oenanthe oenanthe* and/or *O. hispanica*	3
Tarambola	Plover	Gen. *Charadrius* and/or *Pluvialis*	3

Table 7.1 (continued)

Ribeiro's Names	English Common Names	Scientific Names	Total Citations
Tentilhão	Chaffinch	*Fringilla coelebs*	1
Tordo	Thrush	*Turdus viscivorus*	4
Toutinegra	Blackcap	Gen. *Sylvia*	10
Tralhão	Spotted flycatcher	*Muscicapa striata* and/or *Ficedula hipoleuca*	3
Tuinha, Tuinho	Zitting cisticola	*Cisticola juncidis*	3
Verdilhão	European greenfinch	*Carduelis chloris*	1

Dark bars in figure 7.2 show the number of citations identified in each publication. These demonstrate how much each source contributes to the overall data set. In nonfiction, we found more citations on wild birds and, consequently, a larger number of excerpts were selected from nonfiction writings (*Aldeia*, n = 90; *Geografia Sentimental*, n = 62; *O Homem da Nave*, n = 83). Light bars show the contribution of each book to the inventory of species. Once again, nonfiction strongly contributes with different taxonomic units cited (*Aldeia*, n = 40; *Geografia Sentimental*, n = 26; and *O Homem da Nave*, n = 38), but three of the novels also deserve particular attention in this context (*Andam Faunos pelos Bosques*, n = 25; *Terras do Demo*, n = 29; and *A Via Sinuosa*, n = 25).

Thematic Descriptors
The classification with thematic descriptors involves a biological content analysis and an evaluation of the writer's knowledge (see below). As an example of Ribeiro's

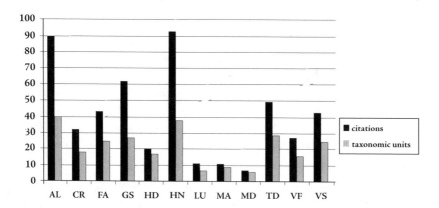

Fig. 7.2. Number of citations (n= 488) and different taxonomic units of wild birds (n=66) in each book. Key: AL, *Aldeia*; CR, *Cinco Reis de Gente*; FA, *Andam Faunos pelos Bosques*; GS, *Geografia Sentimental*; HD, *O Homem que matou o Diabo*; HN, *O Homem da Nave*; LU, *Quando os lobos uivam*; MA, *O Malhadinhas*; MD, *Mina de Diamantes*; TD, *Terras do Demo*; VF, *Volfrâmio*; VS, *A Via Sinuosa*.

detailed knowledge of the green woodpecker and the hoopoe, here is an excerpt classified under the following thematic descriptors: (1) Morphology, (2) Habitat, (4) Nesting, and (7) Other behavior patterns:

> I remember still, shining in black, an impeccably round opening a little smaller than the bunghole of a barrel being excavated by a green woodpecker. Year after year he lived there. When the little nest disappeared, the hole became the private domain of a hoopoe, who came there every spring to breed. Later on, once her young had emerged from the nest with their heads adorned with Sevillian combs, their hail-speckled wings shaking the sky with faltering half-rotations, it was as if an exotic and graceful futility had been knitted from the landscape.[19]

Describing a small pond surrounded by a pasture, Ribeiro recalled the wagtail, rock thrush, common magpie, and the northern wren, wording their behavior patterns as literature, and merging science and poetry. Here is an excerpt classified by the following descriptors: (2) Habitat and (7) Other behavior patterns:

> If you spy from a distance, rarely will you miss, fluttering or foraging about, the wagtail with its tail bobbing up and down, the rock thrush full of suspicion, the adventurer-magpie, and the little wren, which is the smallest of our birds and fears no one.[20]

Another example showing Ribeiro's remarkably accurate knowledge of the lark, the quail, the partridge, the stone curlew, and the starling was classified by the following descriptors: (4) Diet, (5) Migration, (7) Other behavior patterns, and (9) Annual cycle:

> They stuff their crop, the lark, the quail, the partridge, the stone curlew, the starling and especially the dove. If it was not for the bracing morning breeze, a premonition of autumn, these timid and delicate birds could prolong their stay until the sowings.[21]

To the 270 excerpts were attributed 379 descriptors on biological aspects, 66 on timetable and calendar, 70 on the relation between humans and nature, and 51 associated with literary aspects. On the biological aspects thematic descriptors, figure 7.3 shows that the major content is about habitats and behaviors, with a particular focus on habitat, songs and calls, and other behavior patterns.

Considering descriptors on the relation of humans and nature, the analysis of *Hunting* and *Poaching* descriptors is of special importance for understanding the use of faunal resources and the existing local knowledge during the first half of the twentieth century. They correspond to 84 excerpts, and 33 bird taxonomic units are mentioned: *abetarda, açor, águia, alcaravão, andorinha, carriça, codorniz, corvo, cotovia, cuco, estorninho, folexa, gaio, galinhola, gavião, marantéu, mejengra, melro, milhafre, milheira, nebri, pardal, perdiz, peto, pintassilgo, pombo-bravo, poupa, rola, rouxinol, tajasno, tarambola, tordo,* and *tuinho.*

In these excerpts, the main themes are regular depredation of eggs in nests, poaching with traps, falconry, and aims and procedures of legal hunting. The first

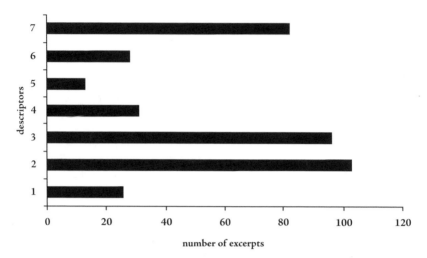

Fig. 7.3. Number of excerpts classified by each descriptor on biological aspects. Key: (1) Morphology, (2) Habitat, (3) Songs and calls, (4) Diet, (5) Migration, (6) Nesting, (7) Other behavior patterns.

two are depicted as negative attitudes and activities that are a threat to wildlife. Ribeiro wrote that the most inauspicious hunters are those who use snares, as "they spend all the morning spying the partridge male where it calls and stays, for trapping its female and getting the laying of eggs."[22] For him, poaching is a primitive activity carried out by certain insensitive and uneducated people, that is, most of the villagers. The activity is also justified due to certain economic difficulties and times of famine.

Although he liked to identify himself with the rural environment, Ribeiro's opinions and behavior in relation to nature differed from most of the villagers, mainly because of his understanding of its noninstrumental value. For instance, birdwatching is one of his favorite pastimes. On his small farm in Soutosa, which he called "my Kruger Park," he decided to protect all the wild animals (with the exception of mice and rats).[23] But he also describes falconry and legal hunting as interesting and traditional leisure activities: "[T]o kill a partridge is more difficult than to produce a good speech in the parliament or to compose a sonnet."[24] In contrast to the poachers, Ribeiro describes hunters as civilized and respectable men. He also commented on hunting regulations, namely provisions adopted by the local commissions: "[I]t matters having these birds for finger's satisfaction of some privileged masters; it does not matter to have these beautiful birds, meanly harmful to agriculture, cheering hills of Portugal."[25] He also criticized hunting calendars for turtle doves because they ignored the habits of the species: "[T]hey name the opening day for the first of September, but in some regions, these birds have not yet migrated then or are migrating at that moment."[26]

Evaluating Ribeiro's Writings as a Source for Local Environmental History

The Writer and the Birdwatcher

By his own account, Ribeiro learned about birds primarily by viewing them himself: "I ignore what has been said on this matter from Buffon onwards. I reason from what I see, just as the countrymen perform arithmetic on their fingers."[27] At his home, he prohibited "to harm birds" and, for this reason, the place became "the heaven of sparrows."[28] But he was an admitted hunter who profited from the practical experience of the activity to observe important facts about nature, especially animal behavior.

Because he was an erudite man, some of Ribeiro's extensive descriptions of the ecology and behavior of some species might also result from his readings of works by authors such as Buffon (1707–1788). Using irony, Ribeiro said that this French naturalist "devotes himself to a sovereign antipathy of an aristocrat"[29] and that "he had judged by the five sores of his embroidered cuffs" that sparrows are "gourmands and impolite."[30] Ribeiro considered the Eurasian woodcock a "sapient bird" and disagreed with Buffon, who referred to it as "stupid, ill-tempered, heavy and sloven."[31] Finally, Ribeiro mentioned the Latin name attributed by Buffon to the turtle dove, "*Columbae turtures.*"[32]

Although we admit Ribeiro's descriptions are his own reading of the environment as he experienced it, his knowledge, his use of realism in his writings, and the ecological accuracy of his texts give us reasons enough to use his information as an important source for local environmental history in Portugal.

Birds as Ornaments and Metaphors

Sometimes Ribeiro mentioned birds as metaphors. He used their imagery to enrich his writing and to elaborate new metaphors. Here are some examples:

+ drawing a line in the sky, the Swallow's flight is as difficult to follow as the designs of God[33] or the life course of an adolescent;[34]
+ the young scholars are compared to a Starling flock[35] or to sparrows when they steal fruits from the trees;[36]
+ goats like freedom as the orioles like figs.[37]

Enthralled by the songs of birds, Ribeiro composed onomatopoeic monologues or dialogues between species. As examples, these are elements of his "soundscape":

+ "preluis! preluis!" the stone curlew has "a lamentable scream, a ringing voice";[38]
+ in the night, "the owl intones its bad song";[39]
+ in the eaves, sparrows cry "Xarriu! Xarriu! Xarriu!";[40]

- ✦   "Ceix! Ceix!" the kingfisher' s cry is a shrill of victory;[41]
- ✦   the golden oriole is a vicious flutist, releasing cheerful eighth notes, in a fascinating chromatic scale, "merry as its clothing."[42]

The golden oriole appears in "colloquium with the jays and with colleagues from one tree to another."[43] Ribeiro represents its songs in understandable sentences with a similar sound effect: "Lá o vi, lá o vi," (in English, "I see him there").[44] He explains that these sentences are onomatopoeias because of the tonic "I."

Ribeiro attributed a special meaning to some bird songs. For example, the crows said "crá-crá," but this was understood by characters according to their role in the story or explained by the narrator as a message to them; when a child passed nearby some of them said "this boy don't leave us in peace!" but the others retorted with "let him go!"[45] And once crows heard a high turbulence in the villages, they would scream, reminding listeners of the deaths of the nineteenth-century Portuguese civil war: "Meat! Meat! Guerrilla is coming back."[46] Finally, more related to the common current needs, and rooted in folklore and local traditional thinking, the chimes of the quail were said to indicate how many wheat seeds each spike would bear that year.

Local Distribution and Abundance of Birds

Birds are often elements of Ribeiro's literary scenarios, both when their passive presence was announced by the writer and when they were portrayed in action, crossing the skies, singing a song, and so on. All together, the list of birds presented in table 7.1 could serve as an inventory of the birds occurring in that region (Lapa and Leomil highlands) during the first half of the twentieth century.

Ribeiro's literary inventory of birds from the past might be compared, according to the previously discussed constraints, with the current distribution of birds recorded in the last edition of the atlas of breeding birds[47] and with the bird study developed in the Leomil highlands.[48] Fifteen species mentioned in the atlas did not occur in Ribeiro's bird inventory listed in table 7.1: the little grebe (*Tachybaptus ruficollis*), the white stork (*Ciconia ciconia*), the grey heron (*Ardea cinerea*), the Egyptian vulture (*Neophron percnopterus*), the little bustard (*Tetrax tetrax*), the common sandpiper (*Actitis hypoleucos*), the roller (*Coracias garrulus*), the great spotted woodpecker (*Dendrocopus major*), the dipper (*Cinclus cinclus*), the dunnock (*Prunella modularis*), the nuthatch (*Sitta europaea*), the short-toed treecreeper (*Certhia brachydactila*), the azure-winged magpie (*Cyanopica cyana*), the hawfinch (*Coccothraustes coccothraustes*), and the corn bunting (*Milaria calandra*). However, these discrepancies are hard to interpret because of the simultaneous variation of scale (in the atlas the two sample map units are larger than the Lapa and Leomil highlands) and time period. In the more recent bird inventory of the Leomil highlands,[49] in a study area included in the region Ribeiro wrote about, two species are absent from Ribeiro's literary inventory of birds in table 7.1: the great spotted woodpecker and the dunnock.

The great bustard is mentioned by Ribeiro but nowadays it does not occur in the area. He suggested that it arrived in winter at the wet pastures of the Leomil

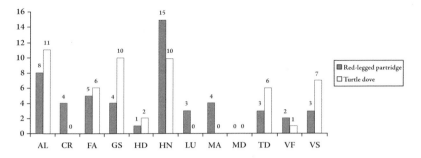

Fig. 7.4. Number of citations of red-legged partridge (in grey) and turtle dove (in white) in each book. Key: AL, *Aldeia*; CR, *Cinco Reis de Gente*; FA, *Andam Faunos pelos Bosques*; GS, *Geografia Sentimental*; HD, *O Homem que matou o Diabo*; HN, *O Homem da Nave*; LU, *Quando os lobos uivam*; MA, *O Malhadinhas*; MD, *Mina de Diamantes*; TD, *Terras do Demo*; VF, *Volfrâmio*; VS, *A Via Sinuosa*.

highlands[50] and mentioned its heavy flight that makes "fuss and volume"[51] when it takes off. The reference to this habitat specialist species could also indicate the dominant landscape in the top of Leomil highlands in Ribeiro's time: a mosaic of seminatural grasslands, field crops, and fallow fields. Nowadays, not only does this species not occur in Beira Alta, but its national distribution is also restricted to the southern and southwestern parts of the country.[52]

The red-legged partridge (n = 52) and the turtle dove (n = 53) are the two most frequently mentioned species in Ribeiro's writings (see fig. 7.4). The partridge is cited in almost all the writings (eleven to twelve) with a maximum in one of the essays (*O Homem da Nave*, n = 15); the turtle dove is more often cited in some writings but not in all of them (eight to twelve), most often in the three essays (*Aldeia*, n = 11; *Geografia Sentimental*, n = 10; and *O Homem da Nave*, n = 10).

These two species were abundant in Ribeiro's day. He wrote that "partridges are thick as the coal dust."[53] Ribeiro's interest in and knowledge of partridges and doves could be explained by the fact that he partially developed his love of nature through hunting as a young man. In his biographic novels *Cinco Reis de Gente* and *A Via Sinuosa*,[54] he reports on his initiation in depredation of nests[55] and hunting.[56] These two species are still very common today and are appreciated as a hunting resource in the area. Without population studies, it is not possible to evaluate the numeric evolution of their effectiveness, but from what we know about landscape changes in the last fifty years,[57] some potential habitat is currently being lost. Furthermore, the expansion of an alien dove species, the collared dove (*Streptopelia decaoto*), could also pose a serious threat to the native turtle dove.

Although this kind of quantitative analysis is valuable, the number of references of species cannot accurately be interpreted as an index of relative abundance in general. For instance, Ribeiro might have mentioned some species more frequently than others for a variety of nonscientific reasons, such as the morphology and behavior of the birds in question, including brilliantly colored plumage (e.g., the golden oriole, the hoopoe), intricate songs and calls (e.g., the nightingale), and close proximity to human habitations (e.g., the sparrow); the important role of a given species in daily activities, like hunting (e.g., the red-legged partridge or the turtle dove; see above) or farming (e.g. the jay or the blackbird, which are infamous crop pests); and knowledge, ethical, and aesthetic options of the writer (e.g., the wren).

Our study of historical data on wild birds that can be gleaned from Aquilino Ribeiro's writings could be expanded in a number of ways. Future studies could take a species by species approach, focusing on such topics as morphology, ecology, or behavior patterns; investigate particular habitats or landscape units; or adopt a cross-cutting approach, exploring "Hunting," "Poaching," "Damages to crops," or other thematic descriptors that directly concern relations between humans and nature.

Such diverse studies of Ribeiro's writings are possible because he had an ecological way of thinking. He was aware of the diversity of life; understood the interdependence among species, and between them and their habitats; and reported on land use changes, criticizing what he saw as abuse of the land. Much of his knowledge can be gathered from his books, whether novels or essays. Based on our study, we argue that his accurate and plausible descriptions of the natural environment constitute a major source of reliable data for Portuguese environmental history. But this does not excuse us from analyzing his writings in the light of other sources, both scientific and nonscientific.

Enquiries, maps, local regulations, photos, paintings, and articles from regional newspapers could be particularly relevant for the period prior to the 1950s. In addition, existing aerial photographs provide us with data on land use, evolution of the landscape, and the dynamics of communities. But, as we pointed out earlier, this study on literature and environment was initiated in order to test the possibilities of filling in important gaps in ecological historical data using evidence from literature, which is, for the time being, an integrative, ongoing process.

Keeping in mind that the use of literature as a source of environmental history depends on the richness of the citations and the position of the writer in relation to nature, future research on this topic must also include detailed treatments of the writer's ideas about the value of nature. Despite Aquilino Ribeiro's lack of scientific training, the results of our study indicated that we are well justified in recognizing him as an important Portuguese naturalist of the early and middle twentieth century.

Resumo

Aquilino Ribeiro (1885–1963), um famoso escritor português do século XX, publicou mais de 50 livros durante a sua vida. Muitas dessas obras são romances, novelas e contos; outros são textos não ficcionais, que incluem reflexões, memórias e ensaios sobre temas históricos e geográficos. A vida selvagem e as descrições paisagísticas são elementos relevantes na sua literatura. Também os personagens desenvolvem actividades relacionadas com a exploração dos recursos naturais, tais como a agricultura, a silvicultura, a caça legal, o furtivismo, a extracção mineira, etc. Por estas razões, ele é frequentemente considerado o escritor que melhor retractou a sua região natal, a Beira Alta (Portugal).

O principal objectivo de um estudo em curso consiste em avaliar textos deste autor como fonte de história ambiental, para um período em que os estudos e registos sobre as questões ambientais são bastante raros, dando ênfase às aves selvagens, grupo para o qual Aquilino Ribeiro manifesta a sua preferência. Este trabalho preliminar aborda o potencial das citações e descrições sobre a morfologia, ecologia e comportamento: (1) para descrever as comunidades e os seus habitats; (2) para reconstituir a história do uso do solo e as relações entre o Homem e a Natureza durante o início e meados do século XX. A partir do registo, selecção e análise das citações relativas às aves selvagens, compreendidas em 9 romances e 3 colectâneas de textos não ficcionais, foi obtida uma lista de 66 diferentes unidades taxonómicas, mencionadas pelos seus nomes comuns. Uma atenção particular é dada aos descritores temáticos "Caça" e "Furtivismo," e às espécies cinegéticas, tais como a Perdiz (*Alectoris rufa*) e a Rola (*Streptopelia turtur*).

Notes

We would like to acknowledge the Luso-American Foundation for Development (FLAD) and the Instituto da Conservação da Natureza (ICN) for supporting the participation of Ana Isabel Queiroz at the NILAS conference in California in the summer of 2001. Our thanks also go to Margarida Fernandes and Luka Clark, who accepted the challenge to translate the excerpts presented here, to António Teixeira for the exchange of historical scientific papers, and to Francisco Moreira for his ornithological advice.

1. Lawrence Buell, *The Environmental Imagination: Thoreau, Nature Writing, and the Formation of American Culture* (Cambridge, Mass.: Harvard Univ. Press, Belknap Press, 1995), 7–8.

2. Aristófanes, *As Aves* (Lisbon: Edições 70, 1989).

3. Faith Medlin, *Centuries of Owls in Art and the Written Word* (Norwalk, Conn.: Silvermine Publishers, 1967); Krystyna Weinstein, *The Owl in Art, Myth, and Legend* (New York: Crescent Books, 1989).

4. Boria Sax, *The Mythical Zoo: An Encyclopedia of Animals in World Myth, Legend, and Literature* (Santa Barbara, Calif.: ABC-CLIO, 2001), 185–87.

5. Hugo de Folieto, *Livro das Aves* (Lisbon: Edições Colibri, 1999).

6. Quoted in John Rowlett, "Ornithological Knowledge and Literary Understanding," *New Literary History* 30, no. 3 (Summer 1999): 625–47.

7. D. H. Lawrence, *Birds, Beasts and Flowers* (1923; reprint, Santa Rosa, Calif.: Black Sparrow Press, 1992).

8. Jeremy Hooker, *Writers in a Landscape* (Cardiff: Univ. of Wales Press, 1996), 76–95.

9. John James Audubon, *Audubon's Birds of America* (New York: Harry N. Abrams, 1978).

10. Philip Shabecoff, *A Fierce Green Fire: The American Environmental Movement* (New York: Hill and Wang, 1993).

11. F. Queirós, "A Contribuição dos Poetas e Prosadores Portugueses para a Génese da Moderna Consciência Ambientalista" (dissertação de mestrado em filosofia da natureza e do ambiente, Faculdade de Letras da Universidade de Lisboa, 2000).

12. A. C. Smith, "A Sketch of the Birds of Portugal," *Ibis* 4, ser. 2, no. 16 (Oct. 1868): 428–60.

13. J. V. Barbosa du Bocage, "Algumas Observações e Additamentos ao Artigo do sr. A. C. Smith Intitulado 'A Sketch of the Birds of Portugal,'" *Jornal de Sciencias Mathematicas, Phisicas e Naturaes* 7 (1869): 1–6.

14. Dom Carlos Bragança's (Charles of Braganza)*Catálogo Ilustrado das Aves de Portugal*, fasc. 1, estampas 1–20 (Lisbon: Imprensa Nacional, 1903), *Catálogo Ilustrado das Aves de Portugal*, fasc. 2, estampas 21–40 (Lisbon: Imprensa Nacional, 1907), and *Catálogo Ilustrado das Aves de Portugal* (Lisbon: Imprensa Nacional, 1983).

15. William Chester Tait, *The Birds of Portugal* (London: Witherby, 1924); J. A. Reis Jr., *Catálogo Sistemático e Analítico das Aves de Portugal* (Porto: Araújo & Sobrinhos, 1931); H. W. Coverley, *H. W. Coverley's Bird Notes—Portugal* c. 1945 (unpublished).

16. Aquilino Ribeiro, *When the Wolves Howl* (New York: Macmillan, 1963).

17. H. Costa, A. Araújo, J. Farinha, M. Poças, and A. Machado, *Nomes Portugueses das Aves do Paleárctico Ocidental* (Lisbon: Assírio & Alvim, 2000).

18. Lars Svensson, Dan Zetterström, Killian Mullarney, and P. J. Grant, *Collins Bird Guide* (London: HarperCollins, 1999).

19. Aquilino Ribeiro, *Cinco Reis de Gente* (1948; reprint, Lisbon: Bertrand Editora e Círculo dos Leitores, 1985), 55.

20. Aquilino Ribeiro, *O Homem da Nave* (1954; reprint, Lisbon: Bertrand Editora, 1968), 28.

21. Aquilino Ribeiro, *Geografia Sentimental* (Lisbon: Bertrand Editora, 1951), 330.

22. Aquilino Ribeiro, *Aldeia—Terra, Gente e Bichos* (1946; reprint, Lisbon: Bertrand Editora, 1964), 107.

23. Ribeiro, *O Homem da Nave*, 147.

24. Ribeiro, *Geografia Sentimental*, 349.

25. Ribeiro, *O Homem da Nave*, 37.

26. Ibid., 53.

27. Aquilino Ribeiro, *Arcas Encoiradas* (Lisbon: Bertrand Editora, 1962), 89—a book that was not included in this study.

28. Ribeiro, *Geografia Sentimental*, 31.

29. Ribeiro, *O Homem da Nave*, 147.

30. Ibid., 160.

31. Ibid., 299.

32. Ribeiro, *Aldeia*, 185.

33. Aquilino Ribeiro, *A Via Sinuosa* (1918; reprint, Lisbon: Bertrand Editora e Círculo dos Leitores, 1985), 138.

34. Aquilino Ribeiro, *O Homem que Matou o Diabo* (1930; reprint, Lisbon: Bertrand Editora e Círculo dos Leitores, 1985), 46.

35. Aquilino Ribeiro, *Terras do Demo* (1919; reprint, Lisbon: Bertrand Editora e Círculo dos Leitores, 1985), 61.

36. Ribeiro, *Cinco Reis de Gente*, 118.

37. Ribeiro, *Aldeia*, 269.

38. Ibid., 281.

39. Aquilino Ribeiro, *Quando os Lobos Uivam* (1958; reprint, Lisbon: Bertrand Editora e Círculo dos Leitores, 1985), 60.

40. Ribeiro, *A Via Sinuosa*, 275.

41. Ibid., 184.

42. Ribeiro, *Geografia Sentimental*, 33.

43. Ibid.

44. Ribeiro, *Aldeia*, 80; Ribeiro, *O Homem da Nave*, 152.

45. Ribeiro, *Cinco Reis de Gente*, 60.

46. Aquilino Ribeiro, *Andam Faunos pelos Bosques* (1926; reprint, Lisbon: Bertrand Editora e Círculo dos Leitores, 1985), 37–38.

47. Rui Rufino, coord., *Atlas das Aves que Nidificam em Portugal Continental* (Lisbon: SNPRCN, Ministério do Plano e da Administração do Território, 1989).

48. J. P. Neves, C. Eira, and T. Múrias, *EIA do Parque Eólico da Serra de Leomil* (Coimbra, Portugal: Relatório Técnico, IMAR, Universidade de Coimbra, 2002).

49. Ibid.

50. Ribeiro, *O Homem da Nave*, 75–76.

51. Ibid., 29.

52. L. G. Elias, L. M. Reino, T. Silva, R. Tomé, and P. Geraldes, *Atlas das Aves Invernantes do Baixo Alentejo* (Lisbon: Sociedade Portuguesa para o Estudo das Aves, 1999).

53. Ribeiro, *O Homem da Nave*, 26.

54. Manuel Mendes, *Aquilino Ribeiro: A Obra e o Homem*, 2d ed. (Lisbon: Arcádia, 1977); Frederick C. H. Garcia, *Aquilino Ribeiro: Um Almocreve na Estrada de Santiago* (Lisbon: Publicações Dom Quixote, 1981).

55. Ribeiro, *Cinco Reis de Gente*, 91.

56. Ribeiro, *A Via Sinuosa*, 188–89.

57. Ana Isabel Queiroz, "Building Landscape Memory through Combined Sources: Commons Afforestation in Portugal," in *From Landscape Research to Landscape Planning: Aspects of Integration, Education, and Application*, ed. Bärbel Tress, Gunther Tress, Gary Fry, and Paul Opdam (Dordrecht, The Netherlands: Springer, 2006), 333–44.

Works Cited

Aristófanes. *As Aves*. Clássicos Gregos e Latinos. Lisbon: Edições 70, 1989.

Audubon, John James. *Audubon's Birds of America*. New York: Harry N. Abrams, 1978.

Barbosa du Bocage, J. V. "Algumas Observações e Additamentos ao Artigo do sr. A. C. Smith Intitulado 'A Sketch of the Birds of Portugal.'" *Jornal de Sciencias Mathematicas, Phisicas e Naturaes* 7 (1869): 1–6.

Bragança, Dom Carlos. *Catálogo Ilustrado das Aves de Portugal*. Fasc. 1, estampas 1–20. Lisbon: Imprensa Nacional, 1903.

———. *Catálogo Ilustrado das Aves de Portugal*. Fasc. 2, estampas 21–40. Lisbon: Imprensa Nacional, 1907.

———. *Catálogo Ilustrado das Aves de Portugal*. Lisbon: Imprensa Nacional, 1983.

Buell, Lawrence. *The Environmental Imagination: Thoreau, Nature Writing, and the Formation of American Culture*. Cambridge, Mass.: Harvard Univ. Press, Belknap Press, 1995.

Costa, H., A. Araújo, J. Farinha, M. Poças, and A. Machado. *Nomes Portugueses das Aves do Paleárctico Ocidental*. Lisbon: Assírio & Alvim, 2000.

Coverley, H. W. *H. W. Coverley's Bird Notes—Portugal*. c. 1945 (unpublished).

Elias, L. G., L. M. Reino, T. Silva, R. Tomé, and P. Geraldes. *Atlas das Aves Invernantes do Baixo Alentejo*. Lisbon: Sociedade Portuguesa para o Estudo das Aves, 1999.

Folieto, Hugo de. *Livro das Aves*. Obras Clássicas de Literatura Portuguesa—Literatura Medieval. Lisbon: Edições Colibri, 1999.

Garcia, Frederick C. H. *Aquilino Ribeiro: Um Almocreve na Estrada de Santiago*. Lisbon: Publicações Dom Quixote, 1981.

Hooker, Jeremy. *Writers in a Landscape*. Cardiff: Univ. of Wales Press, 1996.

Lawrence, D. H. *Birds, Beasts and Flowers*. 1923. Reprint, Santa Rosa, Calif.: Black Sparrow Press, 1992.

Medlin, Faith. *Centuries of Owls in Art and the Written Word*. Norwalk, Conn.: Silvermine Publishers, 1967.

Mendes, Manuel. *Aquilino Ribeiro: A Obra e o Homem*, 2d ed. Lisbon: Arcádia, 1977.

Neves, J. P., C. Eira, and T. Múrias. *EIA do Parque Eólico da Serra de Leomil, Secção Fauna*. Coimbra, Portugal: Relatório Técnico. IMAR, Universidade de Coimbra, 2002.

Queiroz, Ana Isabel. "Building Landscape Memory through Combined Sources: Commons Afforestation in Portugal." In *From Landscape Research to Landscape Planning: Aspects of Integration, Education, and Application*, edited by Bärbel Tress, Gunther Tress, Gary Fry, and Paul Opdam, 333–44. Wageningen UR Frontis Series, vol. 12. Dordrecht, The Netherlands: Springer, 2006.

Queirós, F. "A Contribuição dos Poetas e Prosadores Portugueses para a Génese da Moderna Consciência Ambientalista." Dissertação de mestrado em filosofia da natureza e do ambiente, Faculdade de Letras da Universidade de Lisboa, 2000.

Reis, J. A., Jr. *Catálogo Sistemático e Analítico das Aves de Portugal*. Porto: Araújo & Sobrinhos, 1931.

Ribeiro, Aquilino. *Aldeia—Terra, Gente e Bichos*. Obras Completas de Aquilino Ribeiro. 1946. Reprint, Lisbon: Bertrand Editora, 1964.

———. *Andam Faunos Pelos Bosques*. Edição comemorativa do centenário do nascimento de Aquilino Ribeiro. 1926. Reprint, Lisbon: Bertrand Editora e Círculo dos Leitores, 1985.

———. *Arcas Encoiradas*. Obras Completas de Aquilino Ribeiro. Lisbon: Bertrand Editora, 1962.

———. *A Via Sinuosa*. Edição comemorativa do centenário do nascimento de Aquilino Ribeiro. 1918. Reprint, Lisbon: Bertrand Editora e Círculo dos Leitores, 1985.

———. *Cinco Reis de Gente*. Edição comemorativa do centenário do nascimento de Aquilino Ribeiro. 1948. Reprint, Lisbon: Bertrand Editora e Círculo dos Leitores, 1985.

———. *Geografia Sentimental*. Obras Completas de Aquilino Ribeiro. Lisbon: Bertrand Editora, 1951.

———. *O Homem da Nave*. Obras Completas de Aquilino Ribeiro. 1954. Reprint, Lisbon: Bertrand Editora, 1968.

———. *O Homem que matou o Diabo*. Edição comemorativa do centenário do nascimento de Aquilino Ribeiro. 1930. Reprint, Lisbon: Bertrand Editora e Círculo dos Leitores, 1985.

———. *O Malhadinhas* (and *"A Mina de Diamantes"*). Obras Completas de Aquilino Ribeiro. 1922 and 1958. Reprint, Lisbon: Bertrand Editora, 1995.

———. *Quando os lobos uivam*. Edição comemorativa do centenário do nascimento de Aquilino Ribeiro. 1958. Reprint, Lisbon: Bertrand Editora e Círculo dos Leitores, 1985.

———. *Terras do Demo*. Edição comemorativa do centenário do nascimento de Aquilino Ribeiro. 1919. Reprint, Lisbon: Bertrand Editora e Círculo dos Leitores, 1985.

———. *Volfrâmio*. Edição comemorativa do centenário do nascimento de Aquilino Ribeiro. 1944. Reprint, Lisbon: Bertrand Editora e Círculo dos Leitores, 1985.

———. *When the Wolves Howl*. New York: Macmillan, 1963.

Rowlett, John. "Ornithological Knowledge and Literary Understanding." *New Literary History* 30, no. 3 (Summer 1999): 625–47.

Rufino, Rui, coord. *Atlas das Aves que Nidificam em Portugal Continental*. Lisbon: SNPRCN, Ministério do Plano e da Administração do Território, 1989.

Sax, Boria. *The Mythical Zoo: An Encyclopedia of Animals in World Myth, Legend, and Literature*. Santa Barbara, Calif.: ABC-CLIO, 2001.

Shabecoff, Philip. *A Fierce Green Fire: The American Environmental Movement*. New York: Hill and Wang, 1993.

Smith, A. C. "A Sketch of the Birds of Portugal." *Ibis* 4, ser. 2, no. 16 (Oct. 1868): 428–60.

Svensson, Lars, Dan Zetterström, Killian Mullarney, and P. J. Grant. *Collins Bird Guide*. London: HarperCollins, 1999.

Tait, William Chester. *The Birds of Portugal*. London: Witherby, 1924.

Weinstein, Krystyna. *The Owl in Art, Myth, and Legend*. New York: Crescent Books, 1989.

Chapter 8

The Triumphant Tiger: Short Narratives by Jorge Luis Borges

Susan Braden

> Tyger! Tyger! burning bright
> In the forest of the night,
> What immortal hand or eye
> Dare frame thy fearful symmetry?
> —William Blake

The tiger is a fearsome predator and, to quote G. K. Chesterton, "an emblem of terrible elegance" in innumerable myths and legends in world literature. The world-famous twentieth-century Argentine writer Jorge Luis Borges (1899–1986) believed that the tiger was a symbol that had profound implications concerning the universal relationship of man with nature and with himself. Ecologists know that the tiger is necessary as a predator to hunt and eliminate weak and diseased animals in the forest, helping maintain a balance of nature. Borges establishes a certain symbolic identification with tigers, a process that provides a psychic catharsis that eliminates feelings of powerlessness in the modern world.[1] With Borges as our guide, this chapter will explore the literary ecology of the tiger in the jungle of the mind.

To become familiar with Borges, a master writer who ranks quite high in importance not just for his own writing but also for his influence on many other writers, we travel back in time to the first decade of the last century, and the small house of a working-class family in the heart of Buenos Aires. We shall peek over the shoulder of a small boy who is busily drawing odd-looking tigers. Georgie Borges was a curious boy who read books voraciously. According to the testimony of his mother Leonor, "he used to draw animals, lying on the floor, and he always started backwards, with the paws. More than anything he would draw tigers, which were his favorite animals. When he would go to the nearby zoo (in Palermo) it was very difficult to persuade him to leave."[2] Emir Rodríguez-Monegal said that Borges was obsessed with tigers.[3] One of Borges's first poems was about an Argentine general known as the "Tiger of the Pampas." It is not surprising that one of his first original short stories (published in 1912), "The King of the Forest," would be about a tiger. Borges describes his obsession:

> A famous page of Blake makes of the tiger a glowing fire and
> an eternal archetype of Evil: I prefer to quote Chesterton, who

> defined him as a symbol of terrible elegance. There are no words, moreover, that can be the sum of a tiger, that form which for centuries has inhabited the imagination of man. The tiger has always attracted me. I know that I used to linger, as a child, before their cages at the zoo; the other animals were not important to me. I judged encyclopedias and natural history texts for the quality of their drawings of tigers. When I became familiar with the *Jungle Books* it bothered me that Shere Khan, the tiger, was the enemy of the hero. For all of my life, this curious love has never left me.[4]

Borges must have been thinking of his own childhood experiences when he notes in his prologue to the *Manual de zoología fantástica* (*Manual of Fantastic Zoology*) the curious contradiction of the behavior of a child during his first encounter with animals in the zoo:

> A small child is taken to the zoo for the first time. This child may be any one of us or, to put it another way, we have been this child and have forgotten about it. In these grounds—these terrible grounds—the child sees for the first time the bewildering variety of the animal kingdom, and this spectacle, which might alarm or frighten him, he enjoys. He enjoys it so much that going to the zoo is one of the pleasures of childhood, or is thought to be such. How can we explain this everyday and yet mysterious event?[5]

He goes on to offer two explanations: the child follows the ideal principle of Plato that he had already seen the tiger in a primal world of archetypes, or he follows that of the German philosopher Schopenhauer, who would say that the child looks on the tiger without fear because they are both forms of the same essence, called the Will. In either case, the encounter allows the child to identify himself with the tiger and to unify his consciousness with his instinctive impulses.

It is evident that through the years as young Georgie matured to the adult Borges, the presence of the tiger would manifest itself in many different ways and undergo significant transformations. Between 1914 and 1921, Borges lived with his family in Europe, in Switzerland throughout the Great War, and then afterward in Spain. A voracious reader and true cosmopolite, he synthesized the folklore and legends of Argentine, European, and Eastern traditions and added touches of philosophy, irony, and humor that made his writing unique.

Not only did Borges read Chesterton, Blake, and Kipling, but also the Uruguayan Horacio Quiroga, a master of short story writing who wrote several tales of the tiger in the jungle in Misiones, Uruguay. His own intimate friend Adolfo Bioy Casares wrote a story called "The Hero of Women" in which the disappearance of the beautiful wife of a landowner is linked to a tiger.[6] The fable of Stockton based on the old oriental legend called "The Lady or the Tiger?" written in 1884 was just the type of story that Borges loved: a type of trap from which escape seems impossible but which invites the participation of the reader to invent one. Borges's inspiration led to the creation of the story "Bestiario" by his protégé, Julio

Cortázar, in which the young heroine tricks an abusive relative into being killed by a tiger.

Borges is most famous for his fantastic short stories, which he began to publish in 1943. In the fantastic genre, the lines between fictional reality and the ordinary are ruptured. For Borges, as well as for Blake, the tiger represents a lithe, brutal reality challenging the commonplace; it is Darkness, Fire, Danger, and Time. In his essay "A New Refutation of Time," he expresses his identification with the tiger:

> Time is the substance of which I am made. Time is a river that carries me away, but I am the river; it is a tiger that mangles me, but I am the tiger; it is a fire that consumes me, but I am the fire. The world, alas, is real; I, alas, am Borges.[7]

Significantly, the tiger is not a creature separate from man, but rather Borges and the tiger are one. Unfortunately, as Borges aged and his fame as an author grew, he started to go blind, and his works reflect his struggle to create himself as a poet in his own more limited intimate space. In "Dreamtigers," he narrates how he revisits his childhood tiger, "that striped Asiatic, royal tiger," in his dreams. But the illusion cannot last:

> Then I think: This is a dream, a pure diversion of my will; and now that I have unlimited power, I am going to cause a tiger. Oh, incompetence! Never can my dreams engender the wild beast I long for. The tiger indeed appears, but stuffed or flimsy, or with impure variations of shape, or of an implausible size, or all too fleeting, or with the touch of the dog or the bird.[8]

The desire to create a tiger in his imagination is expressed even more poignantly in another poem in the same book entitled "The Other Tiger." Borges was appointed director of the National Library in Buenos Aires in 1955, the same year in which he completely lost his sight. He describes the vivid image of an imaginary tiger prowling in the library:

> I think of a tiger. The gloom here makes
> The vast and busy library seem lofty
> And pushes the shelves back;
> Strong, innocent, covered with blood and new,
> It will prowl through the forest and its morning. . . .[9]

He meditates on the distance between his world in South America and that of the real tiger on the banks of the Ganges. But neither the tiger in his imagination nor the "paper tiger" that he creates in his poem is a satisfactory replacement for the flesh-and-blood tiger so he proposes a solution to the problem which exists outside of the limits of space and time:

> We shall seek a third tiger. . .
> The other tiger, that which is not in verse.[10]

This tiger, according to Antonio Planells, "is that which the poet longs for, that which symbolizes desire and passion." It is a point of intersection between his material reality and the reality of his dreams.[11]

In the poem "The Gold of the Tigers" from a book with the same title, Borges reflects upon the yellow color of the tiger that is now the only color that his blindness allows him to see:

> O sunsets, O tigers, O wonders
> Of myth and epic,
> O gold more dear to me, gold of your hair
> Which these hands crave to touch.[12]

The last two lines of this poem express Borges's sensual desire to actually touch a tiger, a wish that was realized late in his life during a trip to Animal World in Irvine, California. He wrote about the experience in a short narrative, "The Last Tiger":

> This last tiger is made of flesh and blood. In a show of terrified happiness, I went up to this tiger. Its tongue licked my face and its claws—distracted or caressing—rested on my head. Unlike its predecessors, it had smell and weight. I do not claim that this tiger, which frightened me, is more real than the others, since an oak tree is no more real than the figures in a dream. But I want to thank our friend, the flesh and blood tiger that my senses perceived that morning, whose image comes back to me like those tigers in books.[13]

One of Borges's last published stories was "The Blue Tigers," where the setting is not Argentina but rather the Punjab in Indostan.[14] The protagonist receives news that a rare blue tiger species has been spotted prowling in the forests of the countryside. Knowing that there are no tigers in this region, he travels to the nearest village and tries to engage the help of the locals in pursuit of the blue tiger. The natives continually trick him into going to places where the tiger is never found and he eventually catches on to the fact that they are only taking advantage of him and his money. He climbs to a plateau that they have told him is forbidden, but he only finds some mysterious small smooth blue round stones. He pockets them and returns to the village where he discovers that they multiply and diminish in number without any explanation. He begins to have an obsessive relationship with the stones as he tries in many different ways to calculate mathematically their change in quantity. He dreams of their "divinity"; later he tries unsuccessfully to get rid of them. Finally, in desperation, he gives them to a passing blind beggar as "charity," warning him of their disconcerting characteristics. The beggar tells him that he does not know what kind of charity this is, but he says that by taking the stones his own charity will disconnect the visitor from the knowledge that he seeks: the academician will stay with his "days and nights, with his routine habits, with the world."

The "blue tigers" in this story symbolize the opposite of order and logic; they also symbolize chaos and man's inability to control untamable forces. Chaos is seen here as a superior condition and human routines and even the concept of time a poor illusion which prevents man from understanding the true nature of his relationship to the universe. There is a possible religious symbolism in this story: the blue color of the stones might symbolize heaven and God; the cross that the academician incises into one of the stones is once again an allusion to crucifixion. The cut stone disappears into the rest during a multiplication cycle but then reappears in their midst a few days later, a type of "resurrection" in the midst of chaos. The fact that the round disks are stones also appears to echo the idea of the "rock of ages" and the philosopher's stone. There is also personal symbolism: the academician has many of Borges's characteristics, which are delineated in the autobiographical beginning to the story. However, the beggar who finally releases him from his obsessive torture is blind, like Borges. Moreover his "charity" could be considered that of the universal author who "releases" the reader by leading him/her to personal exploration and catharsis. Once again Borges emphasizes his antithetical nature as a blind poet, a Homer on his own personal odyssey.

A reading of the tiger in Borges's writing is both inspiring and challenging. On the one hand, the tiger represents chaos and the archetypical primitive forces that both inspire and frighten us. The tiger shatters our sense of security and leads us to a sense of primal loss and efforts to recover our original innocence. Whether it be the mind of a child; the library, as in "The Other Tiger"; or simply golden light entering the eye, as in the "Gold of the Tigers," the perfect psychological "safety bubble," once burst, can never be put back together again the same way. For example, in "The Blue Tigers" the academician must rid himself of the multiplying stones or he will go crazy. Tensions build up to an intolerable level, creating the need for release and restoration of harmony, even though it is just an illusion. On the other hand, Borges's admiration for tigers and his inspiration to write about them have always been based on his imagination—they are only "dreamtigers" after all. The power of the real tiger in the jungle cannot be equated with its literary creation and yet the legends, stories, and poems have a power of their own to inspire entire generations of readers to feel awe and admiration of the tiger.

Gary Hoppenstand describes the multifaceted nature of the tiger:

> Tigers can be viewed any number of ways. For the deer, tigers are engines of violent death, yet for the tiger, hunting and killing are merely the means of survival, of living. For the poet and illustrator, tigers are beautifully symmetrical animals, possessing grace, form, color and enigma. For the zoologist, they are a class of predators functioning according to the designs of nature within a particular ecological environment. Death, life, poetic enigma and natural function: all of these concepts define the same thing, contradicting each other yet not being contradictory.[15]

Another fundamental idea of Borges's is that the tiger's complex symbolism reflects the fact that humans do not identify themselves as completely outside of the animal world, but neither do they completely include themselves in it. Man shares characteristics with the animals, but he is "only human" just as the tiger is "only an animal." In spite of the fact that human consciousness has evolved from the limitations of the early days of colonial domination, hubris still seems to keep modern man just beyond reach of true communication with animals. Borges's writings exaggerate this contradiction with a certain literary *mestizaje*: a blend of traditional forms with profound ideas in stories and poems that are both moving and aesthetically pleasing.

Unhappily, the tiger has not benefited from its relationship to us as much as we have from it. The world is coming to grips with the fact that the tiger is an endangered animal on the brink of extinction in most of its former habitat, where it is now rarely seen. According to John Seidensticker, little is known about the overall status, distribution, and ecological needs of the tiger. Management, legislative, and enforcement initiatives have been inadequate.[16] It is ironic, therefore, that while the literary symbolism of the tiger is more important than ever to us as a form of psychic exploration of our connection to nature, we might be the last generation to even be able to contemplate its existence in the wild. The winsome cartoon animal, the paper tiger, even the tiger at Animal World can never compete with the wild tiger, burning bright in the jungle. We must save the tiger that an aging blind Argentine librarian named Borges and each and every one of us dreams about—the one that captures our imagination and thrills us with his powerful golden magnificence.

Notes

I would like to acknowledge the assistance of Professor Dr. Suzanne Jill Levine at the University of California–Santa Barbara in the preparation of this chapter.

1. Joseph Tyler, "From the Fabulous to the Fantastic: The Tiger and Its Fearful Symmetry in the Twentieth-Century Spanish American Short Story," *Romance Languages Annual* 9, no. 1 (1997): 710.

2. Jorge Luis Borges, Miguel de Torre Borges, and Adolfo Bioy Casares, *Borges: Fotografías y manuscritos con 15 relatos* (Buenos Aires: Renglón, 1987), 25.

3. Emir Rodríguez-Monegal, "Symbols in Borges' Works," *Modern Fiction Studies* 19, no. 3 (Autumn 1973): 339.

4. Jorge Luis Borges, *La rosa de Paracelso y Tigres azules* (Madrid: Swan, 1986), 33–34. All translations from the Spanish are my own unless otherwise noted.

5. Jorge Luis Borges and Margarita Guerrero, *Manual de zoología fantástica* (Mexico City: Fondo de Cultura Económica, 1957), 771.

6. Adolfo Bioy Casares, *El héroe de las mujeres* (Buenos Aires: Emecé, 1978), 130–54.

7. Jorge Luis Borges, Alastair Reid, and Emir Rodríguez-Monegal, *Borges, a Reader: A Selection from the Writings of Jorge Luis Borges* (New York: Dutton, 1981), 120.

8. Jorge Luis Borges, *El hacedor* (Buenos Aires: Emecé, 1960), 12.

9. Jorge Luis Borges, *Obras completas* (Buenos Aires: Emecé, 1974), 825.

10. Ibid.

11. Antonio Planells, "The Presence of the Tiger in the Works of Jorge Luis Borges," *Explicacion de Textos Literarios* 18, no. 1 (1990): 6.

12. Jorge Luis Borges, *The Gold of the Tigers* (Buenos Aires: Emecé, 1977), 46.

13. Jorge Luis Borges with María Kodama, *Atlas* (Barcelona: Edhasa, 1986), 457.

14. Borges, *Rosa de Paracelso*, 31–72.

15. Gary Hoppenstand, *Search of the Paper Tiger: A Sociological Perspective of Myth, Formula, and the Mystery Genre in the Entertainment Print Mass Medium* (Bowling Green, Ohio: Bowling Green State Univ. Popular Press, 1987), 9.

16. John Seidensticker, "Saving the Tiger," *Wildlife Society Bulletin* 25, no. 1 (1997): 6.

Works Cited

Bioy Casares, Adolfo. *El héroe de las mujeres*. Buenos Aires: Emecé, 1978.

Borges, Jorge Luis. *The Gold of the Tigers*. Translated by Alastair Reid. Buenos Aires: Emecé, 1977.

———. *El hacedor*. Buenos Aires: Emecé, 1960.

———. *Obras completas*. Buenos Aires: Emecé, 1974.

———. *La rosa de Paracelso y Tigres azules*. Madrid: Swan, 1986.

Borges, Jorge Luis, Miguel de Torre Borges, and Adolfo Bioy Casares. *Borges: Fotografas y manuscritos con 15 relatos*. Buenos Aires: Renglón, 1987.

Borges, Jorge Luis, and Margarita Guerrero. *Manual de zoología fantástica*. Mexico City: Fondo de Cultura Económica, 1957.

Borges, Jorge Luis, with María Kodama. *Atlas*. Barcelona: Edhasa, 1986.

Borges, Jorge Luis, Alastair Reid, and Emir Rodríguez-Monegal. *Borges, a Reader: A Selection from the Writings of Jorge Luis Borges*. New York: Dutton, 1981.

Hoppenstand, Gary. *Search of the Paper Tiger: A Sociological Perspective of Myth, Formula, and the Mystery Genre in the Entertainment Print Mass Medium*. Bowling Green, Ohio: Bowling Green State Univ. Popular Press, 1987.

Planells, Antonio. "The Presence of the Tiger in the Works of Jorge Luis Borges." *Explicacion de Textos Literarios* 18, no. 1 (1990): 1–16.

Rodríguez-Monegal, Emir. "Symbols in Borges' Works." *Modern Fiction Studies* 19, no. 3 (Autumn 1973): 325–40.

Seidensticker, John. "Saving the Tiger." *Wildlife Society Bulletin* 25, no. 1 (1997): 6–17.

Tyler, Joseph. "From the Fabulous to the Fantastic: The Tiger and Its Fearful Symmetry in the Twentieth-Century Spanish American Short Story." *Romance Languages Annual* 9, no. 1 (1997): 710–16.

Chapter 9

Dark Brothers and Shadow Souls: Ursula K. Le Guin's Animal "Fables"

Tonia L. Payne

Ursula K. Le Guin is noted for her science fiction works; however, one of the most intriguing forms she uses is the animal fable. Le Guin uses this form to explore how we construct the "other." Confronting issues around "othering" is a salient characteristic of Le Guin's works in all genres. In many cases, her fiction proposes methods by which difference between self and other can become a source for penetrating relationships rather than rejection or subjugation. Her animal stories, however, more often do not suggest any cure for the problem of othering. Rather, through the readers' alliance with the othered, they demonstrate the negative, destructive aspects of othering, giving readers an emotional experience that clarifies, more profoundly than an intellectual explanation, what othering actually means and why, whenever it appears, it is indeed a problem in need of a cure.

One of the ways Le Guin provides readers with the emotional experience of othering is through shifting our viewpoint, placing her readers in a situation in which we become the other. Because we must, as a consequence, experience being othered, and because we also form an empathic relationship with the characters by whom we are othered, we must question both sides of the equation. Through our emotional experiences of being othered, as both the "rejected" humans of the stories and as we identify with the centralized characters who are othered by humans, we also begin to question our complicity in the othering around us—and, indeed, by us.

Although various "others," human and nonhuman, occur throughout Le Guin's writings, perhaps the most profound examples of othering are found in her animal stories. I equate her animal stories with fables for two reasons. Because the central character—usually the narrator—is an animal, the animals in these stories are given literal authority; they speak for themselves. Speaking animals are one of the hallmarks of fable, certainly of the fables of Aesop that are most familiar to U.S. readers from childhood, who will remember the stories of "The Tortoise and the Hare," "The Fox and the Grapes," and so on. Indeed, part of the *Webster's Collegiate Dictionary* definition of fable states explicitly that a fable is a story "in which animals speak and act like human beings."[1] Another hallmark of fables, also identified by Webster's, is that they are "intended to enforce a useful truth"; that is, they exist to convey some point about the society or behaviors of the culture in which they are constructed. Again, included in most readers' memory of the fables known from childhood is the aspect of the "moral of the story."

Le Guin's tales do not explicitly state a moral, but they contain, nonetheless, a critique of Western, patriarchal, hierarchical society.

A number of critics have noted that the decline of fable in our time is due in large measure to our distance from animals in our daily lives. Consequently, fables are now often dismissed as "merely" stories for children. Nicholas Howe, for example, states, "People in the industrialized West over the last several centuries . . . have grown apart from a diverse company of animals. We live in cities and suburbs with our pets . . . but we have never encountered anything as routinely necessary for the workings of a beast fable as a fox raiding our chicken coop. The ways we live with animals, or do not live with them, affect the stories we can tell about them."[2] Indeed, we have even turned our pets into nonanimals, viewing them as surrogate humans instead, even going so far as to dress them in human clothing and call them our "babies." This separation from animal lives is one aspect of contemporary society that Le Guin critiques in her animal stories.

Indeed, Le Guin's stance in her animal stories is ecofeminist, a view that regards mastery and control of nonhuman nature not as a metaphor or symbol of patriarchal, hierarchical mastery and control of certain humans but as a symptom of the same social illness. As Le Guin explains, "Civilized Man says: I am Self, I am Master, all the rest is Other—outside, below, underneath, subservient. I own, I use, I explore, I exploit, I control. What I do is what matters. What I want is what matter is for. I am that I am, and the rest is women and the wilderness, to be used as I see fit."[3] Le Guin's short stories "Mazes" (1975) and "A Wife's Tale" (1982) and her novella *Buffalo Gals, Won't You Come Out Tonight* (1987) are, of her works to date, the most specific examples of her use of fable as a form. Not only are the central characters in these works speaking animals—in two cases, indeed, even the narrator of the story—but these stories also most clearly require the readers' empathetic identification with the othered, which, as discussed above, is the aspect of these stories that carries the full impact of their implicit critique of U.S. society.

Because the fables most familiar to a general audience are those of Aesop and La Fontaine, which are often (wrongly) considered "merely" stories for children, it is important to emphasize that in Le Guin's stories, the animals are not cartoons, in which the actual animal characteristics are unimportant in constructing the characters. The Webster's definition given above suggests that the animals in fables are merely masks for human behaviors and thoughts, leading to Paul Shepard's definition of fables as "cautionary tales whose one-dimensional animals stereotype . . . human possibilities."[4] Rather, in reading Le Guin's animal stories, it is important to bear in mind aspects of fables pointed out by Howe, when he states that using animals in fables is "the activity of telling stories in words about animals, sometimes with and sometimes without people, in order to point a moral that humans believe should hold throughout the natural world. . . . In this act of fabling, animals can imitate the behaviors of humans, humans can imitate the behaviors of animals, but most of all the genre calls into question all categorical distinction between animals and humans."[5] It is precisely such categorical distinctions that Le Guin's animal stories want us to question. The animals in her stories are shown not as caricatures but as whole characters, multidimensional and complex personalities.

From a Jungian perspective, the communication between humans and animals in folktales can be seen as a metaphor for communication between the rational and instinctive sides of the human self. Le Guin makes note of this Jungian interpretation of folktales in her critical works, most notably in her essay "The Child and the Shadow" (in *Language of the Night*) and her introduction to *Buffalo Gals and Other Animal Presences*. However, Le Guin reworks the "talking animal" tale, giving the nonhuman other its own, separate self. The animals in her stories are like us, rather than symbols for us. Furthermore, in Le Guin's version of the "talking animal" story, the element of companionship has been eradicated. As the discussion below of the story "Mazes" makes clear, whatever communication may be possible, even desirable, between the animal other and the human, in most cases today, the human is no longer able to receive the message. Contemporary Western society has cut itself off from the willingness, and thus the ability, to hear animal voices, and the lessons that might be learned are lost along with the voices of those speaking others. In losing our awareness of those voices outside us, we also lose our awareness of our own internal "other" voices. Le Guin thus implicitly incorporates the Jungian idea of the animal as representing the human "shadow self" while at the same time demonstrating that animals are distinct and bounded individuals in their own right.

Le Guin's animal stories, most especially *Buffalo Gals*, also draw on Native American animal fables, in which the animals are seen to be bearers of messages from a wider world to human beings, rather than pointed aspects of human understanding. In the Native American traditions from which Le Guin draws, human understanding is limited unless it includes awareness of the knowledge held by animals of a world humans cannot experience directly.[6] However, in Native American fables, animals and humans are able to communicate directly; indeed, this is the case in fables and fairy tales from a number of world traditions, in which the speaking animals speak to humans. In Le Guin's animal stories, the animals are tragically unable to communicate with humans, and it is this failure of communication that carries the message to us about our society.

It seems likely, given commentary Le Guin has made about her own works (especially in the introduction to *Buffalo Gals and Other Animal Presences*), that she has created these stories deliberately with the intent to present the "other" side of the coin, to give voice to something apart from the dominant (white male human) voice of contemporary U.S. society. The attitude Le Guin critiques in these stories objectifies nature and "others" anything connected with it, including "primitive" peoples, women, children, human bodies, and, of course, animals. As Le Guin notes, "In literature as in 'real life,' women, children and animals are the obscure matter upon which Civilization erects itself, phallologically. That they are Other is (vide Lacan et al.) the foundation of language, the Father Tongue. If Man vs. Nature is the name of the game, no wonder the team players kick out all these non-men who won't learn the rules."[7] Le Guin sets herself up as one of those others, because she is a woman. However, rather than trying to "learn the rules" of the Man vs. Nature "game," she uses her role as a writer—an artist whose medium is language—to propose a different game with new rules that include those others. Interestingly, she does so by marginalizing humans, or at least marginalizing our rational, Cartesian selves.

Le Guin suggests that the animals in her stories help us to connect with our own otherness. Drawing on Jungian thinking, Le Guin argues that, in traditional fables, animals stand for the human subconscious, because the subconscious, which guides us, is instinctive and therefore "animal." As she explains, "The animal . . . acts with certainty; it acts 'rightly,' appropriately. . . . It is the animal who knows the way, the way home. It is the animal within us, the primitive, the dark brother, the shadow soul, who is the guide."[8] I have used her terms "dark brother" and "shadow soul" in the title of this chapter; the terms are significant because of the familial relationship and intimacy they imply. The animal is the "dark brother" because our familial relationship with that animal is not clear, obvious, or logical, yet Le Guin wants readers to see that it is undeniable. We are kin with the animals. The evocation of the yin-yang symbol is appropriate here; animals are the yang side of our families. The reference to them as "shadow souls" further refers to the denied, repressed aspects of the self, so a reconnection with animal lives requires an acceptance of the yang sides of our own psyches, a refusal to reject or dismiss our own animal selves. The fact that the three stories under discussion here in fact demonstrate a rejection of that sense of kinship, the dismissal of our animal selves, is the more poignant because Le Guin makes the familial, spiritual connection so clear.

In the older fables, animal guides or companions—even animal spouses—are a common trope. In Le Guin's reworking of the animal tale, however, the element of companionship or close relationship has been eradicated, or at least made extremely complex. As I mentioned earlier, contemporary Western society has cut itself off from willingness and ability to hear animal voices, and the lessons that might be learned are lost along with the voices of those speaking others. In her fables, Le Guin shows us that the lack of interspecies communication has tragic ramifications for humans and animals alike. To counteract the contemporary disconnect between humans and animals, Le Guin tells her stories through the animal's point of view. By othering the humans, the empathetic bond that existed between humans and animals in the old tales is at once reestablished and revised. It is reestablished because we empathize with narrating animals; it is revised because those animals do not seem to be speaking to us or for our benefit. We are pushed to the edges of the stories, and the animals take center stage.

"Mazes" is told from the point of view of an unidentified being who attempts to communicate with (apparently) a human scientist, whose only relationship to it is to treat it as a lab rat, trying to "teach" it to push the "right" lever and to run through a series of mazes.[9] The "alien" is explicitly not a lab rat, nor is the story specifically about the mistreatment of animals in laboratories, though that issue is, of course, implicit. The point of "Mazes" stems from the fact that the alien cannot, no matter how hard it tries, communicate its own reality to the observing scientist because the scientist can only hear the answers he or she expects: communication with the other has been denied. This denial seems to stem in large part from the fact that the captive alien is small and nonhumanoid in appearance: the parallel to a lab rat (something that is used to run mazes) suggests that the alien may be a quadruped of similar size. Hence, the scientist makes assumptions about the alien's intelligence and capacity for communication, assumptions in turn based on assumptions about small, furry quadrupeds in labs. The scientist, for all the intelligence and ability as a trained observer that makes her or him a scientist, cannot see that the alien is trying with all its power to please, to reach out. It is communicating in its own way, which the scientist cannot perceive as meaningful.

The misunderstanding is at first mutual: the alien looks for communication in the human's gestures (as its own form of language is through body movement, specifically dance), and only belatedly wonders "if it could be communicating labially."[10] However, the alien realizes it cannot understand the other's language: "If it speaks with its face I cannot understand it, that is too foreign a language."[11] Yet still the alien attempts communication, even being reduced to "a pitifully low level of interpersonal aesthetics": when forced to chose between receiving a shock to its feet or pulling a lever that pelts it with indigestible food, it nearly "goes vertical" and in a rage pulls the knobs off the wall and defecates on them. "The alien took me up at once and returned [me] to my prison. It had got the message, and had acted on it. But how unbelievably primitive the message had had to be!"[12]

The mutual inability to communicate, in spite of the alien's attempts and the human's close observation of it, leads finally, too late, to a small breakthrough. The alien says:

> There were no words, yet there was communication. I saw,
> as it stood watching me, a clear signification of angry sadness. . . .
> Never a word came clear, and yet it told me that it was filled with
> resentment, pity, impatience, and frustration. It told me it was sick
> of torturing me, and wanted me to help it. I am sure I understood it.
> I tried to answer. I tried to say, "What is it you want of me? Only tell
> me what it is you want." But I was too weak to speak clearly, and it
> did not understand. It has never understood.[13]

Unable and unwilling to fit into the scientist's paradigms, the animal in "Mazes" ultimately dies rather than allowing itself to be relentlessly objectified. It dies rather than submitting to the scientist's demands that it conform to his or her conceptualization of it as a mindless creature. Though the story is told from the point of view of the alien, what is being clarified is the human attitude toward nonhuman creatures, especially those that are smaller than humans or furry. It indicates the ways in which contemporary humans are blind to the methods of communication of nonhuman others.

The lack of communication between humans and animals is also a key aspect of "The Wife's Story." More traditional in form as an animal fable than "Mazes," the story also suggests that rejection of the other is motivated in large measure by fear—and that such rejection is not the exclusive province of humans. Again, Le Guin is working to demonstrate that categorizations of difference between humans and animals are questionable, and again, the tragedy stems from a mutual inability to communicate across the divide between the human and the animal other. The story is deliberately set up so that the reader will assume, at first, that a human is speaking; the clues that the narrator is not human are subtle, building gradually. The wife, who narrates the story, is married to a partner she clearly loves and who is clearly lovable. However, a problem arises in the dark of the moon, when the husband disappears "when everybody's home asleep" and comes back smelling strange and acting very short-tempered and odd. Eventually, the wife witnesses a horrible transformation:

> I saw the changing. In his feet, it was, first. They got long, each foot longer, stretching out, the toes stretching out and the foot getting long, and fleshy, and white. And no hair on them.
> The hair begun to come away all over his body. It was like his hair fried away all over his body in the sunlight and was gone. He was white all over, then, like a worm's skin. And he turned his face. It was changing while I looked. It got flatter and flatter, the mouth flat and wide, and the teeth grinning flat and dull, and the nose just a knob of flesh with nostril holes, and the ears gone, and the eyes gone blue—blue, with white rims around the blue—staring at me out of that flat soft, white face.
> He stood up then on two legs.
> I saw him, I had to see him, my own dear love, turned into the hateful one.[14]

At this point, the reader realizes that the wife is a wolf and her husband a were-human. Human anatomy, as described from a wolf's point of view, is suddenly made grotesque. Moreover, the reader must feel the other side of the demonization wolves have suffered in human minds. To wolves, humans are "the hateful ones." For both species, the demonization of the other is brought about in part by an inability to communicate, to find a shared experience that will allow the strange to become acceptable. In the end, the wolf wife and her family and neighbors see her transformed husband as an enemy, and, while he is in human form, they chase him down and kill him. When he was a wolf, the husband could love, even marry, a nonhuman creature, but when he is human, the gulf between them is too wide for any communication to exist. The wife cannot know her husband once he has become human; she can only fear him and thus is driven to eradicate the source of her fear, an echo of the historic human response to wolves.

In both these stories, Le Guin turns humans into others to demonstrates how humans "other" animals. The animals feel familiar, like us, not only in their possession of language and their narrative ability but also in the emotions and experiences they describe. Conversely the humans are made into others; in the eyes of the animal narrators, the humans are strange, repulsive, and incomprehensible. The fact that both narrators are ultimately incapable of communicating with or accepting the human other highlights the contemporary disconnect from animal lives. However, because Le Guin tells the stories from the other's point of view, she suggests that we might be able to shift our own empathic responses, so that others seem less strange, more familiar—in the literal sense of the word: more like family.

Buffalo Gals, Won't You Come Out Tonight is another fascinating and complex exploration of the barrier between human and nonhuman others. In this case, the main point of view is that of a human, but one who is already doubly othered: a female child named Myra. Sole survivor of a plane crash, she is taken in by an animal community, especially by Coyote, who brings her to live with the other animals. Myra alone of the humans in these three stories is able to communicate with animals directly—indeed, she becomes part of the animal community in a very real sense. However, we must bear in mind that she is already an other, so her apparent bridging of the gap between human and animal has been largely accomplished before she comes in contact with the animals of the story. In effect, she completes the identification already necessitated by her status as a female and as a child, fully joining the animal community her human society suggests she is already allied with.

The other main character of the story, Coyote, is similarly liminal; Coyote exists on the fringes of both animal and human society, penetrating the boundaries between them but fully accepted in neither. She and Myra are able to form their close relationship largely, the story suggests, because they both live very close to those edges. Coyote is, of course, a significant character in certain Native American cultures as well, though in Le Guin's hands the character is female, rather than male, and Coyote's "trickster" aspects are downplayed here. However, Coyote's role as a go-between is significant in both Native American traditions and in Le Guin's story, though the outcome of that role is tragically different in *Buffalo Gals.*

The ways in which Myra specifically penetrates the boundaries between human and animal societies is made apparent in a central event in the novella. Myra has lost one eye in the crash, and the animals hold a ceremony in which they replace it with an eye made of pitch-pine sap. Afterward, what she sees is affected by whether she uses only her human eye or both eyes together: "If she shut the hurting eye and looked with the other, everything was clear and flat; if she used them both, things were blurry and yellowish, but deep."[15] The new animal-given eye provides depth perception, though not clarity. This suggests a metaphor for a possibly appropriate mode of perception; in this story, Le Guin is suggesting a method for overcoming the negative aspects of othering. The struggle for "clarity" in understanding is a hallmark of Western society, and especially Western science, yet that rational, logical approach to the cosmos has been criticized for leaving out the blurry, indefinable "deep" aspects of existence, such as emotion, spirit, and dream. Myra's nonhuman eye is, in effect, an incorporated animal guide, one that helps her see the world "rightly, appropriately." The animal aspects of our own psyches—usually identified as being childlike, primitive, or feminine and consequently of less value than logic and clarity—are precisely those that Le Guin suggests we must reconnect with if we are to establish a more viable relationship with others, and with ourselves. Through the metaphor of Myra's pitch-pine eye, Le Guin suggests the ways in which we might hope to alter our own sight so that it incorporates both clarity and depth, both human and animal ways of seeing.

It should be noted, however, that even before Myra receives the new eye, her vision of the world has changed. When Coyote first finds Myra, the child sees Coyote as a coyote, as an animal. Coyote can speak to her, and she understands, but on the way to the animal village Myra has a transformative experience:

> The child turned. She saw a coyote gnawing at the half-dried-up carcass of a crow, black feathers sticking to the black lips and narrow jaw.
>
> She saw a tawny-skinned woman kneeling by a campfire, sprinkling something into a conical pot. She heard the water boiling in the pot, though it was propped between rocks, off the fire. The woman's hair was yellow and grey, bound back with a string. Her feet were bare. The upturned soles looked as dark and hard as shoe soles, but the arch of the foot was high, and the toes made two neat curving rows. She wore bluejeans and an old white shirt. She looked over at the girl. "Come on, eat crow!" she said.[16]

The pun here is instructive. Not only is Myra invited to shed her human inhibitions by eating the unappetizing carrion that makes up a coyote's regular diet—not even a dead pigeon or chicken, but crow—she is also invited to thereby apologize with humility for her (human) errors, eating metaphoric crow.

From this time on, Myra sees the animals as human people, wearing clothes and living in houses, and the food that she eats is food that is familiar to her, not a rotting crow carcass but dried salmon mush. However, she retains the awareness that these people are not humans, and tries to understand the way she sees them. Alone of the humans in these stories, Myra is able to communicate with animals. It seems her ability to do so arises partly from her own status as an other and partly from the trauma of the crash and her injuries. It is significant that her life literally depends on her ability to communicate with the animals; lost in the desert Southwest, without their wisdom and guidance, she would certainly die. Myra thus demonstrates in concrete terms the underlying message of these stories: we need some level of communication with the world's animals in order to ensure their survival and our own.

In spite of Myra's individual ability to converse with animals, however, it is clear in this story that modern society has lost that ability, and again, this lack brings about a tragic end. Throughout the story, Coyote is seen as strange by the rest of the animal community because she is willing to interact, albeit peripherally, with humans, and it is her willingness to approach these others—us—that proves her downfall. She and Myra come across some food, which Coyote takes to be an offering to her. She eats it, but in fact it is loaded with strychnine, and she dies a horrible death, leaving Myra, who has begun to call her Mother, alone and bereft. After burying Coyote, Myra looks back at the human town. "'I hope you all die in pain,'" she says,[17] and at that moment it is hard for the reader not to share her condemnation of them, of us.

One cannot read these stories without being profoundly disturbed, in large measure because one's own kind are clearly the enemy, the hated ones, the evil other. It is difficult to read such works and not feel either cringing apology or a desire to defiantly assert one's difference from those "others" who are so cruel and vile. However, *Buffalo Gals* offers a kind of hope, again using Myra as an exemplar for the rest of us.

Myra eventually does return to human society, to her father, who has been searching for her, but she is told that she need not completely lose her connection with the animal people she has come to love so intimately: "'Go on, little one, Granddaughter,' Spider said. 'Don't be afraid. You can live well there. I'll be there too, you know. In your dreams, in your ideas, in dark corners in the basement.'"[18] This is literally true; spiders will, in fact, always live in our basements, but the equation of dreams and "dark corners of the basement" also draws on Jungian symbolism. Our "dark brothers" and "shadow souls" survive in dreams—Jungian territory—and the "dark corners of the basement" are, in addition to their literal truth, metaphoric representations of the subconscious mind. Spider Grandmother's statement thus functions as a reminder to readers of both the literal and metaphysical ways that animals pervade our lives, regardless of our awareness of them. As Paul Shepard says, "Animals are among the first inhabitants of the mind's eye. They are basic to the development of speech and thought. Because of their part in the growth of consciousness, they are inseparable from the series of events in each human life, indispensable to our becoming human in the fullest sense."[19]

Human othering of animals—whether in fact or fiction—may place humanity in a unique and privileged realm, but it also walls humanity off from the rest of the cosmos, robbing humans of connection with the universe and with our own interior lives. Through the experiences in Le Guin's animal stories, the reader is implicitly urged to reconsider her or his own relationship with the natural world, with the other, and to discover means of connection that dissolve alienation while retaining differentness as a thing of value. As Le Guin says, "Our curse is alienation, the separation of yang from yin."[20] In Le Guin's animal stories, we are, in effect, being urged to question the sources of that alienation, to discover ourselves as others and to be aware of the many levels of awareness possible to us.

Notes

1. *Merriam Webster's Collegiate Dictionary*, 10th ed.

2. Nicholas Howe, "Fabling Beasts: Traces in Memory (In the Company of Animals)," *Social Research* 62, no. 3 (Fall 1995): 641–60, Expanded Academic ASAP, Nassau Community College Library, http://elt.sunynassau.edu.

3. Ursula K. Le Guin, "Women/Wilderness," in *Dancing at the Edge of the World: Thoughts on Words, Women, Places*, by Ursula K. Le Guin, 161–64 (1986; reprint, New York: Grove Press, 1989), 161.

4. Paul Shepard, *The Others: How Animals Made Us Human* (Washington, D.C.: Island Press, 1996), 96.

5. Howe, "Fabling Beasts."

6. It is worth noting that Le Guin's parents were noted anthropologists Alfred and Theodora Kroeber. Perhaps more important to the echoes and convergences with Native American beliefs in Le Guin's works are the personal relationships she had with two of her father's collaborators, whom she refers to as her "Indian uncles." For more on those relationships, see Le Guin's essay "Indian Uncles," in *The Wave in the Mind: Talks and Essays on the Writer, the Reader, and the Imagination*, by Ursula K. Le Guin (Boston: Shambhala, 2004), 10–19.

7. Ursula K. Le Guin, introduction to *Buffalo Gals and Other Animal Presences*, by Ursula K. Le Guin (1987; reprint, New York: Penguin-Roc, 1990), 9.

8. Ursula K. Le Guin, "The Child and the Shadow," in *Language of the Night*, by Ursula K. Le Guin (New York: G. P. Putnam's Sons, Perigee Books), 67.

9. An interesting discussion of this story appears in Manfred Jahn's essay "'Speak, Friend, and Enter': Garden Paths, Artificial Intelligence, and Cognitive Narratology," in *Narratologies: New Perspectives on Narrative Analysis*, ed. David Herman (Columbus: Ohio State Univ. Press, 1999), 167–94.

10. Ursula K. Le Guin, "Mazes," in Le Guin, *Buffalo Gals and Other Animal Presences*, 73–74.

11. Ibid., 75.

12. Ibid.

13. Ibid., 75–76.

14. Ursula K. Le Guin, "The Wife's Story," in Le Guin, *Buffalo Gals and Other Animal Presences*, 81.

15. Ursula K. Le Guin, *Buffalo Gals, Won't You Come Out Tonight*, in Le Guin, *Buffalo Gals and Other Animal Presences*, 31.

16. Ibid., 21.

17. Ibid., 58.

18. Ibid., 60.

19. Paul Shepard, *Thinking Animals: Animals and the Development of Human Intelligence* (New York: Viking, 1978), 2.

20. Ursula K. Le Guin, "Is Gender Necessary?" in *Language of the Night*, by Ursula K. Le Guin (New York: G. P. Putnam's Sons, Perigee Books), 169. Pertinent to this discussion as well is Le Guin's essay "American SF and the Other," also in Le Guin, *Language of the Night*, 99: "If you deny any affinity with another person or kind of person," she states—and I am sure she would be happy to add "or animal"—"you

have made it into a thing, to which the only possible relationship is a power relationship. And thus you have fatally impoverished your own reality. You have, in fact, alienated yourself."

Works Cited

Howe, Nicholas. "Fabling Beasts: Traces in Memory (In the Company of Animals)." *Social Research* 62, no. 3 (Fall 1995): 641–60. Expanded Academic ASAP. Nassau Community College Library. http://elt.sunynassau.edu.

Jahn, Manfred. "'Speak, Friend, and Enter': Garden Paths Artificial Intelligence, and Cognitive Narratology." In *Narratologies: New Perspectives on Narrative Analysis*, edited by David Herman, 167–94. Columbus: Ohio State Univ. Press, 1999.

Le Guin, Ursula K. "American SF and the Other." In Le Guin, *Language of the Night*, 97–100.

———. *Buffalo Gals and Other Animal Presences*. 1987. Reprint, New York: Penguin-Roc, 1990.

———. *Buffalo Gals, Won't You Come Out Tonight*. In Le Guin, *Buffalo Gals and Other Animal Presences*, 17–60.

———. "The Child and the Shadow." In Le Guin, *Language of the Night*, 59–71.

———. "Indian Uncles." In *The Wave in the Mind: Talks and Essays on the Writer, the Reader, and the Imagination*, by Ursula K. Le Guin, 10–19. Boston: Shambhala, 2004.

———. "Is Gender Necessary?" In Le Guin, *Language of the Night*, 161–69.

———. *Language of the Night*. New York: G. P. Putnam's Sons, Perigee Books, 1979.

———. "Mazes." In Le Guin, *Buffalo Gals and Other Animal Presences*, 69–76.

———. "The Wife's Story." In Le Guin, *Buffalo Gals and Other Animal Presences*, 77–83.

———. "Women/Wilderness." In *Dancing at the Edge of the World: Thoughts on Words, Women, Places*, by Ursula K. Le Guin, 161–64. 1986. Reprint, New York: Grove Press, 1989.

Shepard, Paul. *The Others: How Animals Made Us Human*. Washington, D.C.: Island Press, 1996.

———. *Thinking Animals: Animals and the Development of Human Intelligence*. New York: Viking, 1978.

Part 3
Holy Dogs and Scared Bunnies

Animals in Art and Religion

Introduction

Laura Hobgood-Oster

Whether in the form of a postmodern bunny or a legendary dog saint in the Middle Ages, animals serve as a medium for human expression and definition. Throughout human history they have provided a lens through which humans define and understand ourselves. So a dog lying on a sofa in a cartoon from the *New Yorker* uncovers the human quest for self (and other) analysis while a real dog with obsessive-compulsive disorder teaches us how we can live with and care for a true other. The chapters in this section suggest that one need only look for animals and images of them appear; they are there, just too often invisible to eyes that are not looking for them. Certainly animal pictures, metaphors, and stories carry various meanings and differing levels of significance. Still, their very presence points back at the humans who picture them. So "why look at animals?" as John Berger asks in his seminal work by the same title.[1] The chapters in this section investigate animals as symbols expressing meaning for human culture and as subjects in and of themselves, but subjects defined by their interactions with humans.

The authors incorporate four quite different methodologies and styles. Approaches move from art history to history of religions to clinical psychology to pastoral theology. They cover cartoons, sacred art and legend, postmodern art, and the enactment of religious beliefs. As a whole, however, these four chapters raise issues of the centrality of animals as symbols and as more than symbols. Animals serve as metaphors in human literary and artistic constructions, but they are also subjects with their own voices, lives, and meanings. Discovering and articulating some of the ways animals function in multileveled and complex categories of human thought is the underlying theme that runs through all these chapters.

It has been argued, and widely accepted, that animals are neither capable of symbolic interaction nor of taking the role of the other because they lack language.[2] But serious challenges to this position have been offered by myriad contemporary scholars, including those who contribute chapters to this section.[3] Hobgood-Oster, Roy, Alden, and Jones all pose questions similar to those suggested by Steve Baker in *Picturing the Beast:* "What place does the animal hold in our imagination, and how are we to understand the uses to which our imaginative conception of the animal is put? Above all, why is it that our ideas of the animal—perhaps more than any other set of ideas—are the ones which enable us to frame and express ideas about *human* identity?"[4]

What do the cartoons in the *New Yorker* and the bunnies in the art of Ray Johnson express about human identity? How do the relationships between saints and animals or between a particular human and her troubled companion dog alter human conceptions of the sacred? Animals, in all of these cases, are not meaningless images—unlike many animal images in contemporary culture. A dog used as a marketing tool to sell tacos or a cow employed as a picture to sell chicken are meaningless images as far as the animal is concerned.[5] In other words, these images do not mirror reality for the lives of the animals themselves but reflect simple utility for human economic endeavors (selling a product or an idea). However, the animals discussed in these chapters are full of meaning; they function symbolically. They are not accessory or tool alone, but integral, as animals, to their own and human cultural constructions of identity.

In addition to animals as symbols, some of the animals of Roy's sermon and Hobgood-Oster's historical analysis are, arguably, actors themselves, even while they carry the weight of symbolic representation. This is yet another step in claiming the significance of animals in human legends and stories. As such, it suggests a certain empowerment of animals not dependent solely upon human meanings and designations. So as metaphor, symbol, subject, and companion these animals emerge in the work of the meaning-full.

Lions, St. Thecla, asses, St. Anthony, birds, St. Francis, pigs, and a "holy greyhound" take center stage in Laura Hobgood-Oster's chapter, "Holy Dogs and Asses: Stories Told through Animal Saints." Hobgood-Oster asks if animals can be counted among the saints in Christianity and proceeds to investigate this question by examining the hagiographies (stories of the lives of saints) and pedagogical sacred artworks of popular religion. She suggests that while dominant Christianity, in its primarily patriarchal structure, takes no real account of other-than-human animals, popular sources (particularly premodern ones) tell a different story and reveal a different picture. Such "artwork, hagiography, oral traditions . . . and important legends reveal a close connection between humans and the natural world." Sometimes animals function symbolically or metaphorically, but they often also "exhibit agency and play an active role in the unveiling of the holy."

Hobgood-Oster's primary sources for these stories are the lives of saints from the second to the sixteenth centuries C.E. and popular religious art, viewed by the masses in churches, throughout the Christian areas of Europe. Hobgood-Oster organizes the images into four categories: animals as exemplars of piety, animals as sources of revelation, animals as saintly martyrs, and animals as the primary intimate other. She concludes that "retelling stories of animals as saints could evoke radical attempts at reconstructing Christianity and help to promote critical reflection on human-animal relationships."

The second chapter in this section is of a different genre—a sermon first preached at St. John's Lutheran Church in Baltimore, Maryland. "Paw Prints on Preaching: The Healing Power of Biblical Stories about Animals" continues the theme of animals and religion. Susan Carole Roy begins her chapter with a story about Freckles, the "obsessive-compulsive cocker spaniel" with whom she shares her life. She then suggests that biblical texts place Freckles in the "company" of a "divine cloud of four-legged witnesses," including Balaam's ass. The primary question posed by Roy is "What . . . does the Holy One invite us to see lurking in the shadows of our theology through the eyes of animals?"

She offers several possible responses. For example, she presents findings that link violence among humans with human violence to animals. Roy argues that animals "can teach us that what affects one part of the web of life often affects other parts as well." She claims animals as "part of God's story . . . a story about animals, humans, and creation and a multitude of expressions of the holy." Including animals in human stories and intimately connecting them to human lives, particularly with the blessing of religion, could significantly alter human perceptions of the role of animals. And, as significantly, animals could alter human perceptions of the divine. This chapter resonates with some of the ideas in Hobgood-Oster's chapter: animals become windows into divine reality when and if humans are open to this possibility, as are the numerous saints discussed by Hobgood-Oster and the theologians Roy cites.

Another approach to the role and perception of animals is presented by Anne Alden in "Personification of Pets: The Evolution of Canine Cartoons in the *New Yorker*." She compares the total numbers and types of canine cartoons published in the *New Yorker* from 1925 to 2002 and suggests that the trends in dog imagery in the *New Yorker* reflect the "significant changes in how companion animals have been regarded by society" over this period. As a clinical psychologist, she also introduces ideas about mental and physical health benefits of pet ownership, particularly in relationship to the changing role of pets who are "increasingly viewed as significant members of the family, in some cases having equal status with children."

Alden finds that the total number of dog cartoons remained fairly steady from the 1920s through the 1960s. From the 1970s onward, however, there was a dramatic increase in dog cartoons. She also differentiates the types of cartoons, specifically focusing on ones that picture anthropomorphic dogs ("defined as dogs shown with human characteristics or behavior"). After outlining the particular presentation of dogs in each decade, Alden concludes that there is a significant "trend towards anthropomorphism" in the cartoons that reflects the changing role of dogs in society as a whole. So in the 1920s, 4 percent of dog cartoons were anthropomorphic, but by the 1990s, 67 percent were anthropomorphic. Such a trend is evident in the cartoons and, according to Alden, in the human-pet relationship as well. In the *New Yorker*, cartoon dogs appear, simultaneously, as mirrors of themselves in relationship to humans and as vehicles for critical social commentary. Looking at the evolution of these cartoons provides a window into the shifting U.S. pet-human culture.

Muffet Jones also reviews visual images in her chapter "Snakes and Bunnies: The Postmodern Animal in the Art of Ray Johnson," analyzing the functions of several animals in the visual representations of the twentieth-century artist Ray Johnson. She suggests that Johnson was "essentially postmodern," even though he worked during the end of the modern era, and bases her theory, in part, on the roles that several animals play in Johnson's art. She states that "his 'adoption' of animal personas as a kind of private symbolism and his refusal to cite animal images within a traditional framework of meaning," while problematic for contemporary viewers, helped usher in a new stage in the history of art.

Jones focuses on the bunny and the snake, two animals that played different but prominent roles in Johnson's art. Johnson's "bunnyhead" functioned as a surrogate for Johnson, "often accompanying his signature or replacing it in correspondence." His "bunny lists" included names of various acquaintances. These would be labeled below a repeated sequence of the same bunny image, "giving identical images different names" and thus problematizing ideas of identity. Snakes, on the other hand, appear as more abstract figures and, according to Jones, function as "an *imago* of the condition of alterity under which artists often labor."

Jones concludes with several significant questions and observations. First, "What is a postmodern animal?" She answers that a postmodern animal "is no longer the object/animal of human history, but one which begins to occupy the same place outside history that postmodernism argues humans do." And for Ray Johnson, "the bunnies, snakes, turtles, and snails all inhabited the same internal world." They were "self-aware images that participated in the alterity of the artist." In other words, Jones suggests that the animals in Johnson's representations move into the postmodern world. Therefore, the boundaries and hierarchies that divided animals from humans under modernism and Cartesian dualism are eroded through Johnson's art.

It could be claimed that the erosion of boundaries, as referenced in Johnson's art, binds these four chapters together as well. Animals bring a framework, provide a mode of comprehension to the otherwise inexplicable, in all of these cases. Animals, as pointed out by Jones, become equal partners in meaning-making. They provide the lens for the cartoonist, the hidden self for the artist, the expression of the human in an other-than-human form.

Together these chapters take into consideration a wide range of media through which human-animals relationships are expressed. Religious tales link animals to the divine, while cartoons help human animals analyze our own condition and our links to other animals. Artists express themselves through animals, and the stories of saints sometimes tell themselves in animal voices. And, in many instances, animals are agents, subjects rather than objects. They are acting, not only acted upon by humans. In other words, whether it be through a "holy dog" or a "scared bunny," human religious traditions and artistic endeavors rely, at some point, on animals. So why look at animals? Because the human might become more explicable through the animal—and what is religion or art but the quest to explain ourselves?

Notes

1. John Berger, "Why Look at Animals?" in *About Looking*, by John Berger (London: Writers and Readers, 1980), 1–26.

2. See George Herbert Mead, *Mind, Self and Society from the Standpoint of a Social Behaviorist* (Chicago: Univ. of Chicago Press, 1962).

3. See Carol J. Adams, *The Sexual Politics of Meat: A Feminist-Vegetarian Critical Theory* (New York: Continuum, 1990); Janet M. Alger and Steven F. Alger, "Beyond Mead: Symbolic Interaction between Humans and Felines," *Society and Animals* 5 (1997): 65–81; Steve Baker, *Picturing the Beast: Animals, Identity, and Representation*, new ed. (Urbana: Univ. of Illinois Press, 2001); Berger, "Why Look at Animals?"; and Clifton P. Flynn, "Battered Women and Their Animal Companions: Symbolic Interaction between Human and Nonhuman Animals," *Society and Animals* 8 (2000): 99–127.

4. Baker, *Picturing the Beast*, 6.

5. A Chihuahua served for years as the "spokesdog" for the fast-food chain Taco Bell and cows cover posters for Chick-Fil-A (another fast food chain), encouraging people to eat more chicken (with words that are invariably misspelled).

Works Cited

Adams, Carol J. *The Sexual Politics of Meat: A Feminist-Vegetarian Critical Theory.* New York: Continuum, 1990.

Alger, Janet M., and Steven F. Alger. "Beyond Mead: Symbolic Interaction between Humans and Felines." *Society and Animals* 5 (1997): 65–81.

Baker, Steve. *Picturing the Beast: Animals, Identity, and Representation*, new ed. Urbana: Univ. of Illinois Press, 2001.

Berger, John. "Why Look at Animals?" In *About Looking*, by John Berger, 1–26. London: Writers and Readers, 1980.

Flynn, Clifton P. "Battered Women and Their Animal Companions: Symbolic Interaction between Human and Nonhuman Animals." *Society and Animals* 8 (2000): 99–127.

Mead, George Herbert. *Mind, Self and Society from the Standpoint of a Social Behaviorist.* Chicago: Univ. of Chicago Press, 1962.

Chapter 10

Holy Dogs and Asses
Stories Told through Animal Saints

Laura Hobgood-Oster

St. Anthony, the founder of monasticism, thought he was the first monk to live the solitary life until he heard of Paul the Hermit. In the third century c.e., Paul left human society and headed for the desert, where he lived in a cave for sixty years. Anthony decided to find the hermit. As the legend goes, a wolf "came to meet him" and proceeded to lead him to Paul's cave. The hermit refused to speak to Anthony but, finally convinced of his sincerity, embraced him. Soon, another animal entered the scene:

> When it was time for food, a crow flew down, carrying a loaf formed of two halves. Anthony wondered at this, but Paul told him that God provided him daily with food: this day the quantity was doubled to take care of the guest.[1]

Somehow the crow knew of Anthony's presence and brought enough food for both of these early Christian saints. During his time in the wilderness, Paul's companions had all been animals. They knew his location, led the wandering Anthony to the hermit, provided Paul with nourishment, and served as his only companions. Paul died shortly after the encounter and Anthony determined to bury him even though he lacked the means. But animals again came to his service. Two lions appeared, "dug a grave, and, when the saint was buried, went back to the forest."[2]

Such appearances of other-than-human animals in the hagiography of the Christian tradition are thought to be rare.[3] But a careful probing of the stories reveals more animal epiphanies than this religion, often classified as extremely anthropocentric, would seem likely to incorporate. This chapter seeks to recover lost strands of silenced animal voices and multiple roles animals have played as agents of the divine in the history of Christianity.[4]

After studying many written texts and examining numerous visual representations, a framework for understanding the inclusion of animals emerges. Animals appear as saints, as sacraments, as revealers of the divine, as bearers of God, or as *imitatio Christi* (imitators of Christ). In these roles, animals act, are acted upon, and enact the will of the divine. Amazingly, their agency and power, their action as subjects in their own right, is prominent in countless stories and is central in numerous images.

As the history of Christianity became intertwined with that of patriarchal and imperialistic Mediterranean and European powers, the dominant forms of

Christianity became increasingly anthropocentric.[5] Animals and their stories ceased to have a significant voice in the Christian choir. Christianity, along with the majority of interlocked European cultural systems, severed ties with the rest of nature in a process that culminated during the scientific revolution. Thus an alienation from any being other than the human, or the humanlike Divine, was embedded in these dominant forms of Christianity. Whereas the presence of animals had been integral to various forms of Christianity in their earlier manifestations, the proclamations of such theologians and philosophers as René Descartes struck the final blow to the inclusion of animals in the circle of Christian religious dialogue. Humans, ascendant for centuries, began to understand themselves as the only subjects worthy of divine consideration. All other animals were simply tools for human use. This hierarchical ranking was interlocked with the myriad systems of oppression that traveled with European imperialism to the rest of the world.

Articulating the significant role animals have played throughout the scope of Christian history strengthens the process of ending the interlocked dominations. It also provides one of many perspectives that have the potential to influence the development of a renewed, biocentric Christianity.[6] Because other-than-human creatures as varied as wolves, crows, crickets, cattle, hinds, spiders, and birds figure into some of the prominent stories of Christian history and legend, the community of Christian subjects expands to include, potentially, every species.

Representation and Animals in Christianity

Distinct cultural patterns and symbol systems shape human experiences of and relationships to other living beings in our environments. Patterns are encoded in visual representations (a pig is presented as a strip of bacon), in many languages (animals are referred to as "it" rather than as "he" or "she"), and in daily, pragmatic ritual performances (a homeless animal is often "put to sleep" and treated as a nuisance).[7] Christianity in its European and North American settings has informed many of these cultural patterns and symbol systems in profound ways. Animals are now widely regarded as subordinate, irrational, soul-less beings whose primary purpose is based on a theory that places human beings at the top of a hierarchy. Animals exist for human consumption, labor, and aesthetic or emotional pleasure alone. Intrinsic value and direct relationship between animals and the sacred is denied. This cultural pattern results from a transformation of understanding, a departure from traditions in which animals once engaged humans and God differently within Christianity.

Christianity grew out of religious traditions found in the Mediterranean world two thousand years ago. Judaism, mystery religions, myriad pagan traditions, and the official religion of the Roman Empire, to name just a few, provided sources for early forms of Christianity. As they developed, diverse forms of Christianity incorporated various aspects of these traditions and their belief systems. From this process a rather ambiguous place was forged for animals in Christian traditions. Each of these religious traditions included and excluded animals in various ways, thus influencing the inclusion and exclusion of animals in Christianity.[8]

A few examples of Christianity's incorporation of animals and animal symbolism from other religions should suffice to establish historical and cultural influence and syncretism. Lions, long revered in Mediterranean religious and cultural traditions, retain that role as they enter Christian liturgical space. Whether they are guardians at gateways, such as the "lion's gate" of Mycenae (c. 1250 B.C.E.), or flanking a goddess, such as those discovered by Marija Gimbutas (c. 6500–5500 B.C.E.), lions (and lionesses) held central positions in religious imagery.[9]

Another example is the ass, a complex and extremely significant example. The ass displays both the differentiation of newly developing Christianity from official Roman religion and, simultaneously, the borrowing of images from classical traditions by some of the first Christian artists. Jesus' entry into Jerusalem on the back of a donkey is prominent in this early art. The image contrasts with those of emperors and nobility, who enter in chariots and/or mounted on regal horses. Such a contrast is deliberate, it seems, as the humility of Jesus is displayed. Simultaneously, the ass connects Christianity to Roman traditions. As Thomas Mathews states, "Early Christian art is rich with Dionysiac associations." He also points out that in "classical art the ass is common in Dionysiac processions, whether carrying Hephaistus, the divine smith, on his entry to Mt. Olympus, or Silenus, Dionysus' aged mentor. . . . In addition, a mule, offspring of an ass and a horse, is the common transport of Dionysus himself."[10]

But dominant Christianities, in their formalized, official, and primarily patriarchal structures, take no real account of other-than-human animals. The major theological works of such figures as Thomas Aquinas, John Calvin, and Karl Barth, the central doctrines and creeds of both the Roman Catholic and Orthodox Churches, as well as the primary themes of Protestant world views, focus on human beings and the human relationship with the divine. Humans are of primary concern, with little or no regard for other animals.

Yet premodern sources tell a different story, reveal a different image. The artwork, hagiography, oral traditions (later recorded in written form), and important legends reveal a close connection between humans and the natural world. Stories and images of animals abound and these animals are not always or only symbolic or metaphoric. Often the animals presented in words and images are sacred; they exhibit agency and play an active role in the unveiling of the holy.

What is the context for animal saints and why, over the course of the last few centuries, have these stories disappeared? It could be argued that most of the examples I present here are stories of animals with saints, not animals as saints. However, when one attends to the roles of the actors, particularly the active roles of the animals in these stories, the roles are often reversed. Through their agency, animals subvert the "power" and "control" of the human saint and elevate the status and piety of the animal saint. Who is the saint or who are the saints in each story? That is sometimes left to the interpretation of the hearer of the story, viewer of the image, or witness to the event.

The primary sources for these stories are the lives of saints from the second to the sixteenth centuries C.E. and religious images throughout the Christian areas of Europe during the same period. My work focuses on religious imagery in popular art, displayed in churches where masses of common people see and interpret its meaning, and on the legends of saints, which were, and arguably still are, popular with common Christians. A tracing of these stories and images suggests that certain patterns reveal cultural continuities and shared symbols. The four patterns or categories into which I organize these shared symbols are animals as exemplars of piety, animals as sources of revelation, animals as saintly martyrs, and animals as the primary intimate other.

Animals as Exemplars of Piety

Lions abound in Christian legend and symbol. For centuries, they stood on either side of many bishops' seats in cathedrals and framed the doors of many churches, including the church in which the young St. Francis was baptized, San Ruffino in Assisi, Italy. One of the most amazing lions appears in the "Acts of Paul."[11] An early fragment, in Coptic, tells of a lion approaching Paul as he prayed. The lion lay down at the apostle's feet and Paul, never missing an opportunity to convert, asked the lion what he wanted. The lion replied, "I want to be baptized." Paul took him to a river and immersed him three times. The lion then greeted Paul with "Grace be with you." The lion finally departed into the countryside.[12] Baptism, the Christian sacrament that confirms an active choice of belief and initiates one into the Christian community, is, in this story, requested by and granted to a lion.

Lions also provide protection for Thecla, a companion of Paul in his journeys at the time of her martyrdom:

> And when the beasts were exhibited they bound her to a fierce lioness. . . . And the lioness, with Thecla sitting upon her, licked her feet; and all the multitude was astonished. . . . And Thecla . . . was stripped and received a girdle and was thrown into the arena. And lions and bears were let loose upon her. And a fierce lioness ran up and lay down at her feet.[13]

A series of animals, some of whom meet their own demise, encounter Thecla during the numerous attempts to execute her. Eventually the lioness dies protecting Thecla.[14]

But what about the inclusion of animals in other central Christian sacraments, particularly the Eucharist? Apparently, animals have been invited to partake in this ritual as well. In Donatello's image *Miracle of the Mule* (Bronze, parcel gilt, Basilica del Santo, Padua), the scene is the celebration of the Eucharist, the central act of many forms of Christian worship. Included in this scene are St. Anthony, a crowd of onlookers, and a mule, who is kneeling before the host, the body and blood of Christ.[15] Here this penultimate liturgical moment in most Christian worship rituals, this sacrament, is most fully adored by a mule. Anthony of Padua (1195–1231), often dubbed the greatest preacher of his time, was a young Franciscan who preached to fish much as his predecessor, Francis, preached to the birds. The miracle of the mule suggests the incorporation of animals into both the liturgy and the sacramental life of the Church. The image appears in highly acclaimed works of art, such as Donatello's, and on the walls of baptisteries frequented by the most common of people, such as the Baptistery in Siena.[16]

A similar pattern is revealed throughout the stories of the life of Francis of Assisi (1181/2–1226). Myriad animals relate with Francis, and many artistic renderings of his life include birds, wolves, and donkeys in company with the saint. Even images of Francis in ecstasy, at the height of mystical union with the divine, include animals.

But a particularly poignant tale reveals the piety of the birds:

> As St. Francis spoke these words to them, all those birds began to open their beaks, and to stretch out their necks, and to open their wings, and reverently to bow their heads to the ground, and to show by their motions and by their songs that the holy father had given them very great delight. St. Francis rejoiced with them and was glad and marveled much at so great a multitude of birds and at their most beautiful diversity, and at their attentiveness and fearlessness, for which he devoutly praised the Creator in them.[17]

An "infinite multitude" of birds (Francis addresses them as "little sisters") gather and attentively listen to Francis as he preaches about their blessedness and their need to praise God.

According to two of Francis's biographers, he "blessed them, and having made the sign of the cross, gave them leave to fly away to another place . . . nor did one of them move from the spot until he made the sign of the cross over them and gave them leave." Upon leaving, another symbol of piety emerges as "all those birds soared up into the air with wondrous songs and then divided themselves into four parts after the form of the cross Saint Francis had made over them."[18] The birds then proceed to announce their own belief:

> One band flew toward the East, and one toward the West, and one toward the South and the fourth toward the North, and each company went singing marvelous songs. Thus they signified that, just as St. Francis, the Standard-bearer of the Cross, had preached to them, and made over them the sign of the Cross, according to which they separated themselves toward the four quarters of the world, so the preaching of the Cross of Christ, renewed by St. Francis, was about to be carried through all the world by him and by his friars. Moreover, these friars, like the birds, possess nothing of their own in this world but commit their lives wholly to the providence of God.[19]

Of course, the Christian imperialistic implications and difficulties of this passage are apparent, but the amazing indication of birds as committing their lives to God shifts anthropocentric paradigms significantly. The birds became role models for the human friars, it seems.

Francis was not the first and not the last to recognize that birds and other creatures comprise a congregation worthy of preaching. Not only do they hear the word, but they are capable of response to it. The birds are infinitely capable of worship and, apparently, of belief in God.

Another animal whose piety testifies to those around is a cricket. For eight days in a row, Francis and the tree cricket sang praises together. The saint would call on the cricket to sing and praise the Creator with him, at which point the cricket would leave the tree and join Francis. But Francis knew that the cricket should return to regular life, and after their days of joint praise passed, he gave the cricket leave.[20]

One of the primary scenes attesting to animals as exemplars of piety is also one of the most powerful symbolic-visual sets of images in Christian history— stories of the nativity of Jesus. These stories include images of adoring animals surrounding the manger. Cattle, sheep, donkeys, and the occasional dog or horse prove uncanny in their ability to recognize the revelation of incarnation at the nativity.[21] Indeed, some images depict humans as much less aware of the nature of the incarnation than were the animals. Images carved in marble, ivory, and stone from the earliest generations of Christianity show the donkey and the cow nuzzling the baby Jesus. In some of these, the donkey is obviously kissing him. Others depict all of the humans in the scene turned away from the infant, but the cow and donkey still gaze at him attentively; often they are smiling. The animals' affinity for the sacred is obvious, and their incorporation into scenes of piety is dramatic.

Animals as Sources of Revelation

Animals have also been direct sources of revelation, messengers of the divine to human beings. Most particularly, animals have been the bearers or carriers of the incarnation of the sacred—the bearers of Christ.

While hunting one day, a Roman soldier, Placidus, came upon a herd of deer. One of these, a large stag, impressed the soldier with his incredible size and beauty. As the stag ran into the dense woods, the soldier approached, pondering how to capture this animal. Suddenly he noticed a cross with the image of Jesus between the antlers of the deer. The voice of the divine came from the stag's mouth and said:

> O Placidus, why are you pursuing me? For your sake I have
> appeared to you in this animal. I am the Christ, whom you worship
> without knowing it. Your alms have risen before me, and for this pur-
> pose I have come, that through this deer which you hunted, I myself
> might hunt you.[22]

The next morning, the vision appeared to him again, with the stag as the vehicle of revelation. The soldier changes his name to Eustace and becomes Christian. His tale relates yet another animal saint.[23] Years later, when Eustace, along with his family, was placed in the arena for martyrdom during the reign of Hadrian (c. 120 C.E.), a ferocious—and very hungry—lion served as the imperial death weapon of choice. But the lion came out peacefully, lowered his head, and adored the soon-to-be martyrs rather than kill them.

A similar story is told of St. Julian, who had "unwittingly" killed his parents:

> When this Julian, noble by birth, was young, he went out one day to hunt and began to chase a stag whose trail he had picked up. Suddenly, by the will of God, the stag turned to face him and said: "Are you tracking me to kill me, you who are going to kill your father and mother?" Filled with dread at hearing this, and fearing that what he had heard from the stag might indeed happen to him, he left everything and went away secretly.

Needless to say, the young man did, accidentally, kill his parents. But this horrid act led him to establish a hospice in order to work out his penance. He and his wife spent their lives "full of good works and almsgiving."[24]

St. Francis Xavier (1506–1552) tells of a related vision of the divine. During a mighty storm in the Moluccas, Xavier tried to calm the waves by holding his crucifix over them, but a huge wave swept it overboard. Once safely on shore, Xavier saw a large crab coming toward him, carrying the cross in his pincers—the bearer of the most sacred symbol of the divine.[25]

The image of the donkey, already a focus in the nativity images addressed above, is central in general visual, Christian imagery. The donkey, referred to as the bearer of the salvation of the world, carries Mary, the mother of Jesus, when she is pregnant and traveling to Bethlehem. Next, the donkey carries Mary and Jesus to safety in Egypt when the infant is being pursued by Herod the Great. Various images show Mary and Joseph feeding the donkey and gazing at him attentively.[26] Finally, the donkey bears Jesus on his back during the triumphant entry into Jerusalem before Jesus' execution. The depiction of this scene is one of the most prominent in early Christianity. In fact, it could be argued that Christianity, as a whole, elevated the status of the ass. When others mock Jesus or fail to notice the signs of revelation, the donkey comes through—adoring, worshiping, and carrying the incarnate God.[27]

Animals as Martyrs and Servants

The most striking images of animals in the hagiography are those of animals as martyrs and animals as servants. The martyr, or witness, was and is elevated as the most faithful of all Christians. Following the example set by Jesus, martyrs claimed a second and ultimate baptism in blood. Their stories were told throughout Christianity to strengthen the commitments of believers facing oppression. But some of these martyrs are not just symbolically but literally sacrificial lambs.

One of the most fascinating martyr-saints is Guinefort. The stories of his heroic martyrdom and of the healings that took place at his shrine influenced generations of believers in southern France. Guinefort, a trusted dog, was left alone with an infant. When the father returned he saw blood covering the room and surrounding the infant's crib. Guinefort sat next to the crib, blood around his mouth. Immediately the man took an arrow and shot Guinefort in the heart. Approaching the crib, he saw that his child was unharmed. Below the crib was the body of a dead snake who had been trying to get to the infant. Guinefort had saved the child's life.

The primary textual traditions about Guinefort come from *De Adoratione guinefortis Canis:*

> This recently happened in the diocese of Lyons where, when I preached against the reading of oracles, and was hearing confession, numerous women confessed that they had taken their children to Saint Guinefort. As I thought that this was some holy person, I continued with my enquiry and finally learned that this was actually a greyhound, which had been killed in the following manner. . . . The peasants, hearing of the dog's conduct and of how it had been killed, although innocent, and for a deed for which it might have expected praise, visited the place, honoured the dog as a martyr, prayed to it when they were sick or in need of something.[28]

Étienne de Bourbon (d. 1262), an inquisitor, recorded the above account in his narrative supporting Guinefort's designation as a heretic. He had the dog "disinterred, and the sacred wood cut down and burnt, along with the remains of the dog." Apparently a dog cannot be an official saint, though he can be an official heretic.

Records vary, but some indicate that sick children were brought to the dog's shrine until the nineteenth century. Guinefort, a martyr, received the popular designation of "saint," a title usually reserved for human animals. The official designation of saint was never bestowed upon Guinefort.

In the year 406, Paulinus, a monk and a priest, read a poem honoring St. Felix on his birthday. The poem features animals as the principal characters in a series of miracle tales. Christianity had denounced animal sacrifice, primarily as a mode of differentiation from Roman religious systems, but the ritual continued, particularly in rural areas. At the tomb of Felix, in southern Italy, the practice had been Christianized and served as a way to distribute food to the poor who would gather at the tomb to collect meat from the sacrificed animals.

The first tale is of a horse "seemingly endowed with human reason" who provided a "holy sign" and became a "source of wonder for those in attendance."[29] This inspired horse intervened as his master attempted to take the best portions of a hog that he had sacrificed rather than leave them for the poor. The horse threw his greedy master to the ground and then carried the sacrifice back to the tomb. Power and compassion are central to this horse-saint's piety.

A second story comes from this same tradition and relates the miracle of a rather plump pig. She had been vowed to Felix at birth, but because of her girth she is unable to walk the distance to the shrine. Her masters take two smaller piglets in her place, but when they arrive the pudgy pig was on the altar offering herself as sacrifice. Obviously, the sacred had been revealed in and through the pig, who, by some accounts, placed her throat on the blade, willingly offering her life as food that others might live. A similar story tells of a heifer who walks without a harness to the altar and "undefiled by the yoke and offering its neck to the axe, about to provide food for the poor from its slaughtered body, joyously it poured out its blood in fulfillment of its masters' vows."[30] Parallels between the sacrificial role of these animals and that of the figure of Jesus, particularly in their theological connotations, prove both striking and potentially controversial since the blood of the animals shares a place on the table with the blood of Jesus.

Of course, the lamb is a pervasive visual and liturgical symbol of sacrifice and piety, oftentimes replacing the figure of Jesus and other disciples. A beautiful example is the seventh-century apse of Sant' Apollinare in Classe that portrays all of the twelve traditional disciples as sheep.[31] So the symbol of animals as sacrificial victims and even as savior is central to Christianity. But the stories of Felix move these animals into active roles, symbolic and actual in their life of sacrifice.

Another common representation of animals as servants comes at the time of death and burial. A story similar to that of Paul and Anthony tells of another lion assisting in the burial of a saint. St. Mary of Egypt (c. fifth century C.E.), a hermit and ascetic, had lived in the desert for years, eating only the lentils and meager supply of bread to which she had access. A monk, Zosimus, came across this figure of holiness as he traversed the desert. One year, he served her the Eucharist and promised to bring this sacrament to her the next year as well. When he came back, he found her dead.

> Zosimus tried to dig a grave but could not. Then he saw a lion meekly coming toward him and said to the lion: "This holy woman commanded me to bury her body here, but I am old and cannot dig, and anyway I have no shovel. Therefore you do the digging and we will be able to bury this holy body." The lion began to dig and prepared a suitable grave, and when that was finished went away like a gentle lamb.[32]

With care and tenderness, the lion dug a perfect hole for Mary, the ground was blessed, and she was buried there.

Another story connected to a Felix includes spiders as heroes. While preaching, Felix, a bishop, found himself being pursued by persecutors, so he proceeded to hide:

> He slipped through a narrow opening in the wall of a ruined house and hid there. In a trice, by God's command, spiders spun a web across the space. The pursuers, seeing the web, thought that no one could have gone through the opening, and went on their way.[33]

Later Felix was killed by a group of boys he taught; apparently they were less compassionate than the spiders.

Animals as Primary Other in Relationship

Finally, there are numerous stories of animals as the primary other in relationship to humans throughout the Christian tradition. Obviously many of the hermits and desert dwellers mentioned throughout are in the company of an animal or animals. In addition, anchoresses who lived cloistered, often as solitaries, would be permitted one cat in their cell. But one of the most popular stories of saint-animal companionship is that of St. Jerome, a Father of the Church.

Jerome (345–420) lived in the wilderness, probably close to Bethlehem, while translating the Bible from Greek into Latin. He lived with some other monks and many animals, including dogs, hens, sheep, and donkeys. On an otherwise normal day, a great lion came into the monastery courtyard. Needless to say, all the monks scattered, except for Jerome. He noticed that the lion was limping and welcomed him in the spirit of hospitality that pervades most monasteries. Jerome healed the lion, who decided to remain with Jerome. The adventures of Jerome and the lion continue, but suffice it to say that on the death of the saint, the lion grieved without ceasing.

This is not the only such account. The story of St. Giles (d. c. 710) and the hind is tender and tragic. Giles, who had cured many, became a solitary living in a cave close to a beautiful spring. But he was only a solitary in terms of his relationship with people, because as the story goes "for some time he was nourished with the milk of a hind" or doe. Eventually, a group of hunters pursued her and she took refuge with Giles in his cave. She was "whining and whimpering . . . not at all like her," so Giles went out and, hearing the hunt, prayed that God would save this doe, the "nurse" God had provided.

This happened again and again, until finally, on the third day, the king brought a bishop along with him to survey the situation. This time, "one of the huntsmen shot an arrow into the cave," wounding Giles as he knelt in prayer for the life of the doe.[34] When the king searched for the doe, he found Giles, who still had the arrow in him. The saint survived and the king granted him land for a monastery.[35]

St. Blaise, a bishop, also decided to live the life of a hermit. He "retired to a cave," where "birds brought him food, and wild animals flocked to him." These animals would not leave "until he had laid hands on them in blessing," which indicates that Blaise understood the animals worthy of blessing and the animals understood the significance of the ritual. In addition, Blaise offered them healing, and "if any of them were ailing, they came straight to him and went away cured."[36]

Conclusions

Can animals be counted among the saints in Christianity? They have served as the locus for revelation, been exemplars of piety, offered themselves as martyrs and servants, and, in their relationships with others, have been the source of agape—the love of the divine. Thus, the sacred history, though often obscured, suggests that animals may indeed be counted among the holy ones in the Christian tradition. Of course, the functional world view for these animal-human-divine relationships reveals a significantly different historical context in many cases. Humans and animals were intimately related in everyday life during the periods when these stories were developed. In contrast, Euro-American culture of the early twenty-first century is a culture alienated from the natural world and other animals in most manifestations. Popular images of animals have morphed into human projections on a vast scale—from *The Lion King* to cultlike pedigree-dog shows to mass-produced flesh for food, with the actual dead animal being an utterly absent referent. These differences could, arguably, render the relevance of such animal stories impotent.

But even in those different cultural contexts of early Christianity saints provided an alternative relationship. Andrew Linzey, one of the few contemporary theologians to address the issue of animals, suggests this possibility in his book *Animal Theology:*

> We need to remember that the challenge of so many saints in their
> love and concern for even the most hated of all animals, was in
> almost all cases *against* the spirit of their times. Christian authorities
> have been forgetful or indifferent to the claims of animals, or per-
> haps more accurately, simply misled by *ad hoc* theological specula-
> tions.[37]

Such subversive stories of liberation for animals were required throughout the first sixteen centuries of Christianity. Interestingly, these stories of animals are connected to the stories of the most pious, the holiest, of all—saints.

I suggest that retelling stories of animals as saints could evoke radical attempts at reconstructing Christianity and help to promote critical reflection on human-animal relationships. In her introduction to a volume of women's writings in American religion, Rosemary Skinner Keller states, "Until history is revised, neither the writer nor the readers can imagine how a different story of the tradition will change their lives or the shape of history itself. When history is revised, the writer and the reader are led to new beginning points for interpreting their heritages. Neither person can accept the old story as it was told before!"[38]

Notes

1. Jacobus de Voragine, *The Golden Legend: Readings on the Saints* (Princeton, N.J.: Princeton Univ. Press, 1993), 84–85.

2. Ibid.

3. For ease of discussion, I use the term "animal" to refer to other than human animals throughout this chapter while acknowledging that human beings are animals as well. I also acknowledge that, in so doing, I am perpetuating the hierarchical

ranking of "humans" over "animals." This is not intended, but our language limits me at this point.

4. It would probably be more realistic to speak of "Christianities" (in the plural) because there are so many varieties of Christianity in the world, and this has been the case since the first century c.e. One "Christianity" has never existed. Attempts to oversimplify traditions by placing them into one category have led to broad generalizations and misunderstandings of diverse Christianities.

5. For an overview of this general theme, see H. Paul Santmire, *The Travail of Nature: The Ambiguous Ecological Promise of Christian Theology* (Philadelphia: Fortress, 1985).

6. At the beginning of the twenty-first century, Christianities are the primary religious system for approximately one-third of the human population—two billion of the earth's six billion people. Biocentric Christianities, therefore, are needed to shift religious sensibilities in the midst of the impending, and already present, environmental crises, in my opinion. Numerous Christian theologians are contributing to this transformation. Among them are: Karen Baker-Fletcher, *Sisters of Dust, Sisters of Spirit* (Minneapolis: Fortress, 1998); John Cobb, *The Earthist Challenge to Economism* (London: Macmillan, 1999); John Cobb and Herman Daly, *For the Common Good* (Boston: Beacon, 1989); Andrew Linzey, *Animal Gospel* (Louisville, Ky.: Westminster John Knox, 2000); Andrew Linzey, *Animal Theology* (Urbana: Univ. of Illinois Press, 1994); Jay B. McDaniel, *Earth, Sky, Gods, and Mortals* (Mystic, Conn.: Twenty-Third Publications, 1994); Charles Pinches and Jay B. McDaniel, eds., *Good News for Animals? Christian Approaches to Animal Well-Being* (Mary-knoll, N.Y.: Orbis, 1993); Sallie McFague, *The Body of God: An Ecological Theology* (Minneapolis: Fortress, 1993); Larry Rasmussen, *Earth Community, Earth Ethics* (Maryknoll, N.Y.: Orbis, 1996); Larry Rasmussen and Dieter Hessel, *Earth Habitat: Eco-Injustice and the Church's Response* (Minneapolis: Fortress, 2001); and Rosemary Radford Ruether, *Women Healing Earth* (Maryknoll, N.Y.: Orbis, 1996).

7. Carol J. Adams in her book *The Sexual Politics of Meat: A Feminist-Vegetarian Critical Theory* (New York: Continuum, 1990) provides an outstanding analysis of representations of animals in the "meat" industry and of the connections between these representations and those of the female body.

8. In the book I am currently writing, an entire chapter, "Holy Dogs and Asses: Animals in the History of the Christian Tradition," covers the influences of these religious traditions and their views of animal-human connections on Christianities.

9. For information on the lion's gate of Mycenae, see George E. Mylonas, *Mycenae: Rich in Gold* (Athens: Edkotike Athenon S.A., 1983); for information on Marija Gimbutas, see Marija Gimbutas, *The Civilization of the Goddess: The World of Old Europe* (San Francisco: HarperCollins, 1991).

10. Thomas Mathews, *The Clash of Gods: A Reinterpretation of Early Christian Art* (Princeton, N.J.: Princeton Univ. Press, 1993), 45.

11. "The Acts of Paul" exists only in large fragments. A widely accepted compilation is available in *The Apocryphal New Testament*, ed. J. K. Elliott (Oxford: Clarendon Press, 1999).

12. "The Acts of Paul," in *The Apocryphal New Testament*, ed. J. K. Elliott (Oxford: Clarendon Press, 1999), 378–79.

13. "The Acts of Paul and Thecla" (a subtext in "The Acts of Paul"), chaps. 28, 33, 369–70.

14. Another interesting question, based on Paul's choice to baptize a lion by water, is whether the lioness that dies defending Thecla receives baptism by blood—thus the actual status of a martyr?

15. This image has been reprinted in several publications, including John Pope-Hennessy, *Donatello Sculptor* (London: Abbeville Press, 1993) and the publications of the cathedral of St. Anthony in Padua, Italy.

16. I have gathered these images from churches—rural and urban, small and large—throughout Italy. While some of these are reproduced in various art history publications, others are not.

17. Ugolino Di Monte Santa Maria, *The Little Flowers of St. Francis of Assisi* (New York: Vintage Books, 1998), 37.

18. Edward A. Armstrong, *Saint Francis: Nature Mystic; The Derivation and Significance of the Nature Stories in the Franciscan Legend* (Berkeley and Los Angeles: Univ. of California Press, 1973), 59.

19. Di Monte Santa Maria, *Little Flowers of St. Francis*, 37.

20. The earliest sources for the life of Saint Francis are available in Marion Habig, ed., *St. Francis of Assisi: English Omnibus of the Sources for the Life of St. Francis* (Quincy, Ill.: Franciscan Press, 1991).

21. While I was writing a version of this chapter in March 2001, cattle and sheep in Europe, Argentina, and some parts of the United States were being slaughtered en masse because of the fear of the potential impact of contagious diseases on the profits of the livestock industry. Few, if any, of the slaughtered animals had been proven to carry these diseases, some of which are not even fatal to the animals, though they do destroy the animals' "market value."

22. De Voragine, *Golden Legend*, 266–67.

23. The concept of animals communicating with humanlike voices had a precedent in Christian scripture—Balaam's ass (Numbers 22:28–35).

24. De Voragine, *Golden Legend*, 127–28.

25. G. Duchet-Suchaux and M. Pastoureau, *The Bible and the Saints: Flammarion Iconographic Guides* (Paris: Flammarion, 1994), 154.

26. The cathedral of Siena is adorned with thirteenth-century sculptures by Nicola Pisano. Animals are portrayed throughout his series of sculptures depicting scenes from the life of Jesus.

27. For more information on "asses" in biblical texts, see Susan Carole Roy's chapter in this volume, "Paw Prints on Preaching: The Healing Power of Biblical Stories about Animals." She addresses the story of Balaam's ass (Numbers 22:21–35).

28. Jean-Claude Schmitt, *The Holy Greyhound: Guinefort, Healer of Children since the Thirteenth Century* (Cambridge, Mass.: Cambridge Univ. Press, 1983), 5.

29. Dennis Trout, "Christianizing the Nolan Countryside: Animal Sacrifice at the Tomb of Saint Felix," *Journal of Early Christian Studies* (Fall 1995): 286.

30. Ibid., 287.

31. This basilica is located south of Ravenna on the eastern coast of Italy.

32. De Voragine, *Golden Legend*, 229.

33. Ibid., 91.

34. Ibid., 148–49.

35. Richard McBrien, *Lives of the Saints* (San Francisco: Harper, 2001), 357.

36. De Voragine, *Golden Legend*, 151.

37. Linzey, *Animal Theology*, 66–67.

38. Rosemary Radford Ruether and Rosemary Keller, eds., *In Our Own Voices: Four Centuries of American Women's Religious Writing* (San Francisco: Harper, 1995), 3.

Works Cited

"The Acts of Paul" and "The Secondary Acts of Paul" (including "The Acts of Paul and Thecla"). In *The Apocryphal New Testament*, edited by J. K. Elliott, 350–89. Oxford: Clarendon Press, 1999.

Adams, Carol J. *The Sexual Politics of Meat: A Feminist-Vegetarian Critical Theory*. New York: Continuum, 1990.

Armstrong, Edward A. *Saint Francis: Nature Mystic; The Derivation and Significance of the Nature Stories in the Franciscan Legend*. Berkeley and Los Angeles: Univ. of California Press, 1973.

Baker-Fletcher, Karen. *Sisters of Dust, Sisters of Spirit*. Minneapolis: Fortress, 1998.

Cobb, John. *The Earthist Challenge to Economism*. London: Macmillan, 1999.

Cobb, John, and Herman Daly. *For the Common Good*. Boston: Beacon, 1989.

De Borchgrave, Helen. *A Journey into Christian Art*. Minneapolis: Fortress, 2000.

Di Monte Santa Maria, Ugolino. *The Little Flowers of Saint Francis of Assisi*. Translated by W. Heywood. New York: Vintage Books, 1998.

Duchet-Suchaux, G., and M. Pastoureau. *The Bible and the Saints: Flammarion Iconographic Guides*. Paris: Flammarion, 1994.

Gimbutas, Marija. *The Civilization of the Goddess: The World of Old Europe*. San Francisco: HarperCollins, 1991.

Habig, Marion, ed. *St. Francis of Assisi: English Omnibus of the Sources for the Life of St. Francis.* Quincy, Ill.: Franciscan Press, 1991.

Hobgood-Oster, Laura. *Holy Dogs and Asses: Animals in Christianity.* Forthcoming, Univ. of Illinois Press.

Linzey, Andrew. *Animal Gospel.* Louisville, Ky.: Westminster John Knox, 2000.

———. *Animal Theology.* Urbana: Univ. of Illinois Press, 1994.

Mathews, Thomas. *The Clash of Gods: A Reinterpretation of Early Christian Art.* Princeton, N.J.: Princeton Univ. Press, 1993.

McBrien, Richard. *Lives of the Saints.* San Francisco: Harper, 2001.

McDaniel, Jay B. *Earth, Sky, Gods, and Mortals: Developing an Ecological Spirituality.* Mystic, Conn.: Twenty-Third Publications, 1994.

McFague, Sallie. *The Body of God: An Ecological Theology.* Minneapolis: Fortress, 1993.

Mylonas, George E. *Mycenae: Rich in Gold.* Athens: Edkotike Athenon S.A., 1983.

Pinches, Charles, and Jay B. McDaniel, eds. *Good News for Animals? Christian Approaches to Animal Well-Being.* Maryknoll, N.Y.: Orbis, 1993.

Pope-Hennessy, John. *Donatello Sculptor.* New York: Abbeville Press, 1993.

Rasmussen, Larry. *Earth Community, Earth Ethics.* Maryknoll, N.Y.: Orbis, 1996.

Rasmussen, Larry, and Dieter Hessel. *Earth Habitat: Eco-Injustice and the Church's Response.* Minneapolis: Fortress, 2001.

Ruether, Rosemary Radford. *Women Healing Earth.* Maryknoll, N.Y.: Orbis, 1996.

Ruether, Rosemary Radford, and Rosemary Keller, eds. *In Our Own Voices: Four Centuries of American Women's Religious Writing.* San Francisco: Harper, 1995.

Santmire, Paul. *The Travail of Nature: The Ambiguous Ecological Promise of Christian Theology.* Philadelphia: Fortress Press, 1985.

Schmitt, Jean-Claude. *The Holy Greyhound: Guinefort, Healer of Children since the Thirteenth Century.* Translated by Martin Thom. Cambridge, Mass.: Cambridge Univ. Press, 1983.

Trout, Dennis. "Christianizing the Nolan Countryside: Animal Sacrifice at the Tomb of Saint Felix." *Journal of Early Christian Studies* (Fall 1995): 281–98.

Voragine, Jacobus de. *The Golden Legend: Readings on the Saints,* Vols. 1 and 2. Translated by William Granger Ryan. Princeton, N.J.: Princeton Univ. Press, 1993.

Chapter 11

Paw Prints on Preaching

The Healing Power of Biblical Stories about Animals

Rev. Susan Carole Roy

> The donkey saw the angel of the Lord standing in the
> road, with a drawn sword in his hand; so the donkey
> turned off the road, and went into a field; and Balaam
> struck the donkey, to turn it back onto the road.
> —Numbers 22:23

Biblical stories about people and animals, such as the story of Balaam and the donkey, are rich sources of spiritual insight. Thirteenth-century mystic Mechtild of Magdeburg penned one such spiritual insight when she declared, "The day of my spiritual awakening was the day I saw and I knew I saw all things in God and God in all things."[1] Those of us who live with companion animals know that some spiritual insights come from our relationships with those animals. Even if we do not share our lives with a companion animal, such as a cat or a dog, we share the world with millions of living creatures, all of whom have something to teach us.

Freckles, an obsessive-compulsive cocker spaniel with whom I share my life, is one such animal. His obsessive-compulsive behavior finds expression in licking walls, household appliances, and needy opportunistic cats. As the shadows dance across shiny surfaces in the brilliance of the morning sun, Freckles attempts to befriend the shadowy figures by licking, scratching, and barking at the ever-elusive reflections.

Only Freckles knows the first five years of his life story prior to being rescued from mangy, matted, ear-infected homelessness. He is a cute dog with a distinctly teddy bear appearance. He is content to watch his canine housemate eat his food, though he does not extend this privilege to his feline companions. This is no doubt a species thing. He stalks squirrels despite being attached to a six-foot leash. He knows where all the neighborhood cats live along his route to the park. He must be coached to go in a desired direction when he becomes obsessed with going a particular way.

Freckles attracts needy household cats desiring affection. One cat, Hagar, is particularly lazy and manipulative when it comes to self-care and personal hygiene. Hagar has discerned certain advantages to living with a dog compulsively obsessed with licking. The cat throws herself at Freckles, forcing him to wash her face.

Once her face is visibly damp, Hagar is satisfied. Freckles, however, is obsessive-compulsive. He cannot stop licking. He will put his paw over Hagar to hold her down so that he can continue to lick her face until she eventually wriggles free.

When Freckles came to live with me, I did not understand his attraction to shiny surfaces. Only after living with him for a while did I realize that he sees reflections in these surfaces, and only then did I learn that Freckles often sees what I would otherwise miss—the very shadows of life and what lurks within them: a squirrel, a cat, a reflection, a truth to ponder, a moment to savor.

Freckles has company among the divine cloud of four-legged witnesses. The Old Testament book of Numbers tells a story about an animal, a nameless donkey, with seemingly sharper theological eyesight than a man by the name of Balaam. Three times in this story the donkey sees the angel of the Lord with a drawn sword preparing to kill Balaam. Three times this nameless, faithful, wise donkey takes evasive action on behalf of this unseeing human. First, the donkey veers off into a field. Second, the donkey attempts to squeeze past the menacing angel. And third, when there is no other option, the donkey simply lies down, submitting to the holy presence towering in front of him.

Balaam, who does not see his own story unfolding in the shadows of the larger story, beats the donkey for each lifesaving evasive action. The donkey is given voice by the Lord to confront Balaam: "Am I not your donkey, which you have ridden all your life to this day? Have I been in the habit of treating you this way?" (Numbers 22:30) Balaam is convicted and given sight to see the angel of the Lord standing in the road, with a drawn sword in his hand. And the angel of the Lord delivers the divine comical punch line: "If it [the donkey] had not turned away from me, surely just now I would have killed you and let it live" (22:33). In polite theological language, the angel has just called Balaam an "ass."[2]

This story, omitted in the revised common lectionary, is a story about a human, an animal, and God.[3] Perhaps it is revealing that it is not included in the designated Sunday readings of most churches. Jay McDaniel writes:

> Many Christians find themselves enriched by a sense of kinship with animals and the Earth, and yet unable to experience Christianity, at least, in its institutional and doctrinal expressions, as supportive of such kinship. It is as if they live in two worlds: an "animal and Earth connected world" that is spiritually linked with fellow creatures and with the Earth, and a "Christian world" that highlights human-divine relationship at the expense of animals and the Earth. Caught in a spiritual schizophrenia, these Christians develop a dissatisfaction with the Christianity they know.[4]

The story about Balaam and the donkey is just one of many stories about humans, animals, and God that fill the Old and New Testaments. The book of Genesis reminds us that God created the animals and saved them along with Noah and his family. God is concerned about the animals, as evidenced by God's remark to the prophet Jonah: "And should I not be concerned about Nineveh, that great city, in which there are more than a hundred and twenty thousand persons who do not know their right hand from their left, and also many animals?" (Jonah 4:11). And in the Gospel of Luke, the animals welcome Jesus' birth in a stable (Luke 2:7). In the story of Balaam and the donkey, the human character is eventually given sight to see what the animal character first saw, namely, the angel of the Lord. How might our eyes also be opened through these stories to glean spiritual insights from the animals around us, some of whom may be angels or messengers of the Lord? What might we learn from the shadows Freckles chases?

We might see that some spiritual insights lurk in the very shadows of our theology as theologians struggle to understand how humans and animals relate. Contributing to this struggle is the very history of human-animal relationships, characterized by a wide range of feelings, attitudes, and beliefs about animals. Susan McHugh paws through the political, social, cultural, and economic impact of the human-dog relationship in her book *Dog*. She suggests that dog breeds were, and to some extent still are, indications of human nobility and social, as well as economic, status.[5] The mutt, on the other hand, has long been considered the dog of the common person.[6] Considering the political, social, cultural, and economic ramifications of the human-dog relationship informs practical ministry and adds to what we see lurking in the shadows.

As a parish pastor in Baltimore in the mid-1990s, I experienced a certain prejudice from the more affluent toward the human-animal bond among the economically disadvantaged. As I developed programs to help low- or no-income parishioners maintain this significant relationship with a companion animal, I encountered an attitude that those who cannot economically provide for a companion animal should not share their life with one. And yet, that animal may be the sole source of support for that person in an otherwise often hostile human world. Even the programs developed to assist with low-cost spay and neutering are based on middle-class economic and social skills such as access to transportation, checking accounts, telephones, calendars and schedules, and the ability to process information upon which the fee is determined, such as species, gender, size, and weight. The wide range of experiences and beliefs that people hold about companion animals has major ramifications for any ministry or social program designed to support the human-animal bond.

James Serpell, in his book *In the Company of Animals: A Study of Human-Animal Relationships*, considers some of the negative attitudes toward human-animal relationships. Serpell notes a tendency to

> denigrate the human practice of keeping animals for companionship by implying either that pets are merely substitutes for people; that pet-keeping is an unnecessary, and therefore, wasteful activity, or that it is a sort of pathological condition arising from the human tendency to respond in a nurturant, parental manner to young or dependent-seeming animals.[7]

He notes that none of these prejudicial notions about pet keeping is substantiated by available evidence:

> Far from being perverted, extravagant, or the victims of misplaced
> parental instincts, the majority of pet-owners are normal rational
> people who make use of animals to augment their existing social
> relationships, and so enhance their own psychological and physical
> welfare.[8]

Further complicating the understanding of our relationship with companion animals is how we respond to pet overpopulation by killing and our general disconnect from the slaughter of animals for food. Alan Beck and Aaron Katcher pick up this discussion in their book *Between Pets and People* when they identify the conflict between animals kept as pets and animals that are food sources. They argue that we cannot consider animals as members of the family, surrogate children, and confidants and then resolve overpopulation by killing millions of unwanted animals annually. They also identify a confounding issue in human history when large-scale human extermination has been described as killing people like animals:

> The urban denial of animal death is part of the conceptual problem,
> but the major impediment to clear thought is the status of pets as
> people. People do not want to think about giving an animal the sta-
> tus of a person and then killing it "like an animal." This process of
> stripping animals of their human status is too close to a similar pro-
> cess: the act of stripping human beings of their human status before
> killing them.[9]

Freckles, and the other animals with whom we share our lives, may enlighten us to consider the choices we make concerning the foods we eat and the way we, as a nation, resolve pet overpopulation.

The somewhat ambiguous understanding of human-animal relations throughout history is certainly paralleled in theology. A vast body of theology exists that is often inconsistent and ambiguous in understanding the very nature of the human-animal bond from the perspective of faith. Andrew Linzey points out:

> It is not that the Christian tradition has faced the question about
> animals and given unsatisfactory answers, rather it is that the ques-
> tion has never really been put. We do not have books devoted to a
> consideration of the theological significance of animals. We do not
> have clearly worked-out systematic views on animals. The thinking,
> or at least the vast bulk of it, has yet to be done. Even Aquinas,
> Calvin and Luther work essentially in an ad hoc manner when it
> comes to animals. It is not the animal issue which is their sole or
> even major concern in their writings and thus in almost all cases
> they cannot be said to have a worked-out position.[10]

Despite a recent rise in popularity among churches in favor of services blessing the animals, most often commemorating the Feast of St. Francis on October 4, animals are still largely missing from contemporary preaching and parish programming.

Some of the confusion about our relationship with animals for the faith community may come from the account of creation found in Genesis 1:26:

> Then God said, "Let us make humankind in our image, according
> to our likeness; and let them have dominion over the fish of the sea,
> and over the birds of the air, and over the cattle, and over all the wild
> animals of the earth, and over every creeping thing that creeps upon
> the earth."

Douglas John Hall, in his book *Imaging God: Dominion as Stewardship*, suggests that "the image of God/the likeness of God" became "almost a pretext for all sorts of speculation concerning the original condition of the human creature and its essential nature."[11] He references the work of Paul Ramsey's *Basic Christian Ethics* in which Ramsey "distinguishes between two primary interpretations of the *imago* concept, one he names the 'substantialist or ontological' concept, the other the 'relational' concept."[12] According to the substantialist view, Hall explains, the human species possesses certain characteristics or qualities that render it similar to the divine being. Rationality, for example, became identified as one such quality that, according to some early church fathers, humans possess but animals lack. The substantialist concept became one way of defining what it means to be human in comparison to other creatures.

On the other hand, "the relational conception conceives of the *imago* as an inclination or proclivity occurring within the relationship. To be *imago Dei* does not mean to have something but to be and do something: to image God."[13] The sixteenth-century reformers, such as Martin Luther, rejected the substantialist theory. Hall believes "Luther had been moved in a fundamental way by the relational character of the whole biblical testimony."[14] (See below for more on Luther's views on animals and religion.)

Hall is just one theologian among a growing number seeking to define how we relate faithfully as humans with all creatures. Other theologians working extensively in the area of animals and religion include Andrew Linzey, Jay McDaniel, and Carol Adams.[15] And feminist theologians such as Carol Adams are exploring what may be learned of significant otherness from the perspective of feminist theology. In their essay subtitled "Table Talk and Animals," Adams and coauthor Marjorie Procter-Smith connect animals as other to myriad, oppressed others in theological systems:

> When new theological subjects appear, we must confront our own
> situation. Poor people direct us to our complicity in gaining wealth
> at their expense; people of color direct us to the white racism in our
> economic and cultural system; women challenge the sexist benefits
> of a patriarchal system. And what would animals as theological subjects
> do? They would require of us that static and universal categories

be eliminated, that we cease believing in their lack of consciousness and sociality. They would have us confront the way we benefit from their oppression.[16]

In bringing feminist theory to the present discussion, Adams points us to yet another spiritual insight that may be as elusive as the shadows Freckles chases.[17] Spiritual insights may hold unique meanings for each of us, shaped as we are by personal experiences.

What else does the Holy One invite us to see lurking in the shadows of our theology through the eyes of animals? What else might we learn from the shadows that Freckles chases? We might see that animals share in the story of redemption, though this has been debated, mainly because of the way in which theologians have understood what it means for humans to be created in the image of God. Psalm 36:6 proclaims, "Your righteousness is like the mighty mountains, your judgments are like the great deep; you save humans and animals alike, O Lord." In the book of Jonah, the king of Nineveh includes animals in the act of fasting and repentance (Jonah 3:6ff). Paul in his letter to Romans, chapter 8, proclaims that all creation waits in expectation of redemption. Martin Luther, perhaps informed by his dog, Topel, painted an animal-inclusive picture of heaven:

There will be no carnivorous beasts, or venomous creatures, for all such, like ourselves, will be relieved from the curse of sin, and will be to us as friendly as they were to Adam in Paradise. There will be little dogs, with golden hair, shining like precious stone.[18]

Even so, Luther did not explicitly engage the subject of animals and religion, and in some instances his writing was less favorable toward animals.[19]

The Catholic scholastic Thomas Aquinas argued that animals lack rational souls and thus cannot be saved.[20] According to Luther's interpretation of Scripture, however, salvation is a free gift from God and is not dependent upon human initiative or intellect. For those of us obsessive and compulsive about our relationship with God, Luther reminds us that we are made okay with God by God's grace through faith.

The question people most often ask me as a pastor working with companion animals is about animals and salvation. Though this question, too, could be the subject of a whole chapter, we should acknowledge the importance of this question and bring it out from the shadows into the open air of discussion. In addition, we may see the death of a companion animal as the significant loss that it often is and respond in a pastoral manner.[21] A second spiritual insight we might glean from both the biblical story about animals and our personal relationship with animals is that spiritual insights may take time and emerge gradually from an openness to the "other." Greater appreciation of and attention to the multifaceted dimensions of the human-animal bond, such as end of life and grief issues, may be a result of spiritual insights learned in relationship with a companion animal.

What else might we see lurking in the shadows of our theology when we consider life through the eyes of animals? What else might we learn from the shadows Freckles chases? Job tells us:

> But listen to the animals, and they will teach you; the birds of the air,
> and they will tell you; ask the plants of the earth, and they will teach
> you; and the fish of the sea will declare to you. Who among all these
> does not know that the hand of the Lord has done this? In his hand
> is the life of every living thing and the breath of every human being
> (Job 12:7–10).

Freckles has taught me to live with the imperfection of a saliva line demarcating licked surfaces in my house. And with a dog equally imperfect, who is so obsessed with chasing shadows and licking the garage door that he routinely forgets to do his business outside. He has taught me to share responsibility for nurturing multiple cats. He has taught me attentiveness to the shadows—to those things I might otherwise miss in life. He has taught me to value the unique in each animal and human. He has taught me awe and reverence for God's beauty, love, and compassion. As Mechtild of Magdeburg suggested nearly a thousand years ago, "The truly wise person kneels at the feet of all creatures."[22]

Freckles has taught me to live with his obsessive-compulsive disorder (OCD). Medications and behavior modification were minimally successful. Those who live with or know someone with a condition like OCD understand that this is a serious condition. During a consultation with an animal behaviorist, Freckles even licked the shiny surface of the video lens recording his behavior. He also licked bacteria off the clinic walls during the same visit, requiring yet another trip to the vet. OCD is a serious condition that can be costly in its toll on relationships, employment, and general well being, not to mention home equity. Companion animals with chronic, life altering conditions may also serve to encourage people living with similar challenges.

A vast body of literature exists about animal-assisted therapy, documenting how animals help us heal and learn. Therapy animals serve in rehabilitation facilities encouraging patients to recover from illnesses and injuries and visit the elderly in nursing homes and children in residential treatment facilities.[23] I was privileged to learn firsthand about animal-assisted therapy from Aaron Katcher and James Serpell, pioneers in the study of the human-animal bond, when I served as a chaplain intern in clinical pastoral education at the Veterinary Hospital at the University of Pennsylvania.

What Freckles has taught me is a variation of animal-assisted therapy, namely, animal-assisted spirituality. Freckles has taught me spiritual lessons such as patience, love, and seeing the holy in the ordinary and the extraordinary. Animal-assisted spirituality is not new. The medieval bestiaries were moral lessons using animals to teach faith values. Stories in Scripture about animals, humans, and the holy have much to teach us. The use of stories about animals in preaching is also not a new phenomenon. Medieval preaching styles of tenth- to fifteenth-century England show that preachers of different periods used aspects of animal lore such as the figurative, the moral, and the entertaining in their sermons.[24] Animals have been messengers of God's Good News throughout the ages. Parishioners who live with companion animals often tell me how appreciative they are to hear animals included in contemporary preaching. And yet a true reverence for animals must be maintained, else they become purely utilitarian instruments of faith. Animals are significant regardless of what they may teach us. A third spiritual insight that we might glean is that the Divine may have many manifestations, some with fur, feathers, or scales.

What else might we see lurking in the shadows of our theology when we consider life through the eyes of animals? What else might be lurking in the shadows that Freckles chases? The story of Balaam and the donkey is a story of human violence toward an animal. In fact, Balaam exhibits a classical compulsion to continue the violent act of beating the donkey as his response to the donkey's action on three consecutive occasions.

Randall Lockwood, Phil Arkow, and Frank Ascione pioneered studies concerning the connections among various forms of violence.[25] Lockwood, vice president of training initiatives at the Humane Society of the United States, was instrumental in developing the organization's First Strike Campaign, designed to educate the public, teachers, social service agents, law enforcement officers, veterinarians, and now religious leaders about the connections among child abuse, domestic abuse, and animal abuse. Evidence is mounting that violent acts are not separate and distinct but part of a cycle. In one study of fifty-three New Jersey pet-owning families involved with physical or sexual abuse or neglect, researchers found that "in 47 (88%) of the families in which physical child abuse took place, animal abuse also occurred."[26] Animals can teach us that what affects one part of the web of life often affects other parts as well.

A significant spiritual insight for institutional religion is the need to attend to both the spiritual and physical. Leaving an abusive relationship is not easy. One role that the church can play is to recognize the need to at least be knowledgeable about the presence of animal welfare organizations in their community and the presence of Safe Havens designed to protect animals so that all those affected by violence can escape without breaking yet another important bond of support and love.

What are we to do with the spiritual insights we gain from animals? Luther often spoke of faith active in love. If we allow these insights to become active in love, we may envision parish ministries to people with companion animals. We may envision faith communities that act harmoniously with the world of nature and animals. We may envision animal-friendly congregations that extend prayers and support to the human-animal bond. We may envision parishioners who open their homes and hearts to animals who need a safe foster home so that their humans may escape the horrors of domestic violence. We may envision a world of faith active in love in which angels do not call us "asses" because we have, at long last, gleaned spiritual insights from the donkeys and the dogs.

Freckles has left his paw prints on my heart and a saliva line on my walls. His story is a part of my story. My story is a part of his story. And our story is a part of God's story. God's story is a story about animals, humans, and creation and a multitude of expressions of the Holy. And a little-told story about a nameless donkey and a man named Balaam invites us to see a God who surprises us anew in the shadows of life.

Appendix
Numbers 22:21–35

So Balaam got up in the morning, saddled his donkey, and went with the officials of Moab.

God's anger was kindled because he was going, and the angel of the Lord took his stand in the road as his adversary. Now he was riding on the donkey, and his two servants were with him. The donkey saw the angel of the Lord standing in the road, with a drawn sword in his hand; so the donkey turned off the road, and went into the field; and Balaam struck the donkey, to turn it back onto the road. Then the angel of the Lord stood in a narrow path between the vineyards, with a wall on either side. When the donkey saw the angel of the Lord, it scraped against the wall, and scraped Balaam's foot against the wall; so he struck it again. Then the angel of the Lord went ahead, and stood in a narrow place, where there was no way to turn either to the right or to the left. When the donkey saw the angel of the Lord, it lay down under Balaam; and Balaam's anger was kindled, and he struck the donkey with his staff. Then the Lord opened the mouth of the donkey, and it said to Balaam, "What have I done to you, that you have stuck me these three times?" Balaam said to the donkey, "Because you have made a fool of me! I wish I had a sword in my hand! I would kill you right now!" But the donkey said to Balaam, "Am I not your donkey, which you have ridden all your life to this day? Have I been in the habit of treating you this way?" And he said, "No."

Then the Lord opened the eyes of Balaam, and he saw the angel of the Lord standing in the road, with his drawn sword in this hand; and he bowed down, falling on his face. The angel of the Lord said to him, "Why have you struck your donkey these three times? I have come out as an adversary, because your way is perverse before me. The donkey saw me, and turned away from me these three times. If it had not turned away from me, surely just now I would have killed you and let it live." Then Balaam said to the angel of the Lord, "I have sinned, for I did not know that you were standing in the road to oppose me. Now therefore, if it is displeasing to you, I will return home." The angel of the Lord said to Balaam, "Go with the men; but speak only what I tell you to speak." So Balaam went on with the officials of Balak.

Notes

This chapter originated as a sermon I first preached at St. John's Lutheran Church in Baltimore, Maryland, on July 22, 2001. The text for the sermon comes from Numbers 22:21–35 and may be found in the appendix at the end of this chapter.

All biblical texts quoted in this chapter are from the New Revised Standard Version (Bruce M. Metzger and Roland E. Murphy, eds., *The New Oxford Annotated Bible NRSV* [New York: Oxford Univ. Press, 1999]).

1. Matthew Fox, *Wrestling with the Prophets: Essays on Creation Spirituality and Everyday Life* (New York: HarperCollins, 1995), 91.

2. For more about language and animals, see Susan McHugh, *Dog* (London: Reaktion, 2004), 48–56.

3. A lectionary is a list of Bible passages for reading, study, or preaching in services of worship. The term is most commonly applied to Scripture readings for Sundays and holy days.

4. Jay B. McDaniel, "A God Who Loves Animals and a Church that Does the Same," in *Good News for Animals? Christian Approaches to Animal Well-Being*, ed. Charles Pinches and Jay B. McDaniel (Maryknoll, N.Y.: Orbis Books, 1993), 75.

5. McHugh, *Dog*, 58–126.

6. Ibid., 127–70.

7. James Serpell, *In the Company of Animals: A Study of Human-Animal Relationships* (Cambridge, Mass.: Cambridge Univ. Press, 1986), 147.

8. Ibid.

9. Alan Beck and Aaron Katcher, *Between Pets and People: The Importance of Animal Companionship* (West Lafayette, Ind.: Purdue Univ. Press, 1996), 25.

10. Andrew Linzey, *Christianity and the Rights of Animals* (New York: Crossroads, 1989), 23–24.

11. Douglas John Hall, *Imaging God: Dominion as Stewardship* (1986; reprint, Eugene, Oreg.: Wipf & Stock, 2004), 88. See also Matthew Scully, *Dominion* (New York: St. Martin's Press, 2002).

12. Hall, *Imaging God*, 98.

13. Ibid.

14. Ibid., 99.

15. For more information on animals and religion, see Andrew Linzey's *Animal Gospel* (Louisville, Ky.: Westminster John Knox Press, 1998), *Animal Rites: Liturgies of Animal Care* (Cleveland: Pilgrim Press, 1999), *Animal Theology* (Urbana: Univ. of Illinois Press, 1994), and *Christianity and the Rights of Animals*; Andrew Linzey and Dorothy Yamamoto, eds., *Animals on the Agenda: Questions about Animals for Theology and Ethics* (Urbana: Univ. of Illinois Press, 1998); Jay B. McDaniel, *Earth, Sky, Gods, and Mortals: Developing an Ecological Spirituality* (Mystic, Conn.: Twenty-Third Publications, 1990); Jay B. McDaniel, *Of God and Pelicans: A Theology of Reverence for Life* (Louisville, Ky.: Westminster/John Knox Press, 1989); Carol J. Adams, ed., *Ecofeminism and the Sacred* (New York: Continuum, 1993), *Neither Man nor Beast: Feminism and the Defense of Animals* (New York: Continuum, 1994), and *Prayers for Animals* (New York: Continuum, 2004); Christopher Manes, *Other Creations: Rediscovering the Spirituality of Animals* (New York: Doubleday, 1997); Stephen Webb, *On God and Dogs: A Christian Theology of Compassion for Animals* (New York: Oxford Univ. Press, 1998); and Robert N. Wennberg, *God, Humans,*

and Animals: An Invitation to Enlarge Our Moral Universe (Grand Rapids, Mich.: William B. Eerdmans, 2003).

16. Carol J. Adams and Marjorie Procter-Smith, "Taking Life or Taking on Life? Table Talk and Animals," in Adams, *Ecofeminism and the Sacred*, 298–99.

17. See also Donna Haraway, *The Companion Species Manifesto: Dogs, People, and Significant Otherness* (Chicago: Prickly Paradigm Press, 2003).

18. Thomas S. Kepler, ed., *The Table Talk of Martin Luther* (New York: World, 1952), 328–29.

19. For more information, see Scott Ickert, "Luther and Animals: Subject to Adam's Fall?" in Linzey and Yamamoto, *Animals on the Agenda*, 90–99, and Jaroslav Jan Pelikan, ed., *Lectures on Genesis*, vol. 1 of *Luther's Works* (St. Louis: Concordia, 1958).

20. Thomas Aquinas in Linzey, *Christianity and the Rights of Animals*, 36.

21. For more information about grief and loss in the human-animal bond, see William J. Kay, Herbert A. Nieburg, Austin H. Kutscher, Ross M. Grey, and Carole E. Fudin, eds., *Pet Loss and Human Bereavement* (Ames: Iowa State Univ. Press, 1984); Gary Kowalski, *Good-Bye, Friend: Healing Wisdom for Anyone Who Has Ever Lost a Pet* (Walpole, N.H.: Stillpoint, 1997); Laurel Lagoni, Carolyn Butler, and Suzanne Hetts, *The Human-Animal Bond and Grief* (Philadelphia: W. B. Saunders, 1994); Jamie Quackenbush and Denise Graveline, *When Your Pet Dies: How to Cope with Your Feelings* (New York: Pocket Books, 1985); and Wallace Sife, *The Loss of a Pet* (New York: Howell Book House, 1993).

22. Fox, *Wrestling with the Prophets*, 87.

23. For more information about animal-assisted therapy, see Jacqueline J. Crawford and Karen A. Pomerinke, *Therapy Pets: The Animal-Human Healing Partnership* (New York: Prometheus Books, 2003); Bruce Fogle, ed., *Interrelations between People and Pets* (Springfield, Ill.: Charles C. Thomas, 1981); Clinton R. Sanders, *Understanding Dogs: Living and Working with Canine Companions* (Philadelphia: Temple Univ. Press, 1999); and Cindy C. Wilson and Dennis C. Turner, eds., *Companion Animals in Human Health* (Thousand Oaks, Calif.: Sage Publications, 1998).

24. Deborah J. McFarland, "Animal Lore and Medieval English Sermon Style" (Ph.D. diss., Univ. of Florida, 1980).

25. For more information about animals and violence, see Frank R. Ascione and Phil Arkow, eds., *Child Abuse, Domestic Violence, and Animal Abuse: Linking the Circles of Compassion for Prevention and Intervention* (West Lafayette, Ind.: Purdue Univ. Press, 1999).

26. Phil Arkow, "The Correlation between Cruelty to Animals and Child Abuse and the Implications for Veterinary Medicine," in *Cruelty to Animals and Interpersonal Violence: Readings in Research and Application*, ed. Randall Lockwood and Frank R. Ascione (West Lafayette, Ind.: Purdue Univ. Press, 1998), 410.

Works Cited

Adams, Carol J., ed. *Ecofeminism and the Sacred*. New York: Continuum, 1993.

———. *Neither Man nor Beast: Feminism and the Defense of Animals*. New York: Continuum, 1994.

———. *Prayers for Animals*. New York: Continuum, 2004.

Adams, Carol J., and Marjorie Procter-Smith. "Taking Life or Taking on Life? Table Talk and Animals." In *Ecofeminism and the Sacred*, edited by Carol J. Adams, 295–310. New York: Continuum, 1993.

Arkow, Phil. "The Correlation between Cruelty to Animals and Child Abuse and the Implications for Veterinary Medicine." In *Cruelty to Animals and Interpersonal Violence: Readings in Research and Application*, edited by Randall Lockwood and Frank R. Ascione, 409–14. West Lafayette, Ind.: Purdue Univ. Press, 1998.

Ascione, Frank R., and Phil Arkow, eds. *Child Abuse, Domestic Violence, and Animal Abuse: Linking the Circles of Compassion for Prevention and Intervention*. West Lafayette, Ind.: Purdue Univ. Press, 1999.

Beck, Alan, and Aaron Katcher. *Between Pets and People: The Importance of Animal Companionship*. West Lafayette, Ind.: Purdue Univ. Press, 1996.

Crawford, Jacqueline J., and Karen A. Pomerinke. *Therapy Pets: The Animal-Human Healing Partnership*. New York: Prometheus Books, 2003.

Fogle, Bruce, ed. *Interrelations between People and Pets*. Springfield, Ill.: Charles C. Thomas, 1981.

Fox, Matthew. *Wrestling with the Prophets: Essays on Creation Spirituality and Everyday Life*. New York: HarperCollins, 1995.

Hall, Douglas John. *Imaging God: Dominion as Stewardship*. 1986. Reprint, Eugene, Oreg.: Wipf & Stock, 2004.

Haraway, Donna. *The Companion Species Manifesto: Dogs, People, and Significant Otherness*. Chicago: Prickly Paradigm Press, 2003.

Ickert, Scott. "Luther and Animals: Subject to Adam's Fall?" In *Animals on the Agenda: Questions about Animals for Theology and Ethics*, edited by Andrew Linzey and Dorothy Yamamoto, 90–99. Urbana: Univ. of Illinois Press, 1998.

Kay, William J., Herbert A. Nieburg, Austin H. Kutscher, Ross M. Grey, and Carole E. Fudin, eds. *Pet Loss and Human Bereavement*. Ames: Iowa State Univ. Press, 1984.

Kepler, Thomas S., ed. *The Table Talk of Martin Luther*. New York: World, 1952.

Kowalski, Gary. *Good-Bye, Friend: Healing Wisdom for Anyone Who Has Ever Lost a Pet*. Walpole, N.H.: Stillpoint, 1997.

Lagoni, Laurel, Caroyln Butler, and Suzanne Hetts. *The Human-Animal Bond and Grief*. Philadelphia: W. B. Saunders, 1994.

Linzey, Andrew. *Animal Gospel*. Louisville, Ky.: Westminster John Knox Press, 1998.

———. *Animal Rites: Liturgies of Animal Care*. Cleveland: Pilgrim Press, 1999.

———. *Animal Theology*. Urbana: Univ. of Illinois Press, 1994.

———. *Christianity and the Rights of Animals*. New York: Crossroads, 1989.

Linzey, Andrew, and Dorothy Yamamoto, eds. *Animals on the Agenda: Questions about Animals for Theology and Ethics*. Urbana: Univ. of Illinois Press, 1998.

Lockwood, Randall, and Frank R. Ascione, eds. *Cruelty to Animals and Interpersonal Violence: Readings in Research and Application*. West Lafayette, Ind.: Purdue Univ. Press, 1998.

Manes, Christopher. *Other Creations: Rediscovering the Spirituality of Animals*. New York: Doubleday, 1997.

McDaniel, Jay B. *Earth, Sky, Gods, and Mortals: Developing an Ecological Spirituality*. Mystic, Conn.: Twenty-Third Publications, 1990.

———. "A God Who Loves Animals and a Church that Does the Same." In *Good News for Animals? Christian Approaches to Animal Well-Being*, edited by Charles Pinches and Jay B. McDaniel, 75–102. Maryknoll, N.Y.: Orbis Books, 1993.

———. *Of God and Pelicans: A Theology of Reverence for Life*. Louisville, Ky.: Westminster/John Knox Press, 1989.

McFarland, Deborah J. "Animal Lore and Medieval English Sermon Style." Ph.D. diss., Univ. of Florida, 1980.

McHugh, Susan. *Dog*. London: Reaktion, 2004.

Pelikan, Jaroslav Jan, ed. *Lectures on Genesis*. Vol. 1 of *Luther's Works*. St. Louis: Concordia, 1958.

Quackenbush, Jamie, and Denise Graveline. *When Your Pet Dies: How to Cope with Your Feelings*. New York: Pocket Books, 1985.

Sanders, Clinton R. *Understanding Dogs: Living and Working with Canine Companions*. Philadelphia: Temple Univ. Press, 1999.

Scully, Matthew. *Dominion*. New York: St. Martin's Press, 2002.

Serpell, James. *In the Company of Animals: A Study of Human-Animal Relationships*. Cambridge, Mass.: Cambridge Univ. Press, 1986.

Sife, Wallace. *The Loss of a Pet*. New York: Howell Book House, 1993.

Webb, Stephen. *On God and Dogs: A Christian Theology of Compassion for Animals*. New York: Oxford Univ. Press, 1998.

Wennberg, Robert N. *God, Humans, and Animals: An Invitation to Enlarge our Moral Universe*. Grand Rapids, Mich.: William B. Eerdmans, 2003.

Wilson, Cindy C., and Dennis C. Turner, eds. *Companion Animals in Human Health*. Thousand Oaks, Calif.: Sage Publications, 1998.

Chapter 12

Personification of Pets

The Evolution of Canine Cartoons in the *New Yorker*

Anne Alden

Cartoons provide a portrait of society's foibles, current obsessions, and attitudes. With a few quick strokes of the pen, they can satirize and provide social commentary far more succinctly than many a long diatribe on the same subject. Viewed in the context of history, cartoons stand as an incisive distillation of popular opinion and social mores over time. For this chapter, I examined the portrayal of dogs in *New Yorker* cartoons over the past century as a reflection of changes in attitudes toward companion animals and the changing role of dogs in American society.

As a form of popular culture, comic art has been described as reflecting what is currently happening in our society[1] and providing a "social history" of the time.[2] Given the popularity of both cartoons and pets, the dearth of research on dog cartoons is surprising. Betty Carmack, who examined syndicated comics from 1984 to 1995 in the *San Francisco Chronicle*, studied the realistic representational images of human-pet interaction, and concluded that the "overall roles pets play in their humans' lives" and "the widely held values by humans toward companion animals . . . are all portrayed through comic art."[3] Harold A. Herzog and Shelly L. Galvin studied animal-related stories and photographs in four American tabloid magazines. They agree that the way animals are depicted in the media could provide information about "social attitudes towards other species."[4] Furthermore, they argue that the portrayal of animals reflects "the roles that animals have had in human cultural and psychological life" since the beginning of civilization.[5] I argue that an analysis of cartoons, one of the most popular and democratic of art forms, can provide information about the public's attitudes toward companion animals over time.

A cultural icon in the literary world, the *New Yorker* magazine has long been known for the popularity of its cartoons. In the magazine's first few decades, its cartoons primarily featured realistic-looking dogs engaged in normal dog behavior, usually in passive roles in relationships with humans. In contrast, the last thirty years have seen the emergence of dogs as anthropomorphized subjects of cartoons, often pictured as equals in interactions with humans.

Because I examined one American magazine, which reflects the tastes and idiosyncrasies of a specific readership, results are not generalizable to the world at large. That said, *New Yorker* cartoons are also published as books, greeting cards, and calendars, so they reach a larger population. Furthermore, the Cartoon Bank (www.cartoonbank.com), an online business division of the *New Yorker,* sells reprints of cartoons from a catalog of more than eighty-five thousand images, and a report by the Media Industry Newsletter (MIN) in 2001 estimated that the Cartoon Bank had 2.5 million page views on their web site per month.[6] Therefore, *New Yorker* cartoons are seen by a much larger and more diverse audience than the magazine's readership.

Due to limitations in length, the primary purpose of this chapter is descriptive, illustrating a trend toward increasingly anthropomorphic portrayal of dogs in cartoons and demonstrating how this has coincided with a current tendency toward anthropomorphism in human-pet relationships.[7] An in-depth analysis of the concept and meaning of anthropomorphism in cartoons is beyond the scope of this chapter.[8]

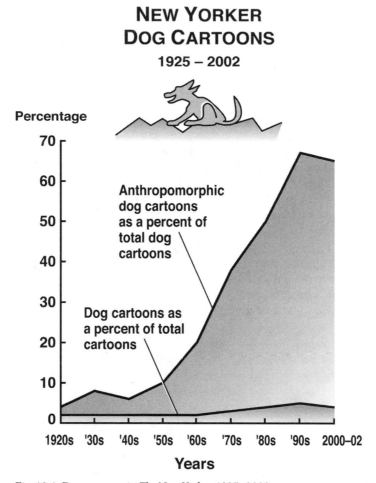

Fig. 12.1. Dog cartoons in *The New Yorker*, 1925–2002.

Method

To analyze changes in dog cartoons from 1925 to 2002, I looked at dog cartoons as a percentage of total *New Yorker* cartoons, and anthropomorphic dog cartoons as a percentage of total dog cartoons for each decade. I also conducted a qualitative examination of dog cartoons, looking specifically at changes in how dogs were portrayed from the 1920s to 2002.[9]

Results

From the 1920s through the 1960s, dog cartoons represented roughly 2 percent of all cartoons in the *New Yorker*. Dog cartoons increased substantially in the 1970s, 1980s, and 1990s, with the highest numbers occurring in the 1990s, when dog cartoons represented 5 percent of all cartoons. From 2000 to 2002, dog cartoons were 4 percent of all cartoons. While this increase over many decades was significant, the trend toward anthropomorphism in dog cartoons was by far the most dramatic and consistent change over time. In the 1920s, only 4 percent of dog cartoons were anthropomorphic in nature. In contrast, by the 1990s, the majority of dog cartoons (67 percent) featured dogs behaving like humans in some way. This trend continued through the year 2002 (see fig. 12.1).

An in-depth look at each decade will provide an opportunity to discuss the cartoons in a qualitative way and to view them in the context of the historical events and sociocultural influences of the time.

1920s

In reviewing the cartoons of the 1920s and 1930s, I was surprised by how little they acknowledged the impact of major events, such as the stock market crash in 1929 and the poverty and hardships of the Depression. Instead, the cartoons of this era tended to reflect wild times, showing excesses of drinking and carousing, with many stylized portraits of flappers. Dogs were often pictured as fashionable ornaments for the wealthy, and diminutive breeds, such as Pekinese and toy poodles, predominated. People typically were shown fussing over dogs, taking pictures of them, and buying collars and clothing for them at pet stores. Themes of dog shows and dog grooming were often featured. One cover depicted a woman in curlers seated next to a dog in identical curlers.[10] Another cartoon pictured a small dog flying through the air with the caption: "I've just washed Chico. He's so fluffy, I can't do a thing with him."[11] Many cartoons of the 1920s featured people relating anthropomorphically to pets, but this almost always involved projecting human characteristics onto pets, with dogs continuing to look and act like real dogs. Cartoons of this decade often pictured dogs being treated like family members or children, usually by women. Captions contained terms of endearment for dogs such as "Snookums," and dogs were often spoken to like children, as in "Junior, Come here!"

1930s

Similar to the 1920s, cartoons of the 1930s tended to feature scenes of society at leisure. Cartoons of domestic life showed people assuming dogs had human emotions such as jealousy and resentment. One cartoon featured a woman covering her mouth and whispering to her husband, "Wilmet, I'm going to have a b-a-b-y" while an annoyed-looking dog observed them.[12] One theme in cartoons of the 1930s was the ownership of many dogs. Seven cartoons from this decade pictured people with more than six dogs. A cartoon by George Price showed a man holding ten dogs on leashes with the caption "Well, she has her books and I have my dogs."[13]

Competitive dog shows and breeding also provided themes for several cartoons in the 1930s. After the American Kennel Club (AKC) was founded in 1884, breed standards were established and handbooks on the competitive showing of dogs became popular.[14] Many *New Yorker* captions from this period mentioned a specific breed, such as Irish wolfhound, Mexican hairless, and Skye terrier. Dogs were also shown in a working capacity, with six cartoons of sled dogs, four of search dogs, and eight of hunting dogs with horses. In the 1930s, as in the previous decade, dogs also continued to be pictured as part of the family and often were given a prominent place in family affairs, as in one cartoon by Peter Arno showing disgruntled relatives hearing that a dog would be getting the bulk of a deceased owner's estate.[15]

1940s

From 1939 through the mid-1940s, there were several cartoons picturing scenes related to the war, such as dogs chasing a military truck and military police coming to the door looking for a misbehaving dog. There were thirteen cartoons picturing St. Bernards rescuing people in the snow. One cartoon showed a woman volunteering her dachshund at a recruiting office, saying, "I thought perhaps he'd be good for crawling under things."[16] A very strange cartoon of a war-related scene in 1940 depicted the eating of dog meat. A reporter was pictured writing a story for *Time* magazine's foreign news desk and typing, "Dog meat has been eaten in every major German crisis at least since the time of Frederick the Great, and is commonly referred to as 'blockade mutton.'" The reporter then goes to a pet store to buy a dog and takes the dog to a restaurant displaying the sign "We cook special dishes to your order." After sitting back down at his typewriter, he types that the dog meat he has just eaten was "tough, gamy, strong-flavored."[17] In *The Companion Species Manifesto*, Donna Haraway discusses the emergence of the term "companion animal" in the mid-1970s in the United States. "Generally speaking," she notes, "one does not eat one's companion animal (nor get eaten by them); and one has a hard time shaking colonialist, ethnocentric, ahistorical attitudes towards those who do (eat or get eaten)."[18] Perhaps, then, this cartoon could be interpreted as anti-Nazi commentary, portraying Germans as barbarian "dog eaters" during World War II. However, one puzzling aspect is that the U.S. reporter has himself just eaten dog meat. Because of the current status and popularity of dogs as pets, it is hard to imagine a cartoon with this subject being published today. Certainly it is likely that the *New Yorker* would receive some negative mail from readers if it did so.

After World War II, the field of advertising was evolving and consumer spending began in earnest.[19] Reflecting this trend, a cartoon in 1949 showed a dog performing in a radio commercial.[20] Many cartoons pictured the urban lifestyle of dog owners in New York. One cartoon showed a dog walker in the city with six dogs on leashes.[21]

1950s

During the 1950s, a dramatic increase in pet ownership coincided with the baby boom and suburban development. According to Bruce Fogle, the role of dogs changed significantly at this time, as they began to be kept indoors. Before World War II, dogs typically lived in yards and were brought inside only on the coldest nights of winter. In the years following the war, "dogs moved into our homes, and our hearts," according to Fogle, because food was plentiful and cheap and because women emerged as a social force in Western countries and brought a more empathic orientation toward animals.[22]

At this time, animal rights groups concentrated their efforts on protecting domestic animals.[23] The 1950s featured several cartoons of ASPCA trucks and one of a dog pound truck rounding up stray dogs. Overall, there was a slight decrease in the number of dog cartoons in the 1950s compared to earlier decades. Interestingly, many cartoons had a negative slant, depicting dogs as a nuisance or exhibiting bad behavior. One cartoon showed a dog barking and charging at an angry postman,[24] and another showed a man pretending to like a dog to impress a woman, then kicking the dog when the woman's back was turned.[25] Other cartoon captions show men saying, "I'll be damned if I'll shake hands with him!"[26] and "Sure, why not? How about a *third* [TV] set for the damned dog?"[27] Almost all of the negative cartoons of the 1950s pictured men getting angry at dogs, which is interesting in light of Fogle's assessment that a new sentience regarding animals was led by women at this time.[28] Perhaps these cartoons reflect strains associated with increases in dog ownership, particularly in scenes where some members of the family feel more positively than others about the addition of a dog to the household.

1960s

Concomitant with the continued increase in pet ownership during the 1960s and 1970s, the regulation of household pets, especially dogs, became stricter. This was particularly true in cities, where complaints of animal waste and noise resulted in pet bans and "scoop laws" requiring dog owners to clean up after their pets.[29] In 1966, Congress passed the Animal Welfare Act, which was aimed at ensuring humane treatment of all animals, including pets. This legislation was also enacted to protect animal research subjects in experiments. Also in the 1960s, the Equal Pay Act was passed by Congress and the Civil Rights Act was amended to include gender.

In a humorous parallel to the nascent women's movement and the questioning of roles in the 1960s, several cartoons portrayed themes of people in a defined "master" role, such as one cartoon with a woman saying to her dog, "Guess what, Mr. Corbett is going to be our lord and master,"[30] and another caption with a dog saying, "I'm leaving you master."[31] Perhaps parodying the prominence of behaviorism in the field of psychology at this time, a cartoon pictured one dog angrily saying to another dog, "How can I talk to you? I give you *ideas*, and all I get back is

"How can I talk to you? I give you <u>ideas</u>, and
all I get back is conditioned responses!"

Fig. 12.2. From *The New Yorker*, Feb. 1, 1969, p. 37. © The New Yorker Collection 1969 William Steig from cartoonbank.com. All Rights Reserved.

conditioned responses"[32] (see fig. 12.2). Another cartoon delivered a commentary on evolutionary biology, featuring a man saying to his dog and cat, "And how are you lower animals getting on?"[33]

1970s

In contrast to earlier decades, the 1970s saw a large increase in the number of dog cartoons. Partly this was influenced by the first publication of cartoons by George Booth in 1969. He left an indelible stamp on the magazine and has become one of the most recognizable of the *New Yorker*'s cartoonists. Although Booth never owned a dog, he grew up in a farm community where dogs and cats were yard animals, not pets.[34] This may account for the typically peevish and independent attitudes of dogs in Booth cartoons; they are rarely portrayed as servile or obsequious. While the 1970s had lots of cartoons showing dogs in anthropomorphized roles, Booth cartoons often capture the essential character of dogs just acting like dogs. An example is a scene featuring a bull terrier with close-set eyes, frantically scratching at fleas with one leg. Another cartoon pictured a psychotic-looking dog going through a ritualized routine of scratching the pavement with each hind leg then barking at nothing in particular (see fig. 12.3).[35] In addition to being known for his psychotic-looking dogs, Booth is known for his portraits of chaotic households with eccentric people and many dogs.

In the 1970s, major trends included continued advances in civil rights legislation. The passage of the Equal Rights Amendment (which was subsequently not ratified) resulted in increasing numbers of women and minorities entering the work force and asserting their rights. In a humorous parallel, *New Yorker* cartoons of the 1970s showed a similar assertion of rights by dogs, which was a major change from previous decades. Dogs were portrayed talking and behaving like humans in the 1970s. One cartoon showed a disgruntled dog painting a sign reading "Beware of Me."[36] Cartoons also showed dogs talking to other dogs. Dogs were pictured having meetings in boardrooms, playing chess with cats, and, in one cartoon, thrusting out a paw and saying to a human, "Shake hands."[37]

New Yorker cartoon editor Robert Mankoff offered his interpretation for these increasingly anthropomorphic cartoons:

> In general, it was part of a whole cultural cartoon trend. Of course, there's the fad of all the cat books, in the late seventies. And I guess the culture became more pet-centric, and we started to project onto pets all these feelings and emotions, the cat people being the first instance of it, and then the environment for these cartoons would be very congenial, because people were already anthropomorphizing their pets to such an extent.[38]

Fig. 12.3. From *The New Yorker,* July 26, 1976, p. 45. © The New Yorker Collection 1976 George Booth from cartoonbank.com. All Rights Reserved.

As further evidence of the society's growing fascination with dogs at this time, the magazine *Dog Fancy* made its debut in 1970.

1980s

The 1980s saw a continued increase in dog cartoons in the *New Yorker*, and dogs were often shown in human roles. Cartoonist Charles Barsotti, for instance, frequently portrayed dogs experiencing very human feelings, such as jealousy, anger, and distress. Cartoons of the 1980s often portrayed dogs as best friend and member of the family, as in one cartoon showing a man and his dog at home with the caption "Zack Brillard and Live-In Companion."[39] Dogs were depicted as having human emotions and talking to humans, and they were pictured in human roles. Several captions exemplified this, such as one where a dog says, "I'm your pet, but you don't own me"[40] and another picturing a dog saying, "I just want you to know Ted, that I think you're a good boy, too."[41]

According to most of the *New Yorker* cartoonists I spoke with, all animal cartoons have gotten more anthropomorphic over time, starting in the late 1970s.[42] This trend included the work of cartoonist Gary Larson, known for his many cartoons featuring life from the animal's perspective. Larson's cartoon strip *The Far Side* was syndicated in newspapers across the United States from 1979 to 1995. His particular breed of anthropomorphism—animals that seem superior to humans, or at least more aware—was complex and perhaps most similar in style to *New Yorker* cartoons. One *New Yorker* cartoon illustrating this situation depicts a dog who appears more socially adept than the humans he lives with, captioned: "Once again I find myself in the rather awkward position of having to ask one of you for a biscuit."[43]

David Lavery described what he termed the "radical anthropomorphism" of Larson's cartoons:

> *Far Side* animals exhibit human characteristics. . . . But the final effect is not, as in the didacticism of Aesop, the sentimentalism of Disney, or the very commercial anthropomorphism of Snoopy, Garfield, Opus, et al., to deny the creature world its own reality.[44]

Charles Minahen echoed Lavery's assessment, characterizing the creatures in Larson's cartoons either as humanized animals or "humanimals," who mesh human and animal traits in various combinations or as "anihumans," humans with a little something missing.[45]

Similar to dogs in Larson's cartoons, *New Yorker* cartoon dogs in the 1980s were shown exhibiting human cognitive abilities in animal situations and, conversely, pictured in human situations with an animal's sensibility. Both *The Far Side* and *New Yorker* cartoons parodied the human assumption that animals are similar to us and understand everything we say. One *New Yorker* cartoon with this theme pictures a man saying to his dog, "When I get home tonight, remind me to call about the furnace."[46]

The type of anthropomorphism in *The Far Side* and *New Yorker* cartoons seems markedly different than the "disnification" of animals described by Steve Baker in *Picturing the Beast*.[47] Baker argued that when the animal is put into visual form, the basic process of disnification serves to "render it stupid."[48] In contrast, both *The Far Side* and *New Yorker* dog cartoons of this time period defined a new type of anthropomorphic humor in which animals are presented as complex and sympathetic characters on equal terms with, and often superior to, humans.

As a backdrop to this trend of increasingly anthropomorphic cartoons, the structure of families changed significantly in the 1980s, a decade with high divorce rates, more single-parent families, and fewer children than in previous decades.[49] Several studies commented on the changing role of pets, suggesting that pets were being increasingly viewed as significant members of the family, in some cases having equal status with children.[50]

Supporting this increased interest in pets, research citing both physical and mental health benefits of pet ownership resulted in reversals of earlier pet bans imposed in many areas.[51] Among the benefits cited in research studies of pet owners were lowered blood pressure, lower incidence of depression, and increased social interactions with others.[52] In 1981, the White House Conference on Aging adopted a resolution calling on federal, state, and local governments to support legislation allowing the elderly to keep their companion animals. California, Maryland, New York, and other states later enacted laws protecting the rights of elderly tenants to own pets.[53]

1990s

The 1970s, 1980s, and, especially, the 1990s reflected increasing scholarly and popular interest in the study of the human-animal bond. Among the many books commenting on the human-animal relationship were *Dog's Best Friend: Annals of the Dog-Human Relationship*, by Mark Derr; *Understanding Dogs: Living and Working with Canine Companions*, by Clinton R. Sanders; *Why the Wild Things Are: Animals in the Lives of Children*, by Gail Melson; and *Children and Animals: Social Development and Our Connections to Other Species*, by Gene Myers.

Animal-assisted therapy emerged as a specialty niche in the field of psychology at this time. Reflecting the increasing public interest in dogs, several new magazines appeared, among them, *The Bark*, which began publication in 1998, and *Animal Fair*, which began in 1999.

Further attesting to the popularity of dogs, new pet superstores contributed to the billions per year spent by consumers on their pets. Spending more than doubled from $17 billion in 1994 to $34.4 billion in 2004 for the care, feeding, and entertainment of companion animals.[54] Today dogs have their own burgeoning industry of special dog gyms and parks, dog spas, exclusive dog photographers and dog schools, dog psychiatrists, and dog day-care centers.[55] People spend thousands of dollars on medical care when pets become ill, including high-tech procedures and surgeries that rival the cost of human health care.[56]

"On the Internet, nobody knows you're a dog."

Fig. 12.4. From *The New Yorker,* July 5, 1993, p. 61. © The New Yorker Collection 1993 Peter Steiner from cartoonbank.com. All Rights Reserved.

Surveys have found that 75 percent of pet owners consider their companion animals like children, 92 percent consider them members of the family, and almost 50 percent of women surveyed report that they rely more on their pet for affection than on their spouse or children.[57] Even the language regarding dogs has been hotly debated. The city of Berkeley, California, adopted an ordinance in 2001 to call people "animal guardians" rather than "owners."[58]

This dramatic change in how people see companion animals has occurred only over the past few decades, concurrent with an estimated 40 percent growth in dog ownership since 1988.[59]

Reflecting these trends, in the 1990s the number of dog cartoons in the *New Yorker* significantly increased. Cartoons showed dogs having both human and animal characteristics and exhibiting the subtleties of complex thinking. One of the *New Yorker's* most popular and often reprinted cartoons showed two dogs in front of a computer with one dog saying to the other, "On the Internet, nobody knows you're a dog" (see fig. 12.4).[60] Regarding the timeliness and phenomenal popularity of this cartoon, former cartoon editor Lee Lorenz commented on the mix of both human and doglike characteristics portrayed: "Not only are the dogs talking like people, but they also realize they are dogs, and they are hiding behind the computer to disguise that."[61]

Many cartoons reflected this mix of both animal and human characteristics, including humanlike angst. An example was a two-panel cartoon first showing a drowning person yelling, "Lassie get Help!" and then in the next panel picturing Lassie on a psychiatrist's couch.[62] Another cartoon showed a dog walking alongside his owner and thinking, "It's always good dog, never great dog."[63] In the 1990s, dogs were pictured being demanding and reflecting the indulgences of our time, as in a cartoon showing a dog nudging his water dish and saying, "This isn't tap water, is it?"[64] Dogs were also pictured handling technology with aplomb, as in a cartoon of a dog on a cell phone saying, "Ok, I'm sitting, what is it?"[65]

Anthropomorphism in the 1990s

Human-Pet Relationships

The anthropomorphic portrayal of dogs in New Yorker cartoons has paralleled the changing role of dogs in society, with pets over the past few decades assuming a more humanlike function in the lives of people, often regarded as substitute children, personified by owners, and viewed as providing more emotional and social support for people than in the past. In The New Work of Dogs, Jon Katz argues that while dogs have served a variety of roles in the past, in the last decade or so they have taken up a whole new kind of work as emotional healers. Katz argues that dogs now do more psychological work in a society in which people are increasingly isolated and have started to depend on dogs to provide nurturance and support.[66] According to James Serpell, anthropomorphizing companion animals is an almost universal trait in pet owners.[67] He cites as evidence people's current tendency to regard pets as children, giving them human names, dressing them in designer fashions, and spending billions of dollars on the care and entertainment of pets.

Serpell feels that in evolutionary terms, anthropomorphism can have both beneficial and harmful consequences for dogs. On the positive side, when a caretaker interprets the behavior of a companion animal anthropomorphically, it allows the pet to be a source of social support for the owner. Serpell views anthropomorphism as necessary to the ability to see the animal as having emotions, feelings, and being able to provide social support in ways such as "loving" the owner.[68] However, overly anthropomorphizing pets can also have negative consequences for animals. Katz suggests that perhaps we are expecting too much from dogs—expecting them to anticipate our every need and provide emotional and psychological comfort—when they are not meant to do this. One potentially harmful result could be owners punishing dogs or abandoning them to shelters when they do not measure up to unrealistic expectations.[69] Serpell cautions that anthropomorphizing dogs could also result in behavior problems, with dogs becoming overly dependent and unable to think on their own. Furthermore, anthropomorphic selection in breeding could be deleterious to the dog's health, producing both physical and behavior problems.[70]

Dog Cartoons

So how does one interpret this phenomenon of anthropomorphism currently found in both human-pet relationships and in dog cartoons? One might argue that anthropomorphic trends in dog cartoons are the result of individual cartoonist preferences or changing styles. However, *New Yorker* cartoon editor Robert Mankoff makes a persuasive argument for public tastes and societal attitudes playing an influential role in determining cartoon content: "It's a little bit Darwinian. Cartoonists have to sell cartoons. People have a great, great weakness for dog and cat cartoons, and I don't know if that accounts so much for the popularity of cartoons as for the popularity of pets. You don't get that many cartoons about spiders who are anthropomorphic."[71]

Providing support for this view, several *New Yorker* cartoonists said their source of inspiration is what they observe around them every day.[72] Certainly anthropomorphism is abundantly evident in human-pet relationships and could provide material for cartoon humor. However, even if a cartoonist's favorite subject was anthropomorphic dogs, this would not necessarily influence cartoon trends. The cartoonists I spoke with uniformly agreed that frequent rejection is an inevitable part of a cartooning career. Longstanding and popular *New Yorker* cartoonist Sam Gross told me that on average he draws eight hundred new cartoons a year, and in 2001 he sold only nineteen.[73] The *New Yorker* receives a thousand cartoon submissions per week, and fifteen to twenty of those are then selected for the magazine. Ultimately, cartoonists do not determine what gets published in the magazine; editors choose which cartoons will be published, basing their decisions on a number of factors.

In an article titled "Gravity and Levity," Ed Ayres argues that cartoons are an expression of public opinion, noting that "cartoons don't work unless the humor taps into an anxiety that is shared, or implicitly understood, by most of the people who see it."[74] Discussing a *New Yorker* cartoon about global warming, he stated that the appearance of this cartoon in the magazine suggested a general awareness and concern about this problem on the part of the public. He added, "In recent months, I've seen a surprising number of such cartoons, suggesting that there may be a growing responsiveness to critical sustainability issues."[75]

In a similar example of responsiveness on the part of cartoonists, the 1990s were characterized by the emergence of a number of syndicated comic strips and animated television shows featuring anthropomorphic animal characters. Among these were *New Yorker* cartoonist J. C. Duffy's newspaper comic *The Fusco Brothers*, which has been nationally syndicated since 1989 and includes a talking wolverine in the cast of characters. The comic strip *Sherman's Lagoon* by J. P. Toomey was first syndicated in 1991 and features an anthropomorphic shark and other sea creatures. The strip *Mutts* began in 1994 and includes animals as diverse as dogs, birds, crustaceans, a Sphinx, and a cat with a pet snail. The *Mutts* comic has addressed topics such as animal welfare and protection. Its creator, cartoonist Patrick McDonnell, is active in animal advocacy, serving on the board of the Humane Society of the U.S. In 1995, the syndicated comic *Rhymes with Orange* by Hilary Price was first published, and *Get Fuzzy* by Darby Conley began in 1999. Both these comic strips feature a talking dog and cat as main characters. *The Family Guy*, an animated television show created by Seth MacFarlane, also premiered in 1999. It includes an anthropomorphic family dog who smokes, sips cocktails, and is more intelligent than most of the humans in the family.

Finally, providing evidence for a general Zeitgeist in anthropomorphic dog cartoon humor, in the 1990s some *New Yorker* and *Far Side* cartoons pictured nearly identical scenes, illustrating a similar mix of human and dog features. Examples included a Larson cartoon of a canine talk show featuring "Dogs that drink from the toilet bowl"[76] and a similar *New Yorker* cartoon of a canine talk show host saying to a dog guest, "I understand you've learned some new tricks since you were here last."[77] Another example was a Larson cartoon of a dog saying to his owner, "Stan, I'd like a place of my own"[78] and a comparable *New Yorker* cartoon picturing a dog saying to his owner, "I do like it here, but I'm ready for my own apartment."[79]

In summary, several nationally syndicated comics and cartoons featuring anthropomorphic animals emerged in the 1990s, at the same time that the *New Yorker* published the greatest numbers of anthropomorphic dog cartoons. Since people enjoy cartoons featuring subjects they care about, it seems likely that the success of these comics and cartoons reflect the changing interests and attitudes of the viewing public.

Conclusion

The years since the *New Yorker* began in 1925 have been characterized by significant changes in how companion animals have been regarded by society. It is clear that in the last few decades, dogs have come to assume a more prominent role in the lives of people and are now often regarded as companions and family members. Both lay and scholarly writing has commented on this dramatic change in people's attitudes toward dogs. Like many sociocultural trends, this growing appreciation for and interest in dogs has been reflected in the popular press and in the visual media, including *New Yorker* cartoons.

Supporting the phenomenon of the growing popularity of dogs, I found an increase in numbers of *New Yorker* dog cartoons published in the 1970s, 1980s, and 1990s, and an increase in dogs pictured in human roles, compared with earlier decades. Lending support for the view that the popular media reflects societal attitudes, Harold A. Herzog and Shelly L. Galvin have argued that their research on animal images in the tabloid press may more accurately reflect people's attitudes toward cats than more rigorous scientific surveys.[80] They cite a sociological study by Stephen Kellert from 1980 that surveyed a random sample of more than three thousand people, asking how they felt about different animals. The respondents ranked cats eleventh in preference, between turtles and ladybugs. In contrast, in Herzog and Galvin's study, cats ranked second in the distribution of species found in tabloid stories that were related to human-animal affection, a ranking more in keeping with statistics showing the immense popularity of cats in the United States.

As the cartoonist's best friend and muse, dogs seem to provide limitless comedic possibilities. They have ushered us through the various decades, allowing us to laugh at our own foibles without judgment. From the Depression era through world wars, the baby boom, and suburban sprawl, and into the current era of technology, dogs have been pictured as loyal companions and best friends. Along the way, cartoons have shown them facing human challenges with a particular brand of doglike ingenuity and good humor.

What accounts for the tremendous popularity of these cartoons? Perhaps anthropomorphic dog cartoons make what would be harsh messages about human weakness easier to accept. Several cartoonists and editors I interviewed agreed with this notion, feeling that we regard dogs with a general good will that softens the critical social commentary delivered by cartoons.[81]

Indeed, if we project our human qualities onto dogs in these cartoons, then our human foibles are also set against the doglike characteristics of loyalty, trust, and faithfulness. Perhaps these positive qualities associated with dogs make us more accepting of our human frailties. Given this possibility, anthropomorphic dog cartoons may even serve to increase our self-awareness while restoring our faith in our own humanity.

Notes

1. Betty Carmack, "Realistic Representations of Companion Animals in Comic Art in the U.S.A.," *Anthrozoös* 10, no. 2–3 (1997): 118.

2. Judith O'Sullivan, *The Great American Comic Strip* (Boston: Little, Brown, 1990), 10.

3. Carmack, "Realistic Representations," 118.

4. Harold A. Herzog and Shelly L. Galvin, "Animals, Archetypes, and Popular Culture: Tales from the Tabloid Press," *Anthrozoös* 5, no. 2 (1992): 77.

5. Ibid.

6. MIN's New Media Report, "The New Yorker's Cartoonbank.com Merchandises Self-Expression," *MIN's New Media Report* 7, no. 17, Aug. 27, 2001.

7. For further discussion of anthropomorphism in human-pet relationships, see Alexa Albert and Kris Bulcroft, "Pets, Families, and the Life Course," *Journal of Marriage and the Family* 50, no. 2 (1988): 543–52; Ann O. Cain, "Pets as Family Members," in *Pets and the Family*, ed. M. B. Sussman (New York: Haworth Press, 1985), 5–10; Jessica Greenebaum, "It's a Dog's Life: Elevating Status from Pet to 'Fur Baby' at Yappy Hour," *Society & Animals* 12, no. 2 (2004): 117–35; Jon Katz, *The New Work of Dogs: Tending to Life, Love, and Family* (New York: Random House, 2003); and James A. Serpell, "People in Disguise: Anthropomorphism and the Human-Pet

Relationship," in *Thinking with Animals: New Perspectives on Anthropormophism,* ed. Lorraine Daston and Greg Mitman (New York: Columbia Univ. Press, 2005), 121–36.

8. For further discussion of the meaning of anthropomorphism, see Steve Baker, *Picturing the Beast: Animals, Identity, and Representation,* new ed. (Urbana: Univ. of Illinois Press, 2001); John Berger, "Why Look at Animals?" in *About Looking,* by John Berger (New York: Pantheon Books, 1980), 1–26; Linda R. Caporael and Cecilia M. Heyes, "Why Anthromorphize? Folk Psychology and Other Stories," in *Anthropomorphism, Anecdotes, and Animals,* ed. Robert W. Mitchell, Nicholas S. Thompson, and H. Lyn Miles (Albany: State Univ. of New York Press, 1997), 59–73; Stewart Elliott Guthrie, "Anthropomorphism: A Definition and a Theory," in *Anthropomorphism, Anecdotes, and Animals,* ed. Robert W. Mitchell, Nicholas S. Thompson, and H. Lyn Miles (Albany: State Univ. of New York Press, 1997), 50–58; R. Lockwood, "Anthropomorphism Is Not a Four Letter Word," in *Perceptions of Animals in American Culture,* ed. R. J. Hoage (Washington, D.C.: Smithsonian Institution Press, 1989), 41–56; and Mary Midgley, *Animals and Why They Matter* (Athens: Univ. of Georgia Press, 1983).

9. For a more complete explanation of methods and results, see Anne Alden, "Anthropomorphism in *New Yorker* Dog Cartoons across the Twentieth Century" (Ph.D. diss., Alliant International Univ., 2004), 25–35.

10. Julian de Miskey, *New Yorker,* Sept. 17, 1927, front cover.

11. Ethel Plummer, *New Yorker,* Sept. 4, 1926, 23.

12. Peter Arno, *New Yorker,* Jan. 24, 1931, 14.

13. George Price, *New Yorker,* Feb. 13, 1937, 74.

14. Juliet Clutton-Brock, "Dog's Best Friend," *Times Literary Supplement* 4916, June 20, 1997, 6.

15. Peter Arno, *New Yorker,* Dec. 2, 1939, 23.

16. Helen Hokinson, *New Yorker,* Apr. 24, 1943, 17.

17. Carl Rose, *New Yorker,* Dec. 14, 1940, 34.

18. Donna Haraway, *The Companion Species Manifesto: Dogs, People, and Significant Otherness* (Chicago: Prickly Paradigm Press, 2003), 14.

19. Mary F. Corey, *The World through a Monocle: The New Yorker at Mid-Century* (Cambridge, Mass.: Harvard Univ. Press, 1999), 8.

20. Sam Corbean, *New Yorker,* Apr. 4, 1949, 31.

21. Claude Smith, *New Yorker,* Mar.13, 1948, 66.

22. Bruce Fogle, "The Changing Roles of Animals in Western Society: Influences upon and from the Veterinary Profession," *Anthrozoös* 12, no. 4 (1999): 234.

23. M. H. Cooper, "America's Pampered Pets," *Congressional Quarterly Researcher,* Dec. 27, 1996, 1139.

24. Perry Barlow, *New Yorker,* July 19, 1958, 20.

25. Sam Cobean, *New Yorker,* Mar. 4, 1950, 19.

26. Barney Tobey, *New Yorker*, Dec. 27, 1952, 21.

27. Barney Tobey, *New Yorker*, Feb. 13, 1954, 27.

28. Fogle, "Changing Roles of Animals," 234.

29. Cooper, "America's Pampered Pets," 1139.

30. Frank Modell, *New Yorker*, Dec. 27, 1969, 21.

31. Warren Miller, *New Yorker*, Oct. 26, 1968, 145.

32. William Steig, *New Yorker*, Feb. 1, 1969, 37.

33. Lee Lorenz, *New Yorker*, Oct. 4, 1969, 154.

34. Lee Lorenz and George Booth, *The Essential George Booth* (New York: Workman, 1999), 74–75; David Owen, "Booth Country: The Cartoonist's Life Is Everything It's Cracked up to Be," *New Yorker*, Dec. 7 and 14, 1998, 138.

35. George Booth, *New Yorker*, July 26, 1976, 45.

36. Tom Smits, *New Yorker*, Jan. 28, 1974, 70.

37. Dean Vietor, *New Yorker*, Oct. 28, 1974, 76.

38. Robert Mankoff, pers. comm., Jan. 11, 2002.

39. Robert Mankoff, *New Yorker*, Feb. 27, 1984, 45.

40. Arnie Levin, *New Yorker*, Feb. 13, 1984, 67.

41. Stan Hunt, *New Yorker*, Jan. 11, 1982, 39.

42. Anne Alden, "*The New Yorker* Cartoon World," *The Bark* 18 (Spring 2002): 52.

43. Michael Maslin, *New Yorker*, Sept. 12, 1988, 108.

44. David Lavery, "Aesop after Darwin: The Radical Anthropomorphism of 'The Far Side'" (paper presented at the Popular Culture Association of the South annual meeting, Knoxville, Tenn., Oct. 1988), 1.

45. Charles D. Minahen, "Humanimals and Anihumans in Gary Larson's Gallery of the Absurd," in *Animal Acts: Configuring the Human in Western History*, ed. Jennifer Ham and Matthew Senior (New York: Routledge, 1997), 233.

46. George Booth, *New Yorker*, Apr. 26, 1982, 112.

47. Baker, *Picturing the Beast*, 174.

48. Ibid.

49. U.S. Bureau of the Census, *Marital Status and Living Arrangements: March 1982*, Current Population Reports, Series P-20, No. 380 (Washington, D.C.: Government Printing Office, 1983); U.S. Bureau of the Census, *Household and Family Characteristics: March 1984*, Series P-20, No. 398 (Washington, D.C.: Government Printing Office, 1984); U.S. Bureau of the Census, *1970 Census of the Population, Subject Reports, Marital Characteristics* (Washington, D.C.: Government Printing Office, 1985).

50. Albert and Bulcroft, "Pets, Families, and the Life Course"; Anne O. Cain, "A Study of Pets in the Family System," in *New Perspectives on Our Lives with Companion Animals*, ed. Aaron Katcher and Alan Beck (Philadelphia: Univ. of Pennsylvania Press,

1983), 73–81; Aaron Katcher, "Interaction between People and Their Pets: Form and Function," in *Interactions between People and Pets*, ed. Bruce Fogle (Springfield, Ill.: Charles C. Thomas, 1981), 41–68; Herbert A. Nieburg, "Psychosocial Aspects of Bereavement," in *Pet Loss and Human Bereavement*, ed. William J. Kay, Herbert A. Nieburg, Austin H. Kutscher, Ross M. Grey, and Carole E. Fudin (Ames: Iowa State Univ. Press, 1984), 65–69.

51. Cooper, "America's Pampered Pets," 1139.

52. A. H. Katcher, E. Friedman, A. M. Beck, and J. Lynch, "Looking, Talking, and Blood Pressure: The Physiological Consequences of Interaction with the Living Environment," in *New Perspectives on Our Lives with Companion Animals*, ed. Aaron Katcher and Alan Beck (Philadelphia: Univ. of Pennsylvania Press, 1983), 351–62; M. Adell-Bath, A. Krook, G. Sandqvist, and K. Skantze, *Do We Need Dogs? A Study of Dogs' Social Significance to Man* (Gothenburg: Univ. of Gothenburg Press, 1979); G. Francis, J. T. Turner, and S. B. Johnson, "Domestic Animal Visitation as Therapy with Adult Home Residents," *International Journal of Nursing Studies* 22, no. 3 (1985): 201–6; L. A. Hart, B. L. Hart, and B. Bergin, "Socializing Effects of Service Dogs for People with Disabilities," *Anthrozoös* 1, no. 1 (1987): 41–44.

53. Cooper, "America's Pampered Pets," 1139.

54. American Pet Products Manufacturers Association, *National Pet Owners Survey* (Greenwich, Conn.: American Pet Products Manufacturers Association, 2004, 2005).

55. C. Siebert, "Citizen Canine," *New York Times Magazine*, Mar. 26, 2000, 46–49.

56. American Animal Hospital Association, *Pet Owner Survey* (Denver: American Animal Hospital Association, 2001); James A. Serpell, "Anthropomorphism and Anthropomorphic Selection: Beyond the 'Cute Response,'" *Society & Animals* 11, no. 1 (2003): 83–100.

57. Serpell, "Anthropomorphism and Anthropomorphic Selection"; R. Gardyn, "Animal Magnetism," *American Demographics*, May 2002, 30–37; American Animal Hospital Association, *Pet Owner Survey* (Denver: American Animal Hospital Association, 1996).

58. P. L. Brown, "The Warp and Woof of Identity Politics for Pets," *New York Times*, Mar. 18, 2001, 4.

59. American Pet Products Manufacturers Association, *National Pet Owners Survey* (Greenwich, Conn.: American Pet Products Manufacturers Association, 2001, 2003, 2004).

60. Peter Steiner, *New Yorker*, July 5, 1993, 61.

61. Lee Lorenz, pers. comm., Jan. 29, 2002.

62. Danny Shanahan, *New Yorker*, May 8, 1989, 43.

63. Alex Gregory, *New Yorker*, July 31, 2000, 40.

64. Bruce Eric Kaplan, *New Yorker*, Aug. 16, 1993, 48.

65. Mick Stevens, *New Yorker*, Aug. 24 and 31, 1998, 117.

66. Katz, *New Work of Dogs*, 15.

67. Serpell, "People in Disguise," 123.

68. Serpell, "Anthropomorphism and Anthropomorphic Selection," 91.

69. Serpell, "People in Disguise," 131.

70. Ibid., 129–30.

71. Robert Mankoff, pers. comm., Jan. 11, 2002.

72. Alden and Woo, "Talk of 'Toon Town," 52.

73. Ibid.

74. Ed Ayres, "Gravity and Levity," *World Watch* 12, no. 6 (1999): 3.

75. Ibid.

76. Gary Larson, *The Far Side Gallery* 5 (Kansas City, Mo.: Andrews and McMeel, 1995), 155.

77. Charles Barsotti, *New Yorker*, Apr. 20, 1981, 32.

78. Larson, *Far Side Gallery* 5, 127.

79. Leo Cullum, *New Yorker*, Jan. 8, 1996, 51.

80. Herzog and Galvin, "Animals, Archetypes, and Popular Culture," 90.

81. George Booth, pers. comm., Apr. 24, 2002; Lee Lorenz, pers. comm., Jan. 29, 2002; Robert Mankoff, pers. comm., Jan. 11, 2002.

Works Cited

Adell-Bath, M., A. Krook, G. Sandqvist, and K. Skantze. *Do We Need Dogs? A Study of Dogs' Social Significance to Man.* Gothenburg: Univ. of Gothenburg Press, 1979.

Albert, Alexa, and Kris Bulcroft. "Pets, Families, and the Life Course." *Journal of Marriage and the Family* 50, no. 2 (1988): 543–52.

Alden, Anne. "Anthropomorphism in *New Yorker* Dog Cartoons across the Twentieth Century." Ph.D. diss., Alliant International Univ., 2004.

Alden, Anne. "The *New Yorker* Cartoon World." *The Bark* 18 (Spring 2002): 52.

American Animal Hospital Association. *Pet Owner Survey.* Denver: American Animal Hospital Association, 1996, 2000, 2001.

American Pet Products Manufacturers Association. *National Pet Owners Survey.* Greenwich, Conn.: American Pet Products Manufacturers Association, 2001, 2003, 2004, 2005.

Ayres, Ed. "Gravity and Levity." *World Watch* 12, no. 6 (1999): 3–5.

Baker, Steve. *Picturing the Beast: Animals, Identity, and Representation*, new ed. Urbana: Univ. of Illinois Press, 2001.

Berger, John. "Why Look at Animals?" In *About Looking*, by John Berger, 1–26. New York: Pantheon Books, 1980.

Brown, P. L. "The Warp and Woof of Identity Politics for Pets." *New York Times*, Mar. 18, 2001, 4.

Cain, Ann O. "Pets as Family Members." In *Pets and the Family*, edited by M. B. Sussman, 5–10. New York: Haworth Press, 1985.

———. "A Study of Pets in the Family System." In *New Perspectives on Our Lives with Companion Animals*, edited by Aaron Katcher and Alan Beck, 73–81. Philadelphia: Univ. of Pennsylvania Press, 1983.

Caporael, Linda R., and Cecilia M. Heyes, "Why Anthropomorphize? Folk Psychology and Other Stories." In *Anthropomorphism, Anecdotes, and Animals*, edited by Robert W. Mitchell, Nicholas S. Thompson, and H. Lyn Miles, 59–73. Albany: State Univ. of New York Press, 1997.

Carmack, Betty. "Realistic Representations of Companion Animals in Comic Art in the USA." *Anthrozoös* 10, no. 2–3 (1997): 108–20.

Clutton-Brock, Juliet. "Dog's Best Friend." *Times Literary Supplement* 4916, June 20, 1997, 6.

Cooper, M. H. "America's Pampered Pets." *Congressional Quarterly Researcher*, Dec. 27, 1996, 1131–51.

Corey, Mary F. *The World through a Monocle: The New Yorker at Mid-Century*. Cambridge, Mass.: Harvard Univ. Press, 1999.

Derr, Mark. *Dog's Best Friend: Annals of the Dog-Human Relationship*. New York: Henry Holt, 1997.

Fogle, Bruce. "The Changing Roles of Animals in Western Society: Influences Upon and from the Veterinary Profession." *Anthrozoös* 12, no. 4 (1999): 234–39.

Francis, G., J. T. Turner, and S. B. Johnson. "Domestic Animal Visitation as Therapy with Adult Home Residents." *International Journal of Nursing Studies* 22, no.3 (1985): 201–6.

Gardyn, R. "Animal Magnetism." *American Demographics* (May 2002): 30–37.

Greenebaum, Jessica. "It's a Dog's Life: Elevating Status from Pet to 'Fur Baby' at Yappy Hour." *Society & Animals* 12, no. 2 (2004): 117–35.

Guthrie, Stewart Elliott. "Anthropomorphism: A Definition and a Theory." In *Anthropomorphism, Anecdotes, and Animals*, edited by Robert W. Mitchell, Nicholas S. Thompson, and H. Lyn Miles, 50–58. Albany: State Univ. of New York Press, 1997.

Haraway, Donna. *The Companion Species Manifesto: Dogs, People, and Significant Otherness*. Chicago: Prickly Paradigm Press, 2003.

Hart, L. A., B. L. Hart, and B. Bergin. "Socializing Effects of Service Dogs for People with Disabilities." *Anthrozoös* 1, no. 1 (1987): 41–44.

Herzog, Harold A., and Shelly L. Galvin, "Animals, Archetypes, and Popular Culture: Tales from the Tabloid Press." *Anthrozoös* 5, no. 2 (1992): 77–92.

Katcher, Aaron. "Interaction between People and Their Pets: Form and Function." In *Interactions between People and Pets*, edited by Bruce Fogle, 41–68. Springfield, Ill.: Charles C. Thomas, 1981.

Katcher, A. H., E. Friedman, A. M. Beck, and J. Lynch. "Looking, Talking, and Blood Pressure: The Physiological Consequences of Interaction with the Living Environment." In *New Perspectives on Our Lives with Companion Animals*, edited by Aaron Katcher and Alan Beck, 351–62. Philadelphia: Univ. of Pennsylvania Press, 1983.

Katz, Jon. *The New Work of Dogs: Tending to Life, Love, and Family*. New York: Random House, 2003.

Larson, Gary. *The Far Side Gallery 5*. Kansas City, Mo.: Andrews and McMeel, 1995.

Lavery, David. "Aesop after Darwin: The Radical Anthropomorphism of 'The Far Side.'" Paper presented at the Popular Culture Association of the South annual meeting, Knoxville, Tenn., Oct., 1988.

Lockwood, R. "Anthropomorphism Is Not a Four Letter Word." In *Perceptions of Animals in American Culture*, edited by R. J. Hoage, 41–56. Washington, D.C.: Smithsonian Institution Press, 1989.

Lorenz, Lee, and George Booth. *The Essential George Booth*. New York: Workman, 1999.

Melson, Gail. *Why the Wild Things Are: Animals in the Lives of Children*. Cambridge, Mass.: Harvard Univ. Press, 2001.

Midgley, Mary. *Animals and Why They Matter*. Athens: Univ. of Georgia Press, 1983.

MIN's New Media Report. "The New Yorker's Cartoonbank.com Merchandises Self-Expression." *MIN's New Media Report* 7, no.17, Aug. 27, 2001.

Minahen, Charles D. "Humanimals and Anihumans in Gary Larson's Gallery of the Absurd." In *Animal Acts: Configuring the Human in Western History*, edited by Jennifer Ham and Matthew Senior, 231–51. New York: Routledge, 1997.

Myers, Gene. *Children and Animals: Social Development and Our Connections to Other Species*. Boulder, Colo.: Westview Press, 1998.

Nieburg, Herbert A. "Psychosocial Aspects of Bereavement." In *Pet Loss and Human Bereavement*, edited by William J. Kay, Herbert A. Nieburg, Austin H. Kutscher, Ross M. Grey, and Carole E. Fudin, 65–69. Ames: Iowa State Univ. Press, 1984.

O'Sullivan, Judith. *The Great American Comic Strip*. Boston: Little, Brown, 1990.

Owen, David. "Booth Country: The Cartoonist's Life Is Everything It's Cracked up to Be." *New Yorker*, Dec. 7, 14, 1998, 130–39.

Sanders, Clinton R. *Understanding Dogs: Living and Working with Canine Companions*. Philadelphia: Temple Univ. Press, 1999.

Serpell, James A. "Anthropomorphism and Anthropomorphic Selection: Beyond the 'Cute Response.'" *Society & Animals* 11, no.1 (2003): 83–100.

———. "People in Disguise: Anthropomorphism and the Human-Pet Relationship." In *Thinking with Animals: New Perspectives on Anthropomorphism*, edited by Lorraine Daston and Greg Mitman, 121–36. New York: Columbia Univ. Press, 2005.

Siebert, C. "Citizen Canine." *New York Times Magazine*, Mar. 26, 2000, 46–49.

U.S. Bureau of the Census. 1983. *Marital Status and Living Arrangements: March 1982.* Current Population Reports, Series P-20, No. 380. Washington, D.C.: Government Printing Office.

———. 1984. *Household and Family Characteristics: March 1984.* Series P-20, No. 398. Washington, D.C.: Government Printing Office.

———. 1985. *1970 Census of the Population, Subject Reports, Marital Characteristics.* Washington, D.C.: Government Printing Office.

Woo, Cameron, and Anne Alden. "The Talk of 'Toon Town." *The Bark* 18 (Spring 2002): 46–51.

Chapter 13

Snakes and Bunnies

The Postmodern Animal in the Art of Ray Johnson

Muffet Jones

Ray Johnson was born in Detroit, Michigan, on October 16, 1927. An artist of great
originality and influence whose experiments with images and language prefigured
pop art and later conceptual movements, he was a singular collagist and the father
of modern mail art.[1] After studying under Joseph Albers at Black Mountain College, Johnson moved to New York City in 1948 and joined company there with artists such as Cy Twombly, Robert Rauschenberg, Jasper Johns, and Andy Warhol.
Johnson was recognized by these and other artists as a unique creative force,
though he increasingly avoided the public eye. His apparent suicide by drowning
in 1995 was considered by some to be his last and greatest performance.

In *The Postmodern Animal*, Steve Baker has attempted to think about animals—
the beings and the symbols—as they are represented in contemporary art and
thought.[2] He uses the work of poststructuralist thinkers such as Lyotard, Derrida,
and Deleuze and Guattari to suggest ways we might talk about animals today that
are more in line with their current incorporation in contemporary art. The animal
"Other" as it might be understood at the beginning of a new age is also the focus
of scholars such as Roy Willis, Tom Regan, and Cary Wolfe. For instance, in his
book *Animal Rites: American Culture, the Discourse of Species, and Posthumanist
Theory*, Wolfe uses animal references in other creative mediums (including a wonderful reading of Jonathan Demme's film *The Silence of the Lambs*) to foreground
the problem of the animal in a postmodern world. And in *Figuring Animals: Essays
on Animal Images in Art, Literature, Philosophy, and Popular Culture*, editors Mary
Sanders Pollock and Catherine Rainwater have selected essays that speak specifically to the complicated ways in which animals have been made a part of the
discourse on popular culture today.[3] This kind of thoughtful scholarship on the
place of animals in contemporary culture is relatively new to the academy and has
provided rich new intellectual ground to till for those grappling with meaning in
animal imagery and with the moral and ethical issues contingent upon the flesh
and blood creatures represented.

I contend that Ray Johnson, working as he was at the end of the modernist era
in art history, was largely overlooked by the art establishment of his time because
his work was essentially postmodern. His "adoption" of animal personas as a kind
of private symbolism (see fig. 13.1) and his refusal to cite animal images within
a traditional framework of meaning made his art problematic for contemporary

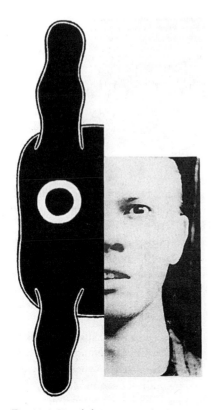

Fig. 13.1. *Untitled: Bunny Ray* by Ray Johnson, 1992, 20 x 9.5", collage, xerographic reproduction on corrugated cardboard. Photograph from the Estate of Ray Johnson, Courtesy Richard L. Feigen & Company.

viewers. At that time, most critics and art writers had no vocabulary or context in which to think about his work. It was consistently described as whimsical or amusing without any real effort at theoretical deconstruction.[4] Now much of his conceptual practice is at home in new art theory, and my own attempt to describe his use of animal images, while certainly not definitive, will at least suggest a new context for positioning Johnson's art.

Animals have traditionally occupied a largely decorative position in art history, much like a vase of flowers or an object fleshing out a landscape. When nineteenth-century artists began to think about painting and representation in a new way, animals began to be exempted from the old visual code, that is, dog = fidelity; game animals being killed or dead = the heroism of man, or, as in Dutch still life, the commercial success and prosperity of man; large wild animals = irrational and dangerous nature.[5] Unmoored from tradition, animals in modern art often floated free of meaning; artists such as Klee and Brancusi used them to explore new forms and mediums, while artists such as Franz Marc tried to infuse them with a nontraditional spirituality.[6] While still participating in modernism's seriousness, women surrealists such as Leonore Fini and Leonora Carrington created images of animals with a "difference."[7] It could be argued that they infused their animals with a unique and personal sensibility, and one that approaches postmodernism's blurring of the lines between self and Other. Still, their animal surrogates have more in common with the anthropomorphic "meaning" attendant on earlier historical animal images than they do with the cool representations of later postmodernism. It is interesting in this context to think of Meret Oppenheim's famous *Le Déjeuner en Fourrure* (Fur-lined tea cup) from 1936. While the intention to "make strange" in the best surrealist fashion was up front at the time, the fact of its appropriation of the animal body juxtaposed with human ingestion begins to approach a postmodern remove. Johnson's own appropriation of a photograph of Oppenheim herself, to which he adds his own ubiquitous bunny ears (see fig. 13.2), completes this ironic reference and illustrates postmodernism's comparative tone. While artists and periods are never clearly delineated, by the 1980s a definite shift in the concerns of the culture could be felt. Steve Baker quotes Hal Foster's dividing of postmodernism into two distinct moments—an initial concern with irony and taking the wind out of high modernism's self-regard and later postmodernism's concern with the real.[8]

So what is a postmodern animal? Consider an animal which is no longer the object/animal of human history but begins to occupy the same place outside history that postmodernism argues humans do, and in which the old hierarchies of meaning begin to break down. In "The Meaning of the Snake," Roy Willis tracks the traditional symbolism of the modern animal to the Cartesian proposition of the duality of mind/spirit versus matter/body.[9] Descartes's "paradigm shift" was set against the received cosmology of medieval theology that proposed man's dominion over the lower animals as part of God's plan. For Descartes, man was also an animal, made of matter, a machine of sorts but inhabited by a reasoning mind. In the new Cartesian world view, animals lacked the higher power to reason, like machines without spirit, and so were destined to be the property of man.[10]

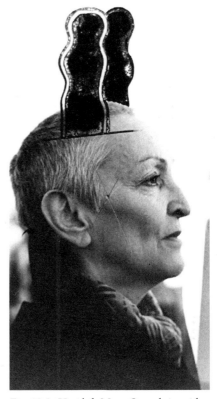

Fig. 13.2. *Untitled: Meret Oppenheim with Bunny Ears* by Ray Johnson, 1994, 9.75 x 5", collage, ink on illustration board. Photograph from the Estate of Ray Johnson, Courtesy Richard L. Feigen & Company.

As such, animals as lower but useful Cartesian machines continued into modern culture until they became the kind of Disneyfied anthropomorphic symbols of the mid-twentieth century. While the animated film *Bambi* served some purpose by suggesting to a young generation that they might begin to think about their moral responsibility toward animals, it is only in the latter part of the twentieth and the beginning of the twenty-first century that a new way of thinking about the human/animal relationship has emerged. Nature has begun to be represented in a nonhistorical, nonhierarchical, nonsymbolic way. Animals as metaphors for human qualities have given way to representations of animals as equal partners in meaning-making—albeit sometimes with surprises in the resultant meanings.

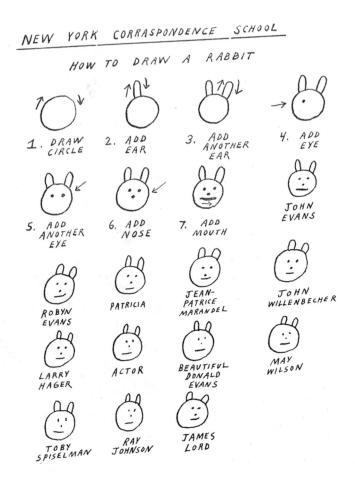

Fig. 13.3. *Untitled: How to Draw a Rabbit* by Ray Johnson, c. 1968, 8.5 x 11", ink on paper. Photograph from the Estate of Ray Johnson, Courtesy Richard L. Feigen & Company.

Both subjects are at risk—literally, ecologically—and both participate finally in the same potential victimization or agency. Both are also at risk as images, as subjects, and both are equally available to reinterpretation. In a poststructuralist, postmodern, post-Cartesian world, the animal/man hierarchy slips—boundaries dissolve and become meaningless. The old paradigms are no longer useful as a way of understanding the world, and it is this sensibility that infuses the work of Ray Johnson.

One of the earliest animal images to be appropriated by Johnson was the rabbit—or bunny, as Johnson most often referred to it. His ubiquitous "bunny-head" functioned largely as an ego-surrogate for Johnson, often accompanying his signature or replacing it in correspondence and mail art. It began as a simple circle with dots for eyes and loops for ears, but by the late 1960s had evolved into a more complicated form with more expressive features (see fig. 13.3). The bunny ears evolved into elongated tubular constructions through a rather complicated series of personal and artistic associations; he designed the flattened circle as the logo for a button shop owned by two lesbian friends and named after Gertrude Stein's book *Tender Buttons*. Combined with a tubular shape suggested by a public relations photo of Shirley Temple dressed in the "leather drag" costume of an aviator, the bunny ear was imbued with the sort of sexual, popular cultural, and personal references that gave Johnson's images the more complex, ironic, and arguably postmodern references that they suggest today.

The function of the rabbit in Johnson's art was largely unrelated to the characteristics usually associated with this animal—timidity, swiftness, prolific sexuality—although when needed, any of these attributes could also be called into play.[11] For instance, Johnson signed a note describing a moment on the streets of

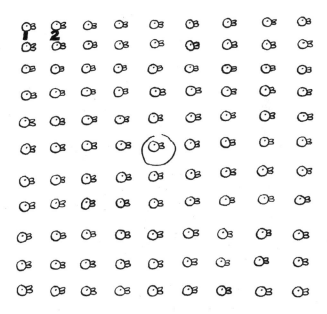

Fig. 13.4. *Untitled: Duck Bunny* by Ray Johnson, c. 1969, 8.5 x 11", ink on paper. Photograph from the Estate of Ray Johnson, Courtesy Richard L. Feigen & Company.

New York when he was chased by would-be muggers "Scared Bunny" with the drawing of a startled-looking bunnyhead beside it.

Johnson also made "bunny lists" with the names of famous artists, writers, and even the relative unknowns of Johnson's personal circle placed under a little figure of the bunnyhead. By giving identical images different names, and the names of persons obviously unrelated to the bunny image they identify, Johnson complicates the very idea of identity and recognition—a completely postmodern strategy. One

Fig. 13.5. *Untitled: Classical Bust with Bunnyhead* by Ray Johnson, n.d. (c. 1980), 13.25 x 10.25 x 8", plaster bust with black paint. Photograph from the Estate of Ray Johnson, Courtesy Richard L. Feigen & Company.

of the early bunny lists also introduces another of Johnson's oblique associations, the rabbit and the duck (see fig. 13.4). On March 26, 1969, at California State University at Sacramento's Art Gallery, Johnson's New York Correspondance [*sic*] School, the name under which his mail art events were held after 1968, sponsored an event titled "A Duck named Andy," during which the eponymous duck, which turned out to be a rabbit, was raffled off. The Andy of the title was, of course, a reference to Andy Warhol, Johnson's friend from his early days in New York. This event had the added significance for Johnson of linking his artistic practice not only with that of Warhol but also with another "master figure" from art history. In *Art and Illusion*, a standard text for young art historians, E. H. Gombrich uses the silhouette of a duck which, when viewed from a slightly different perspective, becomes a rabbit to explain the relativity of perception and the psychological complications of the identification of shapes.[12] In the little bunnyheads that advertise the Sacramento event, Johnson himself creates a simplified version of this bunny/duck with an identification that shifts depending on the viewers' point of view. He enjoyed this linking of rabbits and ducks, then, as a kind of art historical in-joke, but one that referred to not only complicated issues of visual perception and understanding but also the basic issue of identity and representation. Johnson's references were in their very nature conceptual, though usually linked to an objective reality. His associations are often difficult for the uninitiated, especially as the time period during which they were made recedes in the collective memory. But even with a decisive "meaning" out of reach, Johnson's images remain visually rich and satisfying (see fig. 13.5).

The issue of identity, and/or subjectivity, is at the heart of the idea of the postmodern animal. It is part of a more general anxiety that philosophers as well as artists and historians have identified in various ways. With the onset of a new century, and for at least the decade leading up to it, there has been a questioning of old certainties and a feeling of a lack at the center without any concrete ideas to replace them. Some have turned to old systems of politics and midcentury mores to fill the void; in art and academe, the lack itself has been embraced, and the question only remains how best to represent it. In gender studies, the idea of performativity was suggested by Judith Butler, Elizabeth Grosz, and others to describe the shifting of sexual identities and expectations now that the old concepts of dualism, nature versus nurture, and innate drives seem bankrupt.[13] The idea of imitation, or mimicry—to naturalists an old idea when it comes to describing animals—is the site of the lack or anxiety when it comes to the human/animal question. Steve Baker quotes Derrida, who was increasingly concerned with the idea of the animal Other, to outline this issue:

> In all these instances, it might be said that the thing imitated or gestured toward is not so much an animal as a version of the imitator or gesturer—"l'animal que donc je suis," as Derrida has it. In a postmodern age marked by "a deeply felt loss of faith in our ability to represent the real," this is perhaps how the animal is now most productively and imaginatively thought in art—as a thing actively to be performed, rather than passively represented.[14]

The practice of complicating identity was also at work even as Johnson participated in the notions of popular culture and fame that were central to Pop Art in the 1960s. Johnson's appropriation of the famous was much more layered and ironic in tone than that of other Pop artists such as Andy Warhol. Johnson's references to movie stars and other figures in the public eye are always employed with a tongue-in-cheek humor that resonates more with the tone of the postmodern 1990s than that of the still-modern 1960s. His animal images are often combined with pop references in a kind of self-aware amusement that often has an edge even with the laughs. Humor for Ray Johnson is a distancing maneuver; it allows for complicated thoughts or associations to be approached obliquely. Didacticism is not good for art or comedy.

Just as he did with Pop Art, Johnson absorbed other ideas current with New York's cultural avant-garde of the 1950s and 1960s but, again, gave them his own flavor. He became aware of Zen philosophy in New York in the 1950s, first, probably, through John Cage, who lived across the hall from Johnson on Monroe

Fig. 13.6. *Untitled: Nothing Bunnies* by Ray Johnson, c. 1980, 11 x 8.5", xerographic reproduction. Photograph from the Estate of Ray Johnson, Courtesy Richard L. Feigen & Company.

Street. Cage was a disciple of D. T. Suzuki and discussed concepts of chance and nothingness with the young artist fresh from Black Mountain College. Johnson worked for a time at the Orientalia Bookstore, mecca for all things Eastern in New York at that time, and cites or incorporates Zen concepts frequently in his work. Especially influential were the ideas on nothingness he discussed with Cage. He called his early performances "Nothings" and did a series of all white paintings with perforations in response to his conversations with Cage.

Despite images such as *Nothing Bunnies* (see fig. 13.6), another animal is actually more closely linked to Johnson's interest in Eastern thought. Images of snakes and snakes that morph into other animals are employed by Johnson in a more complicated and subterranean way. The unexpected juxtapositions of human and animal images, or animals and wordplay, allow for new meanings and associations to occur much as they do in Zen koans—texts that are meant to jar our consciousness from its everyday patterns, as in, "What is the sound of one hand clapping?" The snake, as such, is a universal symbol which represents widely divergent things for different cultures. Its Judeo-Christian referent—the serpent in the Garden of Eden—is balanced by its Eastern use as a symbol of rebirth or continuity. Hopi Indians saw snakes as the messengers of the gods and held them sacred.[15] For Ray Johnson, the snake's shedding of its skin and the attendant associations of a nature transitory, mutable, and unfixed in meaning were like his own feelings of standing outside the cultural mainstream. Baker suggests that the postmodern artists' use of animal imagery is concomitant with this sense of Otherness, and complicates any simple understanding of either the artist or the animal identity.[16] Johnson's identity as an artist, and one with a particularly problematic relationship to the traditional art market, along with his homosexuality, set him apart

Fig. 13.7. *Untitled: Snake on a Couch* by Ray Johnson, 1986, 6 x 11.5", collage, ink on illustration board. Photograph from the Estate of Ray Johnson, Courtesy Richard L. Feigen & Company.

from his peers and the culture as a whole. The promise symbolized by the snake's ability to shed its skin—shedding identity, shedding meaning, approaching nothingness—was close to Johnson's own desires, at least as they are manifested in his art. His snakes lurch phallically on magazine cutouts of male models; they lounge sensuously with sly smiles on furniture (see fig. 13.7).

Johnson's snake is a knowing, cartoonish creature, yet oddly expressive; it turns the mythic, reverent images of snakes on their head. The image or idea of the snake of Genesis, or even those of contemporary horror films such as *Python*, remains fixed, one-dimensional in meaning (and usually in the West that meaning is "Snake is Evil"—an animal that exists in opposition to humankind, that never has our best interests at heart). Ray Johnson's snakes are more difficult to objectify; the form or drawing of the snake is always consistent and simple, even decorative, but its context shifts and intrudes not only on the human spaces of couches and chairs but also on the integrity of the human body itself. His snakes refuse to be the easily understood animal Other—the boundaries of human/animal duality are blurred and complicated. Unlike his bunnies, his snakes feel more like creatures with a hidden agenda. They are an *imago* of the condition of alterity under which artists often labor in our culture, and as such Johnson often paired the snakes with pictures or references to artists besides himself. *Untitled: John Waters Snake on Chair* appropriates a photo of the head of the iconic gay filmmaker set on the sinuous body of a snake draped over a formal chair (see fig. 13.8). As if this confusion of creativity were not sufficient, Johnson adds a further reference to his own Correspondance [*sic*] School and to another celebrity in the text "Please Send to Paloma Picasso." Snakes on the furniture are as bizarre as the artist is in a society in which artists are often regarded with confusion and distrust, and Johnson in particular was more of an outsider than most. The snakes, however, appear comfortable with their circumstances, and their potency is always suggested. The phallic power of the snakes is not unreservedly sexual; it also suggests creative or artistic power. Johnson's snakes drape themselves over textual references to seminal visual artists such as Yves Tanguy or Duchamp or to writers such as William Burroughs (see fig. 13.9); he links the ancient culture-laden symbol of the snake—and as his personal representative, Johnson himself—to the important creative work of the artists he cites.

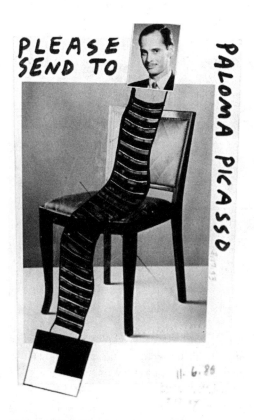

Fig. 13.8. *Untitled: John Waters Snake on Chair* by Ray Johnson, 1992–94, 10 x 8", collage, ink, felt pen on cardboard panel. Photograph from the Estate of Ray Johnson, Courtesy Richard L. Feigen & Company.

The snakes are sometimes transformed into turtles or snails by the addition of a heavy "shell" onto their backs. Now the skin-shedding ani-

Fig. 13.9. *William Burroughs* by Ray Johnson, 1978, 16 x 16 x 1.25", collage, paint on masonite. Photograph from the Estate of Ray Johnson, Courtesy Richard L. Feigen & Company.

mal surrogate takes on a new identity, one able to exist both on land and in the water. William S. Wilson has written of the many images of sea creatures sent to him by Johnson, likening their use on an envelope dropped into the ocean of the postal system as an explicit isomorphism—"a letter is to the postal system as an octopus is to the sea."[17] According to Wilson, a longtime friend and chronicler of Johnson's work, Johnson felt his one true home to be underwater, like a fish, but he could not go home without drowning. Therefore frogs, snails, turtles, and other amphibians became models of an existence that could be both above and beneath the water (see fig. 13.10). Johnson kept the desiccated remains of a blowfish in his studio and sent Wilson many other references to frogs including the famous haiku: "Frog / pond / splash."

Ray Johnson's snakes and bunnies were postmodern animals in a rather arid modern culture. For Johnson, the bunnies, snakes, turtles, and snails all inhabited the same internal world of meaning. His is a personal symbolism useful to him, provocative to us, but not entirely accessible—at least not in the tradition of the old art historical readings of animal symbols. Johnson's snake was certainly not the biblical symbol of the evil of knowledge and transgression, nor even the male/

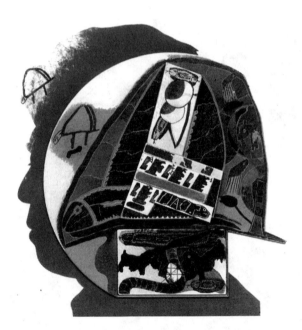

Fig. 13.10. *Untitled: Blue Arakawa* by Ray Johnson, 1976–94, 15 x 15", collage on illustration board. Photograph from the Estate of Ray Johnson, Courtesy Richard L. Feigen & Company.

female immortality symbol of the Ouroboros, devouring its own tail, although he did quote that image on occasion. Johnson's snakes—and bunnies, too—were self-aware images that participated in the alterity of the artist, winking at the discomfort we feel when gazing at the Other and knowing that somehow they are us. When Johnson jumped from the Sag Harbor Bridge on Friday, January 13, 1995, he returned, in a sense, to the watery world of language and meaning that he had pioneered before art history caught up with him. His animals were postmodern in their refusal to be merely "dumb bunnies," always already projecting into a future of more complicated and interesting meanings.

Notes

1. While the practice of artists mailing items to one another was not new with Johnson, he is credited with creating the first network of correspondents among whom the act of mailing was at least as important as the physical object mailed. For more on mail art, see Michael Crane and Mary Stofflet, eds., *Correspondence Art: Source Book for the Network of International Postal Art Activity* (San Francisco: Contemporary Arts Press, 1984).

2. Steve Baker, *The Postmodern Animal* (London: Reaktion, 2000).

3. Wolfe's reading (along with Jonathan Elmer) of Demme's movie can be found in Cary Wolfe, *Animal Rites: American Culture, the Discourse of Species, and Posthumanist Theory* (Chicago: Univ. of Chicago Press, 2003), 97–122. Also see Mary Sanders Pollock and Catherine Rainwater, eds., *Figuring Animals: Essays on Animal Images in Art, Literature, Philosophy, and Popular Culture* (New York: Palgrave Macmillan, 2005). There are many other significant texts that could be recommended here, but the ones I have found to be most useful in addition to those mentioned above are Cary Wolfe, ed., *Zoontologies: The Question of the Animal* (Minneapolis: Univ. of Minnesota Press, 2003); Roy Willis, ed., *Signifying Animals: Human Meaning in the Natural World* (New York: Routledge, 1990); Carl Cohen and Tom Regan, *The Animal Rights Debate* (Lanham, Md.: Rowman & Littlefield, 2001); and Carol J. Adams and Josephine Donovan, eds., *Animals and Women: Feminist Theoretical Explorations* (Durham, N.C.: Duke Univ. Press, 1995). Specific information about Ray Johnson and his work comes from my research in his Estate.

4. Reviews of Johnson's art were usually good but not very thoughtful. Two early exceptions are William S. Wilson, "Ray Johnson: Letter of Reference," *Arts Magazine* 44, no. 4 (Feb. 1970): 28–30, and Henry Martin, "Mashed Potatoes: Henry Martin Looks at the Collages of Ray Johnson," *Art and Artists* 7, no. 2, issue no. 74 (May 1972): 22–25. For other references on Johnson, see my "Selected Bibliography," in *Ray Johnson: Correspondences*, ed. Donna M. De Salvo and Catherine Gudis (Paris: Flammarion and Wexner Center for the Arts, 1999), 214–15.

5. Most surveys of seventeenth-century Dutch art provide references to the symbolic inclusion of animals; see, for instance, Jakob Rosenberg, Seymour Slive, and E. H. ter Kuile, eds., *Dutch Art and Architecture, 1600–1800* (New York: Penguin Books, 1966), 333–45. See Walter Friedlaender, *David to Delacroix* (Cambridge, Mass.: Harvard Univ. Press, 1952), 122–23, for a discussion of animals in nineteenth-century romantic art. For an American take on animal imagery, see Mary Sayre Haverstock, *An American Bestiary* (New York: Harry N. Abrams, 1979). Kenneth Clark's *Animals and Men: Their Relationship as Reflected in Western Art from Prehistory to the Present* (New York: William Morrow, 1977) and Francis Klinger's *Animals in Art and Thought to the End of the Middle Ages* (Cambridge, Mass.: MIT Press, 1971) are good early sources on traditional animal iconography. Also see Francesco Mezzalira, *Beasts and Bestiaries: The Representation of Animals from Prehistory to the Renaissance* (Turin: Allemani, 2001) for a more recent survey.

6. Again, most general art historical discussions of the Blaue Reiter explore Kandinsky's and Marc's spiritual underpinnings for that movement. See, for instance, Sam Hunter and John Jacobus, eds., *Modern Art* (New York: Harry N. Abrams, 1985), 120–22, and Franz Marc, "How Does a Horse See the World," in *Theories of Modern Art: A Source Book by Artists and Critics*, ed. Herschel B. Chipp (Berkeley and Los Angeles: Univ. of California Press, 1968), 178–79.

7. Feminist art historians have increasingly examined the role of women in the surrealist movement. For a general survey, see Whitney Chadwick, *Women Artists of the Surrealist Movement* (London: Thames and Hudson, 1985). For a specific discussion

of the animal imagery of Carrington and Fini, see Georgiana M. M. Colvile, "Beauty and/Is the Beast: Animal Symbology in the Work of Leonora Carrington, Remedios Varo and Leonor Fini," in *Surrealism and Women*, ed. Mary Ann Caws, Rudolf Kuenzli, and Gwen Raaberg (Cambridge, Mass.: MIT Press, 1991), 159–81. Leonore Fini is my particular favorite since we share a passion for Persian cats. I was lucky enough to buy a print by Fini that features her self-portrait with the ears and facial characteristics of a cat and a very erect masculine attribute! Also, Carrington's own *The House of Fear: Notes from Down Below* (New York: G. P. Dutton, 1988) is a direct source for her elaborate animal symbology.

8. Baker, *Postmodern Animal*, 24.

9. Roy Willis, "The Meaning of the Snake," in *Signifying Animals: Human Meaning in the Natural World*, ed. Roy Willis (New York: Routledge, 1990), 247–48.

10. "Man" is the operative word, because women continued to be seen as closer to nature, irrational, instinctual, closer to animals than to men.

11. For more on rabbits and their cultural history, see Susan E. Davis and Margo DeMello, *Stories Rabbits Tell: A Natural and Cultural History of a Misunderstood Creature* (New York: Lantern Books, 2003). Thanks to Dave Aftandilian for that reference.

12. E. H. Gombrich, *Art and Illusion* (New York: Pantheon Books, 1960), 5.

13. See especially Judith Butler's *Gender Trouble: Feminism and the Subversion of Identity* (New York: Routledge, 1990) and Elizabeth Grosz, *Volatile Bodies: Toward a Corporeal Feminism* (Bloomington: Indiana Univ. Press, 1994).

14. Steve Baker, "Sloughing the Human," in *Zoontologies: The Question of the Animal*, ed. Cary Wolfe (Minneapolis: Univ. of Minnesota Press, 2003), 159.

15. Willis, "Meaning of the Snake," 248–49. For more on the serpent in Hopi folklore, see Dave Aftandilian's chapter, "Frogs, Snakes, and Agricultural Fertility," in this volume.

16. Baker, "Sloughing the Human," 147.

17. William S. Wilson, "With Ray: The Art of Friendship," in *Black Mountain College Dossiers*, ed. James Thompson (Raleigh, N.C.: Black Mountain College Museum and Arts Center, 1997), 54–56; and in letters and e-mails to me.

Works Cited

Adams, Carol J., and Josephine Donovan, eds. *Animals and Women: Feminist Theoretical Explorations*. Durham, N.C.: Duke Univ. Press, 1995.

Baker, Steve. *The Postmodern Animal*. London: Reaktion, 2000.

———. "Sloughing the Human." In *Zoontologies: The Question of the Animal*, edited by Cary Wolfe, 147–64. Minneapolis: Univ. of Minnesota Press, 2003.

Butler, Judith. *Gender Trouble: Feminism and the Subversion of Identity*. New York: Routledge, 1990.

Carrington, Leonora. *The House of Fear: Notes from Down Below*. New York: G. P. Dutton, 1988.

Chadwick, Whitney. *Women Artists of the Surrealist Movement*. London: Thames and Hudson, 1985.

Clark, Kenneth. *Animals and Men: Their Relationship as Reflected in Western Art from Prehistory to the Present*. New York: William Morrow, 1977.

Cohen, Carl, and Tom Regan. *The Animal Rights Debate*. Lanham, Md.: Rowman & Littlefield, 2001.

Colvile, Georgiana M. M. "Beauty and/Is the Beast: Animal Symbology in the Work of Leonora Carrington, Remedios Varo and Leonor Fini." In *Surrealism and Women*, edited by Mary Ann Caws, Rudolf Kuenzli, and Gwen Raaberg, 159–81. Cambridge, Mass.: MIT Press, 1991.

Crane, Michael, and Mary Stofflet, eds. *Correspondence Art: Source Book for the Network of International Postal Art Activity*. San Francisco: Contemporary Arts Press, 1984.

Davis, Susan E., and Margo DeMello. *Stories Rabbits Tell: A Natural and Cultural History of a Misunderstood Creature*. New York: Lantern Books, 2003.

Friedlaender, Walter. *David to Delacroix*. Cambridge, Mass.: Harvard Univ. Press, 1952.

Gombrich, E. H. *Art and Illusion*. New York: Pantheon Books, 1960.

Grosz, Elizabeth. *Volatile Bodies: Toward a Corporeal Feminism*. Bloomington: Indiana Univ. Press, 1994.

Haverstock, Mary Sayre. *An American Bestiary*. New York: Harry N. Abrams, 1979.

Hunter, Sam, and John Jacobus, eds. *Modern Art*. New York: Harry N. Abrams, 1985.

Jones, Muffet. "Selected Bibliography." In *Ray Johnson: Correspondences*, edited by Donna M. De Salvo and Catherine Gudis, 214–15. Paris: Flammarion and Wexner Center for the Arts, 1999.

Klinger, Francis. *Animals in Art and Thought to the End of the Middle Ages*. Cambridge, Mass.: MIT Press, 1971.

Marc, Franz. "How Does a Horse See the World." Translated by Ernest Mundt and Peter Selz. In *Theories of Modern Art: A Source Book by Artists and Critics*, edited by Herschel B. Chipp, 178–79. Berkeley and Los Angeles: Univ. of California Press, 1968.

Martin, Henry. "Mashed Potatoes: Henry Martin Looks at the Collages of Ray Johnson." *Art and Artists* 7, no. 2, issue no. 74 (May 1972): 22–25.

Mezzalira, Francesco. *Beasts and Bestiaries: The Representation of Animals from Prehistory to the Renaissance*. Turin: Allemani, 2001.

Pollock, Mary Sanders, and Catherine Rainwater, eds. *Figuring Animals: Essays on Animal Images in Art, Literature, Philosophy, and Popular Culture*. New York: Palgrave Macmillan, 2005.

Rosenberg, Jakob, Seymour Slive, and E. H. ter Kuile, eds. *Dutch Art and Architecture, 1600–1800*. New York: Penguin Books, 1966.

Willis, Roy. "The Meaning of the Snake." In *Signifying Animals*, edited by Roy Willis, 246–52. New York: Routledge, 1990.

———, ed. *Signifying Animals: Human Meaning in the Natural World*. New York: Routledge, 1990.

Wilson, William S. "Ray Johnson: Letter of Reference." *Arts Magazine* 44, no. 4 (Feb. 1970): 28–30.

———. "With Ray: The Art of Friendship." In *Black Mountain College Dossiers*, edited by James Thompson, 1–64. Raleigh, N.C.: Black Mountain College Museum and Arts Center, 1997.

Wolfe, Cary. *Animal Rites: American Culture, the Discourse of Species, and Posthumanist Theory*. Chicago: Univ. of Chicago Press, 2003.

———, ed. *Zoontologies: The Question of the Animal*. Minneapolis: Univ. of Minnesota Press, 2003.

Part 4

Come into Animal Presence

Ethics, Ethology, and Konrad Lorenz

Introduction

David Scofield Wilson

In her poem "Come into Animal Presence," Denise Levertov offers her readers a challenge and a promise: she invites us to learn from the animals "who were sacred and have remained so" that "holiness does not dissolve, it is a presence of bronze," and she promises that we may regain the "old joy" by coming back into that presence.[1] Her invitation is a reminder that many of our best poets and writers have made that journey across species boundaries to share in the presence of nature's creations: Walt Whitman with a live oak ("I Saw in Louisiana a Live-Oak Growing," 1860), Emily Dickinson with "several of nature's people," for whom she feels "a transport / Of cordiality" ("A Narrow Fellow in the Grass," 1891), Henry David Thoreau with a woodchuck he crouches in front of and watches grind its teeth at him (*Journal*, Apr. 16, 1852), and Sally Carrighar with a mouse she hears singing from within her Philco radio, an event so striking and portentous as to convince her that "I could after all be a writer, a nature writer."[2]

Countless authors, scholars, storytellers, naturalists, artists, and scientists have also been drawn into animal presence and have sought ways to express the kinship they feel with nonhuman animals. As Robert Bly argues in his 1980 anthology, *News of the Universe: Poems of Twofold Consciousness*, poets have had to overcome the prejudices of what he terms "the Old Position" in order to rediscover such kinship and to express it without apology. His subtitle comes from six lines by William Blake:

> Now I a fourfold vision see,
> And a fourfold vision is given to me;
> 'Tis fourfold in my supreme delight
> And threefold in soft Beulah's night
> And twofold always. May God us keep
> From Single vision & Newton's sleep![3]

To see as Blake does implies the gift of multiple viewpoints, to see animals, for example, as angels do and Blake did. Or less arcanely, perhaps, as painters, poets, mythmakers, and shamans do, as hunters and wranglers and animals trainers sometimes do, and even as our animal kin themselves do. Scientific and lay observers of animals may gain a deeper and wider appreciation of animal sentience than that imagined by Blake's Newton or other single-minded students of nature.[4]

As Bruce Hackett explains in his chapter in this section, prejudices within the scientific community have made it equally perilous at times for scientists to report on the everyday lives of animals in natural settings and in interaction with their human kin. The relatively new scientific subdiscipline of "ethology" spoke to many of us, to scientists and laypeople alike: we could relate to our animal neighbors, helpers, and pets more comfortably than our education had taught us to trust. In 1965, Sally Carrighar introduced the field to lay readers:

> The new science of ethology—the science of animals' normal behavior—has brought up the whole question of what ways, and to what extent, human beings behave like the simpler creatures from which we evolved. What do we do that they do? What similar impulses (if any) move both animals and men?[5]

Eight years later, Nikolaas Tinbergen, Karl von Frisch, and Konrad Lorenz were made Nobel laureates in medicine "for their discoveries concerning organization and elicitation of individual and social behaviour patterns," which is to say, "ethology."[6]

"In contrast to their naturalist predecessors' representation of animal life as immanently meaningful, ethological accounts are external to any possible vantage point of animals," Eileen Crist argues in her recent book *Images of Animals: Anthropomorphism and Animal Mind*. She continues:

> Despite their intellectual continuity, there is a great disparity between ethologists and naturalists with respect to their uses of language. In contrast to the naturalists' language of the lifeworld, ethologists use a technical vocabulary, in part constructed by themselves and in part appropriated from behaviorist psychology. The linguistic and argumentative edifice created by the pioneer ethologists led to the representation of animals as natural objects. Yet it is quite certain that neither Tinbergen nor Lorenz wanted to "desubjectify" animals.[7]

Nevertheless, the objectifying language they employed distances them from their animal "subjects" and seems to deny those subjects volition or intention. For instance, ethologists speak of "innate releasing mechanisms" within the animals that "release" behavioral responses, rather than of animals *doing* something for their own purposes. This "technical idiom," Crist concludes, "leads to a mechanomorphic view of animals."[8]

And yet, for many of us, animals came alive in a new way when these ethologists studied them. Their behavior seemed to make sense now in terms of field narratives, much as they had in the past in legends, fables, fantasies, and dreams. We looked over von Frisch's shoulder as he watched bees wiggle and dance their messages to fellow bees, and now to humans, about how far and in what direction they could find nectar. We watched with Tinbergen as wasps on Dutch dunes figured out how to find nests hidden from them by him, and we watched as he "fooled" herring gull chicks with mocked-up herring gull heads and beaks ringed in red. And most especially, we followed Lorenz as he squat-walked and quacked his way across the barnyard or swam with his geese in the Danube (see plates 1 and 2 following this introduction). We were charmed and heartened.

The spell of such storytelling by ethologists rests, it seems, on two pre-critical foundations—the authority of animals themselves, living normal lives in the world, and the person of our guide into their world, one we trust to open unto us the "inner lives" of otherwise familiar animals. To ever so many literate and sympathetic friends of animals, Konrad Lorenz took center stage as he told of dogs acting out their so-familiar follies, of jackdaws making themselves at home in a loft, and of baby geese attaching themselves to their "parent." Because Lorenz was so charming a guide, his presence commands equal attention in this volume to that of other animals appearing here as icons, totems, personae, or symbols. Is this "father" of ethology, in short, a totem to be savored, critically?

The spell of Lorenz's storytelling qua science was shattered for some of us years later by revelations that he had a Nazi past and had been less than candid in owning up to his background. Were we now to doubt the advances of ethology because of the political ideology of one of its pioneers? Did ethology need to find a new foundational mythology to replace that built upon Lorenz's persona? Should animal behavior studies carry on without Lorenz, or in spite of his tarnished reputation? And could much of his contribution be saved, cleansed? Those are the questions the contributors to this section explore.

Each of these chapters responds in some way to Boria Sax's book *Animals in the Third Reich: Pets, Scapegoats, and the Holocaust,* in which he relentlessly laid out the case for Lorenz's soiled reputation. The account he tells is presented as history, a genre of storytelling that carries a high degree of authority, especially when written out and published. Written history and its accouterments—footnotes, sources, quotations, bibliography—can be checked by others, verified, collated, compared to other texts. This is the work Sax has done so well, as he demonstrates in the brief account of his findings in this section.

Sax's method of setting cases side by side, as he does in comparing Lorenz's influence on ethology with Wernher von Braun's on the space program of the United States following World War II, or in testing the response to revelations about Lorenz's Nazi past against the response to revelations about Martin Heidegger's Nazism or Bertholt Brecht's Stalinism, allows Sax to complicate a story that seemed at first simple and inescapably black and white. He understands that the force of narratives to organize thought and to move us to act depends not upon reason alone, nor upon written, historical expositions and arguments, but equally upon what the classical rhetoricians called "pathetic proof" and "ethical proof," that is, on the ability of the story to move us and upon the perceived character of the teller to convince us of his or her practical standing within the story. Sax recognizes, for instance, that "one thing Lorenz had in common with Hitler and many others in the Nazi movement was the ability, and inclination, to exploit mythic images." Which is to say that the "sight" of Lorenz the man in the Danube with his geese adds powerfully to the authority of his story and to the plausibility of ethology to future readers. Sax ends, however, by wondering in his chapter in this section, "What will happen to the discipline of ethology now that so much of its foundation myth, intimately associated with Lorenz, seems to be discredited by association with national socialism?" How to answer that question from the point of view of present-day ethologists, cum animal behaviorists, is the problem addressed by Lynette A. Hart in her chapter in this section.

While Sax casts his narrative as history and then raises extrahistorical questions, Hart places the case of Lorenz within a disciplinary framework along with issues of fraud, fabrication, plagiarism, and conflicts of interest. The difference may seem slight, but it allows her to step back, as it were, from focusing on an ethos of evil and to stand instead within the present community of scholars who matter-of-factly bracket the extradisciplinary rhetoric of "ethical proof" and "pathetic proof" and who believe that no one voice can generate a whole mythos and revelation. Hers is a setting in which researchers and critics sift and weigh and reassess what this or that new work contributes to the controlling theory and to the practice of the study of normal animal lives. And hers is the story, or rather a collection of stories, that allows her and us to respect much of what Lorenz discovered and invented as well as to appreciate more fully the founding and practical work of co–Nobel Laureates von Frisch and, especially, Tinbergen:

> While Lorenz was called the father of ethology, it was Tinbergen who became its conceptual pillar. He formulated the framework for the theoretical field of ethology, setting its four aims that pointed toward goals requiring interdisciplinary alliances among ethologists, psychologists, and physiologists.[9]

And it is from Hart that we learn of the work of other important "fathers" of ethology—Ernst Mayr, Frank Beach, Ted Schneirla, Robert Yerkes, and Danny Lehrman—a contribution that enriches our grasp of the collaboration that has generated the science. In the end, Hart concludes that the "conflict with Lorenz sharpened the dialogue among scientists and improved the science, requiring more finely honed arguments from all concerned."

Bruce Hackett brings still another rhetoric to the problem as he positions our story of ethology and ethologists within the contemporary subdiscipline of the sociology of knowledge, wherein all "truths" are cast in quotation marks, emphasizing their dependence upon larger environments of controlling assumptions, in this case the contest between the so-called positivists and pragmatists in science and the arts. Along with the ethologists, psychologists, and physiologists with whom Tinbergen assumes he must collaborate, Hackett adds those in sociology and communications who regularly do fieldwork with human subjects and create "'qualitative' accounts of human conduct." In an analogue of the study of normal animal behavior among ethologists, Hackett draws our attention to qualitative social science's focus on "how things come to be thought of as 'normal'" as opposed to "trying to explain social deviation."

Hackett would agree with Leslie White that it is crucial that we not call what scientists do "science," as if it were a positive, finished product more than an ongoing process. By coining a new term, "sciencing," White points up the crucial interaction between investigators and what they study and how what they learn depends both upon their assumptions about (for instance) the animals they study, on the one hand, and upon the settings and equipment within which and with which they study animals and their behavior.[10] Hackett admits that such a pragmatic approach "will remain for some time on the margins of accredited knowing." Such a "focus on the *relationship* between knower and known produces instances," he says, "of 'legend'—ultimately including, one supposes, those second-degree legends that students of legend-making produce, and that are on display in this volume." Here *social sciencing, sciencing,* and *legending* converge for our edification. And Hackett takes comfort from "studies currently underway of the legends and the folklore of the modern research laboratory itself (tracing, e.g., the vernacular roots of notions such as 'cause' or 'finding' or 'roots')" that "will undoubtedly contribute to humanizing our understanding of the 'disciplines' that confront 'nature' and hopefully hasten the day when the NILAS approach will be taken to be what real 'science' is all about."

In the meantime, the strength of animal studies lies, as in this volume, in our assembling and clustering of diverse discoveries about how we humans have used and abused animals in our legends and life and art and science and in accounts of how dealing with animals has clarified our own aims and trajectories for good or ill in the world. If we have learned anything from the many contributions assembled here, it is that we should expect never to create a "master narrative" of the sort that is so often the aim of the disciplines but rather to learn to abide in the presence of the wild and to learn what Gary Snyder has called "the practice of the wild," toward a multifold vision closer to Blake's and to other poets than to Newton's "Single vision & . . . sleep."[11]

Notes

1. Denise Levertov, "Come into Animal Presence," in *The Life around Us: Selected Poems on Nature,* by Denise Levertov (New York: New Directions, 1997), 34.

2. Both poems by Whitman and Dickinson are widely anthologized but may be found in Wilson Allen Gay, Walter B. Rideout, and James K. Robinson, eds., *American Poetry* (New York: Harper & Row, 1965), 456 and 555–56; for the encounter between Thoreau and the woodchuck, see his journal entry for Apr. 16, 1852, wherever reprinted, but I take my citation from his *Journal* in Henry David Thoreau, *The Works of Thoreau,* ed. Henry Seidel Canby (Cambridge, Mass.: Houghton Mifflin, 1937), 603–4; and for Carrighar, see Sally Carrighar, *Home to the Wilderness* (Cambridge, Mass.: Houghton Mifflin, 1973), 272–75. This remarkable account of her conversion deserves to be more widely known and appreciated. Carrighar looked within the Philco radio from which she had heard the singing and found a mouse's nest, then she called the Zoology Department at the University of California at Berkeley and asked "whether a mouse could sing." She was connected to Dr. Joseph Grinnell, "who said that yes, very occasionally there were singing mice." "I was still attempting to find better words for it," she writes, "when I had to get out of bed and walk up and down because of a thought so startling and exciting: *this* is what I

should write about! Birds and animals! There could be no finer subject than woods and fields, streams, lakes, and mountainsides and the creatures who live in that world. It would be a subject of inexhaustible interest, a supreme joy to be learning to tell it all straight and truthfully."

3. William Blake, November 22, 1802, in *News of the Universe: Poems of Twofold Consciousness*, ed. Robert Bly (San Francisco: Sierra Club Books, 1980), 29.

4. For a fascinating perspective on animal behavior from the point of view of a woman with autism, see Temple Grandin and Catherine Johnson, *Animals in Translation: Using the Mysteries of Autism to Decode Animal Behavior* (New York: Scribner, 2005).

5. Sally Carrighar, *Wild Heritage* (Boston: Houghton Mifflin, 1965), vii.

6. Nobel Foundation, "The Nobel Prize in Physiology or Medicine 1973," http://nobelprize.org/medicine/laureates/1973, accessed June 22, 2005.

7. Eileen Crist, *Images of Animals: Anthropomorphism and Animal Mind* (Philadelphia: Temple Univ. Press, 1999), 89.

8. Ibid., 121.

9. Lynette A. Hart, this volume.

10. Leslie A. White, *The Science of Culture: A Study of Man and Civilization* (New York: Farrar Straus, 1949), 3–21.

11. Gary Snyder, *The Practice of the Wild* (San Francisco: North Point Press, 1990).

Works Cited

Bly, Robert, ed. *News of the Universe: Poems of Twofold Consciousness*. San Francisco: Sierra Club Books, 1980.

Carrighar, Sally. *Home to the Wilderness*. Cambridge, Mass.: Houghton Mifflin, 1973.

———. *Wild Heritage*. Boston: Houghton Mifflin, 1965.

Crist, Eileen. *Images of Animals: Anthropomorphism and Animal Mind*. Philadelphia: Temple Univ. Press, 1999.

Gay, Wilson Allen, Walter B. Rideout, and James K. Robinson, eds. *American Poetry*. New York: Harper & Row, 1965.

Grandin, Temple, and Catherine Johnson. *Animals in Translation: Using the Mysteries of Autism to Decode Animal Behavior*. New York: Scribner, 2005.

Levertov, Denise. *The Life around Us: Selected Poems on Nature*. New York: New Directions, 1997.

Nobel Foundation. "The Nobel Prize in Physiology or Medicine 1973." http://nobelprize.org/medicine/laureates/1973/. Accessed June 22, 2005.

Sax, Boria. *Animals in the Third Reich: Pets, Scapegoats, and the Holocaust*. New York: Continuum, 2000.

Snyder, Gary. *The Practice of the Wild*. San Francisco: North Point Press, 1990.

Thoreau, Henry David. *The Works of Thoreau*, edited by Henry Seidel Canby. Cambridge, Mass.: Houghton Mifflin, 1937.

White, Leslie A. *The Science of Culture: A Study of Man and Civilization*. New York: Farrar Straus, 1949.

Plate 1. Greylag geese following Konrad Lorenz, on whom they have imprinted. Photo by Nina Leen, 1960. © Getty Images. Used with permission. All rights reserved.

Plate 2. Konrad Lorenz swimming with a trio of greylag geese. Photo by Nina Leen, 1964. © Getty Images. Used with permission. All rights reserved.

Plate 3. "The Civilized Man Being Made into a Domestic Pig." Illustration by Högfeldt to an article by Konrad Lorenz, used to show the contrast between degeneration and primitivism. From Boria Sax, *Animals in the Third Reich: Pets, Scapegoats, and the Holocaust* (New York and London: Continuum, 2000): 71, Fig. 5. Courtesy of Continuum International Publishing Group.

Plate 4. Konrad Lorenz, c. 1940. XX. HA Historisches Staatsarchiv Koenigsberg, Nachlass Friedrich Hoffmann, Nr. 3, Bl. 36. Bildarchiv Preussicher Kulturbesitz / Art Resource, NY.

Chapter 14
Konrad Lorenz and the Mythology of Science

Boria Sax

I learned in grammar school, as had generations of American children since the early nineteenth century, that Columbus proved the world was round. That is one story that is now fully discredited, but it shows how myths of science, like those of religion and government, can persist for a long time in the absence of any evidence. Stories, not arguments or utility, give cohesion to the scientific enterprise; they anchor the abstractions of researchers in the human imagination, not only for the public but also for the scientists themselves. At least for a mass audience, the appeal of science may be due less to its rationality or utility than to the narratives it generates, filled with heroes such as Galileo and villains such as the Inquisition. Often years of work are condensed into an epiphany, for example, in the widespread story that Newton conceived of gravity when an apple fell on his head. Like all mythic narratives, these are constantly changing. Whether science ought to be considered a kind of mythology, as many postmodern theorists have suggested, is beyond the scope of this chapter. The development of ethology, at any rate, illustrates how science at least requires mythologies to support it.

Konrad Z. Lorenz (1903–89) was not only a scientist but also a charismatic storyteller. He worked at the time when a new branch of research was being established, a time when the need for foundation myths was especially great. His career illustrates both the powers and dangers of storytelling, particularly when there are no external checks. He made himself world famous and established the discipline of ethology. In addition, he placed the study of animals in the service of Nazi agendas and almost managed to obscure a sordid past until the time of his death.

When Lorenz returned from Soviet captivity after World War II, his involvement with Nazism was widely rumored though not definitively confirmed. When he shared the Nobel Prize in 1973 (though the Nazi hunter Simon Wiesenthal urged Lorenz to refuse the honor, saying that the recipient's support of a brutal dictatorship would dishonor the prize), Lorenz admitted to having, allegedly out of naïveté, used the language of the Nazis. He vehemently denied, however, having joined the Nazi party.

Over the decades the evidence of his involvement with the Nazi movement has steadily accumulated. A few researchers in the 1980s independently discovered proof of his party membership. In the next decade, Ute Deichmann revealed that Lorenz was also a member of the Nazi government's Office of Race Policy. Most significantly, Deichmann and others have shown that Lorenz was involved in a study to determine the suitability of 877 products of mixed Polish-German marriages for "Germanization," in which those considered "asocial" were sent to concentration camps.[1] Had all of this been known at the time of the Nuremberg Tribunal, it is easily possible that Lorenz might have been convicted as a war criminal.

The revelations even now continue to trickle in. An archive opened only in the twenty-first century contains the following statement from Lorenz's 1938 application to join the Nazi party:

> At many conferences and lecture tours I have always and every-
> where made a maximum effort to protest the lies of the Jewish-
> international press about the supposed popularity of Schuschnigg
> and the so-called "rape" of Austria with compelling arguments. I
> have done the same with all foreign visitors to my studio in Alten-
> berg. Finally, I can truthfully say that my entire lifetime of scientific
> work—in which evolutionary, racial, and social-psychological
> questions are of foremost importance—has been in the service of
> National-Socialist thought.[2]

If perhaps Lorenz may have been exaggerating out of opportunism or emotional intoxication, the statement was certainly not without basis. The fundamental concept of his early work, which continued to surface in his books after World War II, was the genetic decline that Lorenz believed came though careless breeding and racial miscegenation. He believed that this was analogous to the degeneration allegedly brought on by domestication in animals, and that it could only be cured through stern eugenic measures such as those being instituted by the Nazis (see plate 3, preceding this chapter).

Just as John B. Watson and B. F. Skinner had used Pavlov's theory of conditioned reflexes to explain almost everything in human and animal behavior, so Konrad Lorenz had applied Oscar Heinroth's theory of imprinting. Conditioned reflexes and imprinting work in almost the same way, as an automatic reaction is triggered by sensory stimuli. Thus the contrast between the two mechanisms is essentially that between environment and heredity.[3] The Nazis sought to rationalize the killing of people such as the mentally ill, Jews, Gypsies, and many others as a means of protecting the genetic pool, but this could only make sense within the context of an extreme biological determinism. Imprinting was a mechanism by which a vast variety of psychological and social characteristics could, theoretically, be inherited. Though the applications did not follow with any inexorable logic, the notion of imprinting was used to help people rationalize the assignment of certain stereotypical mental traits such as greed or heroism to various races, so that sterilizing or killing people became ways of culling unwanted genetic material. Lorenz theorized very freely about imprinting, for example, by saying that "lack of patriotic enthusiasm" was a sign of an "instinctual cripple" who ought not to have children.[4] But students of animal behavior now recognize that imprinting is not nearly as simple as Lorenz had thought.[5] It is not necessarily instantaneous or irreversible, and it is not distinguished sharply from other kinds of learning.

Most of this is old news by now, but there are several puzzles remaining. For instance, how was it possible for Lorenz to keep his support for the Nazi party hidden for so long, even though he had announced it in journals such as *Der Biologe* and *Zeitschrift für Tierpsychologie*, which were far from obscure? Scientists, including victims of the Nazis such as Karl von Frisch and Niko Tinbergen, certainly knew about these publications. Whether out of personal friendship or professional solidarity, they not only kept their mouths shut but also continued to support Lorenz in his career.

More recently, it is puzzling that the membership of Lorenz in the Nazi party has caused little discussion among either the general public or the scientific community. Admittedly, facile moralizing about the Nazi period may now be rather cheap. One cannot easily argue that the discipline of ethology is contaminated by association with a Nazi after our space program in America was directed by Werner von Braun. But if thundering denunciations are not very helpful, thoughtful debate and analysis certainly ought to be. Considering Lorenz's influence, for example, one might ask to what extent the perspectives of the Nazis may still be found in ethology and related fields.

By contrast, revelations about anti-Semitic articles written by literary theorist Paul de Man during Nazi occupation of his native Belgium sparked an intense, and often anguished, debate in literary circles around the end of the 1980s.[6] While no consensus was ever reached, the result was a dramatic decline in the influence of deconstruction, the critical approach that de Man had championed. Though de Man's involvement with the Nazis was far less serious than that of Lorenz, the revelations about Lorenz have received a good deal less attention.

Part of the reason for the lack of attention to his Nazi past was certainly the personal charm of Lorenz, which continues to beguile people even after his death. Quite a few observers who knew Lorenz during the 1930s and 1940s stated that he had the manner of a modest, diligent researcher and did not act like a Nazi. In view of this, we may ask how a Nazi acts. The popular image of Nazis after the war, which persists today, is that of brutal automatons. That idea can be traced back to the Nazis themselves, though as much to their propaganda as their behavior. They fostered a cult of "hardness," and they cultivated a severe, expressionless appearance, such as one may see in countless photographs of Nazi leaders. These people characteristically have sunken cheeks, impassive lips, and a maniacal gleam in their eyes. Lorenz himself has much that sort of countenance in the portrait of him from about 1940 that appears on the cover of the recent book on Lorenz and national socialism by Benedikt Föger and Klaus Taschwer, *Die Andere Seite des Spiegels: Konrad Lorenz und der Nationalsozialismus* (see plate 4). After the defeat of the Nazis, people realized that such an appearance was not a sign of indomitable resolution but of simple brutality. The Nazis themselves were often, however, a good deal more complex than their portraits.

Hannah Arendt challenged the stereotype of the Nazis with her famous theory of the "banality of evil" in *Eichmann in Jerusalem*, first published in 1965.[7] She described Adolf Eichmann, who had headed the Jewish Office of the Gestapo, not as a sadistic monster so much as a faceless bureaucrat. He was a sort of everyman, lacking only the imagination to question orders or to appreciate the horror of his deeds. Scholars now generally do not accept the portrait of Eichmann by Arendt. Contrary to his own claims, as well as those of Arendt, Eichmann did disobey orders by continuing to send Jews to the gas chambers even after his boss Himmler had ordered the killing to stop. There was also something a little self-serving about the theory of Arendt, who was a passionate believer in the moral value of high culture. By equating evil and banality, she implicitly excused artists and thinkers of quality. She would speak with withering contempt for ordinary citizens who had cooperated with the Nazis yet elaborately rationalize the Nazism of a Martin Heidegger or the Stalinism of a Bertolt Brecht.

People constantly attempt to stereotype Nazis, since highly simplified images obscure resemblances between Nazi society and our own. In truth, the characters of the Nazis did not neatly fit into any particular profile. They were not necessarily overtly brutal or even banal. A Nazi could also be a charismatic intellectual such as Martin Heidegger, Carl Schmitt, or, for that matter, Konrad Lorenz. A Nazi might be either brutal or sentimental, bland or fascinating, and almost everything that other people might be. Instead of asking, therefore, whether Lorenz fits some predetermined profile of a Nazi, it would be more useful to ask what this exemplar of Nazism can tell us about the movement. One thing Lorenz had in common with Hitler and many others in the Nazi movement was the ability, and inclination, to exploit mythic images.

Scientific disciplines construct for themselves a mythic past in much the same way as do religious institutions or national entities—a past full of venerated prophets, heroes, and martyrs. For all its aspiration toward objectivity, it is hard to even imagine science apart from stories of such imposing figures as Bruno, Galileo, Kepler, Newton, Darwin, and Einstein. The case of Lorenz shows how difficult it may be to separate the actual work of science from the mythologizing that surrounds it. Lorenz made no discovery comparable to, say, the work of Karl von Frisch in deciphering the dances of bees.[8] Lorenz generalized glibly in both his observations and his theoretical work, for example in his famous, and erroneous, claim that a dog or wolf that had been vanquished in a fight would release an inhibiting mechanism by baring its neck to the victor.[9] Nevertheless, Lorenz has come to represent the discipline of ethology so completely that it is now hard to think of it apart from him.

Even apart from his Nazism, the legacy of Lorenz would need to be reexamined, because his claims were never subjected to the usual scrutiny. As ethologist Bernd Heinrich has remarked, "In the early part of this century, it was generally recognized that Konrad Lorenz knew more about animal behavior than anybody else. That made it easy. If he said that ravens have an innate call that they use when they want others to follow them, it was generally accepted as fact on the basis of his authority."[10] Heinrich makes an interesting mistake in chronology, since Lorenz labored in near obscurity in the early part of the twentieth century, and did not come to be regarded as a major authority until after he joined the Nazi party in 1938. It is remarkable that he was accorded such unquestioned authority so quickly.

The reason seems to be that a cult of Lorenz addressed a need in the emerging science of ethology or, as it was called during the 1930s and 1940s, "animal psychology." To obtain recognition as an authentic science, with all the accompanying advantages in funding and prestige, the discipline needed more than a body of technical literature. It had to appeal not only to the intellect but also to the imagination, just as in the preceding decades Freud had given new status to the discipline of human psychology as much through his mystique as through his discoveries.

Now the emerging discipline of ethology needed a mythic origin, and this was something that Lorenz, in part because of his limitations as a scientist, was best able to supply. During the Third Reich he accomplished this by integrating ethology into the mythopoeic vision of the Nazis. After the collapse of Nazism, however, Lorenz created another myth in which he was to figure even more prominently. This myth was articulated in his popular books, especially *King Solomon's Ring*, which begins:

> As Holy Scripture tells us, the wise King Solomon, the son of David, "spake also of beasts, and of fowl, and of creeping things, and of fishes" (I Kings IV.33). A slight misreading of this text, which very probably is the oldest record of a biological lecture, has given rise to the charming legend that the king was able to talk the language of animals, which was hidden from all other men. Although this venerable tale that he spake to the animals and not of them certainly originated from a misunderstanding, I feel inclined to accept it as truth. . . . I can do it myself, and without the aid of magic, black or otherwise.[11]

Perhaps the life work of Lorenz was actually not so much in science as in the development of an elaborately constructed public persona—the sage who talked to animals and learned from them about the human soul. Students of myth will easily recognize the image of the "master of animals," a common motif in folklore that is identified with such figures as Orpheus and Cernunnos.

In light of what we now know about the Nazi past of Lorenz, however, it may be impossible to think of many of his exploits in the same way. The image of Lorenz perhaps most indelibly fixed in the public imagination is probably of him waddling across the grass with a flock of ducklings (or goslings) following him (plate 1). He had raised the ducklings in an incubator to show that they could be imprinted to follow a person as their parent. In his introduction to *King Solomon's Ring*, Julian Huxley wrote:

> Poor Lorenz being forced to spend hours crouched on his knees or crawling on his hands and feet, and quacking loudly at frequent intervals, if he was to fulfill his role as "imprinted" parent of a brood of ducklings; his assistant suddenly realizing he was talking goose

> instead of duck to the same ducklings, and cutting his goose-talk
> with "no, I mean quah, quah, quah."[12]

It may now, however, be a little difficult to imagine this scene without thinking of what the Nazis called the *Führerprinzip,* or "the principle of leadership," with which the Nazis attempted to impose a hierarchical order on every aspect of society.

One of the many claims of Lorenz that may reflect the Nazi legacy is that the society of jackdaws is absolutely hierarchical. As he stated in *King Solomon's Ring:*

> I can assure you, every single jackdaw of my colony knew each of
> the others by sight. This can be convincingly demonstrated by the
> existence of an order of rank, known as the "pecking order." Every
> poultry farmer knows that, even among these more stupid inhabitants
> of the poultry yard, there exists a very definite order, in which
> each bird is afraid of those that are above her in rank. After some
> few disputes, which need not necessarily come to blows, each bird
> knows which of the others she has to fear and which must show
> respect to her.[13]

But then how should we explain that very often those particular jackdaws which Lorenz considered near the top of the avian hierarchy would not peck those allegedly far beneath them? Lorenz ingeniously explained this by saying it demonstrated the extremes of hierarchy in their society:

> Very high caste jackdaws are most condescending to those of lowest
> degree and consider them merely as the dust beneath their feet;
> the self-display actions of the former are here a pure formality and
> only in the event of too close proximation does the dominant bird
> adopt a threatening attitude, but he rarely attacks.[14]

There are several other possibilities that Lorenz does not appear to consider. One explanation for the observed behavior might be that dominance relations among jackdaws are not necessarily transitive. It may even be that jackdaws do not quarrel as much over rank as over simpler things such as a scrap of food. Lorenz's characterization of jackdaws probably contains elements of truth, but Lorenz was communicating an ideological message by stating his case in such absolute and anthropomorphic terms. He, in effect, made his jackdaws into Nazis with a rigidly pyramidal social structure based on ability to dominate. In the Third Reich and afterward, such descriptions helped to sanction the sort of social order imposed by the Nazis by making it appear natural.[15]

The application of the language drawn from social hierarchies cannot be attributed simply to poetic license or even to anthropomorphism. As Eileen Crist has shown in *Images of Animals,* Lorenz was extremely selective in his use of anthropomorphic terms. He was, in fact, one of the first scientists to write of animal behavior in a theoretical language, which contrasted with the language used to describe human beings. The result, while not entirely deliberate, was to reinforce the Cartesian distinction between the rational behavior of human beings and the mechanical behavior of animals, at least "lower" animals.[16]

Though a strong authoritarian bias runs through all of Lorenz's work, recent research shows him to have been an opportunist rather than a fanatic. Russian archives that were recently opened reveal, for example, that his captors at the end of World War II gave Lorenz many special privileges in return for his work as a propagandist among other prisoners for their sociopolitical ideology.[17] Lorenz is a paradigmatic figure of the latter twentieth century in the way his carefully constructed public image eventually eclipsed both the man and the scientist. In spite of considerable scholarship, Lorenz the man seems unknowable and almost irrelevant. His public image is so well established in our collective imagination that it has so far been largely impervious to assaults from either history or science. This is no longer even unusual for people in public life, from rock stars and pro wrestlers to politicians.

It will be interesting to observe how people will react to revelations about Lorenz over the next few decades. What will happen to the discipline of ethology now that so much of its foundation myth, intimately associated with Lorenz, seems to be discredited by association with national socialism? The discipline is now far too established to be seriously threatened, but we may come to regard it in very different ways. Up to now, the foundation myths of ethology, like the idea that Columbus proved the world is round, continue to be disseminated in spite of a lack of evidence. I believe they will eventually be abandoned, but the process may be very gradual. It is possible that ethology may be entirely absorbed into other disciplines such as sociobiology. It may also be that new foundation myths of ethology will come to center on another scientist such as Darwin, Tinbergen, or von Frisch, who will perhaps be stylized to match the image that Lorenz created. Unprecedented phenomena such as cloning, genetic manipulation, and mass extinctions will doubtless inspire new mythologies, which give us not only a future but also a past.

Notes

1. Ute Deichmann, *Biologists under Hitler* (Cambridge, Mass.: Harvard Univ. Press, 1996), 193–97, 323; Benedikt Föger and Klaus Taschwer, *Die Andere Seite des Spiegels: Konrad Lorenz und der Nationalsozialismus* (Vienna: Czernin Verlag, 2001), 148–60.

2. Föger and Taschwer, *Andere Seite des Spiegels*, 79; translation by the author.

3. James L. Gould, *Ethology: The Mechanisms and Evolution of Behavior* (New York: Norton, 1982), 4–8, 18–21, 50–51.

4. Boria Sax, *Animals in the Third Reich: Pets, Scapegoats, and the Holocaust* (New York: Continuum, 2000), 135.

5. Erika K. Honoré and Peter H. Klopfer, *A Concise Survey of Animal Behavior* (New York: Harcourt, Brace, Jovanovich, 1990), 31–33, 137.

6. Martin Quillan, *Paul de Man* (New York: Routledge, 2001).

7. Hannah Arendt, *Eichmann in Jerusalem: A Report on the Banality of Evil* (1965; reprint, New York: Penguin, 1994).

8. Karl von Frisch, *The Dance Language and Orientation of Bees* (Cambridge, Mass.: Harvard Univ. Press, 1967).

9. Sax, *Animals in the Third Reich*, 90–91.

10. Bernd Heinrich, *Ravens in Winter* (New York: Vintage, 1989), 94.

11. Konrad Z. Lorenz, *King Solomon's Ring: New Light on Animal Ways* (New York: Thomas Y. Cromwell, 1952), xiii.

12. Ibid., x.

13. Ibid., 147.

14. Ibid., 149.

15. Sax, *Animals in the Third Reich*, 42–44.

16. Eileen Crist, *Images of Animals: Anthropomorphism and Animal Mind* (Philadelphia: Temple Univ. Press, 1999), 88–106, 211–22.

17. Föger and Taschwer, *Andere Seite des Spiegels*, 161–75.

Works Cited

Arendt, Hannah. *Eichmann in Jerusalem: A Report on the Banality of Evil.* 1965. Reprint, New York: Penguin, 1994.

Crist, Eileen. *Images of Animals: Anthropomorphism and Animal Mind.* Philadelphia: Temple Univ. Press, 1999.

Deichmann, Ute. *Biologists under Hitler.* Translated by Thomas Dunlap. Cambridge, Mass.: Harvard Univ. Press, 1996.

Föger, Benedikt, and Klaus Taschwer. *Die Andere Seite des Spiegels: Konrad Lorenz und der Nationalsozialismus.* Vienna: Czernin Verlag, 2001.

Frisch, Karl von. *The Dance Language and Orientation of Bees.* Translated by Leigh E. Chadwick. Cambridge, Mass.: Harvard Univ. Press, 1967.

Gould, James L. *Ethology: The Mechanisms and Evolution of Behavior.* New York: Norton, 1982.

Heinrich, Bernd. *Ravens in Winter.* New York: Vintage, 1989.

Honoré, Erika K., and Peter H. Klopfer. *A Concise Survey of Animal Behavior.* New York: Harcourt, Brace, Jovanovich, 1990.

Lorenz, Konrad Z. *King Solomon's Ring: New Light on Animal Ways.* Translated by Marjorie Kerr Wilson. New York: Thomas Y. Crowell, 1952.

Quillan, Martin. *Paul de Man.* New York: Routledge, 2001.

Sax, Boria. *Animals in the Third Reich: Pets, Scapegoats, and the Holocaust.* New York: Continuum, 2000.

Chapter 15

The Ethical and Responsible Conduct of Science and the Question of Political Ideology

Konrad Lorenz in the Field of Ethology

Lynette A. Hart

Issues regarding the irresponsible conduct of science in recent decades have forced the scientific community to attend particularly to violations of ethical issues concerning the management of data, plagiarism, fraud, fabrication of data, and a disrespect for guidelines that protect animal or human subjects participating in research. The use of ostensibly accurate data obtained under cruel or unethical conditions, such as scientific and medical findings from scientists in Japan during World War II[1] or under the Nazi regime, has not been addressed. Even today, there are vestiges of this issue playing out in controversies involving the use of human embryos for medical research.

In this chapter, I focus on ethical questions that have been raised concerning Konrad Lorenz and his activities during the Nazi era as they relate to his historic stature and role in helping establish the field of animal behavior and launching it into public awareness and acceptance. Julian Huxley called Lorenz the father of modern ethology,[2] a field that studies the evolutionary bases of behavior. Indeed, Lorenz was the first "to try to assess what existing science could contribute to our understanding of the normal natural behaviour of animals under undisturbed conditions."[3] His efforts to popularize animal behavior, and to convey to the public the magic of it, continue to affect prevalent views of animals in society today. But how do we regard such accomplishments given the disclosure of possible ethical compromises in his past behavior?

More recent controversies bringing ethics to the forefront have involved compelling accusations of misconduct in 1980 at four major research centers in the United States. These accusations led to the establishment of the Office of Scientific Integrity in 1989, which was replaced in 1992 by the Office of Research Integrity; both offices have focused on fraud, fabrication, and plagiarism.[4] Such cases continue to arise;[5] the Office of Research Integrity has considered over two thousand allegations since 1992, formally investigating about four hundred of these.[6]

In this vigilant climate, the National Academy of Sciences published *On Being a Scientist*, which described the risk of self-deception, the significance of values in science, and the importance of appropriate intentions.[7] Discussions of responsible conduct have sometimes included consideration of the responsible care of animals in research.[8] National Institutes of Health Training grants for graduate and postdoctoral students carry a responsibility for the recipients to provide instruction in the responsible conduct of science. Scientific journals have been confronted with the possible conflicts of interest of their authors, a topic of growing concern.[9]

Related to these major issues is the concern about the scientific findings of those who sympathize with reprehensible causes or have unsavory pasts but did not plagiarize, fabricate, defraud, or directly participate in the abuse of humans or animals for scientific purposes. Konrad Lorenz conducted valuable work with enduring implications. He provided the core ideas for the field of ethology—proposing that the evolution of behavior could be studied with the same principles as the evolution of morphological structures—which has evolved into behavioral ecology, evolutionary psychology, behavioral neuroscience, and developmental psychobiology. However, at least as early as the 1950s, it became evident to leaders within his field that Lorenz had engaged in questionable activities during the Nazi era.

Scrutiny of Lorenz Vis-à-Vis the Nazi Era

Perhaps reflecting the increased emphasis on responsible conduct of science in recent years, the recent book by Boria Sax, *Animals in the Third Reich: Pets, Scapegoats, and the Holocaust*, includes a political biography of Konrad Lorenz—a pillar in the emerging field of ethology during the early Nazi era.[10] This book provides an occasion to examine how scientists, after their ignominious downfall during that era,[11] have dealt with Lorenz, given his involvement with the Nazi regime. Indeed, these issues of inappropriate medical experimentation still resound in Germany, resulting in a recent apology,[12] and continue to limit scientific study.[13] Sax argues (see his chapter in this section) that once Lorenz's contamination with the Nazi regime becomes widely known, his work will lose respect, and that the resulting impact will reverberate adversely throughout the field of ethology. Although Sax bases his criticism of Lorenz (in his book and chapter in this volume) primarily on material reported recently by Ute Deichmann, Benedikt Föger, and Klaus Taschwer,[14] in fact, Lorenz's association with Nazis was discussed openly and has received serious consideration for decades.

In terms of scientific contributions, Konrad Lorenz is credited with two major conceptual advances. He profiled the inherited species-typical bases of behavior, drawing parallels between the biological bases of behavior and body traits such as eye color, plumage, or body size. This aspect of animal behavior is still often conventionally referred to as ethology; it emphasizes the role of natural selection in shaping behavior. Second, he is well known for profiling the sensitive periods for the early experiential effects of imprinting. Later in life he focused upon aggression. He and Niko Tinbergen (among others) were credited with founding ethology, emphasizing field studies of animal behavior, which Lorenz paired with a concern for what he called a behavioral decline as animals were domesticated.

As a scientist highly visible to the public, Lorenz's leadership role and activities during the Nazi era have been scrutinized by philosophers in recent decades, particularly since he received a Nobel prize in 1973. Theodora Kalikow criticized Lorenz's involvement in Nazism, initially in a review of a biography of Lorenz by Alec Nisbett and later in a more extensive analysis.[15] Lorenz's family's beliefs and his professional struggles in Austria, she argues, may have inclined him to accept

Nazism.[16] She criticizes his concept that instinctive behavior patterns play a role in human behavior as in animal behavior and his attempt to draw implications that would contribute to peaceful resolutions of human conflict. She also was critical of his "aesthetic valuational response" to physical characteristics reflecting attractiveness.[17] From his work she extrapolates a concern that Lorenz was duping his colleagues: "Thus those ethologists, sociologists, and popularizers who have adopted Lorenz's traditional biologistic view of society have also accepted, wittingly or unwittingly, its presuppositions, its implications, and its history of use in justifying race-political ways of thought and action."[18] Her concern regarding his influence among scientists is similar in some respects to the sentiments expressed by Sax (in this volume).

Recently, a book published in German has provided biographical data on Konrad Lorenz and his association with Nazism.[19] In reviewing this book, Thomas Potthast points out some additional troubling information—that from 1941 to 1944 in Poland, as a physician and psychiatrist, Lorenz "participated in an investigation of racial psychology of alleged Polish-German *Mischlinge*, separating them into different categories of future usefulness."[20] On the whole, however, Potthast concludes that "not much is new [in the book] except some more telling letters alluding to Lorenz's strong affiliation with German-ness and the biological politics of Nazi Germany" and that the book aims at "the still large camp of naive defenders of the moral and political authority of Lorenz."[21]

Such far-reaching criticism of Lorenz's politics by philosophers and historians has been almost nonexistent from his scientific colleagues. As a notable exception, Peter Klopfer, a scholar of animal behavior and ethology devoted more to the experiential aspects of behavior than the genetical control aspects, has written concerning the politics of ethology. In particular, he has pointed to the political influences on Lorenz and argued that the fundamental ideas of ethology were corrupt.[22] Klopfer's line of inquiry seems to have been largely ignored by his colleagues in animal behavior, however. He stands alone in expressing a view reminiscent of historians Föger and Taschwer and Kalikow, implying that scientists are being misled or even duped by Lorenz's work: "Lorenz defined the fundamentals of ethology, and it is the source of his ideas that we now have reason to believe were corrupt."[23] In his book *Politics and People in Ethology*, Klopfer relays some unappealing and anti-Semitic anecdotes regarding Lorenz.[24]

From a broader scientific perspective, the importance of genetic behavioral predispositions continues as a contentious issue today in disputes involving thinkers such as E. O. Wilson, often termed the father of sociobiology,[25] and Richard Dawkins of "selfish gene" fame partnered against proponents of the learned and environmental determinants of behavior, such as Richard Lewontin and Stephen Jay Gould, arguing on both biologically substantive and moral objections.[26] Although these four spokesmen agree in many respects, Wilson and Dawkins lean more heavily on the importance of genetics, a position sometimes labeled by detractors as social Darwinism. In contrast, Lewontin and Gould favor a greater emphasis on the role of learning and experience.

Not only animal behaviorists but also many of the humanists and social scientists considering these issues sometimes view Lorenz as an important link between Darwin and the philosophical position today held by Wilson and Dawkins. Thus Richard Lerner argued that the ideology of genetic determinism played a role in the Nazis' actions, and he further expressed a concern that E. O. Wilson's book *Sociobiology* represented a rebirth of biological determinism.[27] The sharp, critical tone of Lerner's book was echoed in a responding review that assumed an equally extreme posture of accusation, this time directed against Lerner along with some others.[28] Attacks on Wilson have included a signed statement by respected leaders published in the *New York Review of Books* drawing links to eugenics policies that led to the establishment of gas chambers in Nazi Germany.[29] Stephen Jay Gould, perhaps seeing that these attacks could damage the evolutionary contribution of Darwinism, in his last years pulled back somewhat in criticizing sociobiology.[30]

The contentious issue of genetic versus environmental influences, or nature versus nurture, is a largely dead issue in animal behavior because of the acknowledged interactions between genes and environment. If current advances in molecular biology are any indication, this debate will prove increasingly nonproductive as genes will surely be found that control behavior just as they affect anatomy and physiology. An issue seemingly kept alive by politicians, scientists, and philosophers, how we regard Lorenz now is complicated, which in turn raises philosophical and scientific questions regarding how we might best view his work today. Clearly, the conceptual contributions of Lorenz have almost no relevance to the debate on genes versus environment. Looking through a philosophical lens raises the following questions:

> Does guilt by association with an unsavory regime imply tainted science or conclusions?
>
> Do acts of government implicate others as implicit participants?
>
> Should Lorenz have been tried for war crimes?
>
> Should Lorenz be viewed as a Nazi in the worst sense?
>
> Should we have buried his scientific results (a question that has arisen in more stark terms with the medical findings from concentration camps)?
>
> Since the findings cannot be buried, should we attempt to disqualify the science or discount its value, even parts that have stood the test of time?

I will not address what to do with the information about the Nazi alliances of Lorenz but will consider two questions: (1) Is there an attempt in ethology and animal behavior to bury the work of Lorenz? and (2) Does his work provide such an essential underpinning for the field of ethology that discrediting the work, for whatever reason, would have devastating results to the field? As I will show, a certain contention involving the political past of Lorenz lasted within the field of ethology for decades but was addressed in a circumscribed manner that appears now to have come to a resolution. Critics of Lorenz who were ethologists stopped short of invoking his past alliance with Nazi groups, instead focusing their sharp criticisms on the content of his works. Such attacks, sometimes even vilification, are part of the scientific process and not unique to Lorenz.

In *Animals in the Third Reich*, Boria Sax recounts some of the historical events that place Konrad Lorenz within the context of the Third Reich. As Sax reviews, Lorenz participated in the concepts and social networks of the Third Reich environment, received governmental funding and stature, and voluntarily endorsed some Nazi concepts within his writings. Most people today would agree that Lorenz made grave mistakes in this regard, yet his research contributions were seminal enough to warrant the Nobel Prize in Physiology or Medicine that he shared with Karl von Frisch and Niko Tinbergen in 1973. Lorenz himself acknowledged his previous errors in the form of an apology within an autobiographical statement he provided as a Nobel Prize winner: "I did a very ill-advised thing soon after the Germans had invaded Austria. I wrote about the dangers of domestication and in order to be understood, I couched my writing in the worst of Nazi-terminology. I do not want to extenuate this action. I did, indeed, believe that some good might come of the new rulers. . . . None of us as much as suspected that the word 'selection,' when used by these rulers, meant murder. I regret those writings not so much for the undeniable discredit they reflect on my person as for their effect of hampering the future recognition of the dangers of domestication."[31]

This troubled him, even during the time of the Third Reich. In *King Solomon's Ring*, he retrospectively quotes himself from a paper published in 1935: "'The day will come when two warring factions will be faced with the possibility of each wiping the other out completely. The day may come when the whole of mankind is divided into two such opposing camps. Shall we then behave like doves or like wolves? The fate of mankind will be settled by the answer to this question.' We may well be apprehensive."[32]

Lorenz and His Accomplishments

Using a scientific lens within the field of the study of behavior, we can assess Lorenz's work and its value. Some measures commonly used in such an assessment are (1) laying a groundwork for an emerging field, (2) inspiring others to contribute to the field, and (3) facilitating collaboration with others. Applying these measures to Lorenz, we note that he already was a pioneer in the 1930s and early 1940s. As mentioned elsewhere in this volume, he and Tinbergen offered a view of animals as being fully sentient and helped legitimize fieldwork (Bruce Hackett, this volume).

In many papers and books, Donald Dewsbury has carefully scrutinized the "biogeography of ideas" across North America and Europe during the development of the field of ethology.[33] The field of comparative psychology developed in North America and initially focused on studying the effects of learning on behavior. As an example, the "Chicago Five," a "family" of psychobiologists, worked with

Table 15.1

Number of Times Publications by Lorenz and Some Contemporaries Were Cited in
Other Publications, as of 2001

Scientist	Total Citations	Number of Publications Cited	Most Cited Publication
Konrad Lorenz	3,225 (2,680 English 545 German)	32	*On Aggression,* 1966 (1,214)
Niko Tinbergen	3,824	29	*Study of Instinct,* 1951 (1,401)
Karl von Frisch	101	1	*Dance Language and Orientation of Bees,* 1967 (101)
Daniel Lehrman	695	8	*Quarterly Review of Biology,* 1953 (216)
T. S. Schneirla	308	9	*Army Ants: A Study in Social Organiza-tion,* 1971 (98)

Note: Data were obtained by searching reference citations in the Web of Science data-base. In some cases, the numbers listed in the "Number of Publications Cited" column include the multiple reprinting of papers.

Karl Lashley, a pioneer on the neural basis of learning, at the University of Chi-cago, sharing commonalities in their work, including beliefs that psychology is the study of both behavior and the mind and that understanding cognitive processes is focal to psychology.[34] By contrast, ethology evolved in Europe and emphasized the evolution of behavioral traits; led by Lorenz and Tinbergen, European ethologists were also to some extent seen as emphasizing fieldwork, even though Lorenz did little conventional fieldwork.[35] Over time, on both sides of the Atlantic, the English-speaking and Dutch scientists in particular came to a meeting of the minds as the fields of ethology, animal behavior, and comparative psychology grew into a single discipline, with a melding of the ethological and experiential viewpoints, acceler-ated after World War II by American scientists traveling to Europe.[36] Yet even as late as the 1950s, course work in the field of animal behavior was not prevalent on U.S. campuses. Few colleges or universities in the United States offered courses in animal behavior, and the field was not well known despite the number of scientific contributors to it documented by Dewsbury.[37]

The awarding of the 1973 Nobel Prize to Lorenz, Tinbergen, and von Frisch signaled that animal behavior had become established as a science. It was an acknowledgment of the development of ethology in Europe, a tradition focusing

Table 15.2

Rates (Counts) of References or Indexed Citations to Lorenz and Some Contemporaries in Selected Behavior Texts

Text	Lorenz	Tinbergen	Frisch	Lehrman	Schneirla
Marler and Hamilton, 1966	(25)	1.3 (32)	0.5 (12)	0.4 (10)	0.6 (16)
Klopfer and Hailman, 1967	(6)	1.3 (8)	0.5 (3)	1.3 (8)	0.8 (5)
Hinde, 1970	(13)	1.9 (25)	0.2 (3)	0.5 (7)	0.9 (12)
McGill, 1973	(13)	1.2 (16)	0.5 (6)	0.6 (8)	0.7 (9)
Wilson, 1975	(6)	1.3 (8)	1.2 (7)	0.5 (3)	1.5 (9)
Grzimek, 1977	(33)	0.7 (22)	0.2 (7)	0.1 (3)	0.1 (3)
Alcock, 1979	(5)	1.8 (9)	0.0	0.0	0.0
Goodenough, McGuire, and Wallace, 1993	(8)	1.5 (12)	0.0	0.3 (2)	0.4 (3)
Alcock, 1998	(2)	3.5 (7)	0.0	0.0	0.0
Alcock, 2001	(1)	7.0 (7)	0.0	0.0	0.0

Note: Rates are expressed as a ratio in comparison to mentions of Lorenz. For texts with comprehensive bibliographies, counts are based on the references listed for each author. In other texts, counts are based on citations as indicated by the numbers of pages separately indexed under each author's name.

on the importance of instinct as a driving force in animal behavior.[38] Building on previous scientific work, the characteristics of species reflected the unique sensory worlds in the environments they inhabited, their *Umwelten*,[39] a concept that was evident in Lorenz's work[40] and even today has fresh utility.[41]

It was in such a context that Konrad Lorenz burst into public awareness. He achieved public recognition and inspired young people to love wildlife and to want to enter fields in which they could conduct similar studies. The powerful story of imprinting, with the memorable images of Lorenz's geese following him (see plate 1), crystallized a goal for many students and created an opportunity for people to vicariously appreciate animal behavior. The well-known photographs of Lorenz's head flanked by geese (plate 2) became symbolic of the importance of our relationships with wild animals. Even today, his books outdraw those of his contemporaries in animal behavior. Reflecting his popularity with the public, classic books by Lorenz continue to be listed on Amazon.com and carry fairly high rankings, from about #76,000 to #143,000 (Amazon.com sales rank as of October 6, 2005), far higher than three books each by his Nobel compatriots von Frisch (#253,000 to #861,000) and Tinbergen (#170,000 to #690,000) but much lower than books by well-known leaders in this field, including Charles Darwin's *Origin of Species* (#6,000) and Jane Goodall's *Reason for Hope: A Spiritual Journey* (#25,000).[42]

Ironically, though, Lorenz's scientific articles were published in German and most were not readily available in English. Today, he is relatively seldom cited in the field of animal behavior. Niko Tinbergen is more frequently cited in the scientific literature (table 15.1) and in animal behavior texts (table 15.2). One volume of papers selected by an editorial board of prominent animal behaviorists as being "classics" in the field includes three by Tinbergen, one each by Lorenz and von Frisch, and two by Lehrman.[43] John Alcock, author of a popular textbook in animal behavior, now includes only one sentimental reference to Lorenz's *King Solomon's Ring* in the most current edition of his textbook, while still citing seven references to Tinbergen's substantive work.[44] Tinbergen's four principles describing the aims and methods of ethology remain the field's foundation (see below).[45] Lorenz's hydraulic model of motivation is still well known and frequently appears within a question during doctoral oral exams. His discovery of imprinting in birds remains well known,[46] and it relates to the work of others that continues today.

While Lorenz was called the father of ethology, it was Tinbergen who became its conceptual pillar. He formulated the framework for the theoretical field of ethology, setting its four aims, which pointed toward goals requiring interdisciplinary alliances among ethologists, psychologists, and physiologists. He bridged these various worlds himself and personally created a broader community for ethology that incorporated the productive work on instinct from Europe with the insights added on learning and ontogeny from the United States. Still today, the four basic questions for animal behavior, first outlined by Tinbergen, are causation, including the underlying physiological systems; ontogeny or development, considering the interaction of the animal's genetic endowment with the environment and experiences; functional significance or adaptiveness, reflecting that behavior has been subject to natural selection; and evolution, including the comparative analyses of behavior patterns in related species.[47] The first two aims pertain to the proximate causes of behavior, mechanisms and development, and the second two consider ultimate causes, based on the evolution and adaptive value of behavior.

The historic foundation of ethology has come under sharp criticism from Eileen Crist on a linguistic basis. She argues that by describing their behavior in a technical language, ethologists moved animals from acting as subjects to being objects.[48] Whereas naturalists had used an anthropomorphic perspective, ethologists such as Lorenz presented a mechanomorphic portrayal in technical writings that was theory laden and based on the stimulus-response paradigm of behaviorism. Furthermore, ethology laid a groundwork of skepticism regarding the animal mind, abrogating the continuity and coherence of animal action for something more puppetlike and, at worst, presenting animals as behaving with some foolishness that is starkly involuntary. On the other hand, Crist allows that both Lorenz and Tinbergen assumed a more anthropomorphic stance in their popular works.

Among Lorenz, von Frisch, and Tinbergen, it was Lorenz who most captivated people who love animals. The enticing charm of his love for animals is clearly conveyed in his book *Here Am I, Where Are You: The Behavior of the Greylag Goose:*

> When I was a child, I wanted to be an owl, because owls did not have to go to bed at night. But just at that time, a book . . . made me see that owls had a great handicap. They could not swim or dive, things I had recently learned to do, and I decided right then, that I wanted to join the ranks of the waterfowl instead.
>
> My mother finally yielded to my begging and bought me one of the ducklings, although my father was against it. He felt that trusting a freshly hatched duckling to a six year old boy amounted to cruelty to animals, and he did not expect the duckling to live very long. But in this particular prognosis the great doctor turned out to be wrong. My Pipsa survived for some fifteen years, close to the maximum for a domestic duck. Even in those early days, my future wife and I had some interests in common, and she was given a duckling from the same clutch a day earlier.
>
> I can still remember, as if it were yesterday, squatting on the flagstones of our huge kitchen in Altenberg with the first duckling, just after we bought it. It was standing in front of me with its neck stretched upward and crying in a series of single-syllable distress calls. I tried to comfort it by imitating the special call a mother duck gives to summon her ducklings. The duckling broke off crying and uttered a two-syllable contact call. At that, I backed away on all fours and quacked more actively, upon which the duckling waddled up to me. As it drew near, it uttered the contact call with increasing frequency, and I replied in kind.[49]

Such writing appeals to anyone who loves animals. Lorenz himself became imprinted on and wrote about the greylag geese and their life stories, including their courtship and bonding, their jealousy, grief, and hatred, and he built his life and home around them. He perceived the similarities among animals and humans and readily wrote of the betrothals, marriages, and grief expressed by other animals. His book *On Aggression* includes a groundbreaking chapter titled "The Bond," which presents a framework prescient to the establishment of the field of the human-animal bond, even including a discussion of the essential role of social support and contact for both nonhuman animals and humans.[50]

With this work, he offered himself as a kind of everyman, loving animals and building a lifelong career around them. He expressed feelings that many people have about animals by noting behaviors that suggested animals and humans have similar emotions. Somewhat audaciously, he wrote about animals' emotions and relationships long before the subtleties of animal consciousness were documented, as in the following passage from *Man Meets Dog:*

> In the weeks that immediately followed Bully's death, I really began to understand what it is that makes naive people believe in the ghosts of their dead. The constant sound throughout years of the

dog trotting at my heels had left such a lasting impression on my
brain . . . that for weeks afterwards, as if with my own ears, I heard
him pattering after me.[51]

Complications

Viewed through a scientific lens, the work of Lorenz at the very least sharpened
interaction among scientists. Immediately upon meeting in 1936, Lorenz and
Tinbergen "clicked," as described later by Tinbergen.[52] Both were social catalysts,
enjoying the dynamic dialogues and creative collaborations that science offered.
Tinbergen visited the United States in 1938, meeting Ernst Mayr, Frank Beach,
Ted Schneirla, and Robert Yerkes.[53] Like Lorenz, he had the ability to engage the
public;[54] his descriptions of studying wasps, butterflies, and birds revealed captivat-
ing experiences with animals (which were popularized in animal stories for children).[55] Like Lorenz, Tinbergen illustrated his writing with appealing sketches,
posing and answering questions such as "Why do we watch birds?" The two men
were a match, with Lorenz providing the broad knowledge of a naturalist, innova-
tive ideas, and the ability to share the significance of emotional linkages to animals
with the public. Tinbergen envisioned the perfect elegant experiments to test each
idea, over years honed an overview of the field, bridged the separate fields of ethology in the United States and Europe, and devised a framework for the field of ethology and behavior that clearly established its goals for decades. His warm, engaging
manner recruited young people to the field and was in sharp contrast to the strict
rule-setting attitude pervading the writings of Frank Beach, a comparative psychologist in the United States.[56] Both Lorenz and Tinbergen valued their relationships
with a wide range of other scientists from whom they gained creative grist. Both
lived long, productive lives, perhaps more savored due to their similar experiences
as prisoners of war; Tinbergen was captive for months, and Lorenz for years.

Tinbergen offered a perspective on Lorenz's particular contribution: "Lorenz's
approach appealed by its comprehensive nature. . . . Many more animal types were
considered than before; ethologists aimed at describing and analysing all complex behaviour shown by animals in their natural surroundings; finally they were
interested in function and evolution of behaviour as well as in its causation."[57]

"Lorenz's notion of innate behaviour clashed with the views of most American psychologists, who considered learning, especially early experiences, as the
most important process controlling the development of behaviour of the individual."[58] It was in this context that Danny Lehrman, at the age of thirty-four, tack-
led the theories of Konrad Lorenz in his sweeping critique that remains a classic
today.[59] "He argued," Tinbergen wrote, "that it is heuristically unhelpful to classify behaviour patterns, or parts of them, as either innate or learnt. Instead, the
developmental processes ought to be analysed, even of those behaviours classified
by ethologists as innate. The urge to disentangle such developmental processes is
lulled to sleep by the rigid dichotomous classification of two behaviour types."[60]

Lehrman was a student of Schneirla, who was known to dislike the ethology
of Lorenz and Tinbergen for ignoring individual differences.[61] Although the Nazi

issues were not mentioned in Lehrman's article, evidence suggests that they may have fueled the attack. "Lehrman . . . and Schneirla . . . openly resented Lorenz's alleged Nazi sympathies, these having been revealed in two articles which were not listed in Lorenz's bibliographies for many years."[62] In discussing Lorenz's hydraulic model, Lehrman "hinted at other than empirical influences at play in the construction of the model," revealed in the little-known articles mentioned above.[63] One of these was expanded upon in Lehrman's paper.[64] Interestingly, early drafts of Lehrman's paper (no longer available) apparently addressed Lorenz's Nazi connections, but these points were deleted from the manuscript prior to submission following consultation with colleagues.[65]

For Lorenz, Lehrman's attack struck deep, and he wrote a small book seeking to address some of the criticisms.[66] The sparring persisted across the Atlantic, and anyone hearing Lehrman speak was introduced to these issues. By 1965, Lehrman, an articulate and colorful man, was entrancing students and other audiences with descriptions of his own seminal work, imitating the bow-coo behavior of ring doves and offering incisive arguments for the crucial role of developmental experience in shaping behavior.[67] His papers continue to be cited at a higher rate than his mentor Schneirla, despite Lehrman's premature death in 1972. Not surprisingly, his most-cited paper is the critique of Lorenz he wrote as a young man (see table 15.1).[68]

Through the years, Lehrman continued to expand on the nature-nurture issue, bringing more energy to the discussion of Lorenz's work than one might have expected. While this may have been due to the historical association of Lorenz with the Nazi era, political overtones never entered the verbal or written dialogue. Lehrman worked closely with colleagues at the American Museum of Natural History, including Schneirla, Tobach, and Aronson, all his seniors, emphasizing learning and early experience. Lehrman's work facilitated launching the new field of hormones and behavior in which Beach even stressed a perceived influence of learning on the hormonal control of behavior, a perception that has not been borne out in subsequent research.[69] The conflict with Lorenz sharpened the dialogue among scientists and improved the science, requiring more finely honed arguments from all concerned. Following Lehrman's death, a retrospective discussion of the relationship between Lorenz and Lehrman by colleague Colin Beer carried no allusion to the Nazi issue.[70]

Like Lorenz, Lehrman dazzled with his intellect, but Lehrman's community was within the field, whereas Lorenz was known by the public as well as in the professional arena. Both men built their concepts on studies of birds. In their hands, greylag geese and ring doves shed light on basic principles regarding animal behavior.

Resolution

In 1970, shortly before his premature death, Lehrman offered somewhat of an apology for his attacks on Lorenz:

> When I look over my 1953 critique of his theory I perceive elements
> of hostility. It does fail to express what, even at that time, I regarded
> as Lorenz's enormous contribution to the formulation of the prob-
> lems of evolution and function of behavior, and his accomplish-
> ment in creating a school based upon the conception of species-
> specific behavior as part of the animal's adaptation to its natural
> environment.[71]

Though Schneirla and Lehrman were younger than Lorenz, ironically, they both predeceased him.

Toward the end of his career, Lorenz was recognized for fostering and legiti-mizing the scientific study of the human-animal bond. In Vienna, on the occasion of his eightieth birthday, he was honored at an international symposium for his contributions to the human-animal bond. The symposium was led by the patri-arch of the new field of the human-animal bond, Leo Bustad, dean of the Wash-ington State University School of Veterinary Medicine. Like Lorenz, Bustad had been a prisoner of war in World War II, but in a German camp; he suffered from post-traumatic stress disorder. We do not know, but would guess, that he under-stood that Lorenz had a somewhat checkered past yet chose to take a path of reconciliation and move ahead.

His acknowledgment of Lorenz, whom he called a "true pioneer relative to the human-animal bond,"[72] offered several quotations on the human-animal bond from the writings of Lorenz:

> "The wish to keep an animal usually arises from a general longing for
> a bond with nature." "It seems like a re-establishment of the immedi-
> ate bond with that unconscious omniscience that we call nature."
> "This bond is analogous with those human functions that go hand
> in hand with the emotions of love and friendship in the purest and
> noblest forms." "These behaviour patterns of an objectively demon-
> strable mutual attachment constitute a personal tie." ". . . a bond
> which shows a mysterious relationship to the other bond between
> human beings and which seem to us the strongest and most beauti-
> ful on earth."[73]

With a checkered and unsavory past at best, a collaboration with one of the most evil political enterprises of modern civilization at worst, the legitimate and impor-tant scientific contributions of Lorenz spurred a strong urge within the science of animal behavior to find a resolution. The resulting scientific findings became a uniting element from which everyone benefited.

Lorenz also effectively communicated the importance of animal behavior to a broad public. His popular books captivated many, especially those who related to his careful observations and his love of animals, as well as his tendency to ascribe human emotions such as love and grief to animals.

At least in the case of Lorenz, it seems that rather than the unsavory past burying the science, the science has prevailed and advanced. The unsavory past, while giving animal behaviorists, sociologists, and philosophers of science much grist for the intellectual mill, has been buried. When it comes to the responsible conduct of science, if nothing else, these issues—which have emerged several times and probably will again—profile an area left out of the dialogue, which heretofore has focused on instances of fraudulent science, stolen science, and compromised science arising from financial conflicts of interest. Clearly, Lorenz is not the only prominent scientist with tainted political associations.

Notes

Donald Dewsbury generously shared references and perspectives on this topic and critiqued several earlier drafts; for this, I am deeply grateful. This chapter also has benefited from extensive discussions with Benjamin Hart. David Anderson reviewed and offered helpful suggestions on an earlier draft.

1. Peter Williams and David Wallace, *Unit 731: Japan's Secret Biological Warfare in World War II* (New York: Free Press, 1989); Sheldon H. Harris, *Factories of Death: Japanese Biological Warfare, 1932–1945, and the American Cover-Up* (New York: Routledge, 1994).

2. Julian S. Huxley, "Lorenzian Ethology," *Zeitschrift für Tierpsychologie* 20 (1963): 402–9.

3. Niko Tinbergen, "Ethology," in *The Animal in Its World: Explorations of an Ethologist, 1932–1972*, vol. 2, *Laboratory Experiments and General Papers* (Cambridge, Mass.: Harvard Univ. Press, 1972), 131–32.

4. Department of Health and Human Services, "Office of Research Integrity, U.S. Department of Health and Human Services," 2002, http://ori.dhhs.gov/about/history.shtml, accessed December 16, 2005.

5. See, for example, Constance Holden, "Psychologist Made Up Sex Bias Results," *Science* 294, no. 5551 (Dec. 21, 2001): 2457.

6. Department of Health and Human Services, "Office of Research Integrity."

7. National Academy of Sciences, *On Being a Scientist* (Washington, D.C.: National Academy Press, 1989).

8. NASA, "NASA Principles for the Ethical Care and Use of Animals," 1999, http://www.nal.usda.gov/awic/legislat/nasa.htm, accessed October 5, 2005; Lynette A. Hart, ed., *Responsible Conduct with Animals in Research* (New York: Oxford Univ. Press, 1998).

9. Eliot Marshall, "Journals Joust over Conflict-of-Interest Rules," *Science* 276, no. 5312 (Apr. 25, 1997): 524.

10. Boria Sax, *Animals in the Third Reich: Pets, Scapegoats, and the Holocaust* (New York: Continuum, 2000).

11. Once information was disseminated about the Nazi atrocities, including their cruel and immoral experimentation on humans and animals and their use of technology

to kill great numbers of people efficiently, a widespread suspicion of the scientific and medical community in Germany and Austria at that time was aroused.

12. Robert Koenig, "Max Planck Offers Historic Apology," *Science* 292, no. 5524 (June 15, 2001): 1979–82.

13. Robert Koenig, "Watson Urges 'Put Hitler behind Us,'" *Science* 276, no. 5314 (May 9, 1997): 892.

14. Ute Deichmann, *Biologists under Hitler*, trans. Thomas Dunlap (Cambridge, Mass.: Harvard Univ. Press, 1996); Benedikt Föger and Klaus Taschwer, *Die Andere Seite des Spiegels: Konrad Lorenz und der Nationalsozialismus* (Vienna: Czernin, 2001).

15. Theodora J. Kalikow, "Konrad Lorenz's 'Brown Past': A Reply to Alec Nisbett," *Journal of the History of the Behavioral Sciences* 14 (1978): 173–79; Alec Nisbett, *Konrad Lorenz: A Biography* (New York: Harcourt Brace Jovanovich, 1977); Theodora J. Kalikow, "Konrad Lorenz's Ethological Theory: Explanation and Ideology, 1938–1943," *Journal of the History of Biology* 16, no. 1 (1983): 39–73.

16. Kalikow, "Konrad Lorenz's Ethological Theory," 56.

17. Ibid., 65.

18. Ibid., 72–73.

19. Föger and Taschwer, *Andere Seite des Spiegels*.

20. Thomas Potthast, "Review of Benedikt Föger and Klaus Taschwer, *Die Andere Seite des Spiegels*," *Journal of the History of Biology* 35, no. 1 (2002): 195.

21. Ibid., 195, 196.

22. Peter Klopfer, "Konrad Lorenz and the National Socialists: On the Politics of Ethology," *International Society for Comparative Psychology* 7 (1994): 202.

23. Ibid.

24. Peter H. Klopfer, *Politics and People in Ethology: Personal Reflections on the Study of Animal Behavior* (Lewisburg, Pa.: Bucknell Univ. Press, 1999), 9, 11, 41, 121.

25. E. O. Wilson, *Sociobiology: The New Synthesis* (Cambridge, Mass.: Harvard Univ. Press, 1975).

26. Robert J. Richards, *Darwin and the Emergence of Evolutionary Theories of Mind and Behavior* (Chicago: Univ. of Chicago Press, 1987), 544–45.

27. Richard M. Lerner, *Final Solutions: Biology, Prejudice, and Genocide* (Univ. Park: Pennsylvania State Univ. Press, 1992).

28. J. Philippe Rushton, "Final Solutions: Biology, Prejudice, and Genocide" (book reviews), *Society* 34 (Mar.–Apr. 1997): 78–83.

29. Tom Bethel, "Against Sociobiology," *First Things: A Monthly Journal of Religion and Public Life* 109 (Jan. 2001): 20.

30. Ibid., 23.

31. Konrad Lorenz, "Konrad Lorenz: Autobiography," 1973/2000, http://www.nobel.se/medicine/laureates/1973/lorenz-autobio.html, accessed Aug. 2, 2001.

32. Konrad Lorenz, *King Solomon's Ring: New Light on Animal Ways*, trans. Marjorie Kerr Wilson (New York: Thomas Y. Crowell, 1952), 199.

33. Donald A. Dewsbury, "Americans in Europe: The Role of Travel in the Spread of European Ethology after World War II," *Animal Behaviour* 49 (1995): 1649.

34. Donald A. Dewsbury, "The Chicago Five: A Family Group of Integrative Psychobiologists," *History of Psychology* 5 (2002): 22.

35. Donald A. Dewsbury, "Comparative Psychology and Ethology: A Reassessment," *American Psychologist* 47 (1992): 208–15.

36. Dewsbury, "Americans in Europe."

37. Donald A. Dewsbury, "A Brief History of the Study of Animal Behavior in North America," *Perspectives in Ethology* 8 (1989): 85–122.

38. Konrad Lorenz, "The Establishment of the Instinct Concept," in *Studies in Animal and Human Behaviour* 1, trans. Robert Martin (Cambridge, Mass.: Harvard Univ. Press, 1970), 259–315; Niko Tinbergen, *The Study of Instinct* (Oxford: Clarendon Press, 1951).

39. J. von Uexküll, "A Stroll through the Worlds of Animals and Men: A Picture Book of Invisible Worlds," in *Instinctive Behavior: The Development of a Modern Concept*, trans. and ed. Claire H. Schiller (New York: International Universities Press, 1957), 5–80.

40. Konrad Lorenz, "Companions as Factors in the Bird's Environment," in *Studies in Animal and Human Behavior* 1, trans. Robert Martin (Cambridge, Mass.: Harvard Univ. Press, 1970), 101–258.

41. Correigh M. Greene, Donald H. Owings, Lynette A. Hart, and A. Peter Klimley, eds., "Revisiting the *Umwelt*: Environments of Animal Communication," *Journal of Comparative Psychology* 116, no. 2 (2002): 113–214.

42. Charles Darwin, *The Origin of Species* (1859; reprint, New York: Grammercy, 1998); Jane Goodall with Phillip Berman, *Reason for Hope: A Spiritual Journey* (New York: Warner Books, 1999).

43. Lynne D. Houck and Lee C. Drickamer, eds., *Foundations of Animal Behavior: Classic Papers with Commentaries* (Chicago: Univ. of Chicago Press, 1996).

44. John Alcock, *Animal Behavior: An Evolutionary Approach*, 7th ed. (Sunderland, Mass.: Sinauer Associates, 2001).

45. Tinbergen, *Study of Instinct*; Niko Tinbergen, "On Aims and Methods of Ethology," *Zeitschrift für Tierpsychologie* 20 (1963): 410–33.

46. See, for instance, Konrad Lorenz, "Der Kumpan in der Umwelt des Vogels," *Journal für Ornithologie* 83, nos. 2–3 (1935): 137–215 and 289–413. For an English translation, see Lorenz, "Companions as Factors."

47. Tinbergen, "On Aims and Methods."

48. Eileen Crist, "The Ethological Constitution of Animals as Natural Objects: The Technical Writings of Konrad Lorenz and Nikolaas Tinbergen," *Biology and Philosophy* 13, no. 1 (1998): 61–102.

49. Konrad Lorenz, *Here Am I, Where Are You? The Behavior of the Greylag Goose*, trans. R. D. Martin (New York: Harcourt Brace Jovanovich, 1988), 1–2.

50. Konrad Lorenz, "The Bond," in *On Aggression*, trans. Marjorie Kerr Wilson (New York: Harcourt, Brace & World, 1966), 165–219.

51. Konrad Lorenz, *Man Meets Dog*, trans. Marjorie Kerr Wilson (Baltimore: Penguin Books, 1953), 196.

52. Nikolaas Tinbergen, "Nikolaas Tinbergen—Autobiography," 1973, http://www.nobel.se/medicine/laureates/1973/tinbergen-autobio.html, accessed Aug. 2, 2001.

53. Ibid.

54. Niko Tinbergen, *The Herring Gull's World: A Study of the Social Behavior of Birds* (1953; reprint, New York: Lyons Press, 1989); Niko Tinbergen, *Curious Naturalists* (New York: Basic Books, 1958); Niko Tinbergen, *The Animal in Its World: Explorations of an Ethologist, 1932–1972*, vols. 1 and 2 (Cambridge, Mass.: Harvard Univ. Press, 1972).

55. Niko Tinbergen, *Bird Life* (London: Oxford Univ. Press, 1954).

56. Donald A. Dewsbury, "Rhetorical Strategies in the Presentation of Ethology and Comparative Psychology in Magazines after World War II," *Science in Context* 10 (1997): 367–86.

57. Tinbergen, "Ethology," 133.

58. Ibid., 134.

59. Daniel S. Lehrman, "A Critique of Konrad Lorenz's Theory of Instinctive Behavior," *Quarterly Review of Biology* 28, no. 4 (1953): 337–63.

60. Tinbergen, "Ethology," 135.

61. Dewsbury, "Chicago Five," 27–29.

62. Klopfer, "Konrad Lorenz and the National Socialists," 203.

63. Klopfer, *Politics and People in Ethology*, 58.

64. Lehrman, "Critique," 354.

65. Donald A. Dewsbury, pers. comm., 2002.

66. Konrad Lorenz, *Evolution and Modification of Behavior* (Chicago: Univ. of Chicago Press, 1965).

67. Daniel S. Lehrman, "Interaction between Internal and External Environments in the Regulation of the Reproductive Cycle of the Ring Dove," in *Sex and Behavior*, ed. Frank A. Beach (New York: John Wiley, 1965), 355–80.

68. Web of Science web site, http://isiknowledge.com, accessed October 5, 2005.

69. Benjamin L. Hart, "Gonadal Androgen and Sociosexual Behavior of Male Mammals: A Comparative Analysis," *Psychological Bulletin* 81 (1974): 383–400.

70. Colin G. Beer, "Was Professor Lehrman an Ethologist?" *Animal Behaviour* 23 (1975): 957–64.

71. Daniel S. Lehrman, "Semantic and Conceptual Issues in the Nature-Nurture Problem," in *Development and Evolution of Behavior: Essays in Memory of T. C. Schneirla*,

ed. L. R. Aronson, E. Tobach, D. S. Lehrman, and J. S. Rosenblatt (San Francisco: W. H. Freeman, 1970), 17–52.

72. Leo Bustad, "Symposium Summary," in *The Human-Pet Relationship: International Symposium on the Occasion of the 80th Birthday of Nobel Prize Winner Prof. Ddr. Konrad Lorenz Proceedings* (Vienna: Institute for Interdisciplinary Research on the Human-Pet Relationship, 1985), 166.

73. Lorenz, "Bond."

Works Cited

Alcock, John. *Animal Behavior: An Evolutionary Approach*, 2d ed. Sunderland, Mass.: Sinauer Associates, 1979.

———. *Animal Behavior: An Evolutionary Approach*, 6th ed. Sunderland, Mass.: Sinauer Associates, 1998.

———. *Animal Behavior: An Evolutionary Approach*, 7th ed. Sunderland, Mass.: Sinauer Associates, 2001.

Beer, Colin G. "Was Professor Lehrman an Ethologist?" *Animal Behaviour* 23 (1975): 957–64.

Bethel, Tom. "Against Sociobiology." *First Things: A Monthly Journal of Religion and Public Life* 109 (Jan. 2001): 18–24.

Bustad, Leo. "Symposium Summary." In *The Human-Pet Relationship: International Symposium on the Occasion of the 80th Birthday of Nobel Prize Winner Prof. Ddr. Konrad Lorenz Proceedings*, 166–74. Vienna: Institute for Interdisciplinary Research on the Human-Pet Relationship, 1985.

Crist, Eileen. "The Ethological Constitution of Animals as Natural Objects: The Technical Writings of Konrad Lorenz and Nikolaas Tinbergen." *Biology and Philosophy* 13, no. 1 (1998): 61–102.

Darwin, Charles. *The Origin of Species*. 1859. Reprint, New York: Grammercy, 1998.

Deichmann, Ute. *Biologists under Hitler*. Translated by Thomas Dunlap. Cambridge, Mass.: Harvard Univ. Press, 1996.

Dewsbury, Donald A. "Americans in Europe: The Role of Travel in the Spread of European Ethology after World War II." *Animal Behaviour* 49 (1995): 1649–63.

———. "A Brief History of the Study of Animal Behavior in North America." *Perspectives in Ethology* 8 (1989): 85–122.

———. "The Chicago Five: A Family Group of Integrative Psychobiologists." *History of Psychology* 5 (2002): 16–37.

———. "Comparative Psychology and Ethology: A Reassessment." *American Psychologist* 47 (1992): 208–15.

———. "Rhetorical Strategies in the Presentation of Ethology and Comparative Psychology in Magazines after World War II." *Science in Context* 10 (1997): 367–86.

Föger, Benedikt, and Klaus Taschwer. *Die Andere Seite des Spiegels: Konrad Lorenz und der Nationalsozialismus*. Vienna: Czernin, 2001.

Frisch, Karl von. *The Dance Language and Orientation of Bees*. Translated by Leigh E. Chadwick. 1967. Reprint, Cambridge, Mass.: Harvard Univ. Press, 1993.

Goodall, Jane, with Phillip Berman. *Reason for Hope: A Spiritual Journey*. New York: Warner Books, 1999.

Goodenough, Judith, Betty McGuire, and Robert A. Wallace. *Perspectives on Animal Behavior*. New York: John Wiley & Sons, 1993.

Greene, Correigh M., Donald H. Owings, Lynette A. Hart, and A. Peter Klimley, eds. "Revisiting the *Umwelt*: Environments of Animal Communication." *Journal of Comparative Psychology* 116, no. 2 (2002): 113–214.

Grzimek, Bernhard, ed. in chief. *Grzimek's Encyclopedia of Ethology*. New York: Van Nostrand Reinhold, 1977.

Harris, Sheldon H. *Factories of Death: Japanese Biological Warfare, 1932–1945, and the American Cover-up*. New York: Routledge, 1994.

Hart, Benjamin L. "Gonadal Androgen and Sociosexual Behavior of Male Mammals: A Comparative Analysis." *Psychological Bulletin* 81 (1974): 383–400.

Hart, Lynette A., ed. *Responsible Conduct with Animals in Research*. New York: Oxford Univ. Press, 1998.

Hinde, Robert A. *Animal Behaviour: A Synthesis of Ethology and Comparative Psychology*. 2d ed. New York: McGraw-Hill, 1970.

Holden, Constance. "Psychologist Made up Sex Bias Results." *Science* 294, no. 5551 (Dec. 21, 2001): 2457.

Houck, Lynne D., and Lee C. Drickamer, eds. *Foundations of Animal Behavior: Classic Papers with Commentaries*. Chicago: Univ. of Chicago Press, 1996.

Huxley, Julian S. "Lorenzian Ethology." *Zeitschrift für Tierpsychologie* 20 (1963): 402–9.

Kalikow, Theodora J. "Konrad Lorenz's 'Brown Past': A Reply to Alec Nisbett." *Journal of the History of the Behavioral Sciences* 14 (1978): 173–79.

———. "Konrad Lorenz's Ethological Theory: Explanation and Ideology, 1938–1943." *Journal of the History of Biology* 16, no. 1 (1983): 39–73.

Klopfer, Peter H. "Konrad Lorenz and the National Socialists: On the Politics of Ethology." *International Society for Comparative Psychology* 7 (1994): 202–8.

———. *Politics and People in Ethology: Personal Reflections on the Study of Animal Behavior*. Lewisburg, Pa.: Bucknell Univ. Press, 1999.

Klopfer, Peter H., and Jack P. Hailman. *An Introduction to Animal Behavior: Ethology's First Century*. Englewood Cliffs, N.J.: Prentice-Hall, 1967.

Koenig, Robert. "Max Planck Offers Historic Apology." *Science* 292, no. 5524 (June 15, 2001): 1979–82.

———. "Watson Urges 'Put Hitler behind Us.'" *Science* 276, no. 5314 (May 9, 1997): 892.

Lehrman, Daniel S. "A Critique of Konrad Lorenz's Theory of Instinctive Behavior." *Quarterly Review of Biology* 28, no. 4 (1953): 337–63.

———. "Interaction between Internal and External Environments in the Regulation of the Reproductive Cycle of the Ring Dove." In *Sex and Behavior*, edited by Frank A. Beach, 355–80. New York: John Wiley, 1965.

———. "Semantic and Conceptual Issues in the Nature-Nurture Problem." In *Development and Evolution of Behavior: Essays in Memory of T. C. Schneirla*, edited by L. R. Aronson, E. Tobach, D. S. Lehrman, and J. S. Rosenblatt, 17–52. San Francisco: W. H. Freeman, 1970.

Lerner, Richard M. *Final Solutions: Biology, Prejudice, and Genocide*. Univ. Park: Pennsylvania State Univ. Press, 1992.

Lorenz, Konrad. "The Bond." In *On Aggression*, translated by Marjorie Kerr Wilson, 165–219. New York: Harcourt, Brace & World, 1966.

———. "Companions as Factors in the Bird's Environment." In *Studies in Animal and Human Behavior*, vol. 1, translated by Robert Martin, 101–258. Cambridge, Mass.: Harvard Univ. Press, 1970.

———. "The Establishment of the Instinct Concept." In *Studies in Animal and Human Behaviour*, vol. 1, translated by Robert Martin, 259–315. Cambridge, Mass.: Harvard Univ. Press, 1970.

———. *Evolution and Modification of Behavior*. Chicago: Univ. of Chicago Press, 1965.

———. *Here Am I, Where Are You? The Behavior of the Greylag Goose*. Translated by R. D. Martin. New York: Harcourt Brace Jovanovich, 1988.

———. *King Solomon's Ring: New Light on Animal Ways*. Translated by Marjorie Kerr Wilson. New York: Thomas Y. Crowell, 1952.

———. "Konrad Lorenz: Autobiography," 1973/2000. http://www.nobel.se/medicine/laureates/1973/lorenz-autobio.html. Accessed Aug. 2, 2001.

———. "Der Kumpan in der Umwelt des Vogels." *Journal für Ornithologie* 83, nos. 2–3 (1935): 137–215 and 289–413.

———. *Man Meets Dog*. Translated by Marjorie Kerr Wilson. Baltimore: Penguin Books, 1953.

———. *On Aggression*. Translated by Marjorie Kerr Wilson. New York: Harcourt, Brace & World, 1966.

Marler, Peter, and William J. Hamilton, III. *Mechanisms of Animal Behavior*. New York: Wiley & Sons, 1966.

Marshall, Eliot. "Journals Joust over Conflict-of-Interest Rules." *Science* 276, no. 5312 (Apr. 25, 1997): 524.

McGill, Thomas E., ed. *Readings in Animal Behavior*, 2d ed. New York: Holt, Rinehart and Winston, 1973.

National Academy of Sciences. *On Being a Scientist*. Washington, D.C.: National Academy Press, 1989.

NASA. "NASA Principles for the Ethical Care and Use of Animals." 1999. http://www.nal.usda.gov/awic/legislat/nasa.htm. Accessed October 5, 2005.

Nisbet, Alec. *Konrad Lorenz: A Biography.* New York: Harcourt Brace Jovanovich, 1977.

Potthast, Thomas. "Review of Benedikt Föger and Klaus Taschwer, *Die Andere Seite des Spiegels.*" *Journal of the History of Biology* 35, no. 1 (2002): 194–96.

Richards, Robert J. *Darwin and the Emergence of Evolutionary Theories of Mind and Behavior.* Chicago: Univ. of Chicago Press, 1987.

Rushton, J. Philippe. "Final Solutions: Biology, Prejudice, and Genocide." (Book reviews.) *Society* 34 (Mar.–Apr. 1997): 78–83.

Sax, Boria. *Animals in the Third Reich: Pets, Scapegoats, and the Holocaust.* New York: Continuum, 2000.

Schneirla, T. C. *Army Ants: A Study in Social Organization,* edited by Howard R. Topoff. San Francisco: W. H. Freeman, 1971.

Tinbergen, Niko. *The Animal in Its World: Explorations of an Ethologist, 1932–1972.* Vol. 1, *Field Studies.* Cambridge, Mass.: Harvard Univ. Press, 1972.

———. *The Animal in Its World: Explorations of an Ethologist, 1932–1972.* Vol. 2, *Laboratory Experiments and General Papers.* Cambridge, Mass.: Harvard Univ. Press, 1972.

———. *Bird Life.* London: Oxford Univ. Press, 1954.

———. *Curious Naturalists.* New York: Basic Books, 1958.

———. "Ethology." In *The Animal in Its World: Explorations of an Ethologist, 1932–1972.* Vol. 2, *Laboratory Experiments and General Papers,* 130–60. Cambridge, Mass.: Harvard Univ. Press, 1972.

———. *The Herring Gull's World: A Study of the Social Behavior of Birds.* 1953. Reprint, New York: Lyons Press, 1989.

———. "Nikolaas Tinbergen—Autobiography." 1973. http://www.nobel.se/medicine/laureates/1973/tinbergen-autobio.html. Accessed Aug. 2, 2001.

———. "On Aims and Methods of Ethology." *Zeitschrift für Tierpsychologie* 20 (1963): 410–33.

———. *The Study of Instinct.* Oxford: Clarendon Press, 1951.

U.S. Department of Health and Human Services. "Office of Research Integrity, U.S. Department of Health and Human Services." 2002. http://ori.dhhs.gov/about/history.shtml. Accessed December 16, 2005.

Uexküll, J. von. "A Stroll through the Worlds of Animals and Men: A Picture Book of Invisible Worlds." In *Instinctive Behavior: The Development of a Modern Concept,* translated and edited by Claire H. Schiller, 5–80. New York: International Universities Press, 1957.

Web of Science. http://isiknowledge.com. Accessed October 5, 2005.

Williams, Peter, and David Wallace. *Unit 731: Japan's Secret Biological Warfare in World War II.* New York: Free Press, 1989.

Wilson, E. O. *Sociobiology: The New Synthesis.* Cambridge, Mass.: Harvard Univ. Press, 1975.

Chapter 16
Lorenz and Reduction

Bruce Hackett

When David Wilson informed me of the revelations regarding Konrad Lorenz's contributions to national socialism in Hitler's Germany, then led me to a reading of Boria Sax's fine essay on the topic in his *Animals in the Third Reich*,[1] I was saddened and perplexed and even embarrassed because for years I had cited approvingly Lorenz's canine typology—among other things, Aryans and Semites, it now appears, in dogs' clothing—in *Man Meets Dog*.[2] I had been introduced to *King Solomon's Ring* as an undergraduate, shortly after it appeared in the early 1950s.[3] My campus, Antioch College, and especially its highly regarded Philosophy Department, had been heavily influenced by the thinking of the philosophical pragmatists (John Dewey, in particular), who rejected the reigning positivism—the view that reality is fixed, a priori and "external" to perceiving minds, that scientists are essentially spectators—and saw inquiry in humanistic terms as an unavoidably creative process and who fought efforts to "reduce" the explanation of conduct to the language of physics and chemistry. So we were learning to be critics of positivism and reductionism, and Lorenz, along with Niko Tinbergen and a few others who were offering a fully scientific view of beasts as fully sentient, and who studied animals in their natural settings rather than as frozen slices of tissue under microscopes, was welcomed there.[4]

Those who study beasts "in the field" are not only producing new kinds of beasts; they have helped to legitimate and recruit a number of us in the social sciences into the doing of "field work" and the production of "qualitative" accounts of human conduct. From these undertakings, exciting new directions emerge: humans as well as other animals are portrayed in ways that fit poorly within a behavioristic model that excludes judgment and interpretations of meaning and the "value-neutral" conception of inquiry that was the mirror image of that model begins to wane. Reality itself is now allowed to be multiple, inquiry to be a creative process, and a single person to have a variety of selves—what the sociologist Erving Goffman charmingly referred to as one's "identity kit"—for deployment in a variety of "situations."[5]

These developments elevate all life-forms, plants included, in the conventional sense of making them more mindful and less mechanical, more proactive and less reactive. In sociology, they have contributed to an acceptance of diversity and have helped to shift at least some of our attention away from trying to explain social deviation and toward efforts to find out how things come to be thought of as "normal." These are a few of the ways in which field work has helped to reconstruct our experience of, and hence the reality of, all the animals, humans included, but this is not to say that these changes have been uncontested. This is in part because of our painful bifurcation of qualitative and quantitative research methods—the two being, to paraphrase Arthur Bentley, companionable but infertile—and the fact that "having a metric" is still emblematic of science in conventional thought.

The place of reductionism in mainstream biological work is a related challenge to what I had taken to be the Lorenzian approach. When Marjorie Grene was in the Philosophy Department at the University of California at Davis, she liked to insist that "it has been, and is, the dream, not only of philosophers and physicists, but of biologists as well, that some day all biology will be reduced to physics and chemistry"[6]—the reduction, that is to say, of life to nonlife—and a biochemist acquaintance of mine has acknowledged that in the biological sciences at Davis, at least, "reduction is orthodoxy." Aside from the nagging question of how an assemblage of chemicals could produce an unbiased chemical account of itself, Grene thought reduction tantamount to a degradation of life and even a threat to the defense of human rights: if life is nothing but physics and chemistry, what does it matter what is done *with* life?[7]

With this background, this sense of reductionism as the primary challenge to a more complete and more accurate approach to the study of life and its forms, I was required to confront a putative ally, Lorenz, now caught aiding a very dark force. One not very satisfactory solution to this problem would be to invoke the "multiple selves" doctrine noted above and argue that good and evil and even moral agnosticism can cohabit in the same Austrian naturalist, perhaps especially if the evil can be said to be, as in Hannah Arendt's famous formulation, "banal." Lorenz does not, at least, appear to be a reductionist, unless that would cover his strong commitment to the explanatory power of instinct—a confusing commitment, sometimes, since much of what makes his beasts attractive is their apparent ability to learn and reconstruct. In *King Solomon's Ring*, he does lament (with cosmic irony, perhaps, given his own past) the apparent loss in humans of the instincts that limit intraspecific aggression in other animals, and he appraised the domestication of animals as a form of decline, one that might account for the emergence of human beings in general.

The rejection of an anthropocentric approach to animals in the Third Reich does share with the reductionist program an inclination to "reduce" human beings, if not to their chemistry, then by invidious comparison with other life forms that are said to be as yet wild, unspoiled, pristine. These reductions are also utopian, and broadly influenced by a long Christian (and especially Protestant) tradition that insists that we are "fallen," with redemption possible largely through denial of our "only too human" cravings. The struggle to contain "bias" in scientific work—symbolized by the white lab coat and the metric—makes common sense, but it also denies recognition of how mindful we are and have to be in doing science, that what we call "data" ought properly to be called "capta."[8] The scientist Konrad Lorenz could have benefited from a postpositivist understanding that the very concepts of a primordial instinct or a "wild" animal were productions of "domesticated" creatures.

I have to be careful not to imply that scientists of a reductionist bent would for that reason approve of or even acquiesce in the puritanical cleansing rituals of the Nazi party; the task instead is to urge a certain wariness regarding our own well-intended and taken-for-granted tendency to celebrate "pure" science and to make damaging comparisons between persons and the wild. American society, because of its uniquely deep roots in the Reformation, may be more inclined to these abuses than most; I recently encountered a homely instance in Bill Bryson's complaint, in *A Walk in the Woods*, that the designers of the Appalachian Trail were careful not to allow the trail to pass through any of the many villages or towns that are located near it, in contrast to the typical pattern in Europe, where pristine settings and human settlements are not so clearly segregated.[9] This contrast may seem innocent, but our efforts to prevent the spoilage that surely will result from human contact is a theme, a master narrative, that pervades our culture. Observers from Tocqueville on have noted the American affection for institutions and their reserve regarding traditional forms of authority based on kinship; for all the talk about "family values" it has in the past century—recently, that is to say—become our understanding that the proper place for children during the day is in the school, not the home. The template that shapes our public schools began to emerge as early as the sixth century, when the European religious and monastic orders began to develop in earnest; the school is a secularized and now compulsory form of this cleansing escape from "the world" extended to include children.

It is, of course, an odd formulation that sees the school not as the tamer of children but as the protector of their wildness, but the school equates to the wilderness in the sense that it excludes the "domestication" that Lorenz reviled; it is at home that children are "spoiled." It might also be sobering to think of the schools, albeit hopefully benign and for most of us temporary settings for "concentrating the mind," as concentration camps nonetheless. This would help direct attention, in turn, to the forms, short of Holocaust, that a secular puritanism takes in doing the difficult work of proscribing liberties.

If this reasoning has any value, it might imply that we should look carefully and critically at our implicit tendency to include the smaller members of our own species in the "nature" that by convention if not by definition is limited in its life forms to species other than our own. To do so would be to extend and in effect to celebrate the way in which NILAS formulates the task of understanding the natural world. This is an approach that, unlike Lorenz's, is not puritanical, does not pretend to somehow exclude or disparage our human mind-work from our descriptions of nature but instead makes that work its focus—openly, explicitly, emphatically. It makes bold to stand away from reduction and the institutions it creates—even though, as teachers, many of us will have trouble staying home from school—and because it exhibits that strength it will remain for some time on the margins of accredited knowing. Its focus on the *relationship* between knower and known produces instances of "legend"—ultimately including, one supposes, those second-degree legends that students of legend-making produce, and that are on display in this volume. The process of "peer review" in the established sciences might be seen as an effort to exclude legend from published work, and it is unquestionably important to ensuring the public and social character of knowledge, but it unfortunately also tends to exclude a full appreciation of the manmade and malleable character of what we take to be "real." Studies currently underway of the legends and the folklore of the modern research laboratory itself (tracing, e.g., the vernacular roots of notions such as "cause" or "finding" or "roots") will undoubtedly contribute to humanizing our understanding of the "disciplines" that confront "nature" and hopefully hasten the day when the NILAS approach will be taken to be what real "science" is all about.

Notes

1. Boria Sax, *Animals in the Third Reich: Pets, Scapegoats, and the Holocaust* (New York: Continuum, 2000), 124–36.

2. Konrad Lorenz, *Man Meets Dog*, trans. Marjorie Kerr Wilson (Baltimore: Penguin Books, 1953).

3. Konrad Lorenz, *King Solomon's Ring: New Light on Animal Ways*, trans. Marjorie Kerr Wilson (New York: Thomas Y. Cromwell, 1952).

4. For those unfamiliar with pragmatism, Dewey's most readable overview of his own project is probably *Reconstruction in Philosophy* (Boston: Beacon Press, 1948). Good secondary sources include George Raymond Geiger's *John Dewey in Perspective* (New York: Oxford Univ. Press, 1958) and Richard Bernstein's *Praxis and Action* (Philadelphia: Univ. of Pennsylvania Press, 1971), especially part 3. A particularly welcome, lucid placement of pragmatism in historical perspective is Louis Menand, *The Metaphysical Club* (New York: Farrar, Straus and Giroux, 2001).

5. Erving Goffman, *Asylums* (Garden City, N.Y.: Doubleday, 1961), 20.

6. Marjorie Grene, *The Knower and the Known* (Berkeley and Los Angeles: Univ. of California Press, 1974), 202.

7. In addition to *The Knower and the Known*, students of the relationship between people and other animals will enjoy Marjorie Grene's *Approaches to a Philosophical Biology* (New York: Basic Books, 1968).

8. "Data" is the plural of datum, or "givens"; "capta" is the plural of captum, or "takens."

9. Bill Bryson, *A Walk in the Woods* (New York: Broadway Books, 1998). The concept of a wilderness is of course of much current interest, and I am indebted to Dave Aftandilian for directing my attention to William Cronon's essay "The Trouble with Wilderness; or, Getting Back to the Wrong Nature," in *Uncommon Ground: Rethinking the Human Place in Nature*, ed. William Cronon (New York: W. W. Norton, 1996), 69–90.

Works Cited

Bernstein, Richard. *Praxis and Action*. Philadelphia: Univ. of Pennsylvania Press, 1971.

Bryson, Bill. *A Walk in the Woods*. New York: Broadway Books, 1998.

Cronon, William. "The Trouble with Wilderness; or, Getting Back to the Wrong Nature." In *Uncommon Ground: Rethinking the Human Place in Nature*, edited by William Cronon, 69–90. New York: W. W. Norton, 1996.

Dewey, John. *Reconstruction in Philosophy*. Boston: Beacon Press, 1948.

Geiger, George. *John Dewey in Perspective*. New York: Oxford Univ. Press, 1958.

Goffman, Erving. *Asylums*. Garden City, N.Y.: Doubleday, 1961.

Grene, Marjorie. *Approaches to a Philosophical Biology*. New York: Basic Books, 1968.

———. *The Knower and the Known*. Berkeley and Los Angeles: Univ. of California Press, 1974.

Lorenz, Konrad. *King Solomon's Ring: New Light on Animal Ways*. Translated by Marjorie Kerr Wilson. New York: Thomas Y. Crowell, 1952.

———. *Man Meets Dog*. Translated by Marjorie Kerr Wilson. Baltimore: Penguin Books, 1953.

Menand, Louis. *The Metaphysical Club*. New York: Farrar, Straus and Giroux, 2001.

Sax, Boria. *Animals in the Third Reich: Pets, Scapegoats, and the Holocaust*. New York: Continuum, 2000.

Afterword
Toward a Unity with Nature

Dave Aftandilian and David Scofield Wilson

Throughout this book we have focused on what other animals mean to humans. We have seen the crucial roles that animals have played in folklore, literature, art, religion, and ethology around the world and from prehistory to the present. We have heard about what various humans have thought about house cats and tigers, foxes and dogs, snakes and frogs, asses and reindeer, and more. But we have rarely considered what the animals mean, to themselves and to us, as real animals in the world, rather than just as players drafted into human dramas.

It is often said that we can never really know what it is like to be another human being, let alone a member of another species. But even if that is so, we believe there is still much to be gained from attempting to encounter real animals in their own worlds and to bring our observations of them back to the human realms. This afterword offers some thoughts on how we might better understand animal others in their own rights and what we might do with that understanding once we have gained it.

We also intend this afterword to address a failing we perceive in much academic work: a tendency to divorce theory from practice. In terms of animal studies, totemic literature, therosentience (see below), and so on, we see theory and practice as two sides of one coin, inseparable (if sometimes divergent) approaches to the single goal of bringing humans back to a closer understanding of and relationship with our nonhuman kin. Therefore, we begin by reviewing various little-known theoretical approaches to understanding animals on their own terms and continue with extended discussions of various models we might draw upon to put those theories into practice. Yet within the "theoretical section," you will also find practical advice, and within the "practical section," you will also find theoretical musings. We hope to productively muddy the intellectual waters by combining theory and practice and, in so doing, to encourage others working toward a unity with nature to do the same.

Thinking toward a Unity with Nature

Animal behavior.

Human behavior.

Well-established and productive academic disciplines have made substantial, illuminating discoveries in both areas. In terms of animal life, entomology, zoology, herpetology, ornithology, ichthyology, genetics, statistics, and, of course, ecology have revealed patterns not available to "common sense" and naïve attention. In terms of human life, similarly, psychology, anthropology, ethnology, history, sociology, psychiatry, and statistics have been able to astonish us with discoveries about ourselves and others we could not have come to "naturally."

Scientists of animal and human life have achieved insights in part by disciplining their sympathies and controlling their very human inclination to "read into" the doings of humans and other animals the motivations we have learned to recognize in ourselves (e.g., by avoiding the human tendency to anthropomorphize). And in controlling their own behavior, scientists are better able to distance themselves from their "subjects" by treating them as objects. There are gains and costs to this construction of reality and its embedded linguistic maintenance. Martin Buber (1878–1965), who wrote the classic *I and Thou* sixty-five years ago, termed this distanced relationship between subject and object an "I/It" compound. He went on to claim that "I/It can never be spoken with one's whole being."[1] We learn early to separate our whole being from our object of interest.

Buber dwells in his treatise on the nature and the consequences of life lived with one's self and with God. The I/It relationship maps a neighborhood commonly favored by and inhabited by academic scientists of animal life. A less alienating landscape than that of I/It is that termed I/Thou by Buber. I/Thou embraces a oneness of beings familiar to the unborn at the beginning of human experience and achieved by some in adulthood through discipline, sympathy, and imagination. Buber writes: "Whoever says *You* does not *have* something; . . . But he stands in relation."[2] "The relation to the You is unmediated," he explains; "immediacy" characterizes encounters with the You.[3]

There are those, have always been those, who "speak" with their whole being in this unified way. Shamans and poets and lovers and saints come to mind as ones who stand face-to-face in intimate relationship to another being or presence, as we have read in several of the chapters in this book. The mode is not analytical, but analogical. A shaman dancing as an owl is not, in her or his construction of reality, acting *like* an owl but is *being* owl.

There have always been people who feel a fellowship with creatures, human and otherwise. Classically, legends are tales that purport to be true and in which theromorphic creatures (centaurs, unicorns, harpies, selkies, kitsune, etc.) command presence and slip from human into animal forms and back again. Stories authors tell and parents read to children draw the listener and reader into the presence of other wild beings, be they spiders (E. B. White's Charlotte), fawns (Felix Salten's Bambi), coyotes, or crows. In these tales, too, people discover in themselves depths of fellowship with all manner of very different Thous. To seek out literary, oral, and material presentations of such shared presence is the mission of NILAS (Nature in Legend and Story), the association that organized the 2001 conference from which the pieces in this book are representative attempts to get beyond the analytical to an analogical "unity with nature" in its many forms.[4]

For the past decade or more, we have been studying how animals are revealed in the stories and legends people enjoy and repeat over the millennia. We have recently begun to wonder how to describe what we do. Do we study animal behavior? That casts the animals as objects which we subjects treat, report on, manipulate, admire, fear, or otherwise take to heart and make sense of. But such objectification leaves humans, even when paired with nonhuman animals, separated out. And our naming of nonhuman animals, whether in Latinate binomials or common English, and our shifting of them to emblematic status on military patches or athletic jerseys, reduces them to symbolic *mediations* between our human webs of value and meaning and the actuality of the living creatures on the other side of those symbols.

Human consciousness and its language is a problem: names and categories, such as "pets" or "wildlife," mediate our experience of those animals we would better understand and value for what they may teach us, both about themselves and their kind and about ourselves. Habits of speech and mind lead us to see creatures-in-mind rather than creatures as truly other and fully there. We need to find ways, as poets and storytellers do, to transform everyday language and recontextualize encounters with other creatures in ways that open up the multifold nature of consciousness that Buber envisioned and that the poet William Blake prayed to keep:

> "May God us keep
> From Single vision & Newton's sleep!"[5]

Carefully chosen words and images may allow us to appreciate the twofold condition of our attention to the Thou we encounter in relationship to animal others and at the same time to recognize the actions of our own I in processing and appreciating such encounters. Marianne Moore is our guide, here. In her poem "Poetry," she advises poets to "present / for inspection, 'imaginary gardens with real toads in them.'"[6] By metaphor, then, poets may achieve a sort of double consciousness that stays true to the creature while acknowledging the human's speaking voice and consciousness of self. I think of poems by Robinson Jeffers ("Hurt Hawks"), Mary Oliver ("Water Snake"), Jane Kenyon ("November Calf"), Wendell Berry ("The Peace of Wild Things"), Robert Francis ("Waxwings"), and Denise Levertov ("Come Into Animal Presence"). Also, *mutatis mutandis,* of paintings by Morris Graves ("Blind Bird" and "Joyous Young Pine"), certain Upper Paleolithic cave paintings, Haida totem figures, and more.[7]

Besides poetry and paintings, four other approaches suggest ways we might transcend mediating barriers between human consciousness and the lives of other creatures: the "humanistic anthropology" of Robert Plant Armstrong, the approach of Gregory Bateson to issues of mind in nature, the ways in which Martha Nussbaum and Tibetan and other Buddhists expand mentality to include all sentient beings, and, as already suggested, the I/Thou insights of Martin Buber.

An anecdote from the archives of herpetological history would seem to have anticipated Buber in enjoyment of an I/Thou relationship between three rattlesnakes and their human "friend." Grace Olive Wiley described her way of taming them in her letters to the *Bulletin* of the Antivenin Institute of America in 1929 and 1930. To keep them clean and healthy, she bathed them in warm soapy water twice a week and placed them in a box on the radiator to dry while she cleaned their cage. "They were frightened at first," Wiley wrote, so she handled them gently, moved slowly, and soon they "came to understand and submitted very good-naturedly." She named one male "Huckleberry Finn," another "Stanley," and a female "Ethel." They "all . . . like to be stroked and petted," she wrote. Some individuals showed their fondness for this attention by arching their backs like cats. She let Stanley rest coiled in her lap at night while she sewed.[8] Wiley was the first ever to breed rattlesnakes in captivity. And more to the point here, she modeled for us all an I/Thou kinship with creatures not of our kind, indeed, creatures so seemingly alien that humans commonly flee from or kill them.

Perhaps the most theoretically stimulating analysis of how we may relanguage and reimagine our response to *presence* when we encounter it in legends and myths (or, I would add, in nature) is the work of Robert Plant Armstrong in his trilogy of books on humanistic anthropology. There he takes on the mediating and objectifying quality of much Western cultural thought and feeling, in the humanities as well as in the natural sciences.[9] "The objective of such [humanistic] anthropology," he explains in the first book, "is an answer to the ancient question, *what is man?* This I view as far more interesting as well as more important than the question, *how does man behave?*"[10] If we substitute an "animal presence" for "man" in his formula, we find ourselves asking, What is animal presence? rather than, How do animals behave apart from us, or even with us? In the preface to his second book, Armstrong proposes that "the end [or aim] of what I think of as *real anthropology* is in the deep mid-point of human *being* where there is to be found an understanding, an appreciation, and a compassion for man."[11]

Substituting "nature in legend and story" for "real anthropology," the mission could read thus: "The end of what we do who study nature in legend and story lies at the deep midpoint of human *being*, where there is to be found an understanding, an appreciation, and a compassion for *all beings*," and indeed for such *beings* as we encounter when we meet affecting creatures in art, as in Jeffers's "Hurt Hawks" and Graves's "Blind Bird," but also in such creatures as we may meet face-to-face, as it were, "out in nature." Armstrong's gift to us lies in his appreciation of the way such "affecting presences" work to *immediate* rather than *mediate* relationships between one's own I and the Thous in the world, be they Yoruba Ibeji, prehistoric cave paintings, or, we would add for this project, animal beings we meet in art or the wild.

Thoreau's long and detailed account in his *Journal* of his relationship with a woodchuck he encounters comes to mind:

> As I turned round the corner of Hubbard's Grove, saw a woodchuck,
> the first of the season, in the middle of the field, six or seven rods
> from the fence which bounds the wood, and twenty rods distant. I
> ran along the fence and cut him off, or rather overtook him, though
> he started at the same time. . . . I squatted down and surveyed him
> at my leisure. . . . I talked to him *quasi* forest lingo, baby-talk, at any
> rate in a conciliatory tone, and thought that I had some influence on

> him. He gritted his teeth less. . . . I reached checkerberry leaves to
> his mouth. I stretched my hands over him, though he turned up his
> head and still gritted a little. . . . I respect him as one of the natives.
> . . . I think I might learn some wisdom from him.[12]

Like Armstrong and Thoreau, Gregory Bateson was much taken by the richness of metaphor, seeing it as at the heart of art, poetry, religion, parable, allegory, dreaming, and even science. He called that quality of mind that saw likeness across species—as, say, between the morphology of a frog, a bat, a bird, and a person—"abduction" and found it expressed as well in totemism.[13] For Bateson, the logic of totemism may be expressed in a "syllogism of metaphor" thus: "Grass dies; / Men die: / Men are grass."[14] Such "syllogisms of grass," as he also termed them, lie at the heart of Walt Whitman's *Leaves of Grass* and the heart of much biblical imagery and prophecy: "All flesh is grass" (Isaiah 40:6).

"There are still a few practicing totemites, even in the ranks of professional biology," Bateson reports, expressing his appreciation of totemism in his account of watching Konrad Lorenz lecture:

> To watch Professor Konrad Lorenz teach class is to discover what
> the Aurignacian cavemen were doing when they painted those living,
> moving reindeer and mammoths on the sides and ceilings of their
> caves. . . . [His] posture and expressive movement, his kinesics,
> change from moment to moment according to the nature of the ani
> mal he is talking about. At one moment, he is goose; a few minutes
> later, a cichlid fish. And so on.[15]

What many of the chapters in this volume seem to be have been good at is just such "abduction," that is, at seeing likeness as if horizontally across species, genera, and families, as opposed to up and down the Great Chain of Being. It is just such a poetical or mystical leap that lets Whitman identify with a live-oak ("I Saw in Louisiana a Live-Oak Growing"), with a spider ("A Noiseless Patient Spider"), or with "leaves of grass" as well as with all ranks of men and women.[16] And good storytellers often, like Lorenz, become the creatures they enact. D. S. W. cherishes the memory of seeing a Miwok State Park employee in California demonstrate a bit of roundhouse dance to his class, "becoming an owl" hitching itself sideways along a branch. The class was riveted, as was he.

Totemism may be, then, the goal, or at least the mode, of a new sort of study of nature in legend and story, in art and dance, in song and worship.[17] We tell our disciplinary stories, of course, but listen alertly to the stories told by others and for the "stories told" by beings not of our kind and not even in human tongues. Ursula K. Le Guin offers "therolinguistics" (fr. *ther*, "wild beast" and "linguistics") as a category of wisdom and telling that creatures other than humans employ.[18] We come to understand that all creatures are beings with degrees of mentality, whether porpoises, geese, or cichlid fish. Perhaps we may borrow from Le Guin's lead and talk now of *therosentience*, one animal listening to and at least partially comprehending or understanding another. Therosentience, then, is a dimension of what Thoreau and Wiley encountered in their relationships with a woodchuck and with rattlesnakes.

Martha Nussbaum, professor of law and ethics at the University of Chicago, would suggest that readers encounter both woodchuck and rattlesnake through what she calls "the narrative imagination." In *Poetic Justice*, the earliest of the works in which she testifies to the importance of this catalyst, Nussbaum explains that her conviction grows out of her belief that "storytelling and literary imagining are not opposed to rational argument, but can provide essential ingredients in a rational argument."[19] Consequently, she believes literature and storytelling should be a constant presence, "not only in our homes and schools, shaping the perceptions of our children, but also in our schools of public policy and development studies, and in our government offices and courts, and even in our law schools—wherever the public imagination is shaped and nourished."[20] What "narrative imagination" provides may be summarized as "the ability to imagine what it is like to live the life of another person."[21] When this happens, powerful emotions are evoked, the certainties of the culture story are questioned, and the reader begins to "distrust . . . conventional pieties."[22] Narrative imagination is seen as the key to entering the lives of all others, human and nonhuman: "In the absence of that capacity, the 'long dumb' voices that seek to speak . . . will remain silent."[23]

Just such an appreciation of presence and abduction invokes a Buddhist perspective to the question of both human and other sentience. As one Tibetan Buddhist explains:

> The idea that humans have imaginations and are inventing their world, whereas animals do not project these constructs and therefore are inherently different, goes against the core Buddhist ideals. Buddhists believe that animals are imagining their worlds just as humans do. In both cases, we name things and then assent to the meaning that comes along with the names. "Ignorance" for Buddhists means that we are not aware of the fact that *we* name things and give them their place in the world, their power, their beauty, ugliness, and so on. This is true of all sentient beings and is actually the defining trait of a sentient being according to Buddhist thought. The difference between a person and an animal is like the difference between a baby and an adult, for example—just different developmental stages that we go back and forth between. So the perceived difference between human and animal is like a fiction, because we see it as being a permanent, black-and-white difference, whereas it is actually a difference of degree and of time.[24]

Finally, we must ask, how might such understanding of sentient beings, ourselves and others, generate new studies of nature in legend and story, and spin off curricula, bibliographies? First of all, we must not romanticize animals as incorruptible, as unfallen. Animals, like humans, carry disabling expectations, memories of bad experiences, and commitments to patterns of expectation harmful to their welfare. They may "forget themselves," as may we: Grace Olive Wiley died from a cobra bite in Los Angeles in the 1940s while handling a new arrival at the zoo. She had neglected to keep her antivenin serum and hypodermic in good shape.[25]

The example offered by Wiley's "taming" of her "pet snakes" Huckleberry Finn, Stanley, and Ethel suggests that others of us human beings might be able to "converse," as it were, with rattlesnakes—and other creatures. Knowing that to be possible, we might begin to gather tales, accounts, poems, and stories of others who have similarly conversed with creatures: St. Francis, Seabiscuit's trainer Tom Smith, or Temple Grandin, the high-functioning autistic animal science professor at Colorado State University who "thinks in pictures" and associations, much as many animals may do, rather than primarily in words. This allows her to take "a cow's eye view" of chutes and gates and dip vats and to design cattle ranching and slaughterhouse equipment that does not frighten the cows. In her latest work, Grandin explores the sort of cross-species "conversations" humans may engage in with animals as virtual "translations."[26]

The explorations in the field of animal behavior by Niko Tinbergen certainly demonstrated that he communicated with herring gulls and their chicks, and even with sand-dune wasps.[27] J. Henri Fabre seems to have understood a good deal about the mentality of various insects, and especially of the virtually "addictive" trap which the "mind" of a caterpillar spun out, causing it to follow its own path around and around the lip of a pot after Fabre had tricked it into turning back onto its original, exploratory track.[28] Sally Carrighar demonstrated an extraordinary empathy with all manner of creatures she studied at Beetle Rock.[29] I think of Farley Mowat and a wolf marking off their respective territories with urine.[30]

We as scholars could easily assemble a bibliography and filmography of such totemic associations between beings of different species.[31] We would, ideally, include oral histories of veterinarians, horse handlers, ranchers, pigeon racers, falconers, and the many others who practice cross-species understanding without reflecting very much on their own skills. Hunters may "know" prey in sometimes intimate ways. We may learn from all those who practice cross-species communication, even those we wish shared a different set of values about the importance of others' lives. To collect such stories would help rescue a good deal of what has been dismissed as children's literature, folklore, sentimentalism, and tall tales as parables from which to learn.

In their Newberry Prize–winning book *A View from the Oak*, Herbert and Judith Kohl suggested exercises children and adults might try in order to enter temporarily the *Umwelt* of insects. They blindfolded children, attached antennae to their heads, and encouraged them to crawl around the yard, sensing their environment as ants might.[32] Similar activities are available for visitors to the recently built Hamill Family Play Zoo in Illinois's Brookfield Zoo, which was designed specifically to inspire caring for nature in children and their caregivers.[33] Therosentience, then, can be practiced and, if not mastered, at least acquired as one now acquires a foreign language.

Cultivating Therosentience through Intuitive Knowledge

If we want to come closer to animal presence, if we want to learn to conceive of animals as subjects and agents rather than passive objects, if we want to cultivate therosentience in ourselves and others—how best can we do this?

One way would be to further develop the approaches of a number of scholars who have been seeking new ways to apply critical theory to animal studies over the past several decades.[34] Yet despite our best intentions, just as words (such as Latinate binomials and other technical language)[35] can separate us from the "real animals" we are attempting to describe, so too can our critical theories construct yet another barrier, a barrier built of ideas, between ourselves and "nonhuman animal Others." Perhaps what we need, then, is not just more critical theories but also better *models* for how we can personally (re)connect with real animals on an intuitive level, and help our students, colleagues, friends, and family to do the same.[36]

What counts as a good model for connecting with animals, for moving from an I/it orientation toward animals to an I/thou stance, for accessing therosentience? First, such models should be built on personal experience, observations, and imaginings. Connections to animals based on received wisdom will always be shaky; those based on real, lived human-animal interactions will be the most firmly grounded. (Such connections will be even stronger if they involve more than one of the five senses.) Second, we need to seek models that focus on the particular and the local rather than the abstract and the global. It is much easier to truly connect to the pair of cardinals that built their nest in our backyard than to the ones we see portrayed in Peterson's *Field Guide to the Birds* or in a television nature documentary. Third, we need models that encourage people to see both the similarities and the differences between themselves and animals. It is much harder to separate ourselves from animals, from their lived experiences, from their capacities to experience joy and suffering, if we see them as similar to ourselves. But we also need to understand their differences from us to see them as unique and valuable in their own right. And finally, we need models that help us know animals not just in an intellectual sense but also in an intuitive, emotional sense. Caring for creatures may begin in the mind—for instance, if we learn that a given animal's habitat is severely threatened or that it has unique adaptations to its environment. But if caring does not take root in our hearts, we will have little motivation to seek a connection to other animals beyond the printed page. And it is that lived, intuitive connection to real animals that will help us make our world whole again.

Ethologist (animal behaviorist) Marc Bekoff describes the effort to seek an emotional, intuitive understanding of animals as "minding animals"—minding both in terms of keeping their feelings and welfare in our minds and in terms of thinking of them as having active, thoughtful minds not unlike our own.[37] "By minding animals," Bekoff writes, "we mind ourselves." And minding ourselves "will help make us nicer to one another and nicer to the planet as a whole."[38]

Although one could cite many models that fill these criteria, we will focus on just two here: experiential natural history and storytelling.

Experiential Natural History and Goethean Science

Before there were "natural sciences," there was natural history, making careful observations of plants, animals, and landscapes. For our gathering/hunting ancestors, such observations filled a very practical purpose: survival. But they also served as the basis for human social structures, religious rituals, and creative arts. Indeed, for many cultures, natural history was human history, and vice versa, because the nature/culture boundary was seen as permeable, if in fact it was perceived at all.[39] As the natural sciences became professionalized over the past several hundred years, natural history in the West changed from being an integral part of everyday life to a specialized activity that scientists performed as they collected and classified organisms, constructed taxonomies, and otherwise sought to discern order within the chaotic riot of natural organisms and environments.

Nowadays natural history has been relegated to the back closets of academia. Even in ecology, for a long time one of the closest disciplines to the old ways of natural history, the most highly respected and professionally rewarded ecologists now tend to work not in the field but in the laboratory and on the computer. However, the tide is turning once again, as hobbies related to natural history, such as birdwatching, become increasingly popular and citizen scientists are sought by governmental and nongovernmental organizations around the world to assist in monitoring the health of nature from their own backyards. Now we offer yet another reason to rediscover natural history: its value as a means of understanding nature on an intuitive basis.

There are many different ways to do natural history, of course. At its simplest level, natural history calls for us to pay attention to nature with all our bodily senses: eyes, ears, nose, mouth, fingers. Anyplace is a good place to practice this attentiveness—even the most densely populated urban areas have birds flying overhead, insects and other creatures scurrying across the pavement, weeds cropping up in abandoned lots. In fact, it can be easier to begin rediscovering natural history in urban or suburban areas, where there are not quite so many animals and plants overwhelming our senses all at once. Perhaps even more important, such areas are accessible to many more people than "wilderness" areas and therefore provide an opportunity for *everyone* to experience connection with nature.[40] If you have access to a wide variety of natural areas, places where two habitats come together ("edges")—where a woodland meets a field, for instance—can be especially rich in diverse species and serve as an excellent place to sit and observe. Wildlife is also often drawn to water, so lakes, streams, and other bodies of water can also make excellent observation stations.

While you could begin your explorations in natural history with a backpack full of field guides, you might want to bring along your dog or your child, instead. Just as theories can make it difficult for us to turn off our analytical minds and experience animals directly, so too can field guides lead you to focus on what their authors *think* are the most important or defining characteristics of an animal, rather than what you *feel* to be important based on what your senses tell you.

Consider starting instead with what intrigues you in what you see or hear or smell when you arrive at your observation site. Or let your child's natural sense of wonder guide you, as they pick up different things and ask you what they are, or why the sky is blue, or why birds have feathers but fish have scales. Or follow the keener senses of your dog as it follows scents we can only imagine or points at the tiniest ripple of animal movement within a sea of grass.

Once your first impressions point you to something intriguing about an animal or animals, settle down and record everything you can observe about it. What does it look like? Is it making any sounds? What is it doing? Is it alone or in a group? As much as you can, use your senses to enter the world of the animal you are observing. You might try imitating its calls or its movements to under-

Fig. A.1. Gesture drawings of seven Steller's jays and an American robin by David Scofield Wilson.

stand these aspects of the animal better. Drawing can also be useful in this stage, because it helps us see things that we might otherwise miss. You do not have to be a visual artist to draw—in fact, anyone can make drawings that capture the essence of an object by using a technique called gesture drawing. Instead of looking from object to page and back again, erasing errors and striving for perfection, gesture drawing calls on you to watch the object rather than the page as you draw (see fig. A.1).[41]

After you feel you have recorded enough facts about the animal you have been observing, put down your notes and try to see the animal with your mind's eye. Think about all you have written about the animal, what it looks like, what it sounds like, how it moves. Then imagine what would happen if the animal were not as you have observed it. What if a hawk did not fly, or a trout did not swim? Imagine the animal's life in different seasons, what happened to it before you arrived, and what will happen after you leave. What is the animal's place in time and in the habitat in which you have observed it? Using your imagination as another sense helps you get at aspects of an animal that you could not normally observe—things that are just as true to the animal as the facts you recorded with your other senses, but that add up to more than the sum of a handful of sensorial observations.

These two types of observations are key to Goethe's scientific method. Goethe the poet was also Goethe the natural philosopher, and he developed an alternate, intuitive, nonlinear way to know the world that complemented the analytical scientific mode with which we are more familiar today.[42] His goal was to develop a "schooled subjectivity" that allowed the observer "to meet the phenomenon [or creature] as it is."[43] Since this is essentially our goal in trying to discover real animals, his method might prove fruitful for our contemporary animal studies as well. The first step in Goethe's scientific method is called "exact sense perception" and involves using all your senses actively to investigate the "facts" of a phenomenon. The second step was described in the preceding paragraph, using your imagination to open yourself to an intuitive "knowing" of the phenomenon; Goethe described this as "exact sensorial fantasy." Together these two steps "giv[e] thinking more the quality of perception and sensory observation more the quality of thinking."[44]

In her paper on applying Goethean science to landscape studies, Isis Brook describes two more steps in this process: "seeing in beholding" and "becoming one with the object" under study.[45] With seeing in beholding, the goal is to take a step back and let the phenomenon you are studying express itself through you in more unconscious ways, as if you were using your subconscious as another sense organ. For many, this might inspire an artistic reaction; perhaps a poem might occur to you, or a melody, or a dance move. The final step in a Goethean analysis is to use empathy and intuition to combine the perceptions, imaginations, and inspirations you have experienced so far into an appreciation of the subject that unites you with it, rather than separates you from it, as in the usual objective, reductionist scientific study.

That all might seem pretty abstract, so let us consider a specific example. Say you have chosen to observe a great blue heron in a pond. You might start by watching the heron carefully, noting how it walks, when it moves, and how its feathers ruffle slightly in the wind when it stands very still, as herons have a habit of doing. You might think about the colors of its feathers, or the sudden splash it makes when its long neck uncoils and its sharp beak spears a fish for dinner. All these are exact sense perceptions. Now you might imagine what this standing still heron might look like if it were flying, whether its colors would seem as natural if it were living in a desert instead of near a pond, how old it is, and how long it might live. You might try imagining what the heron would look like to a fish or frog or snake that it might be about to eat, using the perspective of another animal to imagine aspects of the heron you might not ever be able to see yourself. These are examples of exact sensorial fantasy. Perhaps you feel especially inspired by the unexpected combination of the heron's ungainly walk, yet very fluid flying, and compose a poem about that disjunction. Or you might paint a picture that explores the ways in which the heron's coloration suits it perfectly to its environment, poised between blue and gray, sky and water. And finally, you might imagine what it would be like to be a heron, wading through a pond on colorful, stick-thin legs, looking for the telltale wriggle of a meal on the fin, and keeping a wary eye out for floating logs that might turn out to be alligators.

Once you have discovered the great blue heron for yourself in this way, you might want to extend these Goethean observations by reading what others, such as John James Audubon or Arthur Cleveland Bent, have written about the natural history of great blue herons, or by looking for folktales, sacred stories, and legends about them from various cultures.[46] You might even decide to read papers about herons by professional animal behaviorists—or poetry about them. You might seek out photographs or paintings of herons and see if they capture what you observed about them. If not, you might want to create your own artworks that do!

Through his method of schooled subjectivity, his intuitive observations and exact sensorial fantasy, Goethe's scientific observations informed his poetry, and vice versa, resulting in a holistic way of knowing the world that is greater than the sum of its parts. When natural history and story unite in this way in our own work and imaginings, we come closer to the level of insight and empathy we need to bring us into the presence of real animal others.

The Power of Animal Stories

You might also want to try creating and telling stories about great blue herons to understand them more completely and to share your understanding of them with others, which brings us to our second model for reconnecting with animals: storytelling. For our purposes, we define "storytelling" broadly, including not just orally told tales but also written stories and paintings, dances, songs, or other artworks that share stories with their audiences. The key here is not so much the mode of transmission as the content of the stories themselves, and the result we hope to achieve through their telling: reconnecting people to animals.

But why tell stories at all? First and foremost because "stories can accomplish what no other form of communication can—they can get through to our hearts with a message," as Will Rogers puts it.[47] Stories can also heal; they can help bring us back into a harmonious relationship with the world around us.[48] As the Navajo storyteller Yellowman once explained, "It's too easy to become sick, because there are always things happening to confuse our minds. We need to have ways of thinking, of keeping things stable, healthy, beautiful. . . . We keep our lives in order with the stories. We have to relate our lives to the stars and the sun, the animals, and to all of nature or else we will go crazy or get sick."[49] Stories, especially the sacred stories we often call "myths," also have the power to unify past, present, and future through their telling.[50] And finally, stories have the power to teach, gently but persistently, generation to generation. Among the Western Apache, for instance, stories tied to particular places in the landscape are used to "shoot" a moral message into their intended listeners.[51] And the Anishinaubae (Ojibway) of the upper Great Lakes use stories to "[pass] along the tribe's values, beliefs, teachings, traditions, understandings . . . everything."[52]

For many audiences, stories about animals have a special power. For instance, when new undergraduate environmental studies majors at the University of Chicago are asked how they first became interested in environmental issues, many of them say, "By reading *Ishmael*," Daniel Quinn's deeply affecting novel of a wise gorilla and his teachings.[53] Similarly, many adults can still recount the stories they read as children decades ago that sparked their lifelong love of animals, stories such as Henry Williamson's *Tarka the Otter* or Thornton W. Burgess's *Adventures of Jimmy Skunk* from the Mother West Wind series.[54] Filmed stories of animals also have tremendous power to awaken awareness and deepen connection to animals. On the fictional side, *Bambi* and *Free Willy* have inspired thousands of children to see deer and whales in new, more compassionate ways. And Jacques Perrin's recent documentary films do the same for adults and children both, opening our eyes to a magical world that is all the more compelling because it is real—real for the insects living in a field in France that are the heroes of his *Macroscope* and real for the many different species of birds that Perrin's crew filmed using ultralight gliders and other "you are there" technologies in *Winged Migration*.

To better understand the power of animal stories to reconnect people with animal others, it is useful to first identify the different types of animal stories. Susan Marie Frontczak offers the following classification of nature stories, including animal stories:

I.   Stories that depict nature directly to convey facts about nature or natural processes

II. Myths or legends that explain how things came to be in the natural world

III. Stories that use the natural world as an allegory to teach something about human nature or society

IV. Fictional stories that use the human realm as an allegory to teach about nature

> V. Stories that compassionately describe personal experience
>   with nature[55]

As Frontczak notes, any one story may contain elements of more than one of these categories. We would suggest a further distinction specific to animal stories:

> A. Stories that depict animals as being like humans
> B. Stories that depict animals as being different from humans
> C. Stories that depict humans and animals as one

Stories of Type A are especially useful in helping people understand animals, to connect with them and establish relationships with them (such stories are often labeled "anthropomorphic"; see below). Stories of Type B, on the other hand, stimulate our curiosity about animals, and inspire a sense of wonder and mystery. And finally, stories of Type C suggest that both the similarities and the differences between humans and other animals are less important than our practical and mystical unity—practical in the ways we share the same neighborhoods (habitats), for instance, and mystical in the feeling of spiritual oneness that comes from empathetic shapeshifting from human to animal and back again. All three types of stories are necessary to tell the whole story of animals, both in relationship to human society and as living, thinking beings in their own rights and therefore worthy of our respect, caring, and restraint.[56]

We mentioned above that personal experience is the best way to get to really know animals on a deep, intuitive level. Telling stories about them can be a tremendous help in this endeavor. Anyone can tell a story; we all do it when we describe what happened to us that day to our families around the dinner table or when we show friends photos or videos from our vacations. Good, compelling stories often include some or all of the following elements: told in first-person voice, use of present versus past tense, attention to precise details, action grounded in known/familiar places, and intimate knowledge of the subject of the story gained through personal experience and/or careful research.[57]

How can we put the animal storytelling model into practice? Think back to the great blue heron. To tell a story about it, we might decide to focus on a personal experience (Type V, in Frontczak's classification). This experience might have been one of deep communion with a particular heron—a moment when we felt one with it (Type C). Or it might have been a time when we saw just how unique and amazing the heron is—how wonderfully different from us it is (Type B). Stories of personal experience can be tremendously moving, in part because they carry the natural authority of the true experience, expressed in our own first-person voices. Just as many people prefer to see real objects in museums instead of simulations or reproductions,[58] so too do many listeners delight in hearing true stories from the people who lived them.[59]

Here is an example of a Type VB personal experience story told by Aldo Leopold to share a mystical moment when a dying wolf—a wolf that he had helped kill—taught him a lesson about wildlife management:

> We reached the old wolf in time to watch a fierce green fire dying in her eyes. I realized then, and have known ever since, that there was something new to me in those eyes—something known only to her and the mountain. I was young then, and full of trigger-itch; I thought that because fewer wolves meant more deer, that no wolves would mean hunters' paradise. But after seeing the green fire die, I sensed that neither the wolf nor the mountain agreed with such a view.[60]

Leopold could have cited scientific studies showing that without predators, deer populations balloon until the deer exhaust every available food source, and then they starve to death. Or he could have mentioned animal behaviorists' observations that wolf predation may actually improve the quality of ungulate herds by thinning out the old, weak, and diseased individuals. But instead he shared a single moment of personal experience, and the emotional impact on the reader was much greater.

Perhaps you would prefer to leave your own experiences out of your story and instead focus on the great blue heron itself. One option would be to tell a Type I story about the heron in its natural habitat, ideally from the heron's point of view. Here you would begin by combining your personal observations with background reading on the natural history of great blue herons. Then you could personalize your facts into a story about one individual heron.[61] Many children's books focus on individual animals in this way, but so do some adult books, such as Fred Bodsworth's heart-wrenching fictionalized tale about the lonely death of the last living Eskimo curlew, *Last of the Curlews*.[62] Often these stories anthropomorphize their animal heroes, providing them with humanlike appearance (e.g., walking on two legs), emotions, and so forth. Although the term "anthropomorphic" is often used in pejorative terms, to denigrate accounts of animals that attribute a "mental" life and consequent subjectivity to animals or that place animal life and human affairs on equal footing,[63] anthropomorphism can be an effective way to connect people to animals, nurturing understanding through the recognition of the many things humans and other animals have in common: animals need to eat, care for their families, and have a safe place to sleep at night, just like humans.[64]

Frontczak's Type II stories, myths about how animals came to look and behave the way they do today, "provide emotional and narrative hooks that help us . . . distinguish between species of animals. . . . Many of the myths also carry a message about the correct way for humans to behave."[65] Such stories are common among indigenous cultures the world over. For instance, North American Indian tribes have stories that explain "How the Butterflies Came to Be,"[66] "Why Possum Has a Naked Tail,"[67] "How the Fawn Got Its Spots,"[68] and so on. To compose stories like this, think about all the distinguishing characteristics of a given animal that you can remember and write them down. Then pick one of those characteristics to be explained by the story, and mention some of the others in the course of the story to make the animal you are talking or writing about feel more real to your audience. Finally, imagine a wide variety of ways that the characteristic you have chosen could have come to be, and then try a couple different ones to see which might work best in your story.[69]

Integrating Intuitive Understandings of Animals into Research and Teaching

In addition to going in search of real animals through our own personal intuitive knowledge quests, whether through experiential natural history or storytelling or some other model, we can also work to integrate our new understandings of animals into our research and teaching. Different fields are, of course, open to experiential, intuitive research to varying degrees. In some fields, such as cultural anthropology, it is arguably *expected* that researchers open themselves to intuitive experience, even if it may be less acceptable to write about such experiences in formal reports. For instance, to better understand the Koyukon people of the Alaskan boreal forest, ethnographer and naturalist Richard K. Nelson not only lived with the Koyukon and adopted their subsistence lifestyle but also attempted to share their *experience* of the northern forest. Here is an excerpt from a journal entry Nelson published about his encounter with a wolverine in the wilds (a creature also stalked by the Koyukon):

> In the gloom of dusk I saw a shadowy figure slip silently from the trees, not thirty yards from the tent. . . . A wolverine. . . . It was curious and grave, reaching out with its nose, slowly wagging its head, trying for a scent. It lifted one foreleg tentatively, then loped a few steps my way. I looked directly into its eyes and knew that I understood nothing. Then it cringed back, turned its head away, and vanished again into the forest.[70]

Nelson clearly saw the value of combining detailed natural history observations with his own emotional reactions to better understand how the Koyukon might react to a similar encounter with a wolverine (and with other creatures of the boreal forest). By opening himself to a moment of mystical communion with this wolverine, Nelson suddenly understood on an intuitive level why the Koyukon felt wolverines possessed "a dangerous power" that had to be treated with the utmost respect.[71] And this openness, in turn, made Nelson's ethnographic research much more insightful than a detached, "objective" account could have.

Even in fields that are less welcoming of intuitive research methods, we can still find opportunities to bring in such perspectives. Literary scholars or folklorists, for instance, could seek out and recover experiential or totemic animal stories for contemporary audiences. Creating interdisciplinary teams to draw on the varying experiences and expertise of researchers is another way to get at aspects of animals that one researcher alone might not discover. Perhaps even more productive would be teams composed of not just academics but also artists and local residents. Such a team might be charged with exploring a given animal or group of animals in a particular area from their various perspectives and then reporting their observations to a larger group, integrating each other's perspectives, and producing a final report for publication and/or online distribution.

Teaching at all levels also offers rich opportunities for bringing intuitive perspectives on animals into the classroom. (Anna Botsford Comstock pioneered this sort of experiential nature education early in the twentieth century, and her *Handbook of Nature Study* still provides a wealth of ideas for educators.)[72] One obvious activity to try would be to take the class outdoors and to have students engage in some of the natural history and storytelling activities discussed above. Introductory science classes, especially for younger students, as well as introductory biology courses for high school and college students, could easily incorporate the intuitive observation and imagination elements of Goethean science. And syllabuses for introductory literature and/or writing classes could be focused on poems, essays, stories, and novels with animals as heroes rather than objects. (Several useful bibliographies of stories and novels about various animals are posted on the NILAS web site at www.h-net.org/~nilas. See also Marion W. Copeland and David C. Anderson's recent annotated bibliography of novels told from birds' eye views—literally.)[73]

Humane education is another way to encourage students to see animals as agents with feelings worthy of our respect. Through visits to animal shelters, classroom curricula, summer camps, and other activities, humane educators help children learn that part of being a good person is treating animals with respect and compassion, and accepting responsibility for the impacts that our actions have on animal lives. (See the National Association for Humane and Environmental Education's web site at www.nahee.org for more information on humane education.)

In fact, one could argue that all of the approaches discussed in this afterword ought to be thought of as humane education, because of their shared emphasis on teaching us how to pursue more empathic, caring relationships with animals— relationships between I and Thou rather than I and It, as Martin Buber put it. This is an important point, because humane education is often thought of as only for children, when in fact it should be part of a lifelong learning process for all of us.

At the beginning of this afterword, we asserted that there was much to be gained from attempting to understand animals on their own terms—as real animals instead of just representations, as thinking, feeling Thous instead of Its. From accessing therosentience, in other words. One can, of course, learn more about what life is like for nonhuman animals from this endeavor, which may in turn lead to increased compassion for them and perhaps to a commitment to act on their behalf when help is needed. But one can also learn much of value about oneself. For we, too, are animals, and therefore understanding nonhuman animal Others is crucial to understanding ourselves. As Boria Sax has said, "What does it mean to be human? Perhaps only the animals can know."

Notes

1. Martin Buber, *I and Thou*, a new translation, with a prologue and notes by Walter Kaufmann (New York: Simon & Schuster, 1970), 54.

2. Ibid., 55.

3. Ibid., 62–63.

4. The phrase "unity with nature" borrows from the Quaker magazine *EarthLight*, formerly published by its Friends in Unity with Nature committee.

5. William Blake, "November 22, 1802," in *News of the Universe: Poems of Twofold Consciousness*, ed. Robert Bly (San Francisco: Sierra Club Books, 1980), 29.

6. Marianne Moore, "Poetry," in *American Poetry*, ed. Wilson Allen Gay, Walter B. Rideout, and James K. Robinson (New York: Harper & Row, 1965), 804–5.

7. These poems and paintings are all well known and anthologized.

8. Grace Olive Wiley, "Notes on the Texas Rattlesnake in Captivity with Special Reference to the Birth of a Litter of Young," *Bulletin of the Antivenin Institute of America* 3 (1929): 8–14, and Grace Olive Wiley, "Notes on the Neotropical Rattlesnake (*Crotalus terrificus basciliscus*) in Captivity," *Bulletin of the Antivenin Institute of America* 3 (1930): 100–103. See also David Scofield Wilson, "The Rattlesnake," in *American Wildlife in Symbol and Story*, ed. Angus K. Gillespie and Jay Mechling (Knoxville: Univ. of Tennessee Press, 1987), 61–62.

9. See Robert Plant Armstrong's *Wellspring: On the Myth and Source of Culture* (Berkeley and Los Angeles: Univ. of California Press, 1975); *The Affecting Presence: An Essay in Humanistic Anthropology* (Urbana: Univ. of Illinois Press, 1971); and *The Powers of Presence: Consciousness, Myth, and Affecting Presence* (Philadelphia: Univ. of Pennsylvania Press, 1981).

10. Armstrong, *Affecting Presence*, 192.

11. Armstrong, *Wellspring*, xi.

12. Henry David Thoreau, *Journal*, Apr. 16, 1852, in Henry David Thoreau, *The Works of Thoreau*, ed. Henry Seidel Canby (Boston: Houghton Mifflin, 1937), 603–4.

13. Gregory Bateson, *Mind and Nature: A Necessary Unity* (New York: E. P. Dutton, 1979), 141.

14. Gregory Bateson with Mary Catherine Bateson, *Angels Fear: Towards an Epistemology of the Sacred* (New York: Macmillan, 1987), 26.

15. Ibid., 141.

16. Walt Whitman, in *The Oxford Book of American Verse*, ed. F. O. Matthiessen (New York: Oxford Univ. Press, 1950), 124, 143.

17. By "totemism" we do not mean the long discredited anthropological notion that certain indigenous peoples literally believed they were directly descended from various plants or animals—see Claude Lévi-Strauss, *Totemism* (Boston: Beacon Press, 1963)—but rather a "new totemism" along the lines of the "totemic literature" described by Boria Sax in his introduction to part 1 of this book.

18. Ursula K. Le Guin, *Buffalo Gals and Other Animal Presences* (Santa Barbara, Calif.: Capra Press, 1987), 167–75.

19. Martha C. Nussbaum, *Poetic Justice: The Literary Imagination and Public Life* (Boston: Beacon Press, 1995), xiii.

20. Ibid., 2.

21. Ibid., 5.

22. Ibid.

23. Ibid., 121.

24. David Scofield Wilson Jr., pers. comm., July 24, 2003.

25. Wiley, who moved to the Brookfield Zoo in Chicago in 1933, died in 1948 at the age of sixty-four from the bite of her "newest pet," a cobra, at a photographic session (*Time*, Aug. 2, 1948, 15). See also Wilson, "Rattlesnake," 72 n. 32.

26. Temple Grandin, *Thinking in Pictures*, with a foreword by Oliver Sacks (New York: Vintage Books, 1995); Temple Grandin and Catherine Johnson, *Animals in Translation: Using the Mysteries of Autism to Decode Animal Behavior* (New York: Scribner, 2005).

27. Niko Tinbergen, *Curious Naturalists* (1969; reprint, Amherst: Univ. of Massachusetts Press, 1984).

28. J. Henri Fabre, "The Pine Processionary," in *The Insect World of J. Henri Fabre*, ed. Edwin Way Teale (New York: Dodd, Mead, 1966), 10–24.

29. Sally Carrighar, *One Day on Beetle Rock* (1943; reprint, Lincoln: Univ. of Nebraska Press, 1978).

30. Farley Mowat, *Never Cry Wolf* (1963; reprint, Boston: Little, Brown, 2001).

31. NILAS has examples of several such bibliographies and totem groups on its web site, www.h-net.org/~nilas.

32. Herbert Kohl and Judith Kohl, *A View from the Oak* (San Francisco: Sierra Club Books, 1975), 27–28.

33. Dave Aftandilian, "Growing Green Kids," *Chicago Wilderness* 8, no. 1 (Fall 2004): 12–15.

34. For some recent examples, see the sources cited in note 7 in Dave Aftandilian's introduction to this volume.

35. Eileen Crist, *Images of Animals: Anthropomorphism and Animal Mind* (Philadelphia: Temple Univ. Press, 1999), 4–5.

36. Thanks to Deborah S. Rose for sharing her insights into the potential value of models versus theories as explanatory devices.

37. Marc Bekoff, "Minding Animals, Minding Earth: Old Brains, New Bottlenecks," *Zygon* 38, no. 4 (2003), 921; see also Marc Bekoff, *Minding Animals: Awareness, Emotions, and Heart* (New York: Oxford Univ. Press, 2002).

38. Bekoff, "Minding Animals, Minding Earth," 939.

39. Tim Ingold, *The Perception of the Environment: Essays on Livelihood, Dwelling and Skill* (New York: Routledge, 2000), 40–60.

40. William Cronon, "The Trouble with Wilderness; or, Getting Back to the Wrong Nature," in *Uncommon Ground: Rethinking the Human Place in Nature*, ed. William Cronon (New York: W. W. Norton, 1996), 88–90.

41. Kimon Nicolaides, *The Natural Way to Draw: A Working Plan for Art Study* (1941; reprint, Boston: Houghton Mifflin, 1969).

42. Henri Bortoft, *The Wholeness of Nature: Goethe's Way toward a Science of Conscious Participation in Nature* (New York: Lindisfarne Press, 1996), 61–63.

43. Isis Brook, "Goethean Science as a Way to Read Landscape," *Landscape Research* 23, no. 1 (1998): 51, 67–68.

44. Bortoft, *Wholeness of Nature*, 42.

45. Brook, "Goethean Science," 56–57.

46. By "sacred stories" we are referring to what many other authors call "myths." See Dave Aftandilian's chapter on "Frogs, Snakes, and Agricultural Fertility," this volume, note 3, for an explanation of why "sacred stories" is a more appropriate term to use to describe these stories.

47. Will Rogers, introduction to *The Story Handbook: Language and Storytelling for Conservationists*, ed. Helen Whybrow (San Francisco: Trust for Public Land, 2002), 1.

48. Barry Lopez, "Landscape and Narrative," in *The Story Handbook: Language and Storytelling for Conservationists*, ed. Helen Whybrow (San Francisco: Trust for Public Land, 2002), 33.

49. Barre Toelken, *The Dynamics of Folklore*, rev. and expanded ed. (Logan: Utah State Univ. Press, 1996), 124.

50. Joseph Epes Brown with Emily Cousins, *Teaching Spirits: Understanding Native American Religious Traditions* (Oxford: Oxford Univ. Press, 2001), 16.

51. Keith H. Basso, *Wisdom Sits in Places: Landscape and Language among the Western Apache* (Albuquerque: Univ. of New Mexico Press, 1996), 37–70.

52. Basil Johnston, *Honour Earth Mother* (Lincoln: Univ. of Nebraska Press, 2004), xxi.

53. Theodore Steck, pers. comm., Sept. 2004; Daniel Quinn, *Ishmael* (1992; reprint, New York: Bantam Books, 1995).

54. Dave Aftandilian et al., "Favorite Books from Childhood," *NILAS Newsletter*, n.s., vol. 1, nos. 3–4 (2002–3): 52–53, 55.

55. Susan Marie Frontczak, "The Nature of Stories," *NILAS Newsletter*, n.s., vol. 1, nos. 3–4 (2002–3): 5.

56. Joseph Bruchac, *Our Stories Remember: American Indian History, Culture, and Values* (Golden, Colo.: Fulcrum, 2003), 158; Vine Deloria Jr., foreword to *Native American Animal Stories* by Joseph Bruchac (Golden, Colo.: Fulcrum, 1992), xi.

57. Brown and Cousins, *Teaching Spirits*, 55; Frontczak, "Nature of Stories," 6–7.

58. Kathleen McLean, *Planning for People in Museum Exhibitions* (Washington, D.C.: Association of Science-Technology Centers, 1993), 15.

59. Lopez, "Landscape and Narrative," 31–32.

60. Aldo Leopold, *A Sand County Almanac with Essays on Conservation from Round River* (New York: Ballantine Books, 1970), 138–39.

61. Frontczak, "Nature of Stories," 6.

62. Fred Bodsworth, *Last of the Curlews* (1955; reprint, Washington, D.C.: Counterpoint, 1995).

63. Crist, *Images of Animals*, 7 and 209; Kenneth J. Shapiro, "A Phenomenological Approach to the Study of Nonhuman Animals," in *Anthropomoprhism, Anecdotes, and Animals*, ed. Robert W. Mitchell, Nicholas S. Thompson, and H. Lyn Miles (Albany: State Univ. of New York Press, 1997), 293.

64. See Marion W. Copeland's introduction to part 2 of this volume for more on the good work anthropomorphism can do in helping us reconnect to animals through story.

65. Frontczak, "Nature of Stories," 7.

66. Papago in Joseph Bruchac, *Native American Animal Stories* (Golden, Colo.: Fulcrum, 1992), 44–47.

67. Cherokee in ibid., 83–86.

68. Dakota in ibid., 88–90.

69. Frontczak, "Nature of Stories," 7.

70. Richard K. Nelson, *Make Prayers to the Raven: A Koyukon View of the Northern Forest* (Chicago: Univ. of Chicago Press, 1983), 153.

71. Ibid., 149.

72. Comstock distinguishes "nature study" from "natural science" thus: "Nature study is not elementary science as so taught, because its point of attack is not the same; error in this respect has caused many a teacher to abandon nature study and many a pupil to hate it." Anna Botsford Comstock, *Handbook of Nature Study* (Ithaca, N.Y.: Cornell Univ. Press), 5.

73. Marion W. Copeland and David C. Anderson, "Bird Novels: An Annotated Bibliography," *NILAS Newsletter*, n.s., vol. 2, nos. 1–2 (2004): 33–39.

Works Cited

Aftandilian, Dave. "Growing Green Kids." *Chicago Wilderness* 8, no. 1 (Fall 2004): 12–15.

Aftandilian, Dave, et al. "Favorite Books from Childhood." *NILAS Newsletter*, n.s., vol. 1, nos. 3–4 (2002–3): 52–53, 55.

Armstrong, Robert Plant. *The Affecting Presence: An Essay in Humanistic Anthropology.* Urbana: Univ. of Illinois Press, 1971.

———. *The Powers of Presence: Consciousness, Myth, and Affecting Presence.* Philadelphia: Univ. of Pennsylvania Press, 1981.

———. *Wellspring: On the Myth and Source of Culture.* Berkeley and Los Angeles: Univ. of California Press, 1975.

Basso, Keith H. *Wisdom Sits in Places: Landscape and Language among the Western Apache.* Albuquerque: Univ. of New Mexico Press, 1996.

Bateson, Gregory. *Mind and Nature: A Necessary Unity.* New York: E. P. Dutton, 1979.

Bateson, Gregory, with Mary Catherine Bateson. *Angels Fear: Towards an Epistemology of the Sacred.* New York: Macmillan, 1987.

Bekoff, Marc. *Minding Animals: Awareness, Emotions, and Heart.* New York: Oxford Univ. Press, 2002.

———. "Minding Animals, Minding Earth: Old Brains, New Bottlenecks." *Zygon* 38, no. 4 (2003): 911–41.

Blake, William. "Untitled, November 22, 1802." In *News of the Universe: Poems of Twofold Consciousness,* edited by Robert Bly, 29. San Francisco: Sierra Club Books, 1980.

Bodsworth, Fred. *Last of the Curlews.* 1955. Reprint, Washington, D.C.: Counterpoint, 1995.

Bortoft, Henri. *The Wholeness of Nature: Goethe's Way toward a Science of Conscious Participation in Nature.* New York: Lindisfarne Press, 1996.

Brook, Isis. "Goethean Science as a Way to Read Landscape." *Landscape Research* 23, no. 1 (1998): 51–69.

Brown, Joseph Epes, with Emily Cousins. *Teaching Spirits: Understanding Native American Religious Traditions.* Oxford: Oxford Univ. Press, 2001.

Bruchac, Joseph. *Native American Animal Stories.* Golden, Colo.: Fulcrum, 1992.

———. *Our Stories Remember: American Indian History, Culture, and Values through Storytelling.* Golden, Colo.: Fulcrum, 2003.

Buber, Martin. *I and Thou.* A new translation, with a prologue and notes by Walter Kaufmann. New York: Simon & Schuster, 1970.

Carrighar, Sally. *One Day on Beetle Rock.* 1943. Reprint, Lincoln: Univ. of Nebraska Press, 1978.

Comstock, Anna Botsford. *Handbook of Nature Study.* 1911. Reprint, Ithaca, N.Y.: Cornell Univ. Press, 1986.

Copeland, Marion W., and David C. Anderson. "Bird Novels: An Annotated Bibliography." *NILAS Newsletter,* n.s., vol. 2, nos. 1–2 (2004): 33–39.

Crist, Eileen. *Images of Animals: Anthropomorphism and Animal Mind.* Philadelphia: Temple Univ. Press, 1999.

Cronon, William. "The Trouble with Wilderness; or, Getting Back to the Wrong Nature." In *Uncommon Ground: Rethinking the Human Place in Nature*, edited by William Cronon, 69–90. New York: W. W. Norton, 1996.

Deloria, Vine Jr. Foreword to *Native American Animal Stories*, by Joseph Bruchac, ix–xi. Golden, Colo.: Fulcrum, 1992.

Fabre, J. Henri. "The Pine Processionary." In *The Insect World of J. Henri Fabre*, edited by Edwin Way Teale, 10–24. New York: Dodd, Mead, 1966.

Frontczak, Susan Marie. "The Nature of Stories." *NILAS Newsletter*, n.s., vol. 1, nos. 3–4 (2002–3): 5–11.

Grandin, Temple. *Thinking in Pictures*. With a foreword by Oliver Sacks. New York: Vintage Books, 1995.

Grandin, Temple, and Catherine Johnson. *Animals in Translation: Using the Mysteries of Autism to Decode Animal Behavior*. New York: Scribner, 2005.

Ingold, Tim. *The Perception of the Environment: Essays on Livelihood, Dwelling and Skill*. New York: Routledge, 2000.

Johnston, Basil. *Honour Earth Mother*. Lincoln: Univ. of Nebraska Press, 2004.

Kohl, Herbert, and Judith Kohl. *A View from the Oak*. San Francisco: Sierra Club Books, 1975.

Le Guin, Ursula K. *Buffalo Gals and Other Animal Presences*. Santa Barbara, Calif.: Capra Press, 1987.

Leopold, Aldo. *A Sand County Almanac with Essays on Conservation from Round River*. New York: Ballantine Books, 1970.

Lévi-Strauss, Claude. *Totemism*. Translated by Rodney Needham. Boston: Beacon Press, 1963.

Lopez, Barry. "Landscape and Narrative." In *The Story Handbook: Language and Storytelling for Conservationists*, edited by Helen Whybrow, 28–35. San Francisco: Trust for Public Land, 2002.

McLean, Kathleen. *Planning for People in Museum Exhibitions*. Washington, D.C.: Association of Science-Technology Centers, 1993.

Moore, Marianne. "Poetry." In *American Poetry*, edited by Wilson Allen Gay, Walter B. Rideout, and James K. Robinson, 804–5. New York: Harper & Row, 1965.

Mowat, Farley. *Never Cry Wolf*. 1963. Reprint, Boston: Little, Brown, 2001.

Nelson, Richard K. *Make Prayers to the Raven: A Koyukon View of the Northern Forest*. Chicago: Univ. of Chicago Press, 1983.

Nicolaides, Kimon. *The Natural Way to Draw: A Working Plan for Art Study*. 1941. Reprint, Boston: Houghton Mifflin, 1969.

Nussbaum, Martha C. *Poetic Justice: The Literary Imagination and Public Life*. Boston: Beacon Press, 1995.

Quinn, Daniel. *Ishmael.* 1992. Reprint, New York: Bantam Books, 1995.

Rogers, Will. Introduction to *The Story Handbook: Language and Storytelling for Conservationists,* edited by Helen Whybrow, 1–3. San Francisco: Trust for Public Land, 2002.

Shapiro, Kenneth J. "A Phenomenological Approach to the Study of Nonhuman Animals." In *Anthropomorphism, Anecdotes, and Animals,* edited by Robert W. Mitchell, Nicholas S. Thompson, and H. Lyn Miles, 277–95. Albany: State Univ. of New York Press, 1997.

Thoreau, Henry David. *The Works of Thoreau.* Edited by Henry Seidel Canby. Boston: Houghton Mifflin, 1937.

Tinbergen, Niko. *Curious Naturalists.* 1969. Reprint, Amherst: Univ. of Massachusetts Press, 1984.

Toelken, Barre. *The Dynamics of Folklore.* Rev. and expanded ed. Logan: Utah State Univ. Press, 1996.

Whitman, Walt. "I Saw in Louisiana a Live-Oak Growing" and "A Noiseless Patient Spider." In *The Oxford Book of American Verse,* edited by F. O. Matthiessen, 124 and 143. New York: Oxford Univ. Press, 1950.

Wiley, Grace Olive. "Notes on the Neotropical Rattlesnake (*Crotalus terrificus basciliscus*) in Captivity." *Bulletin of the Antivenin Institute of America* 3 (1930): 100–103.

———. "Notes on the Texas Rattlesnake in Captivity with Special Reference to the Birth of a Litter of Young." *Bulletin of the Antivenin Institute of America* 3 (1929): 8–14.

Wilson, David Scofield. "The Rattlesnake." In *American Wildlife in Symbol and Story,* edited by Angus K. Gillespie and Jay Mechling, 41–72. Knoxville: Univ. of Tennessee Press, 1987.

Contributors

Dave Aftandilian is preceptor and program coordinator for the Environmental Studies Program and a Ph.D. candidate in anthropology at the University of Chicago. He is currently writing his dissertation, "Changing Perceptions of Animals in the Prehistoric Lower Illinois Valley and American Bottom: Evidence from Artistic Representations." His research interests include religion and environment, Native American studies, and the role of storytelling in environmental education.

Anne Alden is a postdoctoral fellow at the University of California at Davis. She received her Ph.D. in clinical psychology from Alliant University/California School of Professional Psychology. Her thesis was titled "Anthropomorphism in *New Yorker* Dog Cartoons across the Twentieth Century."

Elisabet Sveingar Amundsen is a *Cand. philol.* student of ethnology at the University of Oslo, Norway, and has participated in the research program "Conservation versus Protection of Natural Resources, 1997–2000" at the Centre for Development and the Environment. Her main research topic, about which she has published several previous articles, has been the cultural history of recreational hunting.

Maria Teresa L. M. B. Andresen is associate professor of landscape architecture at Oporto University in Portugal. She is the author of *Francisco Caldeira Cabral* (2000) and coauthor of "Jardins Históricos do Porto," and is a member of both the Scientific Council of the European Environmental Agency and the IUCN's World Committee on Protected Areas.

Susan Braden is an ESL instructor in the Continuing Education division of Santa Barbara City College. She holds an M.A. in Spanish literature from the University of California–Santa Barbara.

Marion W. Copeland is a tutor and lecturer in the M.S. program at the Center for Animals and Public Policy of Tufts University's Veterinary School and emerita professor of English at Holyoke Community College. Her primary research interests are in literature that foregrounds more than human animals as protagonists, narrators, and major characters. The author of numerous articles and reviews, she has also written two books, *Charles Alexander Eastman (Ohiyesa)* (Boise State University, 1978) and *Cockroach* (Reaktion Books, 2003).

Bruce Hackett is professor emeritus of sociology at the University of California–Davis and the author or coauthor of several papers exploring the social and biological dimensions of household energy consumption.

Lynette A. Hart is professor of population health and reproduction in the School of Veterinary Medicine at the University of California–Davis and director of the University of California Center for Animal Alternatives. She is editor of *Responsible Conduct with Animals in Research* (Oxford, 1998) and coauthor of *Canine and Feline Behavior Therapy* (Lippincott Williams & Wilkins, 2006).

Elizabeth Jane Wall Hinds is professor and chair of English at the State University of New York–Brockport. Her work deals with both the connections and gaps between early and late modern culture—between the transatlantic eighteenth century and the "postmodern" world. Her publications include *Private Property: Charles Brockden Brown's Gendered Economics of Virtue* (Delaware, 1997) and articles on Charles Brockden Brown and Olaudah Equiano. She is also the editor of *The Multiple Worlds of Pynchon's Mason & Dixon: Eighteenth-Century Contexts, Postmodern Observations* (Camden House, 2005).

Laura Hobgood-Oster holds the Elizabeth Root Paden Chair in religion at Southwestern University (Georgetown, Texas). Her publications include *The Sabbath Journal of Judith Lomax*; "Wisdom Literature and Ecofeminism" and "Wells and Water of the Earth" in *The Earth Bible; Crossroads Choices: Biblical Wisdom Literature in the 21st Century* (2000); and *Holy Dogs and Asses: Animals in Christianity* (Illinois, forthcoming). She is also executive editor of *The Encyclopedia of Religion and Nature*.

Muffet Jones is archivist/curator for the Estate of Ray Johnson at Richard L. Feigen & Company in New York City. She has a B.A. in art history from New York University, with honors, and an M.A., M.Phil. from Columbia University. In 2001, she curated "Mind Games: Ray Johnson's Art of Ideas" for Feigen Contemporary in Chelsea. She has also written frequently on Johnson and is currently at work on the first monograph about him. She lives in Brooklyn with two Persian cats and two French bulldogs named Delphine and Didier.

Xiaofei Kang is assistant professor of Chinese Studies at Carnegie Mellon University. She received her Ph.D. from Columbia University in 2000 and specializes in the history and religion of late imperial and modern China. She is also the author of *The Cult of the Fox: Power, Gender, and Popular Religion in Late Imperial and Modern China* (Columbia University Press, 2005).

Ria Koopmans–de Bruijn is East Asian studies librarian in the C. V. Starr East Asian Library at Columbia University. She graduated from Leiden University (The Netherlands) in 1986; for her thesis, she completed a survey of serpent symbolism in Japanese folktales. In addition to serpent folklore, she has also written about historical Dutch-Japanese relations. In 1998, she published the *Area Bibliography of Japan* (Scarecrow Area Bibliographies, No. 14).

Lynne S. McNeill is a Ph.D. candidate and instructor in the Folklore department at Memorial University of Newfoundland. She obtained her master's degree in American studies and folklore from Utah State University in 2002. In addition to animal folklore, her research interests include contemporary legends, supernatural folklore, folk belief, cultural geography, and ethnography.

Tonia L. Payne received her Ph.D. from the Graduate School and University Center of the City University of New York in 1999. Currently, she is an assistant professor in the English Department at Nassau Community College, SUNY. She is the author of "'Home Is a Place Where You Have Never Been': Connections with the Other in Ursula Le Guin's Fiction," in a focus issue on "Nature and the Environment" of *AUMLA: The Journal of the*

Australian Universities Language and Literature Association; "Becoming (An)Other: Ursula Le Guin's Fiction and the Othered Reader," in *JASAT: Journal of the American Studies Association of Texas;* and "'We Are Dirt; We Are Earth': Ursula Le Guin and the Problem of Extraterrestrialism," in *Beyond Wild Nature: Transatlantic Perspectives on Ecocriticism* (Rodopi Press, forthcoming). Her poem "Prairie" was published in *California Quarterly.*

Ana Isabel Queiroz is a Ph.D. student in the School of Sciences, University of Porto (Portugal). She is interested in landscape studies, especially in landscape changes and environmental history, exploring and combining different sources of information. Her background is in environmental conservation and management, and she previously worked as a biologist at the Institute of Nature Conservation in Portugal's Ministry of the Environment.

Rev. Susan Carole Roy received her B.A. from Lawrence University in Appleton, Wisconsin; her M. Div. from the Lutheran School of Theology at Chicago; and is currently completing her dissertation toward a D. Min. at Wesley Theological Seminary in Washington, D.C. She is an ordained pastor in the Evangelical Lutheran Church in America and a board certified chaplain with the Association of Professional Chaplains. She currently serves as director of pastoral care at the University of Maryland Medical Center in Baltimore. She shares her life with several formerly homeless cats and dogs, who are now employed as her spiritual advisors on the human-animal-divine bond.

Boria Sax received his doctorate from SUNY-Buffalo and is the founder of NILAS. His many books include, most recently, *Animals in the Third Reich: Pets, Scapegoats, and the Holocaust* (Continuum, 2000), *The Mythical Zoo: An Encyclopedia of Animals in World Myth, Legend, and Literature* (ABC-CLIO, 2001), and *Crow* (Reaktion Books, 2003). For more information, see his web site at www.boriasax.com.

David Scofield Wilson, an emeritus senior lecturer at the University of California–Davis, earned his graduate degrees in American studies at the University of Minnesota. The author of *In the Presence of Nature* (University of Massachusetts Press, 1978), he taught courses on nature and culture in America and has written on Jonathan Edwards's "flying spiders," poison oak, rattlesnakes, tomatoes, and hot peppers as they served to focus both scientific interest and popular imagination. He recently coedited *Rooted in America: Foodlore of Popular Fruits and Vegetables* (University of Tennessee Press, 1999). An interest in the natural landscape of the West finds expression in his essays on Yosemite, Old Sacramento, and the Sutter Buttes of northern California as places that vivify patterns of value and meaning central to American popular, folk, and elite culture.

Index

Page numbers in **boldface** refer to illustrations and tables.

A

Aesop, xi, xviii, 169–70, 226. *See also* fables

aggression, 278, **282,** 285, 298

agriculture, 64, 68, 74n23, 81n93, 141; and birds, 150; ceremonies related to, 58, 59, 60; and fertility, 66; fields used for, 60, 74n21; pest control in, 54; vs. hunting, 120. *See also* fertility

Alabama: state of, 56, 64, **65**; tribe, 61

Amazon.com, 283

American Kennel Club, 222

American Society for the Prevention of Cruelty to Animals (ASPCA), 223

American Werewolf in London, An, 104

Anasazi, 60

animal-assisted therapy, 211, 215n23, 227

animal behavior. *See* ethology

Animal Fair, 227

animal mind, skepticism regarding, 284. *See also* consciousness, animal

animal rights, xxn7, 38, 102; for domestic animals, 223

animal studies, xii–xvii, xviii–xixn7, xxin21, 89, 263, 313; and critical theory, 310; definition of, xvi; inter-disciplinarity and, xiii; marginaliza-tion of, xi; role of theory and practice in, 303

animals: in art history, 242; human dominion over, 209, 243; and human self-understanding, xiv, 183, 186, 232; kinship with, 172, 206, 259, 306; law and, 120, 223–24, 227; lim-inal, xii, xv, 3, 9–11, 13–14, 175; as metaphors, 2, 38–39, 41, 151, 183–84, 191, 243, 307; in popular culture,

95, 97, 100–101, 103, 219, 241; post-modern, 186, 241, 243–44, 247, 249, 251–52; as saints, 191, 196; slaughter of, 118, 197, 201n21, 208, 309; as subjects vs. objects, xv, xxin16, 89, 183–84, 186, 189–90, 209, 247, 260, 284, 304–5, 310, 317; as symbols, 8, 40–41, 48nn11–12, 89, 91–92, 118, 161–62, 183–84, 190, 192, 193, 195, 197, 249–52. *See also* under specific animals and topics

Animal Welfare Act (U.S.), 223

ant, **282**

anthropocentrism, 91, 92, 189, 190, 298

anthropology, 130n2, 304, 305–6, 318

anthropomorphism: in art, 242–43; avoidance of by scientists, 304; in cartoons, 220, 221, 225–27, 230, 232; consequences of for animals, 229; critiques of, 89; definition of, 89; in Disney cartoons, 227, 243; in human-pet relationships, 220, 230, 232n7; and hybrids, 101; in Larson's *Far Side,* 226–27; meaning of, 233n8; role in understanding animals, xv, 90, 317, 323n64; use of by hunters, 120; use of by Lorenz, 274; use of by naturalists, 284

anthrozoology, xvi

Apache, 143, 315

Apep, 6

Appalachian Trail, 299

Aquinas, Thomas, 191, 208, 210

archaeology, 55, 69–71

Arendt, Hannah, 271–72, 298

Aristophanes, 143

Aristotle, 95, 96

Armstrong, Robert Plant, 305–7

art, 89, 92, 183–86, 263, 303, 306, 307; archaeological artifacts as, 71n4;

What Are the Animals to Us? was designed and typeset on a Macintosh computer system using InDesign software. The body text is set in 10/12 Jenson and display type is set in Neographik. This book was designed and typeset by Stephanie Thompson and manufactured by Thomson-Shore, Inc.